The Essential Middle School

Jon Wiles
University of Montana

Joseph Bondi
University of South Florida

CHARLES E. MERRILL PUBLISHING COMPANY
A Bell & Howell Company
Columbus   Toronto   London   Sydney

Published by
Charles E. Merrill Publishing Co.
A Bell & Howell Company
Columbus, Ohio 43216

This book was set in Helvetica and Avant Garde.
Cover Design Coordination: Will Chenoweth.
Production Coordination: Lucinda Ann Peck.

Photo Credits

Paul Conklin: pages 160 and 186; Jean–Claude LeJeune: pages 48, 80, and 226; Charles
Quinlan: page xiv; Joseph Scolaro: pages 66, 92, 104, and 217; David S. Strickler: pages
18, 126, 258, 290, and 302.

Library of Congress Catalog Card Number: 80–82389
International Standard Book Number: 0–675–08086–X
Printed in the United States of America
1 2 3 4 5 6 7 8 9 10—85 84 83 82 81

This book is dedicated to special people in our lives: our children, Amy and Michael Wiles and Pam, Beth, and Brad Bondi who provide us daily joy,

Our wives, Margaret Wiles and Patsy Bondi, who are marvelous companions, mothers, and teachers,

Our mothers, Hilda Wiles and Virginia Bondi, whom we love and respect as mothers and great school teachers,

Our mentors, too numerous to mention, who taught us how essential the middle school is for emerging adolescent learners.

Contents

Preface

The Essential Middle School is intended for college students preparing to teach, for persons seeking a better understanding of students in the transitional years between childhood and adolescence, and for experienced teachers, administrators, and curriculum leaders responsible for designing and implementing middle schools. The authors also intend this book to be a landmark in the developing trend of the middle school in the United States and other countries. The comprehensive nature of this book affords the reader the opportunity to trace the development of the middle school from its beginnings in the junior high school to its present dynamic structure. In addition, guidelines are presented for future direction of the middle school so that the middle school will remain a significant part of the total educational program of our youth.

Many illustrative materials are included in this text to give the reader a better understanding of the proposals, innovations, and practices of the middle school. The authors are deeply appreciative of the many contributions by practicing middle schools to this book. Without such sharing, progress in the development of quality programs is delayed. It is hoped, as well, that university and college classes under titles such as middle school education, the secondary school, and curriculum development will benefit from the use of these "real" examples and materials.

The Essential Middle School takes the reader through the same steps school personnel might take in planning for a middle school. The book begins with a rationale for the middle school, progresses to the implementation of programs, and ends with the evaluation of the middle school. A thorough description of the emerging adolescent learner is presented with implications for developing appropriate programs and organizational structures for those students. Key ingredients, both human and material, in developing the essential middle school are presented under the following chapter heads: "The Teacher in the Middle School," "The Organization of the Middle School," "Curriculum Leadership in the Middle School," and "Developing Creative Instructional Materials and Learning Environments in the Middle School." Illustrative materials, in addition to those found throughout the text, are included in a major appendix. Suggested Learning Activities and Selected References are provided at the end of each chapter to assist the reader in further study and thinking about the middle school.

The authors are indebted to many persons in the production of this book: our colleagues throughout the nation who encouraged us, practitioners who worked closely with us in the field, and especially the fine editors at Charles Merrill Publishing Company such as Gil Imholz and Cindy Peck who worked closely with us in developing our manuscript. A special note of thanks, too, to our children who provide that extra incentive for wanting to improve the essential middle school.

Acknowledgements

The authors would like to thank the students, parents, teachers, and administrators of Fitzgerald Middle School in Pinellas County, Florida School District for their cooperation in allowing us to photograph them for this book. We would also like to thank our photographer, Mr. Joseph Scolaro, for the excellent photographs used in the text and Mrs. Susan Cornette for her invaluable help in preparing the manuscript.

The authors are also indebted to the many schools and school districts which allowed us to use many of the materials, schedules, and program descriptions illustrated in this book.

Finally, we are grateful to the in-between-agers we have taught and the dedicated teachers and administrators in middle schools and school districts who have helped us acquire the ideas and insights in middle school education that are presented in this book.

An early adolescent is . . .

a canvas to be filled.
a field to be tilled.
clay to be molded.
a bulb to develop.
a diamond to be cut.
a challenge to be met.
a poem to be written.
a song to be sung.
a fragrance to be released.
a life to be saved.
a friend to be made.
a gift to the future.
a bridge to the stars.
a pain in the heart.
a tear in the eye.
energy to be channeled.
a riddle to be solved.
a birdsong in December.
a candle to be lit.
a rain for the sod.
the right hand of God.

_____

Georgia Ensminger, Oldham Middle School, LaGrange, Kentucky. Used with permission.

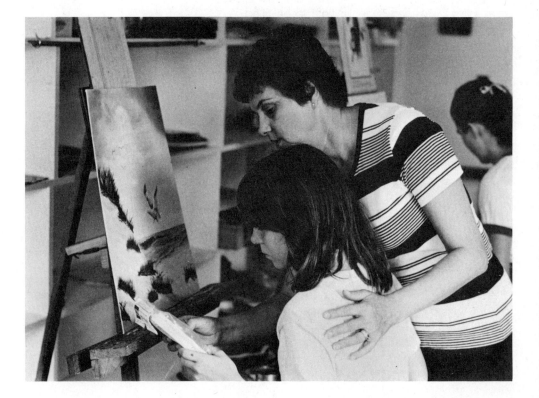

Rationale for the Middle School

A successful middle school depends
more upon faculties than facilities,
more on people than upon the purse

INTRODUCTION

The middle school of the 1980s has emerged from the junior high school. Ironi-
cally, the stated goals of the middle school today are exactly the goals espoused for
the junior high school when it began in 1910. These goals are to provide a
transitional school between the elementary school and the high school and to help
students bridge the gap in their development between childhood and adolescence.

Those persons interested in the middle school concept can better understand
the present middle school by examining the historical development of the junior
high school and its growth.[1] In the first sections of this chapter, we will trace the
emergence and growth of both the junior high school and the middle school. In later
sections, we will present goals for the middle school with criteria for organizing
such a program.

---

[1] John Lounsbury and Gordon Vars, *A Curriculum for the Middle School Years* (New York:
Harper & Row Publishers, 1978), p. 14.

THE JUNIOR HIGH SCHOOL

The rapid growth of the high school in the United States after the Civil War resulted in many patterns of school organization. Some sections of the country operated under an 8–5 plan—eight years of elementary school and five years of high school.[2] Others operated under an 8–4 pattern with eight years of elementary school and four of high school. Still others had six years of elementary school and six years in high school. The 8–4 pattern became popular toward the end of the nineteenth century with the elementary school seen as preparation for high school and the high school serving a college-preparatory function.

In the late 1800s and early 1900s, a number of national committees and commissions were organized to study secondary education. In general, these committees favored moving the secondary program down into the elementary grades. The familiar bulletin, *Cardinal Principles of Secondary Education,* recommended that a school system be organized into a six-year elementary school with a six-year high school designed to serve pupils twelve to eighteen years of age. The *Bulletin* also suggested that secondary education be divided into two periods designated as the junior and senior periods.[3] The influence of colleges on secondary committees and commissions was reflected in the reports of those groups. For instance, the report of the Committee of Ten in 1893, one of the most influential in American education, stressed that high school subjects such as algebra and foreign languages be initiated in the last years of the elementary school. It also suggested a 6–6 pattern of schooling.[4]

While a separate junior high school was advocated in the early 1900s, it was simply thought of as a part of the high school. However, research studies on school dropouts and the psychological theory advanced by G. Stanley Hall began to focus increased attention on adolescent youth. Statements of "individual differences" and "meeting the needs of early adolescents" began to show up in educational literature. The junior high movement was underway.

In 1909, the first junior high school with grades 7–8–9 was introduced. Columbus, Ohio, was the first district to use the term *junior high school.*

In January 1910 Superintendent Frank Bunker of Berkeley, California, reported to the school board that two new junior high schools or introductory high schools would reduce the high dropout rate in the high schools and relieve overcrowded conditions.[5] In 1919, the North Central Association of Colleges and Secondary Schools defined the junior high school as a school in which grades 7, 8, and 9 were placed in a building of their own with their own teaching staff and administrators.

By 1920, approximately 400 junior high schools were in existence and the

---

[2] Alvin Howard and George Stoumbis, *The Junior High and Middle School: Issues and Practices* (Scranton: Intext Educational Publishers, 1970), p. 6.

[3] Commission on the Reorganization of Secondary Education, *Cardinal Principles of Secondary Education,* Bulletin 1918, No. 35 (Washington, D.C.: U.S. Dept. of the Interior, Bureau of Education, 1918), pp. 12–13.

[4] National Education Association, *Report of the Committee of Ten on Secondary School Studies* (New York: American Book Co., 1894), p. 45.

[5] Frank Bunker, *The Junior High School Movement: Its Beginnings* (Washington, D.C.: Roberts, 1935), pp. 10–16.

Figure 1.1
A Middle School in the United States in 1898

number was growing. By the mid-fifties there were approximately 6,500 junior high schools in the United States.

Although the majority of junior high schools were composed of grades 7–8–9, there were a number of other combinations including 8–9, 7–10, and 6–8. A number of 7–12 secondary schools still existed. Indeed, a public "middle school" with grades 5–8 existed in the United States in 1898 (see Figure 1.1).

The curriculum of the junior high school tended to parallel that of the high school. Teacher training institutions also prepared "secondary" teachers for positions in the junior high schools. Very few college courses dealt with pre- or early adolescent behavior. The organization of the junior high school also imitated that of the high school. The emphasis was on mastery of subject matter with the program carried out through departmentalization. Activities such as varsity athletics, cheerleading, proms, marching bands, and even cap-and-gown graduation exercises tended to exert considerable pressures on junior high students. The junior high school was in reality a "junior" high school.

The Carnegie unit credit assigned to grade 9 exerted additional influence on the course offerings of the junior high school. Later, the same argument for controlling the courses in the ninth grade was used to move the ninth grade to the high school and structure 6–8 middle schools.

The junior high school was not without its critics and there were attempts to reform the program and organization of the junior high through the addition of exploratory programs and core teaching. William Gruhn and Harl Douglass conducted a study of the junior high school in the 1940s and developed six basic functions of the junior high school:

> Function One—*Integration*. This is designed to help students use the skills, attitudes, and understandings previously acquired and integrate them into effective and wholesome behavior.
>
> Function Two—*Exploration*. To allow students the opportunity to explore particular interests so that they can choose better choices and actions, both vocational and academic. Students will develop a wide range of cultural, civic, social, recreational, and avocational interests.
>
> Function Three—*Guidance*. To help students make better decisions about vocational and educational activities and help students make satisfactory social, emotional, and social adjustments toward mature personalities.
>
> Function Four—*Differentiation*. To provide differential educational opportunities and facilities in accord with varying backgrounds, personalities, and other individual differences of students so that each pupil can achieve most economically and completely the ultimate aims of education.
>
> Function Five—*Socialization*. To furnish learning experiences intended to prepare students for effective and satisfying participation in a complex social order as well as future changes in the social order.
>
> Function Six—*Articulation*. To provide for a gradual transition from pre-adolescent education to an educational program suited to the needs of adolescent girls and boys.[6]

Gruhn and Douglass, as well as other leaders of the junior high movement such as Leonard Koos, Vernon Bennett, Calvin Davis, Thomas Briggs, and later John Lounsbury, William Van Til, Gordon Vars, and Maurice Ahrens, could not break the junior high school away from the high school mold. After forty years of existence, the deficiencies of the junior high school remained. In the late 1950s and early 1960s the middle school emerged as an alternative to the junior high school.

THE EMERGENCE OF THE MIDDLE SCHOOL

Although the junior high school was under constant fire, no specific major alternative structure was proposed until the middle school captured the public's attention in the early 1960s. Dr. William Alexander helped revive the term *middle school* used in some American private schools and long used in European schools, and gave the term a new set of educational attributes.

---

[6] William Gruhn and Harl Douglass, *The Modern Junior High School* (New York: Ronald, 1956), pp. 31–32.

Four factors led to the emergence of the American middle school. First, the late 1950s and early 1960s were filled with criticisms of American schools, classroom and teacher shortages, double and triple sessions, and soaring tax rates; books like *Why Johnny Can't Read* triggered new concerns about the quality of schooling in the United States. The successful launching of Sputnik in 1957 led to further criticism, especially about the curriculum of elementary and secondary schools. (Sputnik created an obsession for academic achievement especially in science, foreign languages, and mathematics.)

At this time a renewed interest in college preparation led to a call for a four-year high school where specialized courses like computer sciences and microbiology could remain under the direction of the college preparatory school, the high school. Likewise, the inclusion of grades 5 and 6 in an intermediate school promised to strengthen instruction by allowing subject specialists to work with younger students. Many of the first middle schools were organized with grades 5–8.

A second factor leading to the emergence of the middle school was the elimination of racial segregation. *The Schoolhouse in the City* stated that the real force behind the middle school movement in the larger cities (New York City, for example) was the elimination of *de facto* segregation.[7]

A third factor leading to the emergence of the middle school was the increased enrollments of school-aged children in the 1950s and 1960s. The shortage of buildings resulted in double and even triple school sessions in school districts. Because older students in high schools were able to cope with overcrowding better than younger students, the ninth grade was moved to the high school to relieve the overcrowded junior high school. The same rationale was used to relieve the elementary school by moving the fifth and/or sixth grade to the junior high school.

A fourth factor favorable to the emergence of the middle school was the "bandwagon effect." This resulted when one middle school received favorable exposure in books and periodicals, and some administrators determined that the middle school was "the thing to do."

All of the four factors above may not have been the most valid reasons why middle schools were organized, but regardless of the "wrong reasons," educators seized the right opportunities to develop programs designed for the pre- and early adolescent learner.

It is ironic that in the early 1980s the same four factors influencing middle school development exist except for two changes, i.e., the criticism of schools is not directed toward language, science, and mathematics excellence, but toward basic skills in reading and mathematics, and the increased enrollment of the 1950s and 1960s has become a declining enrollment in the 1980s.

Today junior high schools are being reorganized into middle schools to eliminate segregation, to alleviate population and building problems brought on by declining enrollment, to improve basic skills programs in the middle grades, and because "other districts have middle schools and we should too."

Although these are *de facto* reasons for reorganizing junior high schools into middle schools, we believe the following rationale, providing a more relevant and

---

[7] Educational Facilities Laboratories, *The Schoolhouse in the City* (New York: Educational Facilities Laboratories, 1966), p. 10.

appropriate program and learning environment for "transescent"[8] learners, is easier to justify:

1. To provide a program especially designed for the 10–14 year old child going through the unique "transescent" period of growth and development. There is recognition that students 10–14 constitute a distinct grouping—physically, socially, and intellectually.

2. To build upon the changed elementary school. Historically, the post-Sputnik clamor to upgrade schools prepared the way for elementary school personnel to accept the middle school concept. The introduction of the "new" science, the "new" social studies, the "new" mathematics, and the "new" linguistics in elementary schools eroded the sanctity of the self-contained classroom. As part of the reorganization of curriculum that followed Sputnik, elementary teachers tended to cultivate a specific content area in the curriculum. This led to a departure from the self-contained classroom toward more sharing of students among teachers.

3. Dissatisfaction with the existing junior high school. The junior high school, in most cases, did not become a transitional school between the elementary and senior high school. Unfortunately, it became a miniature high school with all the sophisticated activities of the high school. Instruction was often formal and discipline centered with insufficient attention given to the student as a person.

4. To facilitate educational change. A more rapid and comprehensive change is frequently effected by creating a new institution rather than attempting to remodel an older one. Teachers and administrators in a new school, free from the constraints and traditions of an existing school, are more receptive to innovations and new ideas.[9]

Why a Middle School?

Many reasons have been advanced for the existence of the middle school. After examining statements of rationale for numerous middle schools, two basic reasons emerged for their development:

1. A special program is needed for the 10–14 year-old child going through the unique "transescent" period in his growth and development. . . . The widest range of differences in terms of physical, social, and intellectual growth is found in middle school youngsters. Such a wide range of differences calls for an individualized program that is lacking in most junior high schools. The middle school provides for individual differences with the program tailored to fit each child.

---

[8] Donald Eichhorn, *The Middle School* (New York: The Center for Applied Research in Education, 1966), p. 3. "Transescence is the stage of development which begins prior to the onset of puberty and extends through the early stages of adolescence. Since puberty does not occur for all precisely at the same chronological age in human development, the transescent designation is based on the many physical, social, and emotional changes in body chemistry that appear prior to the time when the body gains a practical degree of stabilization over those complex pubescent changes."

[9] A Report of the Special State Committee on the Middle School, *Development of Middle Schools in Florida,* ed. Ed Trauschke (Tallahassee, Fla.: State Department of Education, 1972), pp. 2–4.

2. The middle school through a new program and organization provides for much needed innovations in curriculum and instruction. Through the creation of a new school, the middle school, rather than remodeling the outmoded junior high school, educators have provided an atmosphere for implementing those practices long talked about but seldom effected.[10]

Advantages of the Middle School

Early in the middle school movement, a comprehensive list of sixteen advantages for the middle school were compiled which exist today:

1. It gives this unit a status of its own, rather than a "junior" classification.

2. It facilitates the introduction in grades 5 and 6 of some specialization and team teaching in staff patterns.

3. It also facilitates the reorganization of teacher education which is sorely needed to provide teachers competent for the middle school; since existing patterns of neither the elementary nor the secondary teacher training program would suffice, a new pattern must be developed.

4. Developmentally, children in grades 6–8 are probably more alike than children in grades 7–9.

5. Since they are undergoing the common experience of adolescence, 6th–8th graders should have special attention, special teachers, and special programs, which the middle school permits.

6. It provides an opportunity for gradual change from the self-contained classroom to complete departmentalization.

7. Additional facilities and specialists can be made available to all children one year earlier.

8. It permits the organization of a program with emphasis upon a continuation and enrichment of basic education in the fundamentals.

9. It facilitates extending guidance services into the elementary grades.

10. It helps to slow down the "growing up" process from K–8 because the oldest group is removed from each level.

11. It puts children from the entire district together one year earlier, aiding sociologically their development.

12. Physical unification of grades 9–12 permits better coordination of courses for the senior high school.

13. It eliminates the possibility of some students and parents not being aware of the importance of the ninth grade as part of the senior high school record, particularly in terms of college admission.

14. It eliminates the need for special programs and facilities for one grade and eliminates the problems created by the fact that the ninth grade is functionally a part of the senior high school.

---

[10] Joseph Bondi, *Developing Middle Schools: A Guidebook* (Wheeling, Ill.: Whitehall Publishing Co., 1972), p. 12.

15. It reduces duplication of expensive equipment and facilities for the one grade. The funds can be spent on facilities beneficial to all grades.

16. It provides both present and future flexibility in building planning, particularly when it comes to changing school population.[11]

Functions of a Middle School

Middle schools, both in recognition and numbers, have become a separate intermediate institution in America. Cumulative experience, research, and proof that "the middle school works" have resulted in widespread acceptance of the middle school by children, teachers, administrators, and parents. We have defined the middle school as a transitional school concerned with the most appropriate program to cope with the personal and educational needs of emerging adolescent learners. The ASCD has identified the middle school as an institution which has the following:

1. A unique program adapted to the needs of the pre- and early adolescent student.

2. The widest possible range of intellectual, social, and physical experiences.

3. Opportunities for exploration and development of fundamental skills needed by all while making allowances for individual learning patterns. It should maintain an atmosphere of basic respect for individual differences.

4. A climate that enables students to develop abilities, find facts, weigh evidence, draw conclusions, determine values, and that keeps their minds open to new facts.

5. Staff members who recognize and understand the student's needs, interests, backgrounds, motivations, goals, as well as stresses, strains, frustrations, and fears.

6. A smooth education transition between the elementary school and the high school while allowing for the physical and emotional changes taking place due to transescence.

7. An environment where the child, not the program, is most important and where the opportunity to succeed is ensured for all students.

8. Guidance in the development of mental processes and attitudes needed for constructive citizenship and the development of lifelong competencies and appreciations needed for effective use of leisure.

9. Competent instructional personnel who will strive to understand the students whom they serve and develop professional competencies which are both unique and applicable to the transescent student.

10. Facilities and time which allow students and teachers an opportunity to achieve the goals of the program to their fullest capabilities.[12]

---

[11] Pearl Brod, as reported in Joseph Bondi's *Developing Middle Schools: A Guidebook* (Wheeling, Ill.: Whitehall Publishing Co., 1972), pp. 13–14.

[12] ASCD Working Group in the Emerging Adolescent Learner, *The Middle School We Need* (Washington, D.C.: Association for Supervision and Curriculum Development, 1975), pp. 2–3. Used with permission.

Table 1.1

The Middle School Unique and Transitional

	Elementary	Middle	High
Teacher-Student Relationship	Parental	Advisor	Instructor
Teacher Organization	Self-contained	Interdisciplinary Team	Department
Curricular Emphasis	Skills	Exploration	Depth
Schedule	Self-contained	Block	Periods
Instruction	Student-Directed	Balance	Teacher-Directed
Student Grouping	Chronological	Multi-age Developmental	Subject
Building Plan	Classroom Areas	Team Areas	Department Areas
Psychomotor Development	Skills & Games	Skills & Intramurals	Skills & Interscholastics
Utilization of Media	Classroom Groups	Balance	Individual Study
Guidance	Diagnostic/Dev.	Teacher Helper	Career-Vocational
Teacher Preparation	Child-oriented Generalist	Flexible Resource	Disciplines Specialist

Table 1.1 illustrates the unique and transitory nature of the middle school.

The middle school, then, represents a renewed effort to design and implement a program of education which can accommodate the needs of the preadolescent population. It is a broadly focused program drawing its philosophy and rationale from the evolving body of knowledge concerned with human growth and development. The middle school represents a systematic effort to organize the schooling experience in a way which will facilitate the maximum growth and development of all learners.

The middle school program consists of arrangements and activities which attempt to tie formal learning directly to the developmental needs of the student. To date, identified "developmental tasks" represent the most promising criteria for curriculum development which intersects school activity with learner growth and development.

Developmental Tasks

The school does not represent our society's only mechanism for preservation and adaptation. The family, the church, and the media, all contribute to the educative processes of society. The public school, however, still remains the only formal sanctioned institution created and supported to preserve and promote that society.

A problem that has plagued educational planners throughout this century is how to determine the scope of the school's responsibility in educating children. As social, economic, and political forces have acted on our nation, the dimension of school operation and the role of the school has fluctuated. Today the scope of school responsibilities is immense. The educative process has expanded to serve 45 million pupils each day, or fifteen times as many individuals as were in the armed services at the height of the Vietnam War. With such size has come increasing diversity of both responsibility and concern.

Obviously, public schools cannot continue to expand their concerns and commitments indefinitely. They must, through program planning, identify those areas which can be dealt with within the boundaries of available resources. Schools must develop a focus and set standards for the determination of the curriculum.

One way schools might work responsibly with young people of all backgrounds and capacities has been called the "developmental tasks" of growth. As formulated by sociologist Robert Havighurst in the early 1950s, developmental tasks of human growth represent universal steps in a culture toward achieving adulthood. An assumption made in considering developmental tasks as possible criteria for school planning (and one essential to the acceptance of the middle school rationale) is that the comprehensive development and expansion of human potential is an important concern of the school.

During the past twenty years, developmental psychologists, educators, sociologists, and others have identified many "tasks" regularly encountered by all individuals in our society as they progress from childhood to adolescence. Examples of such tasks are shown in Table 1.2.

While these developmental tasks are only suggestive of the kinds of concerns and needs experienced by young persons between early childhood and adolescence, they do indicate some areas where school programs can intervene meaningfully in the developmental process.

At the early childhood level, representing the corresponding school years from nursery school through the third grade, there might be a focus on the following kinds of needs:

1. *Social Adjustment.* An introduction of institutional living, a building of relationships with other children and adults, the encouragement of socially acceptable behaviors.

2. *Initial Physical Development.* The encouragement of both gross motor skills and specialized tasks associated with the schooling process. Also, the detection and correction of progress-retarding deficiencies, such as visual and learning problems.

3. *An Awareness of Self.* The establishment and awareness of identity as an individual. The development of autonomy, an exploration of roles, the discovery of interests and talents.

4. *Academic Readiness.* Consisting of learning basal knowledge, developing learning skills, establishing symbols literacy, promoting positive attitudes toward schooling.

5. *Sensory Development.* Encouraging expansion of the five senses including aesthetic appreciation and an awareness of environmental beauty. (No priority for importance is intended by the order of these categories.)

Table 1.2
Examples of Developmental Tasks

Adolescence
Emancipation from parent dependency
Occupational projection selection
Completion of value structure
Acceptance of self

Preadolescence
Handling major body changes
Asserting independence from family
Establishing sex role identity
Dealing with peer group relationships
Controlling emotions
Constructing a values foundation
Pursuing interest expression
Utilizing new reasoning capacities
Developing acceptable self-concept

Late Childhood
Mastering communication skill
Building meaningful peer relations
Thinking independently
Acceptance of self
Finding constructive expression outlets
Role projection

Middle Childhood
Structuring the physical world
Refining language and thought patterns
Establishing relationships with others
Understanding sex roles

Early Childhood
Developing motor control
Emerging self-awareness
Mapping out surroundings
Assigning meaning to events
Exploring relationships with others
Developing language and thought patterns

SOURCE: Jon Wiles, *Planning Guidelines for Middle School Education* (Dubuque, Iowa: Kendall/Hunt Publishing Co., 1976), p. 7.

In the intermediate years, corresponding to grades 4–8, the focus of programs might be:

1. *Social Development and Refinement.* To facilitate the acceptance of new roles and responsibilities, to teach the interdependence of individuals in society, to explore social values, to teach basic communications and human relations skills.

2. *Promotion of Physical and Mental Health.* An intensive program of exercise designed to develop conditioning and coordination. An accompanying

component used to promote positive physical and mental health practices. Basic sex education.

3. *Development of Self-concept and Self-acceptance.* To promote feelings of worth in all individuals, to accentuate strengths, to aid in the development of realistic perceptions and expectations of self, to foster increased independence, to assist in values exploration, to explore and expand interests.

4. *Academic Adequacy.* To insure literacy, to aid in the organization needed for academic achievement, to teach skills for continued learning, to introduce knowlege areas, to explore career potentials as they relate to interests, to develop independence and autonomy in learning, to foster critical thinking.

5. *Aesthetic Stimulation.* To develop latent talents in art, music, writing, to promote an understanding of man's aesthetic achievement, to develop a capacity for the satisfying use of leisure time. (No priority for importance is intended by the order of these categories.)

In the secondary school, corresponding to the first years of the high school and perhaps into the post-secondary years (9–13), the following program focus might be utilized:

1. *Social Maturation.* Promoting increased independence and autonomy in decision making, exploring the rights and responsibilities of adulthood and citizenship, studying marriage and family life, exploring socially acceptable means of communication.

2. *Refinement of Health.* Defining and analyzing the meaning of good health for individuals and society, the personalizing of positive health plans, an emphasis on programs of individual health development and maintenance, a study of causation of poor health (drugs, alcoholism, smoking, obesity).

3. *Supporting Self-actualization.* Assisting in value clarification, exploration of careers and education as extensions of individual needs and interests, the correction of minor psychological and emotional problems, the identification and emphasis of personal strengths.

4. *Academic Specialization.* The development of specialization in knowledge and learning skills, an exploration of academic opportunities, the refinement of critical and analytical thinking, an emphasis on the utility of knowledge in everyday living.

5. *Aesthetic Refinement.* The pursuit of quality living, an emphasis of social existence, the refinement of aesthetic talents, the development of satisfying hobbies, an understanding of man's capacities for further achievements. (No priority of importance is intended by the order of these categories.)

Utilizing developmental tasks as criteria for planning school programs suggests some global areas of focus for activity development. Outlined on the next page are some continuums of concern:

Early childhood	Intermediate	Secondary
Social Adjustment	Social Development	Social Maturation
Initial Physical Development	Promotion of Physical Development	Refinement of Physical Health
Self-awareness	Self-acceptance	Self-actualization
Academic Readiness	Academic Adequacy	Academic Specialization
Sensory Development	Aesthetic Stimulation	Aesthetic Refinement

$$\longrightarrow \text{Continuums of Growth in School} \longrightarrow$$

Even though educators must analyze student needs at each level of education, it is interesting to view in isolation the tasks and possible roles of schooling at the intermediate level of education:

Tasks

Late Childhood
Mastery of communication
Building peer relationships
Thinking as an individual
Acceptance of self
Finding means of expression
Role projection

Preadolescence
Handling physical change
Asserting independence
Establishing sex-role identity
Refining peer relationships
Controlling emotions
Constructing a values foundation
Pursuing interest
Use of reasoning capacity
Developing self-concept

School Roles

1. *Social development and refinement*
   Acceptance of responsibility
   Interdependence of individuals
   Exploration of social values
   Human relations
   Communications skills

2. *Promotion of physical and mental health*
   Conditioning and coordination
   Understanding hygiene
   Sex education
   Understanding nutrition

3. *Develop self-concept and self-acceptance*
   Accentuate strengths
   Self-analysis
   Increased responsibility
   Values exploration
   Interest expansion

4. *Academic adequacy*
   Basic literacy
   Organized for academic achievement
   Skills for continued learning
   Introduce knowledge areas
   Explore career potential
   Develop learning autonomy
   Critical thinking

5. *Aesthetic stimulation*
   Develop latent talents
   Promote aesthetic appreciation
   Develop leisure time activities

Matching some of the developmental tasks of late childhood and preadolescence with some of the possible roles of the school during the corresponding grade levels highlights interesting conditions existing in intermediate education. Few programs in the middle grades justify their experiences in terms of student needs. The narrowness of the curriculum in most intermediate schools is a historical hybrid derived from other levels of schooling.

If educational planners choose to use the developmental needs of the students being served as criteria for curriculum development, the school must broaden its definition of an "education." There must be a greater concern of social and emotional dimensions of preadolescent development, since academic preparation and physical development represent only part of the needs of emerging adolescents.

Our growing awareness of the affective dimensions of learning, such as feelings, attitudes, and emotions, suggest that we must deal with preadolescents in a more sophisticated and comprehensive manner. We can no longer afford to ignore the environmental conditions surrounding the schooling process. Further, we must acknowledge that our objectives in formal schooling require altered behaviors as well as a growth in intellect.

It seems obvious that the kinds of administrative and curricular arrangements made by the school at both the building and classroom level will need to be rethought and redesigned. Greater program flexibility and diversity will have to be introduced in all facets of school life. Activity will have to be broadened and enriched.

Establishing an Identity for the Middle School

Education for emerging adolescents has received an intensive re-examination over the past decade. One result has been the verification of a need for a school with a differentiated function for the age group 10–14. That need for a distinct school unlike the elementary, high school, or even the junior high school, is more defensible than ever in light of recent information about growth and development of emerging adolescents. Changing social conditions have also helped establish the need for a school in the middle with an identity of its own. As middle schools have grown in number and quality, a number of common elements have helped establish an identity for the middle school. Here are some of these:

1. Absence of the "little high school" approach.

2. Absence of the "star system" where a few special students dominate everything, in favor of an attempt to provide success experiences for greater numbers of students.

3. An attempt to use instructional methods more appropriate to this age group: individualized instruction, variable group sizes, multi-media approaches, beginning independent study programs, inquiry-oriented instruction.

4. Increased opportunity for teacher-student guidance. (May include a home base or advisory group program.)

5. Increased flexibility in scheduling and in student grouping.

6. At least some cooperative planning and team teaching.

7. At least some interdisciplinary studies, where teachers from a variety of academic pursuits provide opportunities for students to see how the areas of knowledge fit together.

8. A wide range of exploratory opportunities, academic and otherwise.

9. Increased opportunity for physical activity and movement, and more frequent physical education.

10. Earlier introduction to the areas of organized academic knowledge.

11. Attention to the skills of continued learning, those skills which will permit students to learn better on their own or at higher levels.

12. Accent on increasing the student's ability to be independent, responsible, and self-disciplined.

13. Flexible physical plant facilities.

14. Attention to the personal development of the student: values-clarification, group process skills, health and family life education when appropriate, career education.

15. Teachers trained especially for, and committed to, the education of emerging adolescents.

Neil Atkins, a pioneer in the middle school movement, early identified the features of the middle school that distinguish it as uniquely appropriate for the children it serves.[13] Those features include:

Attitudinal Stance. The uniqueness of the middle school comes not so much in grade organization, courses, grouping, or schedules as it does in matters of attitude, perception, and sensitivity. The mission of the school is viewed as neither remedial nor preparatory. The transitional nature of students 10–14 is not only recognized, but also valued. Therefore, the middle school can be characterized as having the capacity to accommodate children whose chronological age is dominated with problems of coping with change—changing interests, personal relationships, and changing bodies.

Operational Flexibility and Innovative Practice. Translated into operational terms, this means the middle school should be characterized organizationally by flexibility, instructionally by individualization, and environmentally by sensitivity to changing needs of the age group it serves. Middle school students are viewed as individuals and not groups for making instructional decisions.

The experimental attitude brought on by increased sensitivity and awareness about children has led to innovative practices and programs in the middle school.

Supportive Instructional Strategies. Another distinguishing feature of the middle school is the shift in emphasis from mastery to utilization of knowledge. Prominent features of the program include diagnostic teaching, individualized instruction,

---

[13] Neil Atkins, "Rethinking Education in the Middle," *Theory into Practice* 7 (June 1968): pp. 118–19.

self-directed learning, and learner-center evaluation. These closely interrelated strategies lead to a central goal of the middle school—namely, supporting the student's effort to move as a learner from dependence to independence. The organizational manifestation of instructional strategies is to remove gradually institutional restraints on movement and use of materials and equipment. Self-concept is strengthened through the power of competence, and a sense of inquiry and commitment to learning is fostered through the choices of alternative courses of action.

SUMMARY

The middle school model for intermediate education evolved from the earlier programs of the junior high school. Although the expressed goals of the junior high school and the middle school are similar, the middle school represents a new and different way of working with emerging adolescent youth.

Historically, the junior high school has tended to imitate the curriculum of the senior high school. By contrast, the middle school was established as a school with its own special identity and organization. The social changes of the 1960s and 1970s, such as fluctuating enrollments, desegregation, and other factors, provided the right opportunities for educators to launch this new school form. Because of its unique structure, the middle school may be able to achieve the early junior high school's goals.

The emergence of the middle school has resulted in a renewed interest in the developmental characteristics of pupils between early childhood and adolescence. These common tasks of growing represent one planning base for conceptualizing the intermediate school program.

We believe that the purposeful design of the middle school program will result in an educational experience highly effective for students in the intermediate years.

Suggested Learning Activities

1. Tracing the history of the junior high school, try to identify those factors that led to the eventual establishment of the middle school.

2. List five differences between the junior high school and the middle school. If the goals of the junior high school and the middle school are basically the same, how is the middle school unique?

3. Write a philosophical statement defending the emerging middle school design. Try to determine what parts of the middle school concept are essential.

Selected References

Alexander, William et al. *The Emergent Middle School.* 2nd edition. New York: Holt, Rinehart and Winston, Inc., 1969.

A.S.C.D. Commission on Secondary Curriculum. *The Junior High School We Need.* Washington, D.C.: Association for Supervision and Curriculum Development, 1961.

A.S.C.D. Working Group on the Emerging Adolescent Learner. *The Middle School We Need.* Washington, D.C.: Association for Supervision and Curriculum Development, 1975.

Center for Urban Education. *The School in the Middle—Divided Opinion on Dividing Schools.* New York: Center for Urban Education, 1968.

Commission on the Reorganization of Secondary Education. *Cardinal Principles of Secondary Education.* Bulletin 1918, no. 35. Washington, D.C.: U.S. Department of Interior, Bureau of Education, 1918.

Howard, Alvin, and Stoumbis, George. *The Junior High School and Middle School—Issues and Practices.* Scranton, Pennsylvania: Intext Educational Publishers, 1970.

Overly, Donald; Kinghorn, Jon; and Preston, Richard. *The Middle School: Humanizing Education for Youth.* Worthington, Ohio: Charles Jones Publishing Co., 1972.

2

The Middle School Student

Nothing is so unequal as the
equal treatment of unequals

INTRODUCTION

The most important group of pupils in our schools today is a diverse group of youngsters caught in the middle years—the years between childhood and adolescence. A growing amount of knowledge is at hand to show that what happens to students between the ages of ten and fourteen determines not only their future success in school, but success in life as well.[1]

Writings on the subject are filled with short, sometimes clever, descriptions of young adolescents—"awkward and clumsy," "filled with turbulent emotions," "displays emerging independence," "trying." Yet, who *are* these young adolescents in the middle grades of our school?

This chapter is designed to give the reader a better understanding of the characteristics of emerging adolescent learners and resultant implications for school programs. It also provides a study of the problems of a modern society that are exerting a profound influence on an impressionable age group.

---

[1] Joseph Bondi, "Caught in the Middle" (Keynote speech, State Conference of the Tennessee Association of Middle Schools, Memphis, August 3, 1978).

19

Figure 2.1
Understanding the Emerging Adolescent Learner

How high is the sky?
Who invented the tie?
Why was I born?
Who am I?
What is the reason?
When is a season?
Where am I going
This I really have to know.

Fred Buckman, Fitzgerald Middle School, Largo, Florida

The poem in Figure 2.1 reflects the uncertainty of the emerging adolescent who is neither boy nor man, neither girl nor woman. Because we often don't understand the behavior of others, we are likely to attribute the worst possible motives to them. This especially holds true for young adolescents. When confronted with normal behaviors of young adolescents, such as loud talking or wearing outlandish clothes, we believe they are done purposively to frustrate or infuriate us. David Elkind, the American child psychologist, has, through the interpretation of his studies and those of Piaget (see Figure 2.2), provided us with insights into the troubling behaviors of emerging adolescents.[2]

---

[2] David Elkind, *A Sympathetic Understanding of the Child: Birth to Sixteen* (Boston: Allyn & Bacon, Inc., 1971). We are grateful to Dr. Elkind for furnishing us background information for this section from a keynote talk delivered at the Annual Conference of the Florida League of Middle Schools, St. Petersburg, Florida, October 1, 1976.

Figure 2.2
Stages of Intellectual Development as Described by Piaget

Stage of Development—Middle Years	7–15 Age Range
Concrete Operations	7–11 years

Ability to think out problems previously "worked" out. Logical thought, e.g., genuine classification, learning to organize objects into a series; reversing operations (as in arithmetic).

a. learns to master logical operations using material with a concrete content,
b. unable to think abstractly about a problem,
c. an understanding of the principle of conservation leads directly to an awareness of reversibility,
d. can use various approaches to the solution of a problem,
e. concerned with the relationship of the parts to the whole,
f. can perform the operation of serializing,
g. language becomes primarily socio-centric while egocentric speech decreases,
h. can comprehend the following four concrete operational groupings:
   i) combinativity
   ii) reversibility
   iii) associativity
   iv) identity or nullifiability

Formal Operations	11–15 years

Comprehension of abstract concepts, e.g., ability to form "ideas" and reason about the future, ability to handle contrary-to-fact propositions, and ability to develop and test hypotheses.

Substage III-A	11–12 to 14–15 years

Appears to be a preparatory stage in which the adolescent may make correct discoveries and handle certain formal operations, but the approach is cumbersome and he is not yet able to provide systematic and rigorous proof.

Substage III-B	14–15 years onward

The adolescent is capable of formulating more elegant generalizations and advancing more inclusive laws; most of all he is able to provide spontaneously more systematic proof, since he can use methods of control.

A higher degree of mastery of the formal operations; he has the ability to make logical combinations in the following ways:

   i) combine by conjunction
   ii) combine by disjunction
   iii) combine by implication
   iv) combine by incompatibility

SOURCE: Table form adapted from Ernest R. Hilgard and Richard C. Atkinson, *Introduction to Psychology,* 4th ed. (New York: Harcourt, Brace and World, 1968). The information presented in the table represents a synthesis of descriptions of Piaget's Theory of Intellectual Development cited in Robert F. Biehler, *Psychology Applied to Teaching* (Boston: Houghton Mifflin Company, 1971), p. 81; and Herbert Ginsburg and Sylvia Opper, *Piaget's Theory of Intellectual Development* (Englewood Cliffs, N.J.: Prentice-Hall, Inc., 1969), pp. 26–206.

A common problem of young adolescents is their tendency to interpret situations more complexly than is warranted. For instance, simple decisions about what slacks or dress to wear are overcomplicated by bringing in extraneous concerns about how and why the clothes were bought in the first place. In school, young adolescents often approach their subjects at a much too complex level and fail in them, not because the studies are too hard, but too simple.

Elkind attributes such behaviors to newly attained thinking capacities made possible through what Piaget calls *formal operations.* Formal operations allow a pupil to hold many variables in mind at the same time, to conceive ideals and contrary-to-fact propositions. But in the young adolescent, these newly attained formal operations often are not under full control. The capacity to think of many alternatives is not immediately coupled with the ability to assign priorities and to decide which choice is best. That is why young adolescents sometimes appear stupid when they are, in fact, too bright.

Formal operations also allow young adolescents to think about other people's thinking. This ability is not always coupled with the ability to distinguish between what is of interest to others and what is of interest to self. Because the emerging adolescent is concerned with all the physical and social changes that are going on, he believes everyone else is as equally preoccupied with his appearance or behavior. Young adolescents, then, surround themselves with an imaginary audience.

The imaginary audience makes young adolescents extremely self-conscious. They believe they are the center of everyone's attention. Fantasies of making a touchdown or singing before a large audience are common imaginary audience fantasies in which the young adolescent is the center of everyone's attention. Groups of young adolescents sometimes contrive to create an audience by loud and provocative behavior. What is of immediate interest to them often annoys adults within listening range. The pervasive imaginary audience of young adolescents accounts for both their self-consciousness and their boorish public behavior.

Vandalism in schools, which seems so irrational, becomes less so when one understands that it is often done with audience reaction in mind. The young vandal speculates how outraged the audience will be when he is committing the act.

The center stage, I-me world of emerging adolescents leads them to believe they are special and not subject to the natural laws that pertain to others. The young girl who becomes pregnant, or the young man who experiments with drugs, believes other people will get pregnant, but not me; other people will become addicted to drugs, but not me.

The *self* is an all-important preoccupation of young people and they assume that what is common to everyone is unique to them. One example is the son who says, "Dad, you just don't know how it feels to be in love," or the daughter who says, "Mom, you just don't know how much I need a new dress."

The reverse preoccupation also occurs. Young adolescents may feel that everyone is concerned with the freckles on their nose. To argue with the young person that he is, in fact, good looking carries little impact because it is arguing with another person's reality.

As young people grow and mature, they begin to share their concerns with others and develop friendships in which intimacies are shared. The tragic, self-destructive behavior of many young adolescents often occurs because they have a sense of loneliness brought on by the belief that their problems are uniquely theirs.

The emerging adolescent often displays hypocritical behavior. For instance, a young adolescent will refuse to allow a brother or sister in his room to borrow things, but will go into his father's study and borrow a typewriter, calculator, or cassette player and not return it. Hypocrisy is but another by-product of formal operations that have not been fully elaborated. The young adolescent is able to conceptualize fairly abstract rules of behavior, but lacks the experience to see their relevance to concrete behavior. The emerging adolescent who believes roles are for everyone else, but not for her, upsets adults who regard such behavior as self-serving. Again, it must be remembered that such behavior results from intellectual immaturity, not from a lack of moral character.

Adolescent idealism often results in the ability to conceive and express high moral principles, but not the ability to find concrete ways to attain them. As adolescents mature and begin to engage in meaningful activities, they learn the need to work toward ideas. The middle school can be a place where young people can become pragmatic without having to become cynical about ideals and moral principles.

Piaget and Elkind have helped middle school educators shift a whole set of behaviors attributed to emerging adolescents from the realm of "bad" to the realm of "behavior typical for the age. . . ." By recognizing that behaviors of middle school students reflect intellectual immaturity, middle school educators can themselves become more rational in their reactions to those students.

CHARACTERISTICS OF EMERGING ADOLESCENTS—IMPLICATIONS FOR THE MIDDLE SCHOOL

Pre- and early adolescents experience dramatic physical, social, emotional, and intellectual changes resulting from maturational changes. More biological changes occur in the body of youngsters between the ages of ten and fourteen than at any other period of life with the exception of their first three years. The middle school has benefited from recent research relating to children going through the major transition from late childhood to adolescence. Those research data have provided additional validated facts about the physiological and psychological dynamics acting in and upon emerging adolescent learners.

When junior high schools were first developed over seventy years ago, only generalized data regarding growth and development of students were available. Although important longitudinal studies featuring the growth and development of boys and girls were conducted between 1930 and 1960, the results of those studies had little impact on the educational program of young adolescents.

The middle school has attempted to use data pertinent to growth and development of ten-to-fourteen-year-olds to justify certain organizational patterns. Unfortunately, some of the data are incorrect. An example is data relating to earlier maturation of girls. Middle school literature is filled with statements purporting to show that American girls are reaching sexual maturity at a younger and younger age. Such statements are often used to justify the moving of sixth and, in some cases, fifth-grade students into the middle school.[3] Recent studies show that the average age at which girls first menstruate, 12.8 years, has not changed over the last thirty years.[4] A major study conducted by the National Institute of Health in

---

[3] J. M. Tanner, "Sequence, Tempo and Individual Variation in the Growth and Development of Boys and Girls Aged 12 to 16," *Daedalus,* 100 (Fall 1971), No. 4, pp. 1–24.

[4] Leona Zacharias, William Rand, and Richard Wurtman, "A Prospective Study of Sexual Development and Growth in American Girls: The Statistics of Menarche," *Obstetrical and Gynecological Survey,* 31 (April 1976), No. 4, pp. 325–27.

1976 reported that no significant difference in age existed in the first menstrual period (menarche) between girls in the study and their mothers. Seven hundred eighty-one girls participated in this study conducted at the Massachusetts Institute of Technology and Massachusetts General Hospital. (Girls in the study were of similar background and about the same height and weight of girls about the same age studied by researchers in 1943, 1954, and 1973.) These new results do not support the belief that each generation is taller and healthier than the last.

Because the transitional years between childhood and adolescence are marked by distinct changes in the bodies and minds of boys and girls, the success of the middle school depends on teachers and administrators understanding each learner and her unique developmental pattern.

In Table 2.1 the reader will be able to study in detail characteristics of emerging adolescent learners together with implications for the middle school.

Table 2.1

Development of Emerging Adolescents and Its Implications for the Middle School

Characteristics of Emerging Adolescents	Implications for the Middle School*
Physical Development	
Accelerated physical development begins in transescence marked by increase in weight, height, heart size, lung capacity, and muscular strength. Boys and girls are growing at varying rates of speed. Girls tend to be taller for the first two years and tend to be more physically advanced. Bone growth is faster than muscle development and the uneven muscle/bone development results in lack of coordination and awkwardness. Bones may lack protection of covering muscles and supporting tendons.	Provide a curriculum that emphasizes self-understanding about body changes. Health and science classes should provide experiences that will develop an understanding about body growth. Guidance counselors and community resource persons such as pediatricians can help students understand what is happening to their bodies. Adaptive physical education classes should be scheduled for students lacking physical coordination. Equipment should be designed for students in transescence to help them develop small and large muscles.
In the pubescent stage for girls, secondary sex characteristics continue to develop with breasts enlarging and menstruation beginning.	Intense sports competition; contact sports should be avoided. Schedule sex education classes; health and hygiene seminars for students.
A wide range of individual differences among students begins to appear in prepubertal and pubertal stages of development. Although the sequential order of development is relatively con-	Provide opportunities for interaction among students of multi-ages, but avoid situations where one's physical development can be compared with others (e.g., gang showers).

Table 2.1—*continued*

Characteristics of Emerging Adolescents	Implications for the Middle School*

Physical Development

sistent in each sex, boys tend to lag a year or two behind girls. There are marked individual differences in physical development for boys and girls. The age of greatest variability in physiological development and physical size is about age 13.

Intramural programs rather than interscholastic athletics should be emphasized so that each student may participate regardless of physical development. Where interscholastic sports programs exist, number of games should be limited, with games played in afternoon rather than evening.

Glandular imbalances occur resulting in acne, allergies, dental and eye defects—some health disturbances are real and some are imaginary.

Regular physical examinations should be provided all middle school students.

Display changes in body contour—large nose, protruding ears, long arms—have posture problems and are self-conscious about their bodies.

Health classes should emphasize exercises for good posture. Students should understand through self-analysis that growth is an individual process and occurs unevenly.

A girdle of fat often appears around the hips and thighs of boys in early puberty. A slight development of tissue under the skin around the nipples occurs for a short time and boys may fear they are developing "the wrong way." Considerable anxiety arises during this natural phase of development which quickly passes.

Films, talks by doctors, and counselors can help students understand the changes the body goes through in the period from childhood to adolescence. A carefully planned program of sex education developed in collaboration with parents, medical doctors, and community agencies should be developed.

Students are likely to be disturbed by body changes. Girls especially are likely to be disturbed about the physical changes that accompany sexual maturation.

Receding chins, cowlicks, dimples and changes in voice result in possible embarrassment to boys.

Teacher and parental reassurance and understanding are necessary to help students understand that many body changes are temporary in nature.

Boys and girls tend to tire easily but won't admit it.

Parents should be advised to insist that students get proper rest: overexertion by students should be discouraged.

Fluctuations in basal metabolism may cause students to be extremely restless at times and listless at others.

The school should provide an opportunity for daily exercise by students and a place where students can be children by playing and being noisy for short periods.

Table 2.1—*continued*

Characteristics of Emerging Adolescents	Implications for the Middle School*

Physical Development

	Activities such as special interest classes and "hands on" exercises should be encouraged. Students should be allowed to physically move around in their classes and avoid long periods of passive work.
Show ravenous appetites and peculiar tastes; may overtax digestive system with large quantities of improper foods.	Snacks should be provided to satisfy between-meal hunger. Nutritional guidance as applied to emerging adolescents should be provided.

Social Development

Affiliation base broadens from family to peer group. Conflict sometimes results due to splitting of allegiance between peer group and family.	Teachers should work closely with the family to help adults realize that peer pressure is a normal part of the maturation process. Parents should be encouraged to continue to provide love and comfort to their children even though they may feel their children are rejecting them.
	All teachers in the middle school should be counselors. Home-base, teacher advisor house plan arrangements should be encouraged.
Peers become sources for standards and models of behavior. Occasional rebellion on the part of child does not diminish importance of parents for development of values. Emerging adolescents want to make their own choices, but authority still remains primarily with family.	The school can sponsor activities that permit the student to interact socially with many school personnel. Family studies can help ease parental conflicts. Involvement of parents in the school should be encouraged. Students should know their parents are involved in the school program but parents should not be too conspicuous by their presence.
	Co-curricular activities should be encouraged. An active student government will help students develop guidelines for interpersonal relations and standards of behavior.
Mobility of society has broken ties to peer groups and created anxieties in emerging adolescent youth.	"Family" grouping of students and teachers can be encouraged to provide stability for students moving to a new school. Interdisciplinary units can be

Table 2.1—*continued*

Characteristics of Emerging Adolescents	Implications for the Middle School*
	Social Development
	structured to provide interaction among various groups of students. Clubs and special interest classes should be an integral part of the school day.
Students are confused and frightened by new school settings.	Orientation programs and "buddy systems" can reduce the trauma of moving from an elementary school to a middle school. Family teams can encourage a sense of belonging.
Show unusual or drastic behavior at times—aggressive, daring, boisterous, argumentative.	Debates, plays, playdays, and other activities should be scheduled at the middle school to allow students to "show off" in a productive way.
"Puppy love years"—show extreme devotion to a particular boy or girl friend but may transfer allegiance to a new friend overnight.	Role playing and guidance exercises can provide students the opportunity to act out feelings. Opportunities should be provided for social interaction between the sexes—parties, games, but not dances in the early grades of the middle school.
Feel the will of the group must prevail—sometimes almost cruel to those not in their group. Copy and display fads of extremes in clothes, speech, mannerisms, and handwriting; very susceptible to advertising.	Set up an active student government so students can develop their own guidelines for dress and behavior. Adults should be encouraged not to react in an outraged manner when extreme dress or mannerisms are displayed by young adolescents.
Strong concern for what is "right," and social justice. Show concern for less-fortunate others.	Activities should be planned to allow students to engage in service activities. Peer teaching can be encouraged to allow students to help other students. Community projects such as assisting in a senior citizens club or helping in a child care center can be planned by students and teachers.
Are influenced by adults—attempt to identify with adults other than their parents.	Flexible teaching patterns should prevail so students can interact with a variety of adults with whom they can identify.
Despite a trend toward heterosexual interests, same-sex affiliation tends to dominate during transescence.	Large group activities rather than boy-girl events should be scheduled. Intramurals can be scheduled so students can interact with friends of the same or opposite sex.

Table 2.1—*continued*

Characteristics of Emerging Adolescents	Implications for the Middle School*
Social Development	
Desire direction and regulation but reserve the right to question or reject suggestions of adults.	The middle school should provide opportunities for students to accept more responsibility in setting standards for behavior. Students should be helped to establish realistic goals and should be assisted in helping realize those goals.
Emotional Development	
Erratic and inconsistent behavior is prevalent among emerging adolescents. Anxiety and fear contrast with reassuring bravado. Feelings tend to shift between superiority and inferiority. Coping with physical changes, striving for independence from family and becoming a person in his own right and learning a new mode of intellectual functioning are all emotion-laden problems for emerging adolescents. Students have many fears, real and imagined. At no other time in development is a student likely to encounter such a diverse number of problems simultaneously.	Students in the middle school should be led in self-evaluation. Activities should be designed to help students play out their emotions. School activity programs should provide opportunities for shy students to be drawn out and loud students to engage in calming activities. Counseling must operate as a part of the learning program rather than as an adjunct to it. Students should be helped to interpret superiority and inferiority feelings. Mature value systems should be encouraged by allowing students to examine options of behavior and to study consequences of various actions.
	Students should be encouraged to assume leadership in group discussions and should experience frequent success and recognition for personal efforts and achievements. A general atmosphere of friendliness, relaxation, concern, and group cohesiveness should guide the program.
Chemical and hormone imbalances during transescence often trigger emotions that are little understood by the transescent. Students sometimes regress to childlike behavior.	Adults in the middle school should not pressure students to explain their emotions, i.e., crying for no reason. Occasional childlike behavior should not be ridiculed by adults.
	The school program should provide numerous possibilities for releasing emotional stress.
Too-rapid or too-slow physical development is often a source of irritation and concern. Development of second-	Appropriate sex education should be provided. Utilizing parents and community agencies should be encouraged in

Table 2.1—_continued_

Characteristics of Emerging Adolescents	Implications for the Middle School*

Emotional Development

ary sex characteristics may create additional tensions about rate of development.	the middle school. Pediatricians, psychologists, and counselors should be called on to assist students in understanding developmental changes.
Are easily offended and sensitive to criticism of personal shortcomings.	Sarcasm by adults should be avoided. Students should be helped to develop values in the solution of their problems.
Students tend to exaggerate simple occurrences and believe their problems are unique.	Socio-drama can be utilized to enable students to see themselves as others see them. Readings dealing with problems similar to their own can help students see that many problems are not unique.

Intellectual Development

Emerging adolescents display a wide range of skills and abilities unique to their developmental patterns.	A variety of approaches and materials in the teaching-learning process should be utilized in the middle school.
Students will range in development from the concrete-manipulatory stage of development to the ability to deal with abstract concepts. The transescent is intensely curious and growing in mental ability.	The middle school should treat students at their own intellectual levels providing immediate rather than remote goals. All subjects should be individualized. Skill grouping should be flexible.
Middle school learners prefer active over passive learning activities; prefer interaction with peers during learning activities.	Physical movement should be encouraged with small group discussions, learning centers, and creative dramatics suggested as good activity projects. Provide a program of learning that is exciting and meaningful.
Students in the middle school are usually very curious and exhibit a strong willingness to learn things they consider to be useful. Students enjoy using skills to solve "real-life" problems.	Organize curricula around real-life concepts such as conflict, competition, peer group influence. Provide activities in both formal and informal situations to improve reasoning powers. Studies of the community, environment are particularly relevant to the age group.
Students often display heightened egocentrism and will argue to convince others or to clarify their own thinking. Independent, critical thinking emerges.	Organized discussions of ideas and feelings in peer groups can facilitate self-understanding. Provide experiences for individuals to express themselves by

Table 2.1—*continued*

Characteristics of Emerging Adolescents	Implications for the Middle School*
	Intellectual Development
	writing and participating in dramatic productions.
Studies show brain growth in transescents slows between the ages of twelve and fourteen.	Existing cognitive skills of learners should be refined and continued cognitive growth during ages twelve to fourteen may not be expected.
	Opportunities should be provided for enjoyable studies in the arts. Self-expression should be encouraged in all subjects.

*The following sources were used by the authors in preparing this section:

Institute for Child Study, College of Education, University of Maryland, "Developmental Characteristics of Children and Youth," Chart, (Washington, D.C.: A.S.C.D., 1975).

R. Havighurst, *Developmental Tasks and Education* (New York: David McKay Co., 1972).

D. Elkind, *A Sympathetic Understanding of the Child: Birth to Sixteen* (Boston: Allyn & Bacon, 1971).

A.S.C.D. Working Group in the Emerging Adolescent Learner, *The Middle School We Need* (Washington, D.C.: A.S.C.D., 1975).

John Kohl, William Caldwell, and Donald Eichhorn, *Self-Appraisal and Development of the Middle School: An Inservice Approach* (The Pennsylvania School Study Council, 1970).

Donald Chase, *Proposed Reorganization Plan for Grades 6, 7, 8* (Glenn Eliyn, Ill.: Hadley Jr. High School, 1978).

The extreme differences in the rate and scale of growth and development among preadolescents is summarized in Figure 2.3. Most of these conditions might be found in a typical eighth grade classroom in the middle school.

Figure 2.3

Portrait of a Thirteen Year Old

6 feet 2 inches in height	or	4 feet 7 inches
So awkward that she trips going up the stairs	or	Olympic gold medal winner with a perfect 10.0 in parallel bar competition
Alcoholic, drug addict	or	Sunday school leader, Little leaguer
Wears mouth braces	or	Competes in Miss Teenage America
Turned off and looking forward to quitting school	or	Curious and enthusiastic learner
Unable to read the comic page	or	Reads the *Wall Street Journal*
Has trouble with whole numbers	or	Can solve geometry problems
A regular in juvenile court	or	An Eagle Scout
Already a mother of two	or	Still plays with dolls

NEEDS SUGGESTED BY GROWTH AND DEVELOPMENT CHARACTERISTICS

The foregoing discussion of physical, emotional, social, and intellectual characteristics of middle school youngsters and the implications for the middle school suggest two terms: *transition* and *difference.* We must develop a school to encompass the transitional nature of the group as a whole and to consider the vast differences within the group.

Middle school youngsters need security on one hand and freedom to experience and explore on the other. They need an environment that protects them from themselves without smothering the "self."

Although variations among individuals are marked, there are certain basic needs which appear to be characteristic of children during these years:

1. The need to be safe and free of threat.
2. The need to be loved.
3. The need to be part of a group with identification and acceptance.
4. The need to be recognized.
5. The need to be independent.

Preadolescence is a restless age. Girls, as well as boys, demonstrate extreme restlessness during the transescent years from childhood to adolescence. The torture of trying to sit still in school is obvious and some children learn to perform remarkable feats of contortion without falling out of their chairs. A school atmosphere in which physical movement is integral to the educative process is of high priority for the preadolescent. Activity-related learning like drawing, designing, constructing, and making displays, as well as moving to and from classrooms and library, and to and from classroom and play centers, are vital to the preadolescent child. A steady grind at the school desk is undesirable at this restless age.

Personal development is beginning to undergo significant, perplexing alterations in the middle school years. Frequently, children commence a self-searching quest, seeking to locate themselves in a shifting social complex—a journey some adults have never completed satisfactorily. Children, with a commitment to fair play, must, nonetheless, struggle to establish a relationship between their own sense of values and the value inconsistencies of others, especially adults.

Transescents are curious, explorative, and interested in many things. They are in the early stages of the conflict between their desires to be independent and the necessity to depend on others. They live in a world of shifting sands—unsure of themselves, unsure of their environment, and the relationship between the two.

Pupils need guidance in the middle years to help them grow and develop into fully functioning individuals. The middle school has been suggested as a school for producing such individuals. Perhaps the message found in the following letter from a junior high school student will help illustrate the needs of youngsters in the middle years:

Who Am I?
I have many things I want
to say but—

No one will listen.
I have many things I want
    to do but—
No one will let me.
There are so many places
    I want to go but—
No one will take me.
And the things I write
    are corrected but—
No one reads them.
Who am I?[5]

EMERGING ADOLESCENTS—VICTIMS OF A CHANGING SOCIETY

Early in this chapter, it was stated that the most important group of students today are pre- and early adolescents, ten to fourteen years old, found in the middle grades of our schools. Normal developmental or maturational changes occurring in this age group create a set of problems unlike those experienced by any other age group. Middle school students of the eighties are also faced with another set of problems, not of their own making. They have become victims of a changing society that no longer provides the nurturing environment emerging adolescents need to grow and to develop into fully functioning adults. They live in a society that has little time or inclination to help them through the traumatic years of transescence. Even though considerable knowledge exists to prove that success in school, and indeed, success in life, depends on what happens to students between the ages of ten and fourteen, this group is the least understood, the least cared for, and the most fragile in our society.[6]

Misunderstood and Neglected

Today's social institutions operate on the premise that all students between the ages of ten and fourteen are difficult, disruptive, obstreperous, and almost impossible to deal with.[7] Parents and educators alike know that youngsters' bodies begin to mature sometime in the middle school years, but don't understand why some students "grow up" early while others are slow to reach physical maturity. Even though physical growth is often traumatic and unpredictable, some parents and

---

[5] Joseph Bondi, *Developing Middle Schools: A Guidebook* (Wheeling: Whitehall Publishing Co., 1972), pp. 22–23.

[6] "Caught in the Middle," Keynote speech delivered by Joseph Bondi, State Conference of Tennessee Association of Middle Schools, Memphis, August 3, 1978.

[7] Karl Stauber, "Early Adolescents: Neglected, Misunderstood, Miseducated," *Foundation News* 18 (Sept.–Oct., 1977): pp. 33–35.

educators are not aware to what extent transescents can be affected by the changes occurring in their bodies. The onset of menstruation, faces breaking out, development of secondary sex characteristics, for example, may create tensions in girls that affect their school performance. Yet girls are expected to display the same behavioral patterns every day. Consider how emerging adolescent girls begin to compete with their mothers in ways mothers don't understand and which may create conflicts at home.

Boys are also affected by a society that leads them to believe men should be tall, broad-shouldered, narrow-hipped, and look like an all-American. Long before puberty, boys know that being tall means being more masculine. Tall, early maturing boys get picked captains of teams, date the prettiest girls, and are chosen class leaders whether they exhibit leadership qualities or not. Often, early maturers are thrust into situations where they are expected to behave like adults socially when they are still mere children.

Life is often difficult for the late maturer, but when he does catch up, he may have gained in the long run from his painful experiences. Late maturers are often more sensitive, more thoughtful, and more understanding in dealing with other people than early maturers. They have had to live with and overcome a big problem of their own.

Adults often treat emerging adolescents as small children. Students are grouped by chronological age and a thirteen-year-old sexually active girl is expected to possess the same basic interests as a thirteen-year-old boy who may still be two years away from puberty. Too many schools maintain age segregation and grade structures based on chronological age rather than on maturational situations.

In addition to physical growth, social changes occur in the middle school years. Emerging adolescents begin to pull away from adults and gravitate toward peers. Evidence of this is found in dress, habits, and language. Yet adults little understand the social transformation of a child from a dependent, obedient, sweet child to an independent, often disobedient, and often ill-tempered young adolescent. Because adults misread signals from our young adolescents, they change and become impatient and short-tempered. Worst of all, they may abdicate their responsibility as adults and parents. They may also quit going to P.T.A. meetings when their sons or daughters reach grade seven, cease visiting the school, and hesitate to show approval or disapproval of their children's behavior. How many parents have called the middle school teacher or principal and said, "I don't know what to do with my daughter; you do something."

Society has created a myth about boys and girls in transescence. That myth is that those youngsters will somehow grow up by themselves and that adults should let them alone until they are mature adolescents.

The survey found in Figure 2.4 was administered to over 5000 middle school students from all socio-economic levels. Students were asked to rank the eleven values (all important values to emerging adolescents) in order from the most important value to the least. Their teachers were also asked to rank in order the values and indicate how they thought students would rank the values. Results of the survey are listed in columns I, II, III in Figure 2.5.

Overwhelmingly, students and teachers chose family security as their most

Figure 2.4
Value Survey Parent–Student

Rank in order of importance.   I am the: _____ Student

Place a number by the first,   _____ Parent
second, third, etc., choices.

Self   **Other**

_____ A comfortable life (nice house, plenty of money)   _____

_____ Equality (brotherhood; equal chance for all, rich or poor, black or white, man or woman)   _____

_____ Family security (family getting along together, all living together, all caring for each other)   _____

_____ Self-respect (liking yourself, feeling good about what you do)   _____

_____ Sense of accomplishment (doing something worthwhile for society; making a lasting   _____
contribution)

_____ Freedom (being independent, having free choice)   _____

_____ Happiness (personal contentment)   _____

_____ True friendship (having friends who are close and loyal)   _____

_____ Exciting life (fun-filled, active, enjoyable)   _____

_____ World at peace (no wars, riots, less crime and violence)   _____

_____ Good education (opportunity to finish high school—go on to college or further training)   _____

Source: Jon Wiles and Joseph Bondi, "Values of Middle School Students," *National Middle School Journal* (May 1979): 2–4.

important value. The results clearly indicate that middle school students do not want their parents to abdicate their responsibility as parents.

The middle school years for ten-to-fifteen-year-olds are years of emotional instability. It is difficult to understand why students are happy one moment and sad the next. Also difficult to understand is why chemical changes in the body trigger certain emotions or how chemical and hormone imbalances affect personalities of emerging adolescents.

Middle school years are "puppy love" years. It has been said that only a middle schooler can meet a person of the opposite sex, go steady, and break up—all through a third person.

A final area of lack of understanding in middle grades is achievement. The widest range of achievement occurs in the middle grades. Students falling a half-year behind grade level in elementary school reading find themselves two to three years behind by the time they reach middle school. Parents don't understand why middle school educators don't eliminate affective programs (such as those that help pupils understand themselves) and simply concentrate on basic skills programs. Parents need help to understand there should be a balance in the curriculum of personal development activities, basic skills programs, and content study.

Emerging adolescents are the least cared for in our society. It is possible to

Figure 2.5
Results of a Value Survey

1. Students*	2. Teachers†	3. As Teachers Believed Students Would Rank‡
Family	Family	World at Peace
Freedom	Self-Respect	True Friendship
Happiness	Equality	Family
Self-Respect	Freedom	Exciting Life
Comfortable Life	World at Peace	Happiness
True Friendship	Sense of Accomplishment	Comfortable Life
Good Education	Happiness	Self-Respect
World at Peace	True Friendship	Freedom
Exciting Life	Good Education	Sense of Accomplishment
Equality	Comfortable Life	Equality
Sense of Accomplishment	Exciting Life	Good Education

*Column one lists values ranked by students.
†Column two lists values ranked by their middle school teachers.
‡Column three lists values in order teachers believed students would rank the values.

SOURCE: Jon Wiles and Joseph Bondi, "Values of Middle School Students," *National Middle School Journal* (May 1979): 2–4.

quantify some of our neglect of this group. Middle schools cannot fulfill all the needs of emerging adolescents; yet some would hold the schools solely responsible for the health and well-being of this age group. Only 5 percent of the generalists practicing pediatrics or family medicine have received training in adolescent health care. Although millions of dollars are spent on juvenile delinquency in the United States, less than 1 percent of grants and research funded by the National Institute for Child Health and Human Development places a primary emphasis on pre- and early adolescents.

Except for 4-H Clubs, most national voluntary organizations and clubs have experienced declining memberships among young adolescents. Too little national research has been conducted on middle school learners. As a result, there seems to be little relationship between what many schools do and what is actually known about young adolescents. The major tasks of the period of life during emerging adolescence include separation, individualization, and commitment; yet there have been few aspects of schooling that have accommodated those tasks. The middle school must do so in the midst of a society that is often too busy to care. Leaders in the middle school must help parents and the community understand that only through their combined efforts will emerging adolescents receive the care and nurture needed to help them make the successful transition from childhood to adolescence.

The Most Fragile Group in Our Society

Middle school students have indeed become victims of a changing society. Social problems in our society have had and are having a profound influence on emerging adolescents. Consider the following:

The American Family Is Changing:[8]

The divorce rate in America is approaching 50 percent, highest in the world.
Over 11 million children beyond age eleven live in a single-parent home.
One of six children in public schools comes from a broken home.
Over 40 percent of divorced, separated, or single women receive no financial assistance from the fathers of their children.
Only 16 percent of American families have the mother at home and the father working.
In 1979, 4.6 million adults moonlighted—the largest number in the history of the United States.
About one in five Americans moves each year.
Along with fewer children in the average family, there are fewer adults as well in the American household.

Television Viewing Is Affecting Life Styles[9]

It is estimated that pre- and early adolescents spend one-third of their waking hours watching television.
T.V. violence has increased. Teenagers charged with committing violent crimes often blame the influence of television.

Juvenile Delinquency Is a Major Problem in Our Society[10]

43 percent of persons arrested for serious crimes in the United States (rape, murder, robbery) are juveniles. Youth crime rose 293 percent from 1960– 1975 and is increasing by more than 10 percent a year.
Although juveniles aged seven to eighteen make up only 20 percent of the population, they account for 43 percent of all arrests for serious crimes. The peak age for committing violent crime is fourteen.
Law education has been mandated for pre- and early adolescents in a number of states.

---

[8] U.S., Department of HEW, "Annual Summary for the United States: Births, Marriages, Divorces, and Deaths," National Center for Health Statistics, *PHS,* 28 (March 14, 1980), No. 12, 80–1120.

[9] U.S., Department of HEW, National Clearing House for Mental Health Information, Annual Report, 1980.

[10] U.S., Department of HEW, National Institute for Child Health and Development, Annual Report, 1980.

Ford Foundation, "Violent Delinquents," Report of Ford Foundation, 9 July 1978.

Table 2.2
Divorces and Marriages in the United States

Year	Divorces	Marriages
1920	171,000	1,274,000
1930	196,000	1,127,000
1940	264,000	1,596,000
1950	385,000	1,667,000
1960	393,000	1,523,000
1965	479,000	1,800,000
1970	708,000	2,159,000
1975	1,036,000	2,126,000
1976	1,083,000	2,154,807
1977	1,091,000	2,178,367
1978	1,228,000	2,243,000
1979	1,170,000	2,317,000

SOURCE: U.S., Department of HEW, "Annual Summary for the United States: Births, Marriages, Divorces, and Deaths," National Center for Health Statistics, *PHS,* 28 (March 14, 1980), No. 12, 80–1120.

Psychologists regard the lack of a stable home as the biggest contributor to delinquency.

Attitude polls reveal parents blame themselves for children getting into trouble and not achieving in school.

Alcoholism Among Teenagers and Pre-Teens Is Increasing at an Alarming Rate[11]

Alcoholism among teenagers increased 800 percent in the years between 1970 and 1980.

Children of alcoholics have a 25–50 percent greater chance of developing that disease. This means 7–14 million children may develop alcoholism if the commonly estimated figure of 10 million adult alcoholics is used.

By the end of the ninth grade, 20 percent of adolescents will suffer a drinking problem.

The Physical Health Status of American Children Is Still Not Good[12]

Although there have been massive governmental investments in health care services, about 20 percent of American children age seven to eleven have serious health problems. Many children do not receive proper health care.

The average age of beginning smokers dropped from age fourteen to ten in the decade from 1970 to 1980. The number of girls between ages thirteen and seventeen who began smoking rose 5 percent in the same decade.

---

[11] U.S., Department of HEW, National Institute on Alcohol and Drug Abuse, Annual Report, 1980.

[12] "Saving the Family," *Newsweek Magazine,* 15 May 1978, pp. 63–86.

Periodic Reports from the American Association for Physical Education and Recreation, 1201–16th St., Washington, D.C. 20036.

Figure 2.6
Adolescent Suicidal Checklist

	Yes	No
1. Student a social isolate, a loner.	____	____
2. Student has deformity or chronic disease.	____	____
3. Student home life unstable over long period.	____	____
4. Student has history of regular student-parent conflict.	____	____
5. Student has recently lost parent or significant person.	____	____
6. Student family experiencing financial troubles.	____	____
7. Student lives in unstable, transitional neighborhood.	____	____
8. Student married at early age (15–20 years).	____	____
9. Student evidences sexual identity crisis.	____	____
10. Student displays sexual promiscuity unchecked by actions of parents.	____	____
11. Student voices feelings of pessimism, worthlessness.	____	____
12. Student appears fatigued, reports insomnia.	____	____
13. Student acts despondent or is unusually quiet.	____	____
14. Student shows accelerating neglect of appearance.	____	____
15. Student reports pressure from parents concerning ability to meet school or social expectations.	____	____
16. Student develops pattern of varied sicknesses during school hours.	____	____
17. Student displays irregular emotional outbursts, anger.	____	____
18. Student displays unusual social anxiety in school.	____	____
19. Student suddenly becomes promiscuous or flirtatious.	____	____
20. Student writes or speaks of suicidal thoughts.	____	____
21. Student becomes unusually aggressive, boastful.	____	____
22. Student begins heavy use of drugs.	____	____
23. Student evidences neglect of school work.	____	____
24. Student unable to concentrate on school work.	____	____
25. Student develops record of excessive absenteeism or unexpectedly drops out of school	____	____

SOURCE: Jon Wiles, "Prescriptions For An Adolescent Suicide," *Transescence* 5 (1977): 23–26.

Mental Health of Youth is a Major Concern in the United States and Other Countries[13]

National mental health sources show that the second leading cause of death among teenagers, after accidents, is suicide. The suicide rate among teenagers doubled in the decade between 1970 and 1980.

School stress in Germany and Japan is the reason most given for teenage suicides in those countries.

[13] U.S., Department of HEW, National Institute of Mental Health, Annual Report, 1980.

Apathy and rejection reflected in our adolescent and post-adolescent society is the major contributing factor to the increase in suicides and attempted suicides in the United States. Insecurity in family life is often given as a cause of teenage suicide. Figure 2.6 provides a checklist for identifying the potential adolescent suicide.

More Youth Are Sexually Active at Earlier Ages[14]

Six hundred thousand girls between the ages of ten and eighteen gave birth to illegitimate babies in America in 1979. One of ten girls will be pregnant before age 18.

There are an estimated 11 million teenage boys and girls that are sexually active, but only 1 million of them are enrolled in family planning clinics. Over 50 percent of the teenage population between ages fifteen and nineteen are sexually active.

Nine years of age is legally considered to be the beginning of childbearing age in most states. Girls' ages of menarche range from 9.1 to 17.7 years. Fifteen percent of babies born to girls in the age group of ten to eighteen were to girls between the ages of ten and thirteen.

Twenty-five percent of babies born with birth defects are born to adolescent mothers.

Two-thirds of teenage marriages end in divorce within five years.

The most frequent reason girls quit school is pregnancy.

The following poem written by a pregnant thirteen-year-old girl in a middle school illustrates the tragic feelings shared by many unwed teenage mothers.

How does it feel to be a teenager and pregnant?

Lonely Death

I remember the fun we once had.
We got our kicks out of being bad.

And remember the time we both skipped school?
Everyone thought that we were cool.

Remember last summer we let nothing take our joy away?
We made out in the barn on top of the hay.

Remember the time you gave me your ring?
I was so happy that I could sing.

And do you remember the kisses we once shared?
And the day you said you'd always care?

Remember the day we went all the way?
You know for that move we must pay.

I'm in a home for unwed mothers.
But what do you care, you've got so many others.

---

[14] U.S., Department of HEW, National Institute of Child Health and Development, Annual Reports, 1977, 1979, 1980.

While writing this I'm fighting the pain—
I'm bearing a child who has no name.

The doctor came in a few minutes ago,
He said there was trouble—
"Oh God, please, no!"

I found out soon he wasn't lying.
The nurse just said that I was dying.

The baby they say will be all right.
But I'll be somewhere else tonight.

(a seventh grader)

HOW STUDENT NEEDS AND INTERESTS ARE IDENTIFIED IN PLANNING A MIDDLE SCHOOL

In developing a middle school, each community should examine the needs and interests of their own students. Surveys, questionnaires, and other means can be used to determine the needs and interests of middle school students. Examples of the efforts of several middle schools are found in the samples in this section. The authors do not suggest that these efforts are applicable to all communities, rather that the approaches used may be of some practical value to communities developing middle schools.

Sample 2.1—Obtaining Background Information about Students

Dear Parent:

The Pine View faculty is planning its curriculum for the new middle school next year.

So we can know more about our students, we are asking them to answer the questions in the following survey. If you do not want your child to participate in this survey, do not return this form to the school.

Thank you very much for your cooperation.

The Pine View Faculty

_____ Grade
_____ Age
_____ Boy, Girl

Questionnaire

1. Are you living with (circle 1 or more) (1. mother, 2. step-mother, 3. father, 4. step-father, 5. _____)

2. How many brothers and sisters do you have living at home?_____

3. How many bedrooms in your home?_____

4. Do you have the following in your home? 1. encyclopedia (yes, no) 2. magazines (yes, no) 3. newspaper (yes, no) 4. color TV (yes, no)

5. Do your parents own a car or truck, if so how many?_____

6. Does your mother work? (yes, no)

7. Do you get enough food for lunch at school? (yes, no)

8. Do you think you are healthy? (yes, no)

9. Which would you prefer in the classroom? (1. desks, 2. tables)

10. Do you think you could be a better student? (yes, no)

11. Do you plan to graduate from high school? (yes, no)

12. Do you plan to go to college? (yes, no)

13. How do you spend most of your free time? (1. reading, 2. making things, 3. working, 4. watching T.V., 5._____)

14. Do you feel your teachers know you? (1. well, 2. fairly well, 3. not so well)

15. Do you find it easy to talk to (1. all your teachers, 2. about half your teachers, 3. less than half your teachers, 4. none of your teachers)

16. I am the happiest when (1. I am alone, 2. I make someone happy, 3. I am having a good time with friends, 4._____)

17. Most people think I am (1. nice, 2. dumb, 3. a snob, 4. _____)

18. I worry the most about (1. being popular, 2. my grades, 3. getting along with my family, 4. money, 5._____)

19. Are your parents too strict? (yes, no)

20. Do you honestly think you are old enough to date? (yes, no)

21. Do you dance? (yes, no)

22. Are you growing into the kind of person you really want to be? (yes, no)

23. Are you anxious to grow up? (yes, no)

24. The future looks (1. good, 2. bad, 3. uncertain, 4. _____)

25. Do you think it is important to have more than two teachers in a day? (yes, no)

26. Would you prefer to be with students in just your grade? (yes, no)

27. Do you prefer to be taught in a small or large group? (_____)

28. Do you understand our grading system? (yes, no)

29. What is your most interesting subject?_____

30. Is there any course you are not taking that you would like to take?_____

31. To whom would you go if you had a problem?_____

Sample 2.2—Finding Out About Student Interests

Next year we hope to have more clubs. These are some suggestions. Check the ones you would like. Write in other suggestions.

_____ Fun cooking

_____ Writing
(poems, stories, plays)

_____ Debate

_____ Active Games

_____ Quiet Games

_____ Square Dancing

_____ First Aid

_____ Scientific Experiments

_____ Typing

_____ Handicrafts

_____ Fun Reading

_____ Stamp Collecting

_____ Astronomy

_____ A club to help me to solve my problems

_____ A club to help me to read better

_____ A club to help me to learn better

_____ A club to help me to decide on my future job

_____ A club to help me to improve my appearance

_____ A club to help me to get along better with other people

_____ A club to help me to write and spell better

_____ A club to help me learn more about _____

_____

_____

_____

_____

_____

_____

_____

_____

_____

_____

_____

_____ Fun Sewing

_____ Travel

_____ Model Cars or Model Planes

Sample 2.3—Student Questionnaire on Individualized Learning

To the Students: We are interested in finding out to what extent the school has been able to individualize your learning to help you learn most effectively in your own way, at your own rate of speed. Your frank answers to the questions below will help us improve our program. Do not identify yourself or your teacher; in no way is this a rating of your classroom teacher.

1. Number of years you have been in school: _____5 _____6 _____7 _____8

    _____9

2. In which of your classes is this questionnaire now being administered to you? (Check one)

    _____ English _____ Science _____ Foreign Language _____ Mathematics

    _____ Social Science

ANSWER THE FOLLOWING QUESTIONS ONLY AS THEY RELATE TO THE SUBJECT YOU HAVE JUST CHECKED.

3. In this subject I find that the pace or speed at which we must cover material is just right for me. _____Yes _____Uncertain _____No

4. In this subject I find that the work I have is not too easy or too hard for me but is just right for me. _____Yes _____Uncertain _____No

5. In this subject I find that the work we have interests me and will be useful in my future. _____Yes _____Uncertain _____No

6. In this subject I feel that the teacher knows me as an individual and tries to suit the work to my ability and interest. _____Yes _____Uncertain _____No

7. I think this subject could be individualized more effectively for me,

---

These sample surveys are but a few of the ways a middle school staff can examine the needs and interests of students. Data can be gathered from test scores to determine achievement levels. I.Q. scores can also be examined to determine mental ability. Information about parents and home life can be gathered from permanent records and from interviewing guidance counselors and social workers. Kinds and numbers of discipline referrals to the office can be documented. Health records can be examined to determine those students in need of special programs such as adaptive physical education classes. Homes can be visited by the staff to learn more about the environment students experience outside of school. Students can be studied to determine intellectual stages of development and physical and social maturational levels. Finally, students can be asked about themselves. Figure 2.7 illustrates the response of an eighth-grade middle school student in Louisville.

The authors encourage middle school teachers and administrators to utilize the guidelines suggested in Chapter 1 and this chapter to conduct a thorough study of the students they will serve. A focus on individualization should follow.

Figure 2.7

What is a Middle Schooler?

What is a middle schooler?
I was asked one day.
I knew what he was,
But what should I say?

He is noise and confusion.
He is silence that is deep.
He is sunshine and laughter,
Or a cloud that will weep.

He is swift as an arrow.
He is a waster of time.
He wants to be rich,
But can not save a dime.

He is rude and nasty.
He is polite as can be.
He wants parental guidance,
But fights to be free.

He is aggressive and bossy.
He is timid and shy.
He knows all the answers,
But still will ask "why."

He is awkward and clumsy.
He is graceful and poised.
He is ever changing,
But do not be annoyed.

What is a middle schooler?
I was asked one day.
He is the future unfolding,
So do not stand in his way.

(An eighth grade middle school student)

SUMMARY

Emerging adolescent learners are characterized by their diversity and their own patterns of development. They are curious, explorative, and interested in many things. They are, more than anything else, physical creatures full of energy and imagination.

The physical, social, intellectual, and emotional changes students experience in the years between childhood and adolescence necessitate a school atmosphere where students can grow and develop into fully functioning mature adolescents. The needs suggested by the characteristics of emerging adolescents must not be ignored in the middle school.

Along with normal maturational changes, the emerging adolescent of the eighties must face societal problems unlike those experienced by students in any other generation. The breakdown of the family and other social changes in American life have led to increased rates of suicide, pregnancies, and alcoholism among pre- and early adolescents. The most impressionable group of students in all of schooling is found in the group between the ages of ten and fourteen, and these students have become victims of a changing society.

Student needs and interests must be examined in planning programs for middle school students. The more knowledge a middle school staff has about the students they serve, the better they can provide the environment necessary for the actualization of the goal of a unique program for each middle school student.

In the next chapter, we shall learn that the middle school teacher is the key figure in reaching the goals of the middle school.

Suggested Learning Activities

1. Conduct a values survey like the one found in Figure 2.4. How do your results compare with those found in Figure 2.5?

2. Develop procedures for studying the students in your middle school. What processes and instruments would you use to gather information about students?

3. Prepare a list of characteristics of emerging adolescents with implications for your middle school program.

4. Develop a position paper on the need for sex education in the middle school.

5. Prepare a slide-tape presentation illustrating various physical, social, intellectual, and emotional characteristics of transescent youth.

6. Prepare an oral presentation for parents that would make them more aware of the social problems affecting middle school students.

Selected References

A.S.C.D Working Group on the Emerging Adolescent Learner. *The Middle School We Need.* Washington, D.C.: Association for Supervision and Curriculum Development, 1975.

Bondi, Joseph. *Developing Middle Schools: A Guidebook.* Wheeling, Ill.: Whitehall Publishing Co., 1972.

Curtis, Thomas; and Bidwell, Wilma. *Curriculum and Instruction for Emerging Adolescents.* Reading, Mass.: Addison-Wesley Publishing Co., 1977.

Elkind, David. *A Sympathetic Understanding of the Child: Birth to Sixteen.* Boston: Allyn & Bacon, Inc., 1974.

Havighurst, R. *Developmental Tasks and Education.* New York: David McKay Co., 1972.

Kohl, John; Caldwell, William; and Eichhorn, Donald. *Self-Appraisal and Development of the Middle School—An Inservice Approach.* University Park, Pa.: Pennsylvania School Study Council, 1970.

Piaget, Jean; and Inhelder, Barbel. *The Psychology of the Child.* New York: Basic Books Publishers, 1969.

Travers, John. *Educational Psychology.* New York: Harper & Row, Publishers, 1979.

3

The Teacher in the Middle School

The teacher we are looking for in the middle school is less the sage on the stage and more the guide on the side

INTRODUCTION

The middle school teacher, more than any other factor, holds the key to realization of the type of effective middle school required for emerging adolescents.[1]

The middle school teacher must have those characteristics that research indicates are good for all teachers. However, because of the ages embraced in the middle school, he is responsible for children who are striking in their diversity. What confronts a teacher in the middle school is a rapidly changing group of children in different stages of development. To identify the teacher needed for the middle school, we will examine five critical areas: personal characteristics, teacher competencies, professional preparation, appropriate teaching strategies, and classroom management and discipline procedures.

---

[1] A.S.C.D. Working Group on the Emerging Adolescent Learner, *The Middle School We Need* (Washington, D.C.: Association for Supervision and Curriculum Development, 1975), p. 18.

PERSONAL CHARACTERISTICS

Although the following characteristics are important for teachers in any school, they are particularly relevant in the middle school:

1. The teacher likes children. Realizing the difficulty in identifying such a person, subjective answers must be relied on: Does she enjoy students who are active, energetic, and loud? Is she flexible and sensitive to quick changes in pupils' moods and needs? Does she establish rapport easily with students?

2. The teacher believes in and practices the middle school concept and philosophy.

3. The teacher displays enthusiasm for and commitment to working with older children and younger adolescents.

4. The teacher possesses a wide variety of skills, abilities, and talents.

5. The teacher sees as his main goal the development of the creative potential of each individual child in the middle school.

6. The teacher is knowledgeable in subject areas and brings them to the level of the learner.

7. The teacher can work effectively in close collaboration with fellow teachers in cooperative planning and team teaching.

8. The teacher has an open mind toward innovation and change.

9. The teacher is alive intellectually, physically, and socially.

10. The teacher is compassionate, tolerant, and flexible.

Perhaps the most important attributes of the middle school teacher are an honest desire to work with this age group, flexibility, enthusiasm, a good sense of humor, compassion, and tolerance.

Flexibility is essential. Middle school teachers must be prepared to make use of intense periods of interest characteristic of the "middlescent." The nature of the middle school requires adaptability on the part of the teacher.

Enthusiasm is another essential. A child tends to emulate the enthusiasm displayed by the teacher. To function most effectively, a middle school should be staffed with teachers who are willing to be enthusiastic about trying new methods and ideas.

A sense of humor is a desirable characteristic. Children in the transitional period between childhood and adolescence are subjected to pressures from parents, peers, and teachers. A teacher's sense of humor in the school environment provides a safety valve for mounting pressures.

A basic ingredient in the personality of teachers of "in-between-agers" is patience. The great disparity in the ability to understand directions and in the length of attention-spans calls for a patient approach by the middle school teacher.

Each middle school child needs at least one person within the framework of the school with whom he can relate. Thus, the teacher becomes a counselor as well as a teacher.

TEACHER COMPETENCIES

In addition to identifying personal characteristics of middle school teachers such as those listed in the previous section, there is a need to identify the specific teacher competencies essential to the success of the middle school. A number of states have moved to a competency-based approach in the preparation of middle school teachers. A pioneer in building such programs is the State of Florida. In 1969, the Teacher Education Advisory Council appointed a task force to draft guidlines for the preparation of teachers for middle schools in Florida. Under the direction of Gordon Lawrence of the University of Florida, twenty of the Teacher Education Council Middle School Competencies, which could be measured, were identified. Those twenty are listed in Figure 3.1.

Figure 3.1
Key Competency Areas for Middle School Teaching

1. Shows awareness of his own behavior patterns and how they are influenced by situations and by his beliefs; awareness of personality characteristics; acceptance of a variety of behavior in others that differs from own.

2. Interacts constructively with other adults and with transescents; shows regard for persons; is approachable, responsive and supportive.

3. Understands the physical development process of the transescent student and organizes his teaching according to that process.

4. Understands the intellectual developmental process of the transescent student and organizes his teaching according to that process.

5. Understands the socio-emotional development process of the transescent student learner and organizes his teaching according to that process.

6. Understands the career developmental process of the transescent student and organizes his teaching according to that process.

7. Understands and applies various theories of the teaching-learning process; analyzes the learning patterns of individual students, prescribes for these and evaluates results.

8. Incorporates a knowledge of group dynamics in his teaching and helps students understand group process: group decision making, leadership skills and peer influence.

9. Promotes positive relationships between the school and the community, between the teacher and parents and between various sub-cultures in the school.

10. Organizes curriculum plans and opportunities appropriate to the middle school (those that facilitate the developmental tasks of transescence and are responsive to community problems).

11. Uses appropriate procedures of managing an instructional program-designing, conducting, evaluating and revising curriculum and instruction.

12. Makes effective presentations using appropriate media.

13. Deals effectively with unusual classroom problems.

Figure 3.1

Key Competency Areas for Middle School Training

14. Counsels individual students, promoting self-direction through indirect guidance.

15. Helps students to consider alternative values and to develop personal workable valuing systems.

16. Teaches students techniques of problem-solving.

17. Provides opportunities and guidance to help students become independent learners (define own goals and problems, identify resources and evaluate outcomes).

18. Designs and conducts group activities according to the kinds of learnings that are facilitated by the different groupings.

19. Has skills of working in cooperative teaching situations with other teachers, paraprofessionals and resource persons.

20. Accepts responsibility of multi-disciplinary instruction: plans thematic and coordinated studies with other teachers and assists them in teaching subjects outside of his own area of specialization.

SOURCE: From Gordon Lawrence, University of Florida—Middle School Project (Gainesville, Fla.: University of Florida, 1974). Used with permission.

Through the work of various doctoral students and researchers, a number of middle school competencies have been validated by those knowledgeable in the middle school. We have listed a number of those competencies at the end of this section (pages 52–56). It is interesting to compare those to the original thirty selected by Lawrence and his colleagues. Because competencies are complex and multidimensional, behavior patterns are not easily measured. Lawrence identified six types of measurement for middle school competencies:

1. Measurement of abstract information—a memory operation. Whether textbook knowledge or firsthand experience, the teacher would be able to describe physical or intellectual developmental traits of emerging adolescents.

2. Conceptual measurement—ability to conceptualize abstract information in operational terms. An example might be the ability of a teacher to use abstract information in writing a lesson plan.

3. Dispositional measurement—the disposition to act in a way to use appropriate abstract information. Measurement of this dimension involves a substantial affective component. An example is evaluating a videotape class activity and measuring the reaction of the viewer to the restless body movement of students.

4. Structured performance—ability to perform a defined task when requested. Such a task might be to plan and conduct a 15 minute lesson during which student talk, as measured by a Flanders System of Interaction Analysis, might be maximized.

5. Performance unconstrained by the measurer—ability to employ certain skills when the situation calls for them. For instance, can a skill be demonstrated on the request of an observer?

6. Measurement of long-term consequences ensuing from performance—defining and measuring a competency by the long-term outcomes it affects in persons or events. Long term pupil growth is hard to measure because a number of factors in addition to the teacher influence pupil growth over a long span of time.[2]

Finally, the authors present for the reader's study a list of teacher competencies developed by Marshall and Holmes. This list, when compared with the Florida list, indicates the primary skills needed for successful middle school teaching.

SELECTED TEACHER COMPETENCIES FOR MIDDLE SCHOOL TEACHERS

1. Possesses knowledge of the pre- and early adolescent physical development which includes knowledge of physical activity needs and the diversity and variety of physical growth rates.

2. Commands knowledge of the pre- and early adolescent intellectual development with emphasis on the transition from concrete to formal levels of mental development.

3. Has a knowledge of a recognized developmental theory and personality theory which can be utilized in identifying appropriate learning strategies for the pre- and early adolescent.

4. Understands the socio-emotional development, including the need to adjust to a changing body.

5. Possesses the necessary skills to allow interaction between individual students as well as the opportunity to work in groups of varying sizes.

6. Understands the cultural forces and community relationships which affect the total school curriculum.

7. Has the ability to organize the curriculum to facilitate the developmental tasks of preadolescence and early adolescence.

8. Understands the transitional nature of grades 5–8 as they bridge the gap between the children of the lower elementary grades and late adolescents and early adults of the upper grades.

9. Possesses the skills needed to work with other teachers and school professionals in team teaching situations.

10. Has the ability to plan multidisciplinary lessons and/or units and teach them personally or with other professionals.

11. Commands a broad academic background, with specialization in at least two allied areas of the curriculum.

12. Possesses the skill to integrate appropriate media, and concrete demonstrations into presentations.

---

[2] Gordon Lawrence, "Measuring Teacher Competencies for the Middle School," *National Elementary Principal* 41 (November 1971): 61–63.

13. Is able to develop and conduct learning situations which will promote independent learning, and maximize student choice and responsibility for follow-through.

14. Possesses the knowledge and skills which will allow students to sort information, set priorities, and budget time and energy.

15. Is able to teach problem solving skills and develop lessons which are inquiry oriented.

16. Has the ability to teach students how to discover knowledge and use both inductive and deductive methods in the discovery of knowledge.

17. Possesses the knowledge and skills necessary to use role playing, simulation, instructional games, and creative dramatics in teaching the content as well as the affective domain in a middle grade classroom.

18. Commands the knowledge and skill needed to organize and manage a classroom which allows individuals to learn at a rate commensurate with their ability.

19. Possesses verbal behaviors which will promote student input in a variety of group settings.

20. Is able to write behavioral objectives and design lessons to effectively conclude the objectives.

21. Has the knowledge and skills needed to diagnose strengths and weaknesses, to determine learning levels of individuals, to prescribe courses of action, and to evaluate the outcomes.

22. Has experiences in innovation and possesses the skill to experiment with teaching techniques to find ones that are most effective in given situations.

23. Is able to teach the communication skills of reading, writing and speaking in all subject areas.

24. Commands knowledge of reading techniques which will enable students to progress and improve their reading in the subject areas.

25. Possesses the skills needed to diagnose reading problems and provide a remedial program in the regular classroom.

26. Has a knowledge of the techniques necessary to promote positive self-concepts and self-reliance.

27. Is able to help students clarify values, consider alternative values, and develop a personal and workable valuing system.

28. Possesses a knowledge of group dynamics and the ability to organize groups which will make decisions and provide their own leadership.

29. Has a knowledge of careers and the ability to help students explore careers.

30. Commands knowledge of several major learning theories and the learning strategies which emanate from the theories.

31. Has a knowledge of how to deal with unusual classroom problems.

32. Possesses skills necessary to effectively manage groups of students in activity settings.

33. Possesses the ability to recognize difficulties which may be emotional and/or physically based.

34. Possesses the knowledge and skills needed to effectively manage abusive and deviant behavior.

35. Works with extracurricular activities in the school.

36. Gathers appropriate personal information on students using questionnaires, interviews, and observation.

37. Provides frequent feedback to students on learning progress.

38. Functions calmly in a high activity environment.

39. Handles disruptive behavior in a positive and consistent manner.

40. Builds learning experiences for students based upon learning skills (reading, math) obtained in elementary grades.

41. Works cooperatively with peers, consultants, resource persons, and paraprofessionals.

42. Exhibits concern for students by listening and/or empathizing with them.

43. Selects evaluation techniques appropriate to curricular objectives in the affective domain.

44. Utilizes value clarification and other affective teaching techniques to help students develop personal value systems.

45. Provides an informal, flexible classroom environment.

46. Cooperates in curricular planning and revision.

47. Evaluates the teaching situation and selects the grouping techniques most appropriate for the situation, large group instruction (100 + students), small group instruction (fifteen to twenty-five students), or independent study.

48. Uses questioning techniques skillfully to achieve higher order thinking processes in students.

49. Can move from one type of grouping situation to another smoothly.

50. Functions effectively in various organizational and staffing situations, such as team teaching, differentiated staffing, and multiage groupings.

51. Selects evaluation techniques appropriate to curricular objectives in the psychomotor domain.

52. The teacher establishes positive relationships with the parents and families of students.

53. The teacher works at understanding, accepting and being accepted by members of the subcultures in the school and the community.

54. The teacher understands the middle school concept and attempts to apply it in the classroom, and in the school as a whole.

55. The teacher manages the classroom with a minimum of negative or aversive controls.

56. The teacher uses himself (herself) as a tool in promoting the personal growth of students and colleagues.

57. The teacher's relationships with colleagues, administrators, and supervisors are harmonious and productive.

58. The teacher is aware of the needs, forces, and perceptions which determine his (her) personal behavior.

59. The teacher maintains a balance between teacher-directed learning and student-directed learning.

60. The teacher's efforts in curriculum and instruction proceed from a problem-solving framework, involving the students in relevant inquiry.

61. The teacher possesses skill in asking questions which encourage student thinking beyond the level of "recall."[3]

PROFESSIONAL PREPARATION

Although most states have either adopted middle school certification requirements or are planning such projects, teacher education institutions have been slow in developing preservice programs to prepare middle school teachers. The decade of the 1970s saw most middle school teachers "re-tooled" to teach in the middle school. Middle school teachers, already certified in either elementary or secondary education, were allowed to add a special middle school certification through completion of required inservice training. The declining enrollment of the late seventies and early eighties, with the subsequent drop in numbers of new teachers required, has resulted in fewer teachers matriculating through preservice teacher preparation programs. As a result, the thrust of teacher preparation for middle school teachers in the 1980s will continue to be in the area of inservice education.

Because many state departments of education and teacher training institutions could not divest themselves from the elementary-secondary syndrome, middle school certifications have typically been housed in either elementary or secondary departments. In seventy years of middle grades education in either the junior high school or middle school, educators have still not been convinced that middle grades education is an entity and deserves equal recognition with the elementary and senior high school.

Middle school leaders in the eighties must continue the fight to establish adequate pre- and inservice training programs for middle school teachers. In later chapters, we will stress the need for strong training programs for administrators and other resource persons in the middle school. We suggest the following middle

---

[3] Adapted from a list identified and compiled by Janelle Marshall, Iowa State University, and Jim Holmes, Fresno, California, and other middle school researchers, 1977.

school teacher training model, developed by the Florida Department of Education, as an excellent example of pre- and inservice education needed for teachers in the essential middle school.

Teacher Education Experiences

A. Underlying Principles

In addition to guidelines for the three phases of teacher education-general education, individual specialization, and professional preparation, the following underlying principles are suggested:

1. Middle school teacher education should promote continuity of educational experience. All aspects of the teacher education program should be closely interrelated to provide a meaningful professional experience for the prospective middle school teacher.
2. Middle school teacher education should assure the development of personal qualities as well as professional abilities.
3. Middle school teacher education should be highly personalized. It is important that the individualization of instruction sought for the middle school should also be a goal of middle school teacher education.
4. Middle school teacher education should be a simultaneous blending of didactic instruction and practical experience. Practical experiences should be coordinated with didactic course work to provide meaningful professional education experiences for prospective middle school teachers.
5. Middle school teacher education should use those principles, techniques, and materials appropriate to middle school teaching insofar as they are consistent with the level of understanding and maturity of prospective middle school teachers.

B. General Education

The preparation of the middle school teacher should include sufficient experiences of a general or liberal education nature to qualify the teacher as a literate, self-directing learner able to understand and interpret current developments in a changing society.

C. Individual Specialization

1. As early as possible in the teacher education program, teacher candidates should have opportunity to study the operation of schools at different levels, so that the individual's choice of middle school specialization is based on special interest in work at this level.
2. Each middle school staff member should have both breadth and depth in preparation. The depth of preparation should be in a curriculum or service in which the person could function as a specialist in team teaching or other instructional organization appropriate to middle school age children.
3. Specialization should be planned for each middle school teacher in terms of his interests, competencies, and pattern of college courses to insure an adequate preparation in the field of specialization.
4. Some experiences in the field of specialization should parallel the school laboratory experiences described below, so as to provide adequate opportunity for relating general professional preparation and individual specialization.

Periodic reviews of each teacher's competencies should be used in determining further training needs.

D. Professional Preparation

1. Basic to the entire program of teacher education for the middle school is study of the characteristics of middle school age children. As continuous and long experience as possible in working with these children is desirable in the program. A combination of laboratory observation, case study, and systematic instruction seems indicated.

2. The middle school teacher should participate in a middle school laboratory experience program of at least one year. These experiences would include observation of teaching and learning situations; involvement in parent conferences and school-community activities; participation in team planning, teaching and evaluation, and other differentiated staff arrangements; direct instruction of individuals, small groups, and variable size classes, and participation in schoolwide and special-interest activities. The program should include both extensive and intensive phases to provide experience with a wide variety of instructional situations.

3. The school laboratory experience should be paralleled by or include experiences of a curriculum and instructional laboratory type. These experiences would include preparation of curriculum objectives, plans and units, and instructional materials; practice in use of a variety of instructional media and resources; development of tests and test analyses; and the use of systematic observation, simulation, and other techniques for developing teacher skills.

4. Paralleling the laboratory experiences should be a professional seminar devoted to developing professional understandings, skills and attitudes for working in the middle schools. Seminar participants in addition to teacher candidates and college professors might include supervising teachers in the laboratory situations and resource personnel as needed and available. Experiences in the laboratory settings would be analyzed with attention to alternative procedures, relationships between schools and units within particular schools, and in general the application of theory and research to practice. The seminar would include opportunities for grouping participants both by curriculum area and across roles.

Program Admission

A. Preservice

1. The institution has a procedure for identifying and selecting candidates for admission to the program for middle school teachers. Sections II and III of these guidelines are used in developing the procedure for admission.

2. Procedures for admission include criteria relating to selection, retention and placement.

3. Procedures provide for individual assessment utilization Section II of these guidelines as criteria. They also provide for a design of an individual program for the applicant which is based on his needs as revealed by this assessment.

4. The assessment should include the capacity of the candidate to complete the program, familiarity with the objectives of the program, an understanding of the competencies, attitudes and skills needed in the middle school teacher and an initial commitment to teaching the middle school child.

5. Procedures provide for candidates to enter the program after completion of an undergraduate program in another area of concentration.

B. Inservice

The inservice teacher for all practical purposes is admitted to the inservice program of a school district when that school district employs the teacher to teach in a middle school. However, admission to certain parts of the inservice program for middle school teachers should follow an organized procedure:

1. The local education agency or school has a cooperatively developed procedure for assessing the inservice needs of middle school teachers.
2. Procedures provide for individual assessment based on Section II of these guidelines and the system's ability to improve the needs revealed. Assessment only includes the competencies in Section II of which the local system is capable of improving through inservice education.
3. Procedures provide for the cooperative development and use of the assessment procedures by teachers, supervisors and administrators.
4. Procedures provide for candidates to use both the local education agency's inservice education program, and institution-based programs.

Follow-Up of Program Participants

A. Preservice
   1. There is a planned program for assessing changes in attitudes and behavior of students as they move through the program.
   2. The program utilizes the results of the assessment procedures to revise individual student programs.
   3. Personnel in cooperating schools participate in the education process.
   4. Evaluation of the effectiveness of the program is accomplished through evidence obtained from former students, the schools in which they work, and the Department of Education. This evidence is based on the stated objective of the program.
   5. The follow-up program includes early leavers as well as those who complete the program.
   6. There is a record of revisions in the program which includes the follow-up data on which the revisions were based.
   7. Data appropriate for preservice/inservice program articulation is shared with the cooperating school system.

B. Inservice Programs
   1. There is a planned program of evaluation of the effectiveness of each inservice education component.
   2. The assessment of competencies developed in the program includes not only changes in teacher behavior, but an assessment of the resultant changes in student behavior.
   3. There is a record of revisions of inservice education components and the evaluation data on which revisions were based.
   4. Personnel from teacher education institutions participate in the evaluation of the program.
   5. Supervisors, principals, and teachers participate in the evaluation of the effectiveness of the program.

6. Follow-up data on the effectiveness of the program is shared with participating teacher education institutions.[4]

APPROPRIATE TEACHING STRATEGIES IN THE MIDDLE SCHOOL

Implementing a new program and organizational pattern will not guarantee the success of a middle school. Teachers must examine the methodology used in the classroom and select appropriate teaching strategies for the middle school. Knowledge of the youngsters in a middle school provides teachers with the background for selecting appropriate teaching strategies. For instance, we know that youngsters between the ages of ten and fourteen cannot sit still for long periods of time. If teachers devise learning situations that involve movement, manipulation of objects, and other forms of active participation, then learning will occur to a greater extent than found in the rigid, non-participating kind of classroom.

As middle school programs have emerged in the past twenty years, systems and instruments have been developed to help teachers look at classroom instruction in a more systematic way. Also, a number of innovations have been developed to improve the ultimate quality of teachers coming out of pre- and inservice training programs. We have identified three of these systems and innovations that are particularly relevant to the middle school: interaction analysis, classroom questions, and independent study. Verbal patterns of teachers are analyzed in a fourth section of this chapter.

Interaction Analysis

Observational systems that measure classroom interaction probably show the most promise as learning devices for preservice and inservice teachers. An observational system is defined here as any systematic technique for identifying, examining, classifying, and/or quantifying specific teaching activities. Of the observational systems available, Flanders' System of Interaction Analysis of verbal behavior is probably the most widely known and used.[5]

Flanders developed a category system that takes into account the verbal interaction between teachers and pupils in the classroom. The system enables one to determine whether the teacher controls students in such a way as to increase or decrease freedom or action. Through the use of observers or by using audio- or videotape equipment, a teacher can review the results of a teaching lesson. Every three seconds an observer writes down the category number of the interaction she has just observed. The numbers are recorded in sequence in a column. Whether the observer is using a live classroom or tape recording for her observations, it is best for the observer to spend ten to fifteen minutes getting oriented to the situation

---

[4] From *Guidelines for Preparation of Middle School Teachers* (Tallahassee, Fla.: Florida Department of Education, 1974), pp. 3–7. Used with permission.

[5] Ned A. Flanders, *Teacher Influence-Pupil Attitudes and Achievement* (Washington: Research Monograph 12, H.E.W., 1965).

before categorizing. The observer stops classifying whenever the classroom activity is inappropriate as, for instance, when there is silent reading or when various groups are working in the classroom, or when children are working in their workbooks.

A modification of the Flanders system of ten categories is a system developed by Hough[6] and used by Bondi and Ober[7] in research studies. That system provides three more categories of behavior than the Flanders system. In the thirteen category system, teacher statements are classified as either indirect or direct. This classification gives central attention to the amount of freedom a teacher gives to the student. In a given situation, the teacher can choose to be indirect, that is, maximizing freedom of a student to respond, or he can be direct, that is, minimizing the freedom of a student to respond. Teacher response is classified under the first nine categories.

Student talk is classified under three categories, and a fourth category provides for silence or confusion where neither a student nor the teacher can be heard. All categories are mutually exclusive, yet totally inclusive of all verbal interaction occurring in the classroom. Figure 3.2 describes the categories in the thirteen category modification of the Flanders System of Interaction Analysis.[8]

The social forces at work in the classroom are so complex that it appears on the surface that it would be difficult to analyze them. The teacher's interaction with middle school students, which is a portion of the total social process, seems almost as difficult to identify. Nevertheless, teacher-pupil contacts have been classified into specifically defined behavioral acts by various researchers who have studied teacher behavior. The Flanders System and other such systems are excellent means of sensitizing middle school teachers to their own verbal behavior in the classroom and helping them monitor their interaction with students.

The importance of analyzing and controlling verbal behavior of middle school teachers is well documented. Nonverbal communication in the classroom is another dimension of teaching that has drawn the attention of researchers. Middle school students are especially cognizant of body messages, both real and imaginary, that their teachers send out.

Nonverbal Communication

Nonverbal communication is often referred to as a silent language. Individuals send messages through a variety of conventional and nonconventional means. Facial expressions, bodily movements, and vocal tones all convey feelings to students. A student may be hearing a teacher verbally praise her work while the teacher's facial expression is communicating disapproval of that work. If a teacher fails to understand the nonverbal message being conveyed to pupils, he may not

---

[6] John B. Hough, "A Thirteen Category Modification of Flanders' System of Interaction Analysis," mimeographed. (Columbus, Ohio: The Ohio State University, 1965).

[7] Joseph Bondi and Richard Ober, "The Effects of Interaction Analysis Feedback on the Verbal Behavior of Student Teachers." A paper presented at the annual meeting of the American Educational Research Association, Los Angeles, February 1969.

[8] Jon Wiles and Joseph Bondi, *Curriculum Development: A Guide to Practice* (Columbus, Ohio: Charles E. Merrill Publishing Co., 1979), pp. 307–8.

Figure 3.2

Description of Categories for a Thirteen-Category Modification of the Flanders System of Interaction Analysis

	Category Number	Description of Verbal Behavior
T E A C H E R **I N D I R E C T**	1	ACCEPTS FEELING: Accepts and clarifies the feeling tone of students in a friendly manner. Student feelings may be of a positive or negative nature. Prediting and recalling student feelings are also included.
	2	PRAISES OR ENCOURAGES: Praises or encourages student action, behavior, recitation, comments, ideas, etc. Jokes that release tension not at the expense of another individual. Teacher nodding head or saying "uh-huh" or "go on" are included.
	3	ACCEPTS OR USES IDEAS OF STUDENT: Clarifying, building on, developing, and accepting the action, behavior, and ideas of the student.
	4	ASKS QUESTIONS: Asking a question about the content (subject matter) or procedure with the intent that the student should answer.
	5	ANSWERS STUDENT QUESTIONS (STUDENT-INITIATED TEACHER TALK): Giving direct answers to student questions regarding content or procedures.
T A L K **D I R E C T**	6	LECTURE (TEACHER-INITIATED TEACHER TALK): Giving facts, information, or opinions about content or procedure. Teacher expressing his or her own ideas. Asking rhetorical questions (not intended to be answered).
	7	GIVES DIRECTIONS: Directions, commands, or orders to which the student is expected to comply.
	8	CORRECTIVE FEEDBACK: Telling a student that his answer is wrong when the correctness of his answer can be established by other than opinions (i.e., empirical validation, definition, or custom).
	9	CRITICIZES STUDENT(S) OR JUSTIFIES AUTHORITY: Statements intended to change student behavior from a nonacceptable to an acceptable pattern; scolding someone; stating why the teacher is doing what he is doing so as to gain or maintain control; rejecting or criticizing a student's opinion or judgment.
	10	TEACHER-INITIATED STUDENT TALK: Talk by students in response to requests or narrow teacher questions. The teacher initiates the contact or solicits student's statements.

Figure 3.2—*continued*

S
T   T
U   A
D   L   11   STUDENT QUESTIONS: Student questions concerning content or
E   K   procedure that are directed to the teacher.
N
T

12   STUDENT-INITIATED STUDENT TALK: Talk by students in re-
      sponse to broad teacher questions which require judgment or opin-
      ion. Voluntary declarative statements offered by the student, but
      not called for by the teacher.

13   SILENCE OR CONFUSION: Pauses, short periods of silence, and
      periods of confusion in which communication cannot be
      understood by an observer.

Indirect-Direct Ratio = categories 1, 2, 3, 4, 5

categories 6, 7, 8, 9

Revised Indirect-Direct Ratio = categories 1, 2, 3

categories 7, 8, 9

Student-Teacher Ratio = categories 10, 11, 12

categories 1, 2, 3, 4, 5, 6, 7, 8, 9

be able to comprehend their responses to him. In analyzing a classroom then, it is just as important to examine *how* the teacher says what he has to say, how he behaves and expresses feelings, as *what* the teacher says, does, and feels. How teachers communicate their perceptions, feelings, and motivations can be identified with facial expressions, gestures, and vocal tones. Such expressions determine in large measure how pupils perceive those teachers.

In examining the significance of nonverbal communication in the middle school, it is important to understand that teaching is a highly personal matter, and prospective and inservice teachers need to face themselves as well as to acquire pedagogical skills. Middle school teachers need to become more aware of the connection between the messages they communicate and the consequences that follow. Middle school teachers also need to capitalize on the nonverbal cues expressed by students as keys to their clarity and understanding. While nonverbal interaction in the classroom is less amenable to systematic objective inquiry than verbal interaction, the meanings pupils give to a teacher's nonverbal message have significance for learning and teaching.

Through continued study of nonverbal behavior, middle school teachers can sharpen, alter, and modify their nonverbal messages they transmit to students. The advantage of adding nonverbal analysis in a study of teaching is that middle school teachers can look at their behavior in two ways—what their behavior means to pupils, and how their behavior is being interpreted by their pupils.

Classroom Questions

In the Flanders or Modified Flanders Systems of Interaction Analysis, one category of behavior deals with questions. That category concerns a teacher asking questions about content or procedure in order to elicit a student response. For the middle school teacher to obtain a greater understanding of her questions, other types of feedback instruments must be used.

The Gallagher-Aschner System of analyzing and controlling classroom questioning behavior has been widely used in preservice and inservice programs. (See Table 3.1.) In their work with the system, Gallagher and Aschner have found that the majority of teacher behavior falls in the first level, cognitive memory, but that even a slight increase in divergent questions leads to a major increase in divergent ideas produced by students.

Table 3.1

The Gallagher-Aschner System—A Technique for Analyzing and Controlling Classroom Questioning Behavior

1. *Cognitive-Memory:* calls for a specific memorized answer or response; anything which can be retrieved from the memory bank.

   1a. What is 2 X 3?
   1b. When did Florida become a state?
   1c. What is a noun?
   1d. At what temperature Centigrade does water boil?

2. *Convergent:* calls for a specific (single) correct answer which may be obtained by the application of a rule or procedure; normally requires the consideration of more than a single quantity of information and/or knowledge.

   2a. What is 30.5 X 62.7?
   2b. How many years was the U.S. under the Prohibition Law?
   2c. Diagram this sentence.
   2d. How many calories are required to melt 160 grams of ice at 0 C?

3. *Divergent:* allows the student a choice between more than one alternative or to create ideas of his own; more than a single answer is appropriate and acceptable.

   3a. What is 10 to three other bases?
   3b. What might have been the effects on the growth of the United States had there not been a Civil War?
   3c. Write a short story about Halloween.
   3d. Design an apparatus that will demonstrate the Law of Conservation of Matter.

4. *Evaluative:* the development and/or establishment of relevant standard of criteria of acceptability involving considerations as usefulness, desirability, social and cultural appropriateness, and moral and ethical propriety, then comparing the issue at hand to these; involves the making of value judgments.

   4a. Is 10 the best base for a number system?
   4b. Was the Civil War defensible?
   4c. Is English the best choice for a universal language?
   4d. Should we continue our space program now that we have landed on the moon?

SOURCE: J. J. Gallagher and Mary Jane Aschner, "A Preliminary Report: Analyses of Classroom Interaction," *Merrill-Palmer Quarterly of Behavior and Development* 9 (1963): pp. 183–94.

The need for helping teachers analyze classroom questions and developing appropriate strategies of questioning indicates that systematic training in the use of questions be made available to middle school teachers. The Gallagher-Aschner and other systems of analyzing and controlling classroom questions should be used in helping train teachers to stimulate productive thought processes in middle school classrooms.

Independent Study and the Role of the Teacher

Independent study demands a look at the role of the teacher and the kind of teacher needed for middle schools. The teacher plays a crucial role in stimulating and supporting independent study in the following ways and situations:

The Teacher as a Supporter of Independent Study. If any independent study is to be effective, the student must develop self-discipline and self-direction. He cannot do this if the teacher views himself as a policeman or spy. Instead, the teacher asks this basic question: Is the student's behavior appropriate for the situation, the learning activity, and the setting?

What is appropriate student behavior?

1. It is not distracting or disturbing others.

2. It is not endangering the student or others.

3. It is helping the student satisfy a worthwhile need. The need to relax and let off steam is worthwhile—given the appropriate setting and means.

If the student's behavior is not satisfactory and appropriate, what can be done?

Sometimes the simplest and best answer is to change the environment, not the behavior. ("Your talking in the library is bothering others. Why not go down to the lounge where you can talk without bothering anyone?")

The basic rule, however, is to use the minimum amount of direction that will enable the student's behavior to become satisfactory. Sometimes a stern look or a quiet word will suffice. Over-reaction should be guarded against.

The Teacher's Role in Stimulating Independent Study.

1. Know the student's interests and appeal to them. But also make a distinct attempt to broaden his interests.

2. Stress the importance of independent study. The student will be unconsciously influenced by your own attitude toward it.

3. Suggest areas for independent study that relate to and emanate from curricular concerns. The best independent study is not extraneous to, but is an intrinsic part of, the curriculum.

4. Stress not what is known about the subject—but what is unknown; not what has been discovered, but what has not been discovered.

5. Pique interest by dropping hints about projects the student might undertake. Resist the temptation to give answers—raise questions instead.

6. Teach the student how to raise the right kinds of questions. Not to deni-

grate serendipity, asking the right questions is, nonetheless, highly important.

7. Set a good example by telling the student the results of your own independent study.

Verbal Patterns of Teachers That Control Pupil Learning in the Classroom

Since 1960, research has provided more and better information about teaching performance. The use of systematic observation is now identifying those teaching behaviors that produce learning in children.

Through the use of various observational instruments, we have identified a number of verbal patterns of teachers that exert great control on pupil learning in the middle school classrooms.

Middle school teachers must like children and share their enthusiasm for new learning.

The first pattern is identified through the use of the Flanders (or modification thereof) System. It is called simply the excessive teacher-talk pattern. This occurs when teachers talk two-thirds of the time or more in the classroom. If teachers are talking more than two-thirds of the time, there is very little time left for students to participate. Middle schools that emphasize extensive student participation in their own learning should encourage the use of feedback from interaction analysis so that teachers can become aware of and able to control the amount of time they talk in the classroom. Just this one use alone renders interaction analysis an effective teaching and supervisory tool.

The second verbal pattern of teachers that controls pupil learning in the classroom is the recitation pattern. Arno Bellack has been a pioneer in describing verbal behaviors of teachers and pupils. Bellack has observed that no matter what the teachers' differences in ability levels or backgrounds are, their actions and responses are much alike.[9] In addition to talking between two-thirds and three-quarters of the time, teachers' major activity is the asking and reacting to questions that call for factual answers from students. As a pedagogical process, the question-answer sequence was recognized fifty years ago when teacher education consisted of considerable training in the skill of asking questions. Unfortunately, this process is still employed, despite the fact that each successive generation of educational leaders, no matter what their differences, has condemned the rapid-fire, question-answer pattern of instruction.[10] Training programs for middle school teachers should develop new processes for keeping teachers from following a similar pattern.

A classroom where recitation is the major activity suggests a high-pressure atmosphere, and also suggests that the teacher is doing most of the work. A large number of questions also means that little attention is being given to individual needs of students. The most that can be found in educational assets from rote recitation are verbal memory and superficial judgment.

By combining the use of the Flanders System with the Gallagher-Aschner System which identifies types of questions asked in the classroom, and Bloom's Taxonomy of Education Objectives (a kind of multidimensional approach), middle school teachers can break the recitation pattern. Again, teachers must be provided with effective feedback which allows them to "read" and modify their own verbal behavior.

The third verbal pattern of teachers that controls pupil learning is called the classroom management pattern. This pattern consists of teacher responses to deviant behavior and teacher communications indicating transitions in learning activities. As will be studied in the next section, Kounin has developed a system for analyzing the classroom management aspect of teaching. Such things as how a teacher notifies pupils of a change in activity and how and when a teacher reacts to deviant student behavior, are aspects of teacher skill in working with pupils which relate to pupil growth. This includes pupil growth in a number of areas, not just in subject matter.

The fourth verbal pattern of teachers that controls pupil learning in the classroom is the teacher-acceptance pattern. This includes teacher acceptance of student ideas and feelings. A number of observational systems have been used to categorize teacher acceptance of ideas and feelings. There is ample evidence that teachers who accept ideas and feelings of students enhance student learning in the classroom. Much work is yet to be done in identifying how teachers react to youngsters of a different race or socio-economic level.

The last verbal pattern of teachers that controls pupil learning is called the flexibility pattern. Most teachers like to think they are flexible individuals who can adjust to any circumstances. Unfortunately, teachers who are products of past learnings are quite often the opposite. Their behavior is so stereotyped that students can often predict accurately how these teachers will react to different student behaviors. Some students, for instance, soon learn that it doesn't pay to ask

---

[9] Arno A. Bellack et al., *The Language of the Classroom* (New York: Teachers College Press, 1966), p. 274.

[10] James Hoetker and William Ahlbrand, Jr., "The Persistence of the Recitation," *American Educational Research Journal* (March 1969): pp. 145–64.

questions in Mr. Jones' room, or know that Miss Smith will always talk 90 percent of the time in her classroom. Nowhere is flexibility of teacher behavior more important than in the middle school.

It is possible for teachers to learn to be more flexible in their verbal behavior. Interaction analysis is also effective in providing teachers with feedback from systematic observations of their verbal behavior. The middle school can provide the setting for teachers to use observational systems to identify and control those verbal behaviors that determine pupil learning.

CLASSROOM MANAGEMENT AND DISCIPLINE PROCEDURES

Classroom Management

Classroom management becomes an important aspect of teaching in the middle school. The changing family structure and increased conflict found in all elements of our society have led to concern about a general breakdown in school discipline and the need for better classroom management. There are a number of ways a middle school teacher can maintain an effective learning environment in the classroom.

Jacob Kounin has found a surprising number of aspects of teacher behavior that relate highly with pupil work involvement in the classroom. An interesting aspect of his work is that much of it is concerned with the management of transitions from one unit to another, rather than from the teaching within a unit. The following are examples:[11]

Group alerting occurs when the teacher notifies pupils of an imminent change in activity, watches to see that pupils are finishing the previous activity, and initiates the new one only when all of the class members are ready. In contrast, thrusting is represented when the teacher "bursts" in on pupil activity with no warning and no awareness of anything but the teacher's own needs.

Stimulus boundedness is represented by behavior in which the teacher is apparently trapped by a stimulus as would a moth by a flame. For example, a piece of paper on the floor leads to interruption of the on-going activities of the classroom while the teacher berates the class members for the paper on the floor or tries to find out how it got there.

Overlappingness is the teacher's ability to carry on two operations at once. For example, while the teacher is working with a reading group, a pupil comes to ask a question about arithmetic. The teacher handles the situation in a way which keeps the reading group at work while he simultaneously helps the child with his arithmetic.

A *dangle* occurs when the teacher calls for the end of one activity, initiates another one, then returns to the previous activity. For example, "Now pupils, put

---

[11] From notes of presentation by Dr. Robert Soar at conference, "The Planning and Analysis of Classroom Instruction," The University of Florida, November 1975, pp. 7–8. For a detailed report of Kounin's work, see Jacob S. Kounin, *Discipline and Group Management in Classrooms* (New York: Holt, Rinehart and Winston, Inc., 1970).

away your arithmetic books and papers and get out your spelling books; we're going to have spelling." After the pupils have put away their arithmetic materials and gotten out their spelling materials the teacher asks, "Oh, by the way, did everybody get problem four right?"

If the teacher never gets back to the new activity which he initiated (for example, if he had never returned to the spelling in the previous example) this would be called a *truncation.*

With-it-ness is the teacher's demonstration of his awareness of deviant behavior. It is assessed both for timing and for target accuracy. Timing involves stopping the deviant behavior before it spreads, and target accuracy involves identifying the responsible pupil. If, for example, an occurrence of whispering in the back of the room should spread to several other children, and at this point the teacher criticizes one of the later class members who joined in, this behavior would be scored negatively both for timing and for target accuracy.

The Kounin examples illustrate the ways teachers can maintain the group and not hinder learning in the classroom. In analyzing classrooms, we must not ignore the techniques of group management that teachers must utilize daily. Teachers must be provided feedback of their own behavior if they are to improve instruction.

Discipline Procedures for Emerging Adolescent Learners

Young middle school teachers enter the classroom filled with such pedagogical terms as *social control, group dynamics, behavior patterns,* and *democratic procedures.* These terms mean little to the worried teacher who must get Johnny to sit down and keep quiet—at least long enough for the teacher to get the day started.

What is good discipline? Certainly not a classroom in which no one speaks but the teacher. A classroom where students respond willingly and quickly to routine requests of the teacher is a well-controlled class. A middle school teacher who can maintain good working conditions and control noise when necessary, without pressure, makes it possible for children to learn.

The 1979 Gallup Poll of the public's attitudes toward public schools indicated, as it had in eight of the last nine years, that discipline was the major problem facing public schools in the nation. Parents still blame themselves for the problems of discipline, motivation, and drug and alcohol addiction that frequently begin in the home.

In spite of the breakdown of the family, and parent acceptance of blame for many student problems, middle school teachers must still cope with the day-by-day discipline problems in the classroom.

We consider the problems of student discipline a major issue in middle school education. Statistics reveal that the prime cause of teacher dropout after a few years is the inability to develop effective discipline procedures.

Teaching in the middle school can be a rewarding and creative experience. It can also be highly frustrating if teacher effectiveness in disciplining students is absent. At no other grade level are students so capable of being uncooperative or disruptive to the teaching-learning process. Teachers who are successful in working with the emerging adolescents often appear to have accomplished a "magic hold" over their students. Closer analysis, however, reveals that such teachers simply have a greater understanding of their students' development, and have structured discipline procedures to fit the students whom they instruct.

Primary among the authors' premises about discipline procedures with emerging adolescents are the following:

1. Most discipline problems experienced in the classroom are natural rather than unnatural acts and, as such, will take care of themselves.

2. The majority of discipline problems in the middle grades can be averted by revising the students' instructional program.

3. The establishment of a clear set of teachers' expectations in the middle grades can make existing discipline procedures more effective over a period of time.

The Significance of the Middle Years

Educators are only now beginning to fully appreciate the significance of the middle school years in terms of eventual adult behavior. The young adolescent is absorbed by a process of immense transformation during which the child is "reborn" as an adult person. This transformation is a precarious balance of social, emotional, physical, and intellectual factors. In most cases, the transformation is successful and a sound and contributing citizen joins the society. Sometimes, however, when identification with society is not successful, a hostile, alienated, and rebellious adult emerges.

Social agencies which deal with problems of adult deviancy point to the transescent period as a critical one for this transformation. The middle years are indeed a watershed for human behavior, and society pays dearly for those who "don't come out right." The criminal, the alcoholic, the insane, the uninvolved nonproductive adult, are a burden to all society.

School programs for emerging adolescents must, then, do all they can to facilitate passage through a difficult period of development. They must accommodate students in their transformation and acknowledge the reality of the stresses experienced by these students.

A Period of Stress

In particular, teachers of the emerging adolescent would do well to resurrect their own experiences at this age. Fond memories come easier than those which are painful, and sometimes it is difficult for teachers to recall the many problems, uncertainties, pressures, and fears of their own early adolescence. Yet today, relationships with parents, peer group pressures, problems of identity, self-image, opposite-sex relationships, and needs for status still form the nucleus of concerns for most young adolescents. The point is that the stress experienced by early adolescents is genuine. Teachers who can "get inside their student," perceptually, will have a greater chance of reacting effectively to his behavior.

When confronted with stressful situations, adults call on previous experience to act in ways which will minimize social and personal pressures. Emerging adolescents, for the most part, do not have such a perspective. Their childhood experiences are inappropriate for the adult world. They react to stressful conditions in unpredictable and inconsistent ways. Often their behaviors are unacceptable to adults and the adult world.

Teachers are most aware of the young adolescents' behavior when that behavior is disruptive to the teaching-learning process or acknowledged norms of the school environment. Teachers hold certain expectations for student behavior and when those expectations are not met, there is an adult reaction. Unfortunately, not all teachers hold the same expectations for student behavior nor react in the same manner to unacceptable behavior.

Disruptive student behavior in the middle school grades is more common than most teachers acknowledge. National statistics on extreme forms of student disruption are shocking, and such statistics often show the young adolescent to be a principal offender.[12] Even in school districts where student misconduct is considered to be a minor problem, a tremendous amount of disruptive behavior and delinquent activity is ignored. It is a rare student indeed who doesn't experience some sort of conflict with teachers and school authorities during the middle grades.

Part of the difficulty in confronting disruption and building effective discipline procedures stems from the lack of a clear definition of the problem itself. "Discipline problems" in schools can range from gum-chewing to outright physical aggression. Until the problem of discipline is clearly defined, establishing effective discipline procedures will remain a hit-or-miss proposition.

Some middle grade students obviously experience greater difficulty in controlling their behavior than others. There are students in every intermediate classroom who are not only unruly but also hostile toward the learning process. They seem to lack self-control and revert to a child-like dependence on physical aggression when confronted by authority. Others, usually habitual offenders of the school codes, seem unable to distinguish between right and wrong. Emerging deviant behaviors seem to achieve full-bloom in the late intermediate years. For many teachers of young adolescents, a major problem is the range of discipline difficulties they confront.

Tasks of Development

A reality in the intermediate grades, besides that of students undergoing a transformation from childhood to adulthood, is that all students are developing physically at their own rates. Unlike other levels of schooling, students in the young adolescent period are unique. This is obvious to the casual observer of size and weight among ten to fourteen year olds. The teacher, however, acknowledges that students differ in ways other than physical appearance. Social maturity, for instance, is uneven among young adolescents. Emotional stability is a variable. The ability to conceptualize and rationalize is strangely individual. Given a roomful of young adolescents, the overriding characteristic is their difference.

Borrowing from sociologist Robert Havighurst's conceptualization, the young

---

[12] The 1974–75 report of the U. S. Senate Sub-Committee on Juvenile Delinquency, chaired by Senator Birch Bayh (D-Indiana), documented extensive vandalism and crime in schools including over 20,000 recorded student assaults on teachers.

adolescent might be perceived as engaged in a set of developmental tasks which must be accomplished as the student passes into adulthood.[13] One task, for instance, is acceptance of a changing body and the accompanying self-image. Another task might be to learn to get along with others in a social setting. A third might be to learn to control emotion and express onself in socially acceptable ways. These many tasks must be confronted by the student individually, and each student has a unique pattern of mastery in dealing with every developmental task.

The concept difficult for many teachers to understand, however, is that few young adolescents are mature in all realms of development. A seventh-grade girl may look 20 years old physically and still act like a child. A small bookish-looking sixth-grade boy may be fully mature only in his intellectual capacity. All students in the intermediate grades are in transition, passing through the young adolescent period and mastering basic social tasks as they go.

If classroom teachers of emerging adolescents can understand this basic fact about their students, they will have a much clearer idea of how they can become more effective in establishing discipline procedures. It is probable that a single and uniform set of regulations in any intermediate classroom *cannot* be applied to all students at all times. The diversity of problems the young adolescent presents makes such a prospect a hopeless task for even the best teachers.

A classic study by John Goodlad and Associates found that most teachers possess a multitude of effective responses to discipline problems in the classroom.[14] These teacher "weapons" include praise, voice control, facial expressions, gestures, finger-snapping, use of physical proximity, touch, isolation, and expulsion from classroom spaces. Subsequent studies indicate that students, too, possess a repertoire of behaviors to counteract such teacher actions. The result, in many classrooms, is that teachers and students engage in games of escalation in terms of disciplining. For students cognizant of this interaction pattern, the most popular "game" is to test or "bait" the teacher without receiving the maximum punishment.

The underlying problem or cause of such a deteriorating situation is that classroom teachers attempt to enforce a uniform code of behavior on all students. The authors believe such a posture is impossible in light of the nature of middle grade students. Only when the "tightest of lids" is applied can a class full of young adolescents be controlled in this manner. Such a classroom, when found, is usually characterized by a lot of discipline and very little real learning!

The authors believe these factors recommend that a highly unique set of discipline procedures must be developed in an intermediate school if discipline is to be effective, and that such a set of procedures must be institutionalized through the school program.

Discipline Procedures Guidelines

In general, there are four thoughts which might serve as guidelines in establishing and enforcing discipline procedures for the young adolescent:

[13] Robert J. Havighurst, *Developmental Tasks and Education,* (New York: Longmans, Green, 1952).

[14] J. Goodlad and M. F. Klein, *Behind the Classroom Door* (Worthington, Oh.: Charles A. Jones Publishing Co., 1970).

1. Discipline procedures must be known to all involved.
2. Discipline procedures must be flexible enough to accommodate differences among students.
3. Discipline procedures must be appropriate to behavior.
4. Discipline procedures must involve others important to the young adolescent.

All too often, the reaction of classroom teachers to a discipline situation is a highly unpredictable event. Even the best teachers have good days and bad days, and it is only human to have slight variance in response to student behavior. But if one thing is needed by emerging adolescents, it is consistency. Their daily lives are a search for patterns to which they can adjust themselves. Teachers who take time to "think through" the concept of discipline with students will eliminate surprise in discipline procedures. Such a predictable pattern will, in turn, eliminate sudden and irrational student responses.

While spelling out discipline relationships is important, it is equally important to acknowledge student differences in the application of punishment. Students are keenly aware of their uniqueness, and their tolerance for "situational application" of discipline will surprise most classroom teachers. If discipline procedures can be thought of as a continuum, rather than as a cause-effect relationship, each student can be helped to be more responsible in the classroom. In some cases, behavior can be modified by continually extending trust and responsibility to students of individual need.

It is important that discipline procedures be appropriate to the behavior exhibited. One of the leading causes of discipline problems in the middle grades is a single teacher response to all conditions. When a teacher applies the same punishment to day-dreaming as to physical aggression in the classroom, students will sense the injustice of the discipline. Continued application of nondiscriminatory punishment will soon place all students in an adverse relationship to the teacher.

Finally, it is critical that whatever the disciplinary procedure, other persons significant to the student be involved. When other teachers, parents, and peers are involved in disciplinary procedures, the act of discipline will be reinforced.

A Discipline Model

Since student behavior in the middle grades is so diverse and everchanging, it is difficult to use behavior as the basis of designing a sound discipline procedure in the classroom. A much more predictable basis for designing discipline procedures is teacher behavior. Wiles has developed a primitive response model which seems to encompass most teacher behavior relating to discipline:[15]

AVOID	SUPPRESS
RESTRUCTURE	DEFUSE

---

[15] Jon Wiles, "School Disruption: In Search of an Adequate Response," *Educational Horizons* 55 (Spring 1977): pp. 124–27.

According to this model, when teachers take action to respond to disruptive student behavior, the intention or strategy of such action is either to avoid the problem, suppress the problem, defuse the problem, or change the environment in an attempt to deal with the cause of the problem.

Examples of avoidance responses are ignoring disruptive behavior altogether or responding in ways which are purposefully unrelated to the behavior being exhibited. For example, a teacher observing one student punching another student might request that everyone open his textbook and begin answering the odd-numbered questions at the end of the chapter.

Examples of suppressive activity on the part of the teacher are the more common punitive measures found in most schools: confiscating personal items, isolating troublemakers, locking bathrooms, and paddling. In the example above, the teacher might respond by giving the "puncher" a squeeze on the neck or by expelling him from the learning space. In suppression responses, the teacher responds to the behavior itself rather than the cause of the behavior.

Teacher responses to disruption which fall into the defuse category also deal with effects. Here the teacher is attempting to take the steam out of a situation. Behavior modification "economies," for instance, seek to lessen the problem by altering the reward pattern of the offender rather than confronting the problem directly. In the foregoing example, the teacher might take the offender out into the hall to "cool off." The teacher hopes that by defusing the situation, behavior will return to acceptable limits.

Finally, teachers may seek to meet the cause of disruptive behavior head-on by identifying the real problem and restructuring the environment so that reoccurrence is lessened. The student who is punching the other may be doing so because he is a frustrated non-reader or because his physical education period is the last of the day. The teacher must choose between continually responding to such behavior or acting to alter the environment so that causation is eliminated.

A model like this one is useful to teachers in gaining perspective on their own style of discipline procedures. By analyzing classroom disruption/response interaction in their learning spaces, they can soon see a pattern. Such insight should lead to effective strategies bearing on what type of response seems appropriate to what kind of behavior.

School-Wide Response Patterns

While there is benefit for every teacher to think about discipline procedures in a systematic way, it is even more important that a school faculty address this concern. Through discussion, a faculty may be able to coordinate its collective response to major types of disruptive behavior. Are there behaviors, for instance, which the whole faculty considers "near sins"? If so, what is an appropriate response which might be collectively communicated to students? Are there behaviors that the school might handle by diversionary tactics? Are some discipline problems so common that they might be considered natural? Are some problems so basic that a change in the school structure is called for?

In particular, we believe that suppression responses are most inappropriate in many cases due to the ever-changing nature of the young adolescent. To confront a student, to suppress a student in the middle grades, should be a tactic of last resort. Such heavy-handedness appears to run counterproductively to the tasks of developing independence, gaining status, and developing self-control. If students are to become adult, they must be given a chance to learn through disciplinary procedures. A restructured school environment and a responsive system of discipline can contribute to such growth and development.

Institutional Activities Which Help

During the past decade, intermediate education has experienced a major renewal. Educational programs have been designed which seek to accommodate student differences and facilitate passage through the early adolescent years. These institutional changes have had a positive effect in reducing student discipline problems. The overall effect of these changes has been to *personalize* education in the intermediate grades. Students have responded well to these efforts.

The changes which have been incorporated into programs for emerging adolescents can be divided into two major categories: (1) to make the instructional program more humane and (2) to make the instructional program more adaptable to student needs. While the ideal condition is for an entire school to adapt such changes, the activities mentioned in the following paragraphs can be implemented by one classroom teacher.

In humanizing educational programs for the young adolescent, teachers have sought to make the school program more personal. One method employed is for teachers to conduct an assessment of the needs of students. To the degree that interests can be determined and a composite of student development outlined, instruction can be designed to serve the learners. Common sense and experience suggest that all persons are receptive to learning which meets their needs.

Another way to humanize programs is to break down large group administrative units into smaller, more intimate groups. In many schools the "school-within-a-school" concept has been used to guarantee that individual students enjoy continuity of social contact during the school day.[16] A dominant theme of the young adolescent period is a feeling of loneliness. Within classrooms, small tasks groups can overcome this problem.

Record-keeping presents another way to make the school program more humane and personal. To the degree that the teacher can monitor growth through effective record-keeping, student needs and problems can be pinpointed and confronted. Such record-keeping should go beyond the maintenance of folders on academic progress and would be most effective if written like entries in a diary.

Schools and teachers within the classrooms can seek to provide greater guidance services for students. To overcome the always large ratio of guidance

---

[16] School-within-a-school is an administrative arrangement whereby students are housed with other students in smaller groups to personalize education. In a school of 1200 students, for instance, there might be four separate student groups of 300 pupils who share the same teachers and space.

counselors to students (1:450 + in most intermediate schools), peer counseling can be encouraged. Such response groups can be used in a number of activities of varying emotional intensity. In classroom settings, teachers can use a form of "teacher-counselor" activity and provide in-the-hall "walking advisement."[17] It is possible in any school or classroom to insure that each student will have an adult with whom she can converse.

Teachers can seek to involve parents to a greater degree in the schooling experience. To assume that lessons in a six-hour school can compensate or overcome the many lessons out-of-school is short-sighted. Teachers need the support and help of parents, and such help is obtainable to the degree that parents are given a meaningful role. Their presence in a classroom setting means additional adult figures and, correspondingly, more adults who can work in small groups with young adolescents.

A second major change that schools and teachers can make is to adjust school programs so that they are more adaptable to student needs. Such adjustments are indicative of teacher understanding of students in the intermediate grades.

One method of making the program more adaptable to the student is to place the curriculum on a continuous progress basis. Such an adjustment allows all students to participate at whatever level of development they possess. In particular, students who are over-aged or repeated failures can become involved without loss of status or suffering humiliation.

Another way of adapting the program is to make the class schedule more flexible within major time periods. In this way, neither the teacher nor student is a slave to the clock, and discussions and activities which strike a responsive chord can be maintained. Such flexibility also teaches time management and allows students to have greater control over their school day.

Yet another way to make the school or class program more adaptable is to "program" constructive and creative outlets into the school day. This can be done by allowing students to earn "free time" in class, or by scheduling exploratory activities which "stretch" the student's experience. Such creative outlets can do much to de-emphasize unfair competition among students and at the same time provide opportunities for all students to find areas of strength.

A fourth way of making the school or class program adaptable is to integrate school and social experiences. Young adolescents have a great need to master social experiences like communicating with others, overcoming shyness, learning manners, and projecting sex roles. The classroom which integrates these strong needs with learning is a classroom with few motivational problems.

Finally, the school can be more adaptive if it will provide more than one way of learning for students.[18] Each teacher has a favored learning style and a preferred delivery system for learning. Rather than exluding those students who don't learn well by traditional methods, teachers can find alternative learning paths for students.

---

[17] The terms *teacher-counselor* and *walking advisement* are used in middle schools to describe a counseling role for the classroom teacher.

[18] The reader is encouraged to read William Glasser's *Schools Without Failure* (New York: Harper & Row, 1969) for an understanding of how to help students gain self-control.

SUMMARY

In this chapter, we have emphasized the position that the teacher, more than any other factor, holds the key to the success of the middle school.

In addition to identifying desirable personal characteristics of teachers that are of a general nature, researchers are now identifying specific teacher competencies necessary for the essential middle school.

Suggestions have been offered for the professional preparation of middle school teachers. It is important that certifying agencies and teacher training institutions revise present training programs to provide a middle school program that is neither elementary nor secondary, but has an identity of its own.

The implementation of a middle school program will only be successful when teachers examine their methodology used in the classroom and are able to select appropriate teaching strategies for the middle school. Several instruments and innovations have been suggested by the authors including interaction analysis of verbal and nonverbal behavior, analyzing and controlling classroom questions, and fostering independent study.

Finally, classroom management and discipline procedures are discussed in detail to give those teaching or working with teachers guidelines for coping with behavioral problems so common in the emerging adolescent years.

Suggested Learning Activities

1. Ask your students to develop a list of personal characteristics of middle school teachers that they most admire.

2. Identify the ten most important teacher competencies of the selected middle school teacher competencies identified in this chapter. Give reasons why you selected the ones on your list.

3. Design an outline of a preservice or inservice training program for middle school teachers. What courses and/or experiences would you include?

4. Use the modified Flanders System or the Gallagher-Aschner System in your classroom to analyze a given teaching-learning situation.

5. Develop a list of discipline procedures for working with emerging adolescents.

Selected References

Alexander, William et al. *The Emergent Middle School,* 2nd ed. New York: Holt, Rinehart and Winston, Inc., 1969.

A.S.C.D. Working Group on the Emerging Adolescent Learner. *The Middle School We Need.* Washington, D. C.: Association for Supervision and Curriculum Development, 1975.

Basile, Joseph, and Shockley, Robert, eds. *A Report on the Proceedings of the West Virginia Conference on Middle Schools and Middle Childhood Education.* West Virginia State Department of Education, 1979.

Bondi, Joseph. *Developing Middle Schools: A Guidebook.* Wheeling, Ill.: Whitehall Publishing Co., 1972.

Flanders, Ned. *Teacher Influence-Pupil Attitudes and Achievement.* Washington, D. C.: Research Monograph 12, HEW, 1965.

Kounin, Jacob S. *Discipline and Group Management in Classrooms.* New York: Holt, Rinehart and Winston, Inc., 1970.

Lawrence, Gordon. *Florida Middle School Models.* Florida State Department of Education, 1972.

Wiles, Jon, and Bondi, Joseph. *Curriculum Development: A Guide to Practice.* Columbus, Ohio: Charles Merrill Publishing Co., 1979.

4

A Program Design
for the Middle
School

The great range of differences
found in middle school students demands
a broad and relevant program.

The program of the middle school should reflect the philosophy of the school itself. It is for this reason that it is difficult to find the same program offered in any two middle schools even within a single school district. There are, however, common elements of a middle school program that can be readily identified. In this chapter we shall examine the elements of program that give the middle school its identity and vitality.

A well-balanced program focusing on personal development, emphasizing skills for continued learning, and utilizing knowledge to foster social competence is essential if we are to serve the diverse group of youngsters found in the middle grades.

The ASCD notes that a good middle school program should provide the following:

1. Learning experiences for transescents at their own intellectual levels, relating to immediate rather than remote academic goals.

2. A wide variety of cognitive learning experiences to account for the full range of students who are at many different levels of concrete and formal operations. Learning objectives should be sequenced to allow for the transition from concrete to formal operations.

3. A diversified curriculum of exploratory and/or fundamental activities resulting in daily successful experiences that will stimulate and nurture intellectual development.

4. Opportunities for the development of problem-solving skills, reflective-thinking processes, and awareness for the order of the student's environment.

5. Cognitive learning experiences so structured that students can progress in an individualized manner. However, within the structure of an individualized learning program, students can interact with one another. Social interaction is not an enemy of individual learning.

6. A curriculum in which all areas are taught to reveal opportunities for further study, to help students learn how to study, and to help them appraise their own interests and talents. In addition, the middle school should continue the developmental program of basic skills instruction started in the elementary school, with emphasis upon both developmental and remedial reading.

7. A planned sequence of concepts in the general education areas, major emphasis on the interests and skills for continued learning, a balanced program of exploratory experiences and other activities and services for personal development, and appropriate attention to the development of values.

8. A common program in which areas of learning are combined and integrated to break down artificial and irrelevant divisions of curriculum content. Some previously departmentalized areas of the curriculum should be combined and taught around integrative themes, topics, and experiences. Other areas of the curriculum, particularly those concerned with basic skills which are logical, sequential, and analytical, might best be taught in ungraded or continuous progress programs. Inflexible student scheduling, with its emphasis upon departmentalization, should be restructured in the direction of greater flexibility.

9. Encouragement of personal curiosity, with one learning experience inspiring subsequent activities.

10. Methods of instruction involving open and individually directed learning experiences. The role of the teacher should be more that of a personal guide and facilitator of learning than of a purveyor of knowledge. Traditional lecture-recitation methods should be minimized.

11. Grouping criteria which involve not only cognitive, but also physical, social, and emotional criteria.

12. As much consideration for who the student is and becomes, his self-concept, self-responsibility, and attitudes toward school and personal happiness, as for how much and what he knows.

13. Experiences in the arts for all transescents to foster aesthetic appreciations and to stimulate creative expression.

14. Curriculum and teaching methods which reflect cultural, ethnic, and socioeconomic subgroups within the middle school student population.[1]

There has been much progress in the past ten years in developing new and exciting programs for emerging adolescent learners; yet still much needs to be done. Whether programs for students in the middle grades are housed in organizational structures called middle schools or are found in upper elementary grades, junior high schools, or secondary schools, the focus of such programs has to be the developmental characteristics of the emerging adolescent learner group itself.[2]

Figure 4.1 on page 84 illustrates the three major program elements in the essential middle school. Each of the three program elements will be discussed in the next sections.

PERSONAL DEVELOPMENT

The personal development element of the middle school program has as a focal point the developmental differences of emerging adolescents rather than their sameness. Developmental age groupings are employed in such a program rather than a chronological-graded concept. Developmental age refers to a student's physical, social, and intellectual maturational levels. The goal of the personal development program element is to provide opportunities for students to understand themselves and others and develop into fully functioning individuals.

Guidance in the Middle School

Guidance is an integral part of the total middle school program. All instructional and special service personnel should be involved in the guidance process.

At no other time in the life of an individual is she likely to encounter as diverse a number of problems simultaneously as the period of time between ten and fourteen years of age. Coping with self-doubt, peer status, and physical changes, as well as struggling with turbulent emotions, emerging independence, and developing sex roles—all are part of the lives of emerging adolescents.

A strong guidance counseling service is needed in the middle school to help emerging adolescents adjust to their changing bodies and environments. Such a guidance-counseling service can be carried out through guidance specialists, support personnel such as psychologists, psychiatrists, and social workers, family teams, homebase teachers, teacher-advisor or advisor-advisee system community agencies, and resource persons.

---

[1] ASCD Working Group on the Emerging Adolescent Learner, *The Middle School We Need* (Washington, D.C.: Association for Supervision and Curriculum Development, 1975), pp. 11–12.

[2] Joseph Bondi, "Programs for Emerging Adolescent Learners," in Robert Leeper, ed., *Middle School in the Making* (Washington, D. C.: Association for Supervision and Curriculum Development, 1974), pp. 17–18.

Figure 4.1

Program Design for the Essential Middle School

I. Personal Development

Guidance—Physical Education—Intramurals—Lifetime Sports—Sex Education—Health Studies—Law Education–Social Services–Drug Education–Special Interests–Clubs–Student Government–Developmental Grouping–Programs for Students with Special Needs–Mainstreaming–Alternative Programs

II. Education for Social Competence

Basic Studies
   Science
   Social Studies
   Mathematics
   Language Arts

Exploratory Studies
   Practical Arts
      Home Economics
      Industrial Arts
      Business—Distributive Education

   Fine Arts
      Music
      Art
      Foreign Language
      Humanities

Environmental Studies
   Outdoor Education

Career Exploration

Consumer Education

Media Study

III. Skills for Continuous Learning

Communication
   Reading
   Writing
   Listening
   Speaking

Mathematics
   Computation
   Comprehension
   Usage

Observing and Comparing

Analyzing

Generalizing

Organizing

Evaluating

Guidance specialists should be assigned to every school with a minimum of one specialist for each 250 middle school students. Guidance specialists or counselors in the middle school must participate in group and individual guidance and work closely with teacher teams and specialists in instructional activities such as valuing exercises and career awareness. Fourteen functions of guidance counselors, as identified by the Florida Department of Education, are listed here:

1. Counseling students, both individually and through skilled use of the group process, on problems of educational, personal, and social and vocational development and adjustment.

2. Familiarizing teachers with the results of varied testing programs and assisting and counseling them in the use of test results.

3. Assisting in orienting the student to become familiar with his new school, its purposes, facilities, rules, and activities in order to adjust better and to further his development.

4. Assisting with small or large group instruction—both in subject areas and in group counseling situations.

5. Securing the testing, interpretation, and subsequent therapy for students with speech, hearing, or health difficulties.

6. Referring students to the visiting teacher for help with the broad range of home problems.

7. Evaluating special needs for children who are underachievers or slow learners.

8. Assisting in determining the appropriate level of learning for each student.

9. Communicating with all service personnel within the school for the maximum benefit to students and children.

10. Participating in team planning sessions and assuming a leadership role in all guidance-related aspects of the learning program.

11. Assisting in determining appropriate diagnostic tests for use in a particular discipline and then being involved in its administration and follow-up.

12. Initiating and providing leadership for parent-team-counselor conferences.

13. Relating students' needs and progress to parents (not necessarily a group conference), thus acting as a liaison between home and school.

14. Preparing reports and collecting information to be used in team-parent conferences which will facilitate communication.[3]

Support personnel such as psychologists, psychiatrists, and social workers must be available to support the staff of middle schools. The complex social-emotional problems of emerging adolescent youth (caused by the breakdown of the family and other social problems) have resulted in increased numbers of youths in need of specialized services.

Family teams are interdisciplinary teams of teachers with common planning time who teach students in a flexible frame of time. Family teams provide family counseling, help develop group affective activities, and encourage a group or family identity of students and teachers.

Homebase is a time where a common group of students can interact with a single teacher over a long period of time. The homebase or homeroom teacher works with students in a number of school-wide activities and serves as a teacher-counselor to students.

A *teacher-advisor* may be any adult in a school who functions in an advisory role with a small group of students. The teacher-advisor meets with a small multiage group periodically. Both structured and unstructured guidance activities are carried out with the group or individuals within the group. The focus is on social and emotional growth of students.

Community agencies and resource persons such as drug-abuse centers, mental health agencies, county health departments, and medical personnel can be utilized to provide services to middle school youth. We have seen many instances where pediatricians are being used as resource persons to help emerging adolescents understand the body changes of transescence. Middle schools cannot possibly meet all the physical, social, or emotional needs of their students and, therefore, must be able to tap the valuable reservoir of community resources available in most school districts.

---

[3] Special State Committee, *Developing Middle Schools in Florida* (Tallahassee, Fla.: Florida Department of Education, 1974), pp. 36–37. Used with permission.

Physical Education

Physical growth and development in emerging adolescents require a physical education program that is tailored for each middle school student. Physical education programs should be offered on a daily basis to all students. Programs such as adaptive physical education programs should be designed to help students cope with maturational problems like awkwardness, underdeveloped psychomotor skills, and weight problems. Handicapped students should be given instruction to help them develop to maximum growth and development. All students should be provided the opportunity to participate in a variety of games, sports, and developmental activities designed to meet their own needs, interests, and abilities.

Intramurals have replaced interscholastic sports programs in many middle schools. Where interscholastic sports programs exist, they have been structured much like intramurals. For instance, contests are scheduled during school time or in the afternoon and all students desiring to play are allowed to play. With the loss of the ninth grade to the high school, middle schools have wisely dropped contact sports such as football.

Lifetime sports like golf, tennis, bicycling, and swimming have been introduced in middle schools to provide for a carry-over into adult life.

Law Education

As a result of alarming increases in youth crime, a growing number of middle schools are introducing law education programs in the curriculum to acquaint emerging adolescents with the functions of law in our society. Several states have mandated law education through legislation.

Health Education

Health education for the middle school student provides an understanding of the human body and how it works as a system. The increased incidence of drug and alcohol abuse as well as venereal disease in pre- and early adolescents makes it imperative that students develop a respect for and desire to take care of their bodies and minds.

To help accomplish this objective, health programs in middle schools may be scheduled as independent courses or incorporated in science or physical education programs. Some of the major topics dealt with include the wise use of products; health information and services; identifying social, mental and physical community resources; keeping one's self free from the threat of accident and disease; growth and development; and family.

Providing for Students with Special Needs

Any plan for the development of a middle program must accommodate students with special needs. Based on existing student populations in middle grades, an average middle school of 720 children would be expected to have the following representation of exceptionalities:

fourteen to fifteen educable mentally handicapped
thirty-six speech and hearing handicapped
seven or eight emotionally disturbed
seven or eight with specific learning disabilities
seven or eight socially maladjusted
one deaf
one or two visually impaired
one or two physically handicapped

Obviously, the characteristics of school population vary from school to school, but the foregoing figures clearly indicate that students with special needs, including the gifted, cannot be ignored. The nature of the exceptionality mandates an individualized approach to instruction. Each child must have a special program designed to meet her needs, and that program must provide for the continuous progress of each student.

Middle school years are years of building self-concept. Students faced with more than the usual number of developmental problems need to feel wanted and capable. Mainstreaming and heterogeneous grouping of students in the middle school are helping to build an awareness of the worth of all students and, likewise, are providing an opportunity for students with special needs to interact positively with other students.

Special Interest Classes

Special interest classes are unique to the middle school. They are an outgrowth of clubs in the junior high school and an expansion of elementary exploratory experiences. Special interest courses are offered in a variety of patterns in middle schools but have the common goal of offering students a variety of affective, psychomotor, and cognitive exploratory experiences above those found in the normal program.

Students can elect to take special interest courses that are taught by teachers with special talents. The courses can run three, six, or nine weeks in length. Some courses may be taught on a semester or yearly basis. Teachers, administrative personnel, and, frequently, community volunteers, help teach special interest courses. Such courses combined with other activity programs like intramurals, school assemblies, and play days do much to create student interest in school as well as to provide valuable exploratory experiences for students. Since pupils participate on a nongraded basis, students are provided an opportunity to interact with students of varying age levels.

The descriptions in Samples 4.1 and 4.2 of the program at Riviera Middle School in Pinellas County, Florida, illustrate the rich variety of experiences a middle school can provide.

Sample 4.1—Riviera Middle School's R E D Program

Management of time and class schedules in a middle school provides the time which can be used in a program of interest activities, developmental or remedial activities, and research activities. Such a program is often called ER & R, or Special Interest, or Enrichment Class. Since our school colors

Sample 4.1—*continued*

are red and white, and since Research-Enrichment-Development produced the acronym RED, our program became known as the R E D classes.

By shortening each of seven periods by a few minutes, we developed an "R Day" schedule for use on the days that these classes met.

Surveys of students and faculty members produced the list of activities attached. The A-B-C lists apportion participation among the activities and insures a variety of experiences for the students.

Registration for R E D classes was effected through the three academic centers by reserving one-third of the membership of each class for each center. Every care was taken that all students took part in R E D classes, and their satisfactory participation was recognized with a certificate.

Sample 4.2—R E D Period Courses

Below are described the various special interest courses being offered in the "R E D" period. Read them over carefully, discuss them with your council teacher and with your parents, and make a list of the numbers of the ten courses you are most interested in. Bring your list of numbers *and this description sheet* back to Council Group.

Activity Number

1. *Applied Mathematics:* A study of the applications of mathematics to social studies, science, athletics, art, home economics, and mechanics. Activities in mapping, use of the slide rule, and independent study and research.

2. *Baby Sitting:* Those who successfully complete this course will receive a Red Cross certificate identifying them as a certified baby sitter.

3. *Basketball—Basic Fundamentals:* Learn and improve your basic skills in basketball through skill drills and game playing.

4. *Beginning Backgammon:* Learn an exciting new game. Develop strategy and compete with other students.

5. *Beginning Typing:* This course is designed to present an introduction to the keyboard and development of correct typing techniques. These skills might be a good way to improve your papers and grades. Students in 8th grade Business Careers *should not* sign up.

6. *Cheerleading:* This course is designed for all cheerleaders. They work on improving their cheers and help others learn cheers. (Cheerleaders will work with 40 additional students every 6 weeks.)

7. *Cheerleading Clinic:* Open to all students who would like to learn cheers and to improve their cheerleading ability.

8. *Chess—Advanced:* This course is for students who already know the moves and rules of the game. Emphasis will be on strategy and improving skills.

9. *Chess—Beginning:* Learn the basic moves and explore the fascinating game of chess.

Sample 4.2—*continued*

10. *Creative Stitchery:* An exploration of various kinds of sewing with emphasis on handwork. Creweling, embroidery, needlepoint and patchwork will also be included.

11. *Creative Communication—Art and Speech:* Participants will do speech and/or art activities such as children's story-telling, puppet theatre, and choral reading. Culmination of activities should be visits to other schools and local organizations to present programs.

12. *Creative Writing:* Write ON! Do you want to write creatively and with purpose? In this course you will create short stories, personal journals, poetry, and biographies. Some may even compose a novel. Depending on this group's work, we may publish a literary magazine containing your best work.

13. *Current American Issues:* To research current American issues for presentation to the rest of the group. Students will be divided into approximately four committees for work on various current problems. Examples of topics are over-population, pollution and the state of the economy. Each group will give a presentation to the class.

14. *Debate:* Students learn to organize their ideas and arguments in a formal manner with the correct debate procedure. Important issues of the day such as politics, environment, and sports will be used in this activity.

15. *Developmental Math:* Acquire a better understanding of the world of math, increase basic skills, and improve your grades. Teacher recommendations required.

16. *Developmental Spanish:* Improve your skills in this subject and improve your understanding of Spain and the Spanish language. Teacher recommendation required.

17. *Dissection—Internal Affairs:* Learn techniques of dissecting by starting with the lower forms such as mollusks and insects. Then progress to more advanced life such as fish and frogs.

18. *Emergency Treatments:* Students learn how to care for someone who has had a heart attack or other emergency. This course could save your life.

19. *Environment—Get Involved:* This course deals with environmental concerns. The activities will be set up to prepare the student to become involved in the functions of his city.

20. *Everything You've Always Wanted to Know About and Not Had Time to Investigate:* This course will offer the opportunity to work on a subject of interest to you from comic strips to archeology. Goals will be determined by contract between students and teacher.

21. *Experiments Can Be Fun:* Interested in Science? Want to do some fun experiments? Here's something that offers a little instruction and a lot of doing. Make things like an electric quiz board, a fire extinguisher, a CO_2 boat and more.

22. *Foreign Language Newspaper:* Improve that language! Help design and publish a foreign language newspaper. Make cartoons, puzzles and illustrations.

Sample 4.2—*continued*

23. *Gardening:* Develop your green thumb, get out in the fresh air, learn to grow your own garden-fresh vegetables. Learn how to cut your family's food costs as you enjoy eating.

24. *Glee Club:* An opportunity for students interested in singing. Boys and girls are welcome to come and learn *how* to sing and how to *enjoy* making music.

25. *Investigating Life Within a Community:* This fun course examines the world of the out-of-doors. We will find out about life in areas around the school, run population counts, explore life cycles, study prey-predator relationships, do soil investigations, and much, much more.

26. *Leathercraft—Candle Making:* This course is designed for students interested in making articles from leather and working on creative candle making.

27. *Pleasure Reading:* This is for students who would like to read and discuss books just for pleasure.

28. *Mass Communications—Advertising—"It Pays to Advertise":* Study the psychology of advertising. What is effective and why? Create your own advertisement using different media.

29. *Mass Media—Recordings:* Discover the history of rock music and the production of today's records.

30. *Mass Media—Slide Production:* Make your own slide show taking pictures with our cameras. Music can then be added to produce a slide-sound presentation. Film, flash cubes, and processing will be paid by the student.

31. *Mass Media—T. V. Production:* In this course we will write, produce, direct and film your own TV show on video tape.

32. *Microbiology:* Stalking the "wee beasties" with the aid of the microscope. Techniques in using microscopes and a study of the world of microlife will be covered in the course.

33. *Model Building:* A perfect chance to design, construct, and assemble model kits. Kits will be purchased by students and made in the shop with assistance from the instructor.

34. *Mysteries of the Sea:* Welcome to the world beneath the sea. Explore the mysterious and dangerous plants and animals that swim in your own back yard. Collection and identification of specimens as well as setting up aquariums will be included in this course.

35. *Puppet Making:* Get involved in story telling, design and make your own puppet shows.

36. *Riviera Leader Corps:* What does it take to be a leader? What does a leader do? Am I one? Could I become one? Join us and find out if you've got what it takes to be one of the best at Riviera!

37. *Rocketry:* Build, construct, and launch rockets. Move into the space age.

38. *Safe Boating:* Discover safe boating through the study of the "rules of the road." Compass reading, chart layouts, equipment (Coast Guard-

Sample 4.2—*continued*

approved) handling in rough water and many other techniques will be learned.

39. *Skinny-Books:* Make your own skinny books from old newspapers, magazines, old books, etc. T-shirts will be given to each student reading 100 skinny books.

40. *The Sound of Rock:* A new kind of band method designed to teach rock music to both stage and concert band students. Open to proficient students and members of advanced band, and open to piano, electric bass guitar, lead and rhythm guitar players who know the fundamentals of playing.

41. *Specialized P.E.:* This is a course open to students who need extra work on their basic P.E. skills. Students will be selected for this course by the P.E. Department.

42. *Story of Florida:* A great chance to look into Florida's colorful history through the use of books, movies, slides and lectures.

43. *Tournament Archery—Bow Hunting:* History of archery, types of equipment available, safety in hunting. We'll also delve into hunting with bow and arrow and bow-fishing.

44. *Veterinary Medicine:* For students interested in animals of all kinds. We will discuss care of animals and explore careers in this field. We will have speakers, films, and field trips.

45. *Volleyball Improvement:* Increase your skills and knowledge of the game of volleyball. Learn the rules and enjoy this team sport.

46. *Who Am I?* This course involves taking a stand on current issues and voicing your opinion. Activities involve working alone and small and large discussion groups. Open-ended problem solving, such as who should live and how to survive on the moon, will be discussed.

47. *Why?* Was Newton a fig? Is Pythagoras an extinct fish? Did some magician wave his wand to cause our number system to appear? Inquisitive? Then investigate R E D period's mathematics research.

48. *World Wide R & R:* Interesting books can be read about different peoples and places in the world. There will be fact-finding sessions along with an exchange of information.

49. *Yearbook and Special Effects:* Students who sign up for this course will be responsible for the production of Riviera's yearbook. Picture taking, layouts and story writing are part of this course.

SOURCE: Riviera Middle School, "Riviera Middle School's R E D Program" (St. Petersburg, Florida, 1975).

The number, variety, and richness of special interest courses depends on the resources of each middle school. Not all middle schools can match the Riviera offerings, but the faculty talent and available community resources found in most middle schools do provide an opportunity for many such activities to be offered. Not only do students and teachers have fun in an activity setting, but they also

A special interest class studies the "science and art of gardening."

learn to interact in a way different from that in a regular course setting. Students and teachers get to know and appreciate each other.

In addition to the normal enriching activities of a special interest program, "special days" can result in personal development growth of students. The listing in Sample 4.3 of special days at a middle school illustrates such offerings.

Sample 4.3—Special Days at I.M.S.

At I.M.S. we plan many special days during the year. Examples follow.

Color Day—On this day everyone dresses in school colors (red and white). We then have an assembly to select a school King and Queen.

Movies—Three days a year we show a full-length feature movie to the children. These movies are in lieu of parties.

Field Day—The entire day is devoted to sporting events and grade competition. A permanent school trophy is engraved with the winning grade. The day is culminated with a faculty egg toss.

Special Lunches—School lunches are served buffet-style complete with silver chafing dishes at Christmas, Thanksgiving, and any special occasions.

Class Breakfast—The eighth grade serves juice and donuts to their classmates and has a grade meeting.

Faculty-Student Games—Each year the teachers play the students in softball, basketball, and volleyball.

Carnival—The students prepare and have a school carnival to raise money for the activity program.

Asolo State Theater—Each year the Asolo players come to the school to present a live production.

Sample 4.3—*continued*

Tournaments—We participate in the spelling bee, basketball, chess, and oratorical contests.

UNICEF—At Halloween we collect in excess of $300 in small change for UNICEF.

Brotherhood Day—This day is devoted to understanding and respecting our fellow man.

Awards—Honor certificates and other special recognition awards are given at all assemblies and especially at the end-of-the-year Awards Assembly.

Many other type days are arranged for the students at I.M.S. depending upon the curriculum units planned and special events that may occur during the year.

Alternative Programs

By the time many students reach middle school, they have been "turned off" by school programs. To provide a program designed to assist those students, many middle schools have designed alternative school programs. Such programs usually are supported by special funds, either federal, state, or local, and are designed to provide a positive environment for cognitive and social-emotional growth. Examples of alternative programs include:

1. Work Study Programs—Students go to school in the morning and are employed in the community part of the afternoon.

2. Time-Out Rooms—In lieu of suspension, students attend a time-out room that is highly structured. Counseling and remedial work is provided. Students have no contact with classmates during the days spent in the time-out room. In-school suspension is a similar program but often does not provide the counseling services.

3. Crisis Intervention Centers—A place for students to get immediate psychological help for severe problems.

4. Special Learning Centers—In lieu of regular classes, a student may attend a special learning center. Such centers provide structured skills programs and affective activities. Students are placed back in regular classes when their expected academic and social goals have been met.

EDUCATION FOR SOCIAL COMPETENCE

In addition to experiences designed for personal development, the middle school must provide courses of studies designed to prepare students for social competence. This phase of the program includes studies in what is often referred to as Basic Studies or Content Courses, and Exploratory Studies. The four content areas of mathematics, science, language arts, and social studies comprise the basic studies of the middle school program. The four studies are generally taught in an academic block of time by an interdisciplinary team of teachers. Exploratory studies include courses in the practical arts and fine arts. Environmental studies, career exploration, consumer education, and media study are other areas of exploratory studies found in the middle school.

Great progress has been made in the last decade to build a balanced and unified curriculum in the middle school. In the beginning years of the middle school movement, sixth grade courses of study were not articulated with those in the seventh and eighth grades. Also, the sixth grade courses were designated as elementary and the seventh and eighth, as secondary. In recent years, efforts have been made by middle school educators to design middle school courses of study that have an identity of their own. Such courses are structured around developmental needs of students and provide for various skill levels of pupils.

The following are examples of content which might be incorporated in the basic studies courses.

Basic Studies—Broad Themes Approach to Language Arts (Sample)

The following are proposed broad unit topics agreed upon by a middle school language arts committee. The units will be developed to include activities in the *grammatical and nongrammatical aspects of language, literature, oral and written composition.*

　I. *Man, A World Citizen*
　　A. Responsibility
　　B. Values
　　C. Citizenship
　　D. Heritage
　　E. Myths, Legends, Tall Tales, Folk Tales

　II. *Man, Communicator of Ideas*
　　A. Languages
　　B. Art Through the Ages
　　C. Mass Media
　　D. Creative Expression—Drama

　III. *Man, A Problem Solver*
　　A. Growing-up
　　B. Prejudices
　　C. Family
　　D. Drugs
　　E. Animals

　IV. *Man, An Explorer*
　　A. Space, Oceanography, Land
　　B. Medicine

C. Sports and Recreation

D. Tools

E. Foods

F. Fashions and Fads

V. *Man Alone in a Crowd*

A. Who Am I?

B. Mysticism

C. Ethics

Each student in the middle school should have an individualized language arts program that involves the development of his reading habits, improves his reading selections, and attempts to meet his individual abilities, needs, and interests.

Social Studies in the Middle School

In moving toward social competence, the middle school student must deal with the social dimension of personal growth which involves a widening understanding of how people behave in today's world. Students are defining themselves, in part, in terms of a relationship to a broader stream of human development. By examining the realities of the social and historical environment of man, middle school students can better understand their role in an increasingly interdependent society. The outlines in Samples 4.4–4.6 of middle school programs are offered as examples of efforts to build a relevant and practical curriculum for middle school students.

Sample 4.4—Social Studies Program for the Middle School

I. Man As an Individual

A. His attitude toward himself

B. His attitude toward and his relationship with others

1. His family and friends
2. His town, state, country, world
3. Prejudices

II. Man Learns About Others

A. People in other states

1. How do they differ from his way of life?
2. How are they alike?

B. People in other countries

1. How do they differ from him?
2. What makes them different from him?
3. How are they alike?

Sample 4.4—*continued*

  C. Man As an explorer

    1. Explorations yesterday and today
    2. The importance of explorations
    3. Changes brought about because of explorations and findings

  D. Important makers of history

    1. World history
    2. American history
    3. Their effects on us today
    4. Current events

  E. Man's geographical relation to the world and to the rest of the country

    1. Geography influences ways of living and means of survival

  F. Man As an inventor

    1. Research goes on today
    2. Man in early civilizations

      a. Stone Age man and his inventions
      b. Greek and Roman civilizations and their innovations

  G. Man As a creator

    1. Arts
    2. Music
    3. Crafts

III. Man As a Lawmaker

  A. Reasons for laws

    1. Crimes
    2. To insure justice
    3. To insure freedoms

  B. Rights and responsibilities of all citizens

    1. All are responsible for making and upholding laws

  C. Compare the structure and organization of local, state, and federal governments

    1. Similarities
    2. Differences

  D. Governments different from ours

    1. Communism
    2. Socialism
    3. Monarchy

IV. Man in Conflict

  A. Man at war

    1. Reasons for wars
    2. After-effects of wars
    3. Advantages and disadvantages of wars

Sample 4.4—*continued*

    B. Man against nature

        1. Pollution
        2. Natural disasters
        3. Extinction of some animals

           a. Man-made
           b. Natural

V. Man and His Needs for the Future

    A. Individual needs for the future

        1. More education will be needed
           a. College
        2. Other types of schools
           a. Mechanical, etc.
        3. Jobs
           a. Finding the type that each is suited for

    B. Physical needs

        1. Food
        2. How to fill more leisure time

    C. Social needs

        1. How to deal with poverty
        2. How to deal with overpopulation

    D. Helping to strive for peace

        1. In one's own country
        2. In the world

BROAD THEMES APPROACH IN SOCIAL STUDIES

SCOPE AND SEQUENCE:

    "Man and His Relations to Man"

First Year
    1. Man as a pioneer and explorer
    2. Man as an inventor
    3. Man as a worker
    4. Man as a sportsman

Second Year
    1. Man and government
    2. Man and citizenship
    3. Man and religion
    4. Man and morals

Third Year
    1. Man as a warrior
    2. Man and prejudice
    3. Man to man
    4. Man and change

Sample 4.5 lists broad unit themes for science in the middle school.

Sample 4.5—Science in the Middle School—Suggested Themes

MAN AND THE WORLD

FIRST LEVEL

I. *Man and His World*

A. How Man Learns About His World

Five Senses—Observational Skills
    Bias
    Recurrence
    Discrepancy
    Sense extensions, i.e., microscope

Graphics and Quantifying—Probability
    Development of Patterns
    Science Attitudes—News, UFO, ESP

Suggested Unit Titles:
Using Five Senses
Discovering Problems
Cycle of Proof
Cultivating Scientific Attitudes
Patterns & Natural Law

B. How Man Behaves Toward (the) His World

Categorizing—Keys
    Identification
    Rec. Properties

Measurement—Precision
    Accuracy
    Length
    Capacity & Wt.
    Time
    Problems in Meas.

Model Building—Atom
    Carbon Chains
    DNA
    Crystals
    Math Models
    Probability Mod.—Heredity
    Solar System

Communication of Data—Language
    Scientific Terminology
    Words!

Sample 4.5—*continued*

Suggested Unit Titles:
    Similarities & Differences
    Units of Measurement Are Man-Made
    Making & Using Models
    Need to Name Things

C. How Man Expects (the) His World to Behave

    Consistency & Uniformity—Projecting Expectations
                           Moon & Stars
                           Relationship among different kinds
                           of change—daily, monthly, annually

    Cause & Effect—Force & Motion
                   Chem. Reactions
                   Superstitions

Suggested Unit Titles:
    Dependable & Predictable World
    Why Do Things Happen?
    How to Resolve Dilemmas

SECOND LEVEL

II. *The Kind of World Man Thinks He Has Found*

D. Man Assumes the Existence of Variation & Change

    Normal Curves—Normal Curves Show Variation
                  Measuring Leaves
                  Success Depends on Variability
                  Which Way Does Wind Blow?

    Directional Variation—Color Gradients
                    Taste Gradients
                    A Gradient in Heating H_2O
                    Topographical Maps

    Extrapolation & Interpolation—Predicting from a Gradient
                           Clockface
                           Growth of Corn
                           Alternate Hypothesis

    Time—Gradient—Natural Selection
                    Variation Human Hands & Feet
                    Competition
                    Species—Competition Quantitative
                    Protective Coloration
                    Selection—Gene Pool

    Repeating Sequences—Animal Life Cycle—Fruit Fly
                        Simple Plant Cycles—Mold, Bacteria
                        Growth Cycles Higher Plants
                        Water Cycle
                        Rock Cycle

Sample 4.5—*continued*

Interacting Changes That Result in Balance
Internal Equilibrium: Wt. Balance in Humans
Chemical Indicators
Equilibrium in Landscape
Balanced Aquarium

Suggested Unit Titles:
Norms & Averages
Variation Can Be Continuous
Judging the Future by the Past
Response to the Challenge of the Environment
Cycles in Nature
An "Almost" Balance That Constantly Approaches Balance

E. Man Thinks in Terms of Relationships Rather Than Absolutes

Measurements Express Relationships—A Balance
Depth and Press
Calories and Degrees
Speed a Relationship

Patterns Govern Relationships—Replication
Communication
We Are What We Are Because—

Frames of Reference Determine Relationships—
What Do We Mean by "Where"?
Illusions
Earth Coordinates

Interdependence Consists of Relationships—
Pond Infusion Culture
Lab Field Trip
Relationship of Acidity and Alkalinity to Yeast Activity
Evaporation
Forest Edge Communities
Interrelationships on School Grounds
City Birds

Heredity & Environment Are Related—Plants & Soil Nutrients
Plants & Light
Human Characteristics—Heredity or Environment

Changes & Rates Are Related—Development of Chick Embryo
Development of Bean Plant
Differential Growth Rate in Humans
Developing Stream Patterns

Sample 4.5—*continued*

Man & His Tools Are Related—Extending Body w/ Tools
Work
Simple Machines
Complex Machines & Utilization
of Outside Energy
Extension of Man's Body—How
It Has Evolved

Suggested Unit Titles:
Quantifying Our Relationships Rather Than Absolutes
We Use Patterns All the Time, So Does Nature
Relativity and Common Sense
Everything Is Dependent on Something Else
Heredity and/or Environment
Changes That Depend on Rates
We Sharpen a Word to Express an Area of Man's Relationships

THIRD LEVEL

III. *Man Finds That His World Has Limits*

F. Science Is Limited by How We Feel about the World

We Can Look at Our World Two Ways—Problems of Conflict
Poetry & Real World
Painting & Pictures
Music & Sound

Complementarity—Structure & Function
Nature of Light
Science & Religion

G. Continuous Discovery—Prognosis of Science Inquiry
Limitations
Moral Obligations

Social Limitations—Political Limitations
Cultural Limitations

Sample 4.6 lists broad unit topics for middle school mathematics.

Sample 4.6—A Mathematics Continuum for the Middle School

1. Origin of Various Numeration Systems (words, symbols, and their meanings)
2. Whole Numbers
   a. Recognition of whole numbers (each student should be able to read or write any number to 1 billion)
   b. Prime, composite, and relatively prime numbers
   c. Computation and related problems of application in equalities and inequalities

Sample 4.6—*continued*

        1) Addition
        2) Subtraction
        3) Multiplication
        4) Division

3. Fractions
    a. Basic understanding of the fraction concept
    b. Computation and related problems of application in equalities and inequalities
        1) Addition
        2) Subtraction
        3) Multiplication
        4) Division
        5) Ratio and proportion

4. Decimal Fractions
    a. Basic understanding of the decimal fraction concept
    b. Computation and related problems of application in equalities and inequalities
        1) Addition
        2) Subtraction
        3) Multiplication
        4) Division

5. Percent, Interest, etc.
    a. Meaning of percent (%)
    b. Computation
    c. Application

6. Statistical Graphs—bar, circle, picture, broken line and smooth line
    a. Reading and interpreting graphs
    b. Construction of graphs from given data

7. Metric System
    a. Length—meter
    b. Capacity—liter
    c. Weight—gram

8. Geometry
    a. Nonmetric geometry
        1) Basic terminology (ray, curve, polygon, parallel lines, etc.)
        2) Elementary constructions
    b. Metric geometry
        1) Perimeter
        2) Area
        3) Volume

9. Directed Numbers
    a. Basic understanding of directed number system
    b. Computation and related problems of application in equalities and inequalities
        1) Addition
        2) Subtraction
        3) Multiplication
        4) Division

Sample 4.6—*continued*

10. Eighth Grade Algebra
    a. Four basic operations of whole numbers and rational numbers
    b. Solution sets for equations and inequalities (all types)
    c. Word problems—reading, interpretation, and translation of data to variable expressions
    d. Polynomials—basic operations of monomials and polynomials, powers
    e. Factoring
    f. Quadratic equations
    g. Algebraic fractions—simple and complex
    h. Graphs and analytic geometry
    i. Systems of linear equations
    j. The real number system
        1) Meaning of square roots
        2) Computation and simplification of square roots
        3) Equations with irrational solutions

Exploratory Studies

Practical Arts

Home Economics is one of the disciplines concerned with strengthening individuals and families. Concepts dealt with in the middle school include these: human development and the family, home management and family economics, foods and nutrition, housing and home furnishings, and textiles and clothing.

Elective or wheel (rotational courses scheduled on a six- or nine-weeks basis) courses in home economics are designed to provide both males and females with preparation for family living through the study of food, environment, and dress. An orientation to occupations such as child care services, food production, management and services, and food production is also a part of home economics courses in the middle school.

Industrial Arts in the middle school consists of a program of instructional and laboratory experiences which provides basic education related to industrial and technical aspects of life. The prevocational aspect of industrial arts provides an orientation to the adult world of work, industrial occupations, economics, and one's self.

Business and Distributive Education courses have become a valuable part of the prevocational study of middle school students. Wholesaling, retailing, agribusiness and marketing services are but a few of the exploratory experiences found in distributive education courses. Typing and data processing have been a part of the "hands on" curriculum built around real job tasks that are found in business education courses in the middle school.

Fine Arts

Music offered as an exploratory experience in middle schools includes a wide variety of music activities including chorus; instrumental music; beginning, intermediate, and advanced band; and orchestra. The emphasis is on enjoyment of music. Students desiring a high degree of mastery can enjoy the opportunity to become skilled in one or more of the vocal or instrumental areas. Instruments such as guitar and strings are popular with middle school students. Music has become a key element in humanities programs, school productions such as musical plays, and in interdisciplinary units of study.

Art, like music, is a high-involvement activity important to middle school students. Middle school art programs should help foster self-expression and enhance visual perception as well as promote the development of aesthetic tasks and interests. Art study can help students develop interests that will provide for the profitable and enjoyable use of leisure time.

Foreign Language exploratory courses are found in many middle schools. Courses include a sociological approach to the study of people, their attitudes, values, customs, art, and music. Students in the middle school may choose from the following based on what is taught in each school: German, Spanish, French, and Latin. In beginning classes, students learn to speak the language. Emphasis is on pronunciation and oral language use. Language labs utilizing the newest media, and often located in learning centers, have helped Foreign Language programs reach many more middle school students. Through creative teaching, foreign language teachers can foster a life-long interest in languages and enrich the lives of their students.

Humanities courses are finding their way into more and more middle schools. Whether taught by a single teacher or humanities team, such courses have finally "related" the arts. Many community resources are brought into play in humanities courses such as community orchestras, Little Theater groups, museums, and art galleries.

Environmental Studies

Outdoor Education experiences are valuable to middle school students. They allow them to move out of the school setting to study nature. Many school districts

Learning to type is a basic skill for many future occupations.

have been able to negotiate the leasing of large tracts of outdoor areas where students can camp, canoe, hike, and enjoy the woods and lakes and streams. The activity and social interaction involved in outdoor education are especially relevant to the emerging adolescent learner.

Environmental studies that include a study of the air, waterways, conservation, pollution, and other ecologically related subjects help middle school students understand how to use the natural resources without destroying them.

Career Education

Career education teachers or occupational specialists are being included as a part of many middle school staffs. Exploring the world of work and increasing occupational awareness can provide students with a base of information to make future educational and career decisions. Several middle schools have created an employment service to give students an opportunity to work in part-time jobs in the community.[4] Students participating in career studies are provided the opportunity to see clearly the relationships between the academic content he is being asked to master and his tentative occupational choices.

Consumer Education

Consumer education has been mandated by legislation in many states. Because considerable advertising is aimed at pre- and early adolescents, students should be provided with an opportunity to study the various products they consume and services they use. One innovative middle school has created a whole grocery store to help students learn about food products. The "store center" is also used to study jobs in food merchandising. Other middle schools are taking consumer education students into the community to study products and services.

Media Study

The influence of television, newspapers, and other media on emerging adolescents has created the need for a study of various media. Middle school students use videotaping equipment, movie and still cameras, newspapers, computers, books and magazines, and find new ways to communicate with others. The creative activities evolving from the use and study of media help improve communication and social skills of emerging adolescents.

Media study can occur in the library or media center, in classrooms, or in the community. Many middle schools have separate media or learning resource rooms where students and teachers can produce media like videotapes, films, slide-tape presentations, audiotapes, transparencies, or books and magazines.

The *librarian or media specialist* is a key instructional leader in the middle school. Warm, exciting media areas enhance the program of the middle school. The librarian or media specialist must be able to work closely with students and teachers or teacher teams in the instructional process.

---

[4] Jerry Bishop, "A Middle School Creates an Employment Service," *Clearing House,* November 1972, pp. 182–84.

Exploratory studies are also an important phase of the middle school program leading toward education for social competence. To experience new and exciting activities through exploration allows emerging adolescent learners to see possibilities that free them from an immediate reality that may not be fulfilling.

The exploration program of middle schools is generally limited not by resources, but by imagination. Creative middle school staffs can design exploratory programs that make the middle school an exciting place in which to teach and learn. One example of a creative staff is the Cloonan Middle School staff, Stamford, Connecticut, which designed the eighth grade unified arts elective program found in Samples 4.7 and 4.8.

Sample 4.7—Cloonan Middle School—Unified Arts

Select according to preference 1–25.
Have a number by every course.

FINE ARTS

1. *Animated Film-Making*
   Creating of actual animated (cartoon type) films beginning with paper cut-outs, clay, and possibly people. Also involves the exploration of filming and camera techniques. Students will use the camera to film their own projects.

2. *Printmaking A–Z*
   A printmaking course that will start with potato prints, found-object prints, linoleum, wood cuts, and conclude with a new printmaking technique called collograph.

3. *String, Wax and Cloth*
   Using string, wax and cloth, learn process such as batik and the dyeing methods of design, using melted wax and cloth, macrame process of knotting string to make belts, wall hangings and string sculptures and rug-making.

4. *Ceramics*
   The craft of designing, building and surface-decorating of clay objects. Make sculptures, pots, plaques, jewelry, bowls and mugs, using slab, coil, pinch and mold techniques.

5. *Designs in Color*
   Learn how to make super-looking designs in color—murals painting, collage and printmaking will be taught along with various other materials. You don't have to be great at drawing to make a great design!

6. *Drawing*
   Learn a better approach to drawing real objects. The class deals with closely looking at things and their shapes and breaking them down to an easier way of drawing them. We will use ink, crayon, pencil, felt-tips and some experimental materials.

7. *Foods and Nutrition*
   This course gives you an opportunity to learn some cooking terms, measuring, meal-planning, shopping, experimenting with new recipes,

Sample 4.7—*continued*

and trying a few old favorites. Learning how foods help the body to grow and develop correctly.

8. *Clothing—Grade Eight*
Students will learn how to use commercial patterns, using patterns that are suitable for themselves or another individual. Students will use patterns and materials that are within their capabilities. One or more garments may be made during the semester, learning many different processes necessary for the construction of these garments.

DRAFTING COURSE OFFERINGS

9. *Design and Layout*
This course will cover original design problems and the organization and development of floor plans. Students will also construct models of the plans they have drawn.

10. *Sketching and Mechanical Drawing*
This course will cover the basis of sketching objects to give a general idea of how an object is shaped. Mechanical drawing using drafting instruments will be dealt with as the course progresses.

INDUSTRIAL ARTS

11. *Metalworking*
This class will consist of basic instruction in the safe operation of power machines and tools; the lathe, milling machine, drill press and shaper. During the course each student will complete a project of his choice taken from several examples.

12. *Welding and Soldering*
This class consists of students being properly instructed in the use of electric arc welding along with soldering of various metals. The student will prepare metals for welding and proceed to weld sheet metals, along with discussion of oxyacetylene welding.

13. *Sheet Metalwork*
The student shall perform a basic layout of the project on sheet metal and make a bill of material. The course will emphasize the importance of this subject for career opportunities.

14. *Woodworking Technology*
In this course the student will learn proper and safe use of tools, develop basic skills in the woodworking field by becoming involved in processes and products of the wood area. Develop insight and understanding of the woodworking area in our culture.

15. *Advanced Woodworking*
This course is only for those students who excelled in woodworking in grade seven. Students will be exposed to career analysis, products of wood, safety, design, hand tool processes, machine processes and consumer values.

Sample 4.7—*continued*

GRAPHICS

16. *Graphics*
    This course will offer students knowledge of the three basic printing methods. Students will incorporate machines and basic design equipment to create projects of practical use.

17. *Advanced Graphics and Design*
    This course recommended for students who have had graphics at least 1 year and have retained that knowledge. Advanced photo-printing and creative graphic designing will be offered.

MUSIC

18. *American Folk Music*
    Emphasis on music from 1776–1976—bi-centennial. This course will include singing, listening, and performing music of this period of America.

19. *Music of the Theater*
    American musical theater, ballet, opera, with emphasis on the Broadway musicals. Students will become acquainted with the music and story and where possible will attend a musical, ballet or opera.

20. *Music of Today*
    Class will include record listening, discussions, strings, and interpretations of the music industry through the use of records, films and when possible, live performances. In addition there will be an emphasis on career possibilities.

21. *Recorder Class*
    This course is designed for the student with no previous instrumental experience who wishes to learn to play an instrument. Students will learn to perform in small ensembles and large groups.

22. *General Music*
    Includes development of vocal forms, development of instrumental forms, singing—the human voice, and elements of music.

23. *Electronic Music Workshop*
    Students will learn tape techniques, operation of tape recorder, amplifier speakers and their relationships. Students will listen to tape compositions, and will create their own works.

24. *Voice Class*
    Concentration will be on learning good vocal technique and learning to perform solos, in small ensembles and large groups.

25. *Modern Music*
    Introduction to 20th century music including Jazz, Rock, Soul, and contemporary classics. This will include listening, performing and composition.

SOURCE: Cloonan Middle School, "Unified Arts" (Stamford, Conn.: Stamford Public Schools, 1976). Used with permission.

Sample 4.8—Cloonan Middle School—Unified Arts

STUDENT NAME: _____ COG/Group: _____

French ⬚
Spanish ⬚

DIRECTIONS: Carefully review the descriptions of the various courses being offered in Music, Fine Arts, and Applied Sciences. Place an X in the box beside the courses you would like to have. You must choose four (4) of the two-period courses, and two (2) of the one-period courses. The total number of periods is seven (7) for *all students*.

	1 PD	2 PDS
Fine Arts:		
Animated Film Making	⬚	⬚
Printmaking A–Z	⬚	⬚
String, Wax and Cloth	⬚	⬚
Ceramics	⬚	⬚
Design and Color	⬚	⬚
Drawing	⬚	⬚
Applied Sciences:		
Food and Nutrition	⬚	⬚
Clothing		
Design and Layout		
Sketching and Mechanical Drawing	⬚	
Metal Working		
Welding and Soldering		
Sheet Metal		
Woodworking	⬚	
Woodworking Technology		
Advanced Woodworking	⬚	
Graphics		
Advanced Graphics and Design		
Practical Arts	⬚	
Building and Home Arts		⬚
Music:		
American Folk Music		⬚
Music of the Theater		⬚
Music of Today	⬚	⬚
Recorder Class	⬚	⬚
General Music	⬚	⬚
Electronic Music Workshop		⬚
Voice Class		⬚
Modern Music		⬚

SOURCE: Cloonan Middle School "Unified Arts" (Stamford, Conn.: Stamford Public Schools, 1976). Used with permission.

SKILLS FOR CONTINUOUS LEARNING

The middle school is responsible for continuing and expanding the instruction of basic communication and computational skills begun in the elementary school. The middle school learner should be encouraged to become more self-directed as a learner and develop her potential to the maximum. Each middle school faculty has the responsibility to develop a skills plan as a part of the total school program. Skills identified by the faculty should be included with content goals for each unit of work in all study areas of the curriculum.

Communication Skills

Reading

All middle school students should be exposed to some type of skill development in reading. Some pupils need extensive remedial work, others need skill development in comprehension, vocabulary, or phonics. Almost all students could benefit from a developmental program that would increase speed and comprehension. Much of skill building in reading can be accomplished through an individualized reading program utilizing a management system that includes diagnosis and prescription. In the middle school, every teacher becomes a reading teacher. Even though special reading teachers and reading labs are available in most middle schools, they must be reinforced by the teaching of reading in all content areas.

Writing

Writing skills should be emphasized in the middle school. The ability to communicate in written form will enhance the chances of academic success of students in later schooling as well as enrich their daily lives. Vocabulary, syntactic, rhetorical, imagination and encoding skills are emphasized in writing programs in the middle school.

Listening

Listening skills are becoming increasingly important in today's society. Students need to develop the skill of listening attentively so they can hear supporting details, listen for enjoyment, predict outcomes, and develop mental imagery. Skills of attending and responding, comprehension, interpretation, and analysis are emphasized in listening skills programs.

Speaking

Speaking skills emphasized in the middle school include skills of statement and response, delivery, use of vocabulary, and organization. The ability to speak before others is an important part of social development in the middle school.

Computation

Computation skills in the middle school include the following:

1. Developing an understanding of basic mathematics concepts.
2. Developing computational skills.
3. Developing the ability to apply understandings and skills to practical situations.
4. Developing the ability to think mathematically, to proceed from known concepts to the discovery of new ideas.
5. Developing an understanding of the logical structure of mathematics, the patterns and relationships which give unity to the subject.

Observing and Comparing

Middle school students should learn to observe with a purpose, i.e., to relate and compare information gained through observation with that gained from other sources.

Analyzing

Middle school students should develop the ability to break down communications into constituent parts in order to make organization of the whole clear.

Generalizing

Emerging adolescents should learn to draw general characteristics or principles from a series of observations, incidents, cases, or readings.

Organizing

Middle school students need to learn to outline and select main ideas, to take notes, to classify facts, pictures, events, and ideas under main categories; and to arrange facts and ideas in sequence.

Evaluating

Students in the middle school should learn to distinguish fact, fiction, and opinion, and be able to compare information from different sources to determine which source of information is most acceptable.

Skills Records

Many middle schools have developed student profile folders that show concepts and skills each student has mastered. The following uses for profile folders have been identified by middle school teachers:

—a basis for grouping
—a basis for individualizing
—a tool for assessing student needs
—a record for transferring students
—a resource for scope and sequence planning
—a reminder of long-range goals
—a record of accountability for both state and district objectives
—a springboard for better use of district guides
—a reference for parent conferences
—a medium for communicating student progress
—a medium of curriculum standardization within the district

We have selected samples of middle school profile folders for you to examine. (See Samples 4.9–4.13)

Sample 4.9—Skill Development in Language Arts

	Language Activity	Grammar & Usage Level I	Grammar & Usage Level II	Grammar & Usage Level III
THINKING	Attention to details Organize materials Draw correct conclusions	Size, shape, sound Alphabet- ize Matching	Expression Group Match Identity	Differenti- ate Categorize Classifying
LISTENING	In con- versation and discus- sion, Poetry	Replying to questions Hear rhyming words	Compari- sons Summarize Listen for own over- worked words	Summariz- ing Listening critically Listen for distin- guishing be- tween two ideas

Sample 4.9—*continued*

SPEAKING	Making introductions Discussions and conversations Vocabulary Play-acting	Make introductions Skits Word pictures	Parliamentary procedure Drama	Panel Critical Analysis Drama
WRITING	Demonstrate ability to complete usage	Cursive letter formation Complete sentences Short paragraphs	Outlining Bibliography Letters (3 kinds) Book Reports Conversations	Write short story Research Letters (3 kinds) Book Reports Write Dialogue Write poetry
READING	To show ability to read for individual needs	Recognize words Recognize sentences Recognize clusters Use table of contents Alphabetize	Evaluate books by contents Proofread all written work	Recognize kinds of sentences Make bibliography Proofread

Sample 4.10—Middle School Mathematics Profile Sheet—Eighth Grade

I. Arithmetic Operations

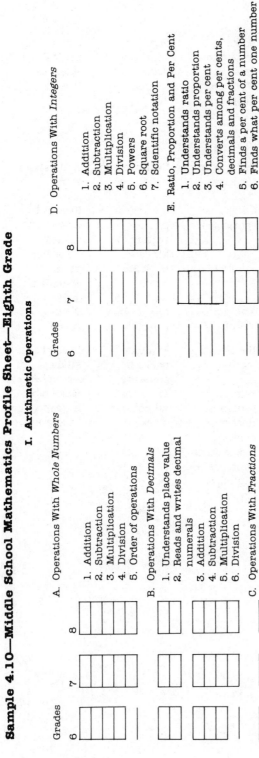

Grades
6 7 8

A. Operations With *Whole Numbers*
1. Addition
2. Subtraction
3. Multiplication
4. Division
5. Order of operations

B. Operations With *Decimals*
1. Understands place value
2. Reads and writes decimal numerals
3. Addition
4. Subtraction
5. Multiplication
6. Division

C. Operations With *Fractions*
1. Addition
2. Subtraction
3. Multiplication
4. Division
5. Knows fractional equivalents

D. Operations With *Integers*
1. Addition
2. Subtraction
3. Multiplication
4. Division
5. Powers
6. Square root
7. Scientific notation

E. Ratio, Proportion and Per Cent
1. Understands ratio
2. Understands proportion
3. Understands per cent
4. Converts among per cents, decimals and fractions
5. Finds a per cent of a number
6. Finds what per cent one number is of another
7. Finds a number when a per cent of it is known.

II. Mathematical Concepts

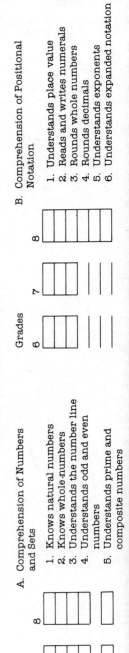

Grades
6 7 8

A. Comprehension of Numbers and Sets
1. Knows natural numbers
2. Knows whole-numbers
3. Understands the number line
4. Understands odd and even numbers
5. Understands prime and composite numbers

B. Comprehension of Positional Notation
1. Understands place value
2. Reads and writes numerals
3. Rounds whole numbers
4. Rounds decimals
5. Understands exponents
6. Understands expanded notation

Sample 4.10—*continued*

II. Mathematical Concepts *(continued)*

Grades

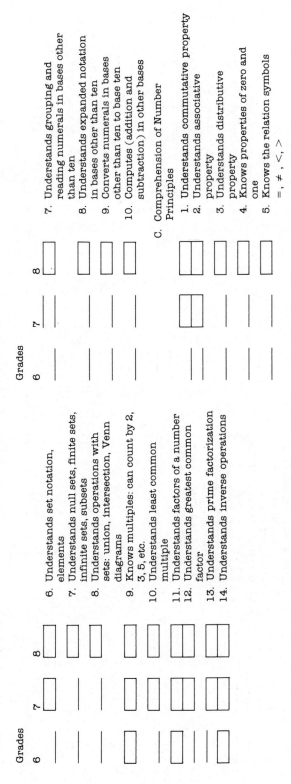

6. Understands set notation, elements
7. Understands null sets, finite sets, infinite sets, subsets
8. Understands operations with sets: union, intersection, Venn diagrams
9. Knows multiples: can count by 2, 3, 5, etc.
10. Understands least common multiple
11. Understands factors of a number
12. Understands greatest common factor
13. Understands prime factorization
14. Understands inverse operations

7. Understands grouping and reading numerals in bases other than ten
8. Understands expanded notation in bases other than ten
9. Converts numerals in bases other than ten to base ten
10. Computes (addition and subtraction) in other bases

C. Comprehension of Number Principles

1. Understands commutative property
2. Understands associative property
3. Understands distributive property
4. Knows properties of zero and one
5. Knows the relation symbols $=, \neq, <, >$

III. Special Topics

Grades

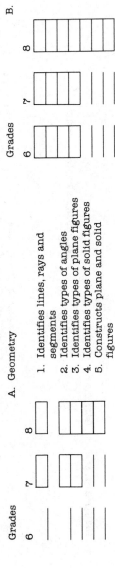

A. Geometry

1. Identifies lines, rays and segments
2. Identifies types of angles
3. Identifies types of plane figures
4. Identifies types of solid figures
5. Constructs plane and solid figures

B. Measurement

1. Knows units of length
2. Knows units of liquid measure
3. Knows units of weight
4. Knows units of time
5. Knows units of metric measure
6. Knows units of area
7. Knows units of volume

Sample 4.10—*continued*

III. Special Topics (*continued*)

Grades

	6	7	8
6. Knows points, lines, planes			
7. Understands ideas of points, lines and planes in space			
8. Constructs line segments, parallel and perpendicular lines			
9. Draws and measures angles			
10. Constructs angles			
11. Constructs bisectors of line segments and angles			
12. Finds length of objects			
13. Finds perimeter of polygons			
14. Finds areas and other dimensions of plane figures			
15. Finds circumference and area of circles			
16. Finds volume of simple solids			

Grades

	6	7	8
8. Knows units of angles and arcs			
9. Knows units of money			
10. Operates with units of measure			
a. Addition			
b. Subtraction			
c. Multiplication			
d. Division			

C. Mathematical Applications

	6	7	8
1. Translates from one "language" or symbolism to another			
2. Solves problems with whole or natural numbers			
3. Solves problems with fractions			
4. Solves problems with decimals			
5. Solves problems with per cent, ratio and proportion			
6. Solves problems with units of measurement			
7. Solves problems with geometry			
8. Reads and interprets graphs			
9. Constructs graphs (circle, bar and line)			
10. Graphs solution sets on a number line			
11. Understands an ordered pair on a coordinate plane			
12. Estimation			
a. Whole numbers			
b. Decimals			
c. Measurement			

Key: X — Mastery
/ — Introduced

Grade level:
4 5 6 7 8 8⁺

Recommendation for grade 9:
_____ Gen. Math _____ Pre-Algebra

Sample 4.11—Profile Sheet in Mathematics

Student's Name _____

	I	II	III	IV	V	VI	VII	VIII	IX	X
Numeration										
Addition										
Subtraction										
Multiplication										
Division										
Fractions										
Decimals										
Per Cents										
Integers										
Measurement										
Enrichment Topics										

Sample 4.12—Reading Skills
Development Checklist—Grades K–8

NOTE: Please date and initial only when mastery has been achieved.

1. Early Reading Skills Program (Generally K-3)

	Date	Teacher's Initials

A. Perceptive Skills

	Date	Initials
1. Reproduces pronounced two and three syllable words	____	____
2. Hears differences in words	____	____
3. Recognizes spoken words with same initial sound	____	____
4. Recognizes spoken words with same final sound	____	____
5. Recognizes likenesses and differences	____	____
6. Has left-to-right eye movement	____	____

B. Vocabulary Skills

1. Recognizes name in print	____	____
2. Names upper case letters	____	____
3. Names lower case letters	____	____
4. Identifies numerals 1–10	____	____
5. Classifies objects and pictures into logical categories	____	____
6. Recognizes words with both upper and lower case letters at beginning	____	____
7. Knows names of letters in sequence	____	____
8. Recognizes 220 Dolch Basic Sight Words	____	____
9. Able to get word meaning from context	____	____
10. Knows basic punctuation marks	____	____

C. Word Analysis Skills

1. Associates consonant sounds with letters	____	____
2. Initial consonants	____	____
3. Final consonants	____	____
4. Medial consonants	____	____
5. Knows digraphs	____	____
6. Two letter blends	____	____
7. Knows the long vowel sounds	____	____
8. Knows endings	____	____
9. Recognizes compound words	____	____
10. Knows common word families	____	____
11. Knows three letter blends	____	____
12. Knows the short vowel sounds	____	____
13. Knows and applies vowel rules	____	____
14. Recognizes little words in big words	____	____
15. Understands use of possessive	____	____
16. Knows contractions	____	____
17. Recognizes root words	____	____
18. Can alphabetize using first and second letter	____	____
19. Knows syllabication rules	____	____

Sample 4.12—*continued*

	Date	Teacher's Initials
C. Word Analysis Skills (cont.)		
20. Knows most common prefixes and suffixes	_____	_____
21. Knows and applies dictionary skills	_____	_____
22. Knows accent rules	_____	_____
23. Recognizes silent letters	_____	_____
24. Knows synonyms	_____	_____
25. Knows antonyms	_____	_____
26. Knows homonyms	_____	_____
27. Knows diphthongs	_____	_____
28. Identifies the names of the days of the week	_____	_____
29. Identifies the names of the months of the year	_____	_____
30. Alphabetizes to 3rd letter	_____	_____
31. Understands multiple meanings of words	_____	_____
32. Recognizes the "schwa" sound	_____	_____
33. Identifies nouns and verbs	_____	_____
34. Understands most commonly used abbreviations	_____	_____
D. Comprehensions Skills		
1. Recalls details from stories read aloud	_____	_____
2. Sequences events logically	_____	_____
3. Follows oral directions	_____	_____
4. Retells a story in own words	_____	_____
5. Follows written directions	_____	_____
6. Recalls main idea from stories read aloud	_____	_____
7. States main idea after silent reading	_____	_____
8. Gives details from stories after silent reading	_____	_____
9. Distinguishes between real and imaginary events	_____	_____
10. Uses context clues	_____	_____
11. Reads without vocalization	_____	_____
12. Reads without head movements	_____	_____
13. Draws conclusions	_____	_____
14. Predicts outcomes	_____	_____
15. Uses table of contents	_____	_____
16. Locates specific information	_____	_____
17. Dramatizes stories read	_____	_____
18. Illustrates stories read	_____	_____
19. Reads for specific purpose	_____	_____
20. Classifies items	_____	_____
21. Uses index	_____	_____
22. Uses various sources for needed information	_____	_____
23. Uses maps and charts	_____	_____
24. Identifies key words and topic sentences	_____	_____
25. Summarizes	_____	_____
26. Selects supporting facts	_____	_____

Sample 4.12—*continued*

		Date	Teacher's Initials
D.	Comprehensions Skills (cont.)		
	27. Identifies mood of selection	___	___
	28. Identifies author's purpose	___	___
	29. Identifies character traits	___	___
	30. Takes notes	___	___
	31. Outlines materials read	___	___
	32. Identifies characters' feelings	___	___
	33. Knows and applies library skills	___	___
	34. Reads orally with understanding and expression	___	___
	35. Identifies story setting	___	___
	36. Makes inferences	___	___
	37. Associates cause and effect	___	___
	38. Identifies similes and metaphors	___	___
	39. Identifies idioms	___	___
	40. Distinguishes between fact and opinion	___	___
	41. Detects and evaluates bias	___	___
	42. Visualizes setting and character	___	___
	43. Reads and interprets maps, charts, graphs, and diagrams	___	___

2. Intermediate Reading Skills Program (Generally 4–8)

		Date	Teacher's Initials
A.	Word Analysis		
	1. Beginning consonant sounds	___	___
	2. Final consonants	___	___
	3. Long vowel sounds	___	___
	4. Short vowel sounds	___	___
	5. Diphthongs	___	___
	6. Letter symbols for consonant blends	___	___
	7. Consonant digraphs	___	___
	8. Symbols for medial consonant sounds	___	___
	9. Silent consonants	___	___
	10. Silent vowels	___	___
	11. Singular vowels	___	___
	12. Compound words	___	___
	13. Root words	___	___
	14. Prefixes	___	___
	15. Suffixes	___	___
	16. Contractions	___	___
	17. Apostrophes	___	___
B.	Vocabulary		
	1. Reads 220 Dolch words	___	___
	2. Matches words with definitions	___	___
	3. Identifies synonyms	___	___
	Identifies antonyms	___	___
	Identifies homonyms	___	___

Sample 4.12—*continued*

	Date	Teacher's Initials
C. Literal Comprehension		
1. Recalls specifics	___	___
2. Follows directions	___	___
3. Story sequence	___	___
D. Interpretative Comprehension		
1. Word definitions	___	___
2. Topic sentences	___	___
3. Main ideas	___	___
E. Critical Comprehension		
1. Distinguishes fact from fiction	___	___
2. Distinguishes fact from opinion	___	___
F. Study Skills		
1. Table of contents	___	___
2. Alphabetical order	___	___
G. Other Word Attack Skills		
1. Graphemic bases, rhyming words	___	___
2. Possessives	___	___
3. Plurals	___	___
4. Syllabication	___	___
5. Plural forms of nouns and verbs	___	___
6. Use of "y" as a vowel	___	___
7. Vowel rules	___	___
H. Comprehension Skills		
1. Cause and effect	___	___
2. Inferences and conclusions	___	___
3. Sight words of grade level	___	___
4. Multiple meanings	___	___
5. Summarizes information	___	___
6. Context clues	___	___
7. Noting details	___	___
8. Critical thinking	___	___
I. Applied Skills		
1. Reads orally with expression	___	___
2. Uses index	___	___
3. Uses glossary	___	___
4. Mood of selection	___	___
5. Classifies into sub-groups	___	___
6. Utilizes dictionary parts	___	___
7. Interprets maps, charts, graphs, and diagrams	___	___
8. Author's purpose and viewpoint	___	___
9. Interprets character's feelings	___	___
10. Library and reference skills	___	___
11. Reading rate	___	___
12. Tailored reading (i.e., skimming)	___	___
13. Outlining	___	___

Sample 4.12—*continued*

J. Language Skills—General	Date	Teacher's Initials
1. Pronoun with antecedent	___	___
2. Creative expression	___	___
3. Readiness	___	___
4. Oral—auditory development	___	___
5. Complete thoughts		
Oral	___	___
Written	___	___
6. Refining sentence structure		
Capitalization	___	___
Punctuation	___	___
7. Nouns/adjectives	___	___
8. Verbs		
Identification	___	___
Usage	___	___
9. Letter writing	___	___
10. Creative writing	___	___
11. Dramatization	___	___
12. Parts of speech	___	___
13. Verb tense	___	___
14. Paragraphs	___	___
15. Developing written language	___	___
16. Examining sentences	___	___
17. Understanding figurative language	___	___

Sample 4.13—Student Profile: Written Skills Checklist—Grades 6–8

Name _____

                Last   First   Middle

Key

X	Satisfactory
1	Needs to improve
0	Fails to achieve minimal skills
	Inappropriate at this time or student not in attendance

Skills

6	7	8	
			Punctuation*
			Capitalization*
			Usage*
			Spelling
			Handwriting

*See supplementary charts.

**Students are to have experience with these forms, but mastery at this grade level is not essential.

Sample 4.13—*continued*

SIXTH YEAR COMPETENCIES

Teacher _____
School Year 19_____–19_____
Late Entry Date _____

6	7	8	
			1. Completes forms
			2. Writes complete sentences
			3. Expands sentences with words and phrases
			4. Combines sentences by embedding
			5. Supplies transitional devices between sentences
			6. Identifies topic sentences
			7. Arranges events in chronological order
			8. Classifies material into logical categories
			9. Completes partial outline
			10. Writes informal letters
			11. Uses appropriate symbols
			12. Uses appropriate library resources
			13. Inserts descriptions into story plot
			14. Writes limericks**
			15. Writes haiku**
			16. GRAMMAR: Form classes N V ADJ ADV

SEVENTH YEAR COMPETENCIES

Teacher _____
School Year 19_____–19_____
Late Entry Date _____

6	7	8	
			1. Writes appropriate one-word modifiers
			2. Writes sensory and physical descriptions
			3. Writes topic sentences
			4. Records steps of process in chronological order
			5. Writes a chronological narrative
			6. Writes paragraphs appropriate to audience, purpose, situation
			7. Takes notes from library resources
			8. Uses appropriate symbols
			9. Writes social notes
			10. Creates new uses and names for common items**
			11. Writes a short story**
			12. Writes cinquains**
			13. GRAMMAR: Sentence patterns N–V N–V–N
			N–V–N–N
			N–LV–N
			N–LV–ADJ

Sample 4.13—*continued*

EIGHTH YEAR COMPETENCIES

Teacher _____
School Year 19_____–19_____
Late Entry Date _____

6	7	8	
____	____	☐	1. Writes in standard English
____	____	☐	2. Expands sentences within paragraphs with words and phrases
____	____	☐	3. Writes sensory and physical descriptions
____	____	☐	4. Builds paragraph outline or list
____	____	☐	5. Uses standard paragraph development
____	____	☐	6. Writes paragraphs appropriate to audience, purpose, situation
____	____	☐	7. Composes a "how to" paragraph
____	____	☐	8. Writes contrasting paragraphs of fact and opinion
____	____	☐	9. Writes a multi-paragraph composition
____	____	☐	10. Supplies transitional devices between sentences and paragraphs
____	____	☐	11. Writes summaries
____	____	☐	12. Writes a business letter
____	____	☐	13. Writes to achieve a specific tone, mood, emotion
____	____	☐	14. Uses figurative language**
____	____	☐	15. Writes a tall tale**
____	____	☐	16. Writes a myth**
____	____	☐	17. GRAMMAR: Phrases and clauses

SUMMARY

In this chapter we have described the program of the middle school as one where learning opportunities are classified under three headings:

Personal Development
Education for Social Competence
Skills for Continuous Learning

Through the use of examples of program offerings in the three areas, we have attempted to show how a diverse and meaningful program can be developed for middle school students.

The challenge of the middle school is to design and implement an effective and relevant program for the emerging adolescent learner. The program must include a planned sequence of concepts, place emphasis on skills and interests needed for continuous learning, provide exploratory experiences, emphasize the development of values, and give special attention to personal development of students.

Suggested Learning Activities

1. Develop an outline of a program designed for the middle school.
2. What courses and activities would you include in a special-interest program?
3. Prepare a statement for a school board on the need for a skills program in the middle school.
4. Develop a rationale for a balanced program in the middle school.
5. Design an advisor-advisee program for your middle school.

Selected References

A S C D Working Group on the Emerging Adolescent Learner. *The Middle School We Need*. Washington, D. C.: Association for Supervision and Curriculum Development, 1975.

Bondi, Joseph. *Developing Middle Schools: A Guidebook*. Wheeling, Ill.: Whitehall Publishing Co., 1972.

Curtis, Thomas, and Bidwell, Wilma. *Curriculum and Instruction for Emerging Adolescents*. Reading, Mass.: Addison-Wesley Publishing Co., 1977.

Hansen, John, and Hearn, Arthur. *The Middle School Program*. Chicago: Rand McNally and Co., 1971.

Kindred, Leslie, et al. *The Middle School Curriculum: A Practitioner's Handbook*. Boston: Allyn and Bacon, Inc., 1976.

Overly, Donald; Kinghorn, Jon; and Preston, Richard. *The Middle School: Humanizing Education for Youth*. Worthington, Ohio: Charles Jones Publishing Co., 1972.

Special State Committee on the Middle School. *Development of Middle Schools in Florida*. Tallahassee, Fla.: State Department of Education, 1974.

5

Organizing for Instruction in the Middle School

You can either knock down walls
or go around them

INTRODUCTION

As we have learned in earlier chapters, middle school teachers and supportive staff, building on a philosophy and knowledge of emerging adolescent learners, have structured a broad and relevant program for the diverse group of students found in the middle grades. To facilitate that program, the middle school organization must present a flexible approach to instruction.

All middle schools consist of five variables—students, teachers, time, space, and media.[1] The skillful manipulation of these variables allows middle schools to provide the flexible program and organization necessary for the diverse group of students they serve. In this chapter we shall see, through examples of various middle school organizations, how flexibility can be realized in the middle school.

---

[1] Joseph Bondi, *Developing Middle Schools: A Guidebook* (Wheeling, Ill.: Whitehall Publishing Co., 1972), pp. 87–90.

For years many intermediate schools have operated under the following assumptions:

1. The appropriate amount of time for learning a subject is the same—forty to sixty minutes in length, six or seven periods a day, for thirty-six weeks out of the year.

2. A classroom group of thirty to thirty-five students is the most appropriate for a wide variety of learning experiences.

3. All learners are capable of mastering the same subject matter in the same length of time. For example, everyone is given the same test on Chapter Five on Friday. Everyone is passed from level one algebra to level two in June.

4. Once a group is formed, the same group is equally appropriate for a wide variety of learning activities.

5. The same material is appropriate to all members of a group. For example, the same assignment is given to the entire group.

6. The same classroom is equally appropriate for a wide variety of learning activities. Conference rooms are not provided for teacher-student conferences. Large group facilities are not provided for mass dissemination of materials. Small group rooms are unavailable for discussion activity, etc.

7. All students require the same kind of supervision.

8. The same teacher is qualified to teach all aspects of his subject for one school year.

The middle school seeks to break this lock-step approach to instruction. Rigid class sizes, inflexible classroom facilities, and lock-step schedules are being challenged. Many middle schools have developed team structures where teams of teachers work with groups of students on a flexible basis. These schools have adopted the position that there is nothing magic about a set number of hours, days, or weeks a child spends in a particular course. Emphasis is placed on designing facilities and schedules to allow for a variety of group sizes which are determined by student needs and the nature of the learning activity. A child's learning progress is determined by mastery of skills or competencies. Students under this performance criteria do not pass on to a second learning level until they have mastered first-level skills.

Ideal school buildings do not always guarantee a flexible organization. Many good middle schools are operating in old buildings designed for conventional high school or junior high programs. Such middle schools are either knocking down walls or going around them. Conversely, some of the most rigid organizations are found in new open-space schools designed especially for middle schools. In such schools, walls, real or imaginary, have risen which leave the schools in a lock-step curriculum.

Here are some of the ways middle schools have attempted to break lock-step organizational patterns.

Flexible Modular Scheduling

A module in a school schedule simply refers to a period of time. Many middle schools have adopted flexible modular scheduling which means that the school day is arranged in modules of time of varying length. Modules may be fifteen, twenty, twenty-five, or thirty minutes in length or longer. The smaller the module, the more flexibility in grouping patterns. For example, operating under a fifteen-minute module plan, an hour can be broken into one, two, three, or four time periods. A thirty-minute module plan would allow for two.

Most middle schools operate blocks of time during the school day where the four academic disciplines of science, mathematics, language arts, and social studies can be taught in longer time periods than a single class period. Such blocks consist of a number of modules grouped together (for instance, seven thirty-minute modules) where four-member teams teach a group of 120–135 students. Blocks of time allow for correlation among the participating disciplines and permit teachers to utilize small- or large-group instruction for varying lengths of time depending on the needs of students. Examples of flexible modular scheduling will be presented later in this chapter.

Team Teaching in the Middle School

Team teaching in the middle school may occur in disciplinary or interdisciplinary patterns. Organizationally, many middle schools have allowed for team teaching by clustering teachers and students in sections of the building and by providing a common instructional block and common teacher-planning time.

New middle school facilities have been built with open-space areas and moveable walls. Older buildings have been renovated for team teaching.

The main difficulties with organizing for team teaching in the middle school are lack of training for teachers, lack of flexible space, and lack of provision of planning time for teachers during the day. Figure 5.1 looks at advantages and disadvantages of teaming.

Figure 5.1
Team Teaching—Why?

Selected Reasons

—Demand for better staff utilization
—Demand for improvement in quality of education
—Diversified student populations
—More sophisticated instructional media resulting from impact of science and technology
—Need to provide a greater variety of educational experiences
—Need for greater individualization

Team Teaching Advantages (For Student)

—Superior teachers are shared by all students
—The team approach permits greater attention to individual students
—Pupils can be grouped in areas of special interest to them
—Pupils become more independent under team teaching
—The team concept can help to build a sense of responsibility in the students
—The team approach provides flexibility to meet the varying needs of the several school populations

Figure 5.1—*continued*

Team Teaching Advantages (Staff)

—Makes more effective use of the professional talents and interests of staff members
—Neutralizes the effect of the poor teacher
—Enables teachers to share information and ideas which help solve problems and improve their professional background
—Provides inservice education opportunities

Team Teaching Advantages (Teaching-Learning Situation)

—Allows students to work across grade lines with subject matter specialists
—Allows better control of pupil-staff ratio through use of large, medium and small grouping
—Provides children with several adult images to study
—Improves correlation of school work, home work, and field experiences
—Makes for flexible scheduling
—Provides a wider range of grouping possibilities
—Provides a wider resource of talent, knowledge, skills and experience from which to derive new educational experiences
—Takes advantage of the fact that the "whole" of the participants working together will be more than the "sum" of the individual staff members working independently

Team Teaching Limitations

—Agreement on the evaluation of individual students
—Arranging time for planning, instructional development and study during the day
—Increased pressure on students resulting from constant upgrading of instruction
—Conflicts resulting from mixing people of different teaching styles
—Providing facilities capable of furnishing the flexibility needed
—Selection of appropriate action regarding student misbehavior
—Teacher insecurity, dread of the unfamiliar often accompany beginning team teaching
—The need for designated leader
—Danger of pupil detachment with the use of large groups
—Tendency to restrict the individual teacher's freedom of action.

Nongrading in the Middle School

If we are going to give more than just lip service to the idea of individualized instruction in the middle school, then we must consider dropping grade-level barriers. Many middle schools retain grade levels for accounting purposes, but devise a curriculum where youngsters are working at school levels in subject areas.

There is a continuum of learning objectives to be mastered in each academic area. Youngsters may find themselves classified as seventh graders, for instance, but are actually doing work that should have been mastered in the third or fourth grade. Other middle schools actually cut across grade lines in grouping youngsters. Some have evolved to a nongraded organization after being initially developed as a graded organization.

A review of Figure 5.2 will help clarify what a nongraded structure should be like in the middle school.

Figure 5.2
A Way of Appraising Nongraded Structure in the Middle School

Graded Structure	Nongraded Structure
A year of progress in subject matter seen as roughly comparable to a child's year in school.	A year of school life may mean much more or much less than a year of progress in subject matter.
Each successive year of progress seen as comparable to each past year or each year to come.	Progress seen as irregular; a child may progress much more rapidly in one year and quite slowly in another.
A child's progress seen as being unified; advancing in rather regular fashion in all areas of development; probably working close to grade level in most subject areas.	A child's progress seen as not unified; she spurts ahead in one area of progress and lags behind in others; may be working at three or four levels in as many subjects.
Specific bodies of content seen as appropriate for successive grade levels and so labeled; subject matter packaged grade-by-grade.	Bodies of content seen as appropriate over a span of years; learning viewed vertically or longitudinally rather than horizontally.
Adequacy of progress determined by comparing child's attainment to coverage deemed appropriate to the grade.	Adequacy of progress determined by comparing child's attainment to ability and both to long-term view of ultimate accomplishment desired.
Inadequate progress made up by repeating work of a given grade: grade failure the ultimate penalty for slow progress. Rapid progress provided-for through enrichment: encouragement of horizontal expansion rather than vertical advancement in work; attempt to avoid moving to domain of teacher above.	Slow progress provided-for by permitting longer time to do given blocks of work; no repetitions but recognition of basic differences in learning rate. Rapid progress provided for both vertically and horizontally; bright children encouraged to move ahead regardless of grade level of work; no fear of encroaching on work of next teacher.
Rather inflexible grade–to–grade movement of pupils, usually at end of year.	Flexible pupil movement; pupil may shift to another class at almost any time; some trend toward controlling shifts on a quarter or semester basis.

INTERDISCIPLINARY TEAMING IN THE MIDDLE SCHOOL

Definition

The interdisciplinary team, as its name suggests, is a combination of teachers from different subject areas who plan and conduct instruction for particular groups of pupils. The aim of interdisciplinary teaming is to promote communication, coordination, and cooperation among subject matter specialists. Students, therefore, will benefit from instruction planned by specialists, and escape the fragmentation which characterizes many departmentalized plans.[2] The interdisciplinary team pattern is common in middle school designs.

---

[2] W. M. Alexander et al., *The Emergent Middle School* (New York: Holt, Rinehart and Winston, Inc., 1968), pp. 107–8.

Rationale

The interdisciplinary team approach is based on at least four premises:

1. That teachers in the middle school need to be specialists in a single subject discipline. With the ever-increasing demands for competency, it is not reasonable to expect a teacher to develop the background of content and method in more than one discipline to the level of effectiveness attainable when only one discipline is required.

2. That, while paying attention to the need for teacher competency in single discipline, it is well to keep in mind the child-centered philosophy emphasized over the years in the elementary school. The elementary teacher tends to know relatively few youngsters rather completely, and they know her well.

3. That the teacher team organizational pattern adds a new dimension, a stimulation resulting from the interaction of teachers who are planning together for the same youngsters.

4. That the team organization, because of its format, allowed many opportunities to progress in the direction of large and small-group instruction and independent study.[3]

Working together, teachers in an interdisciplinary team deal with individual student problems, consult with specialists, integrate subject areas, and consider other school-related topics. Below is an outline of professional activities of an interdisciplinary team.

Professional Activities of Interdisciplinary Teams

Consideration of individual children:

1. Behavior and emotional problems
2. Evaluation of progress
3. Meeting with parents to discuss an individual child
4. Changing schedules within the team to accommodate the needs of all children

Consultation with specialists:

1. Guidance counselor
2. Psychologist
3. Speech teacher
4. Visiting teacher
5. Reading specialist
6. School nurse
7. Teacher of handicapped and gifted
8. Principal, assistant principal, or curriculum coordinator
9. Teachers of foreign languages, art, music, physical education

---

[3] G. F. Vars, *Common Learnings* (Scranton: International Textbook Co., 1969), pp. 84–85. Used with permission.

Correlation of subject areas:

1. Each teacher describes coverage to date
2. Each teacher submits for discussion papers written by pupils in each subject area
3. Plan correlations around subject matter and skills. For example, conservation in social studies and science; written expression in all fields
4. Exchange materials

Discussion of school-related topics:

1. Student council
2. Assemblies
3. Corridors
4. Homerooms
5. Cafeteria
6. Marking and reporting[4]

Advantages

The interdisciplinary team approach to planning and implementing instruction possesses some distinct advantages over a self-contained teaching pattern. Some of those advantages are listed below.

1. More than one teacher with the knowledge of scheduling, use of instructional materials, grouping and instructional methods benefits individual student learning.
2. Curriculums among subject areas can be coordinated so that students can relate one subject to another. Leads to greater breadth of understanding for students—"sees" more relationships.
3. Teachers can better understand individual differences in students when more than one person is making observations and evaluations and, therefore, can "cope" with those differences more effectively; discipline problems are more easily handled; guidance for the student is discussed among the team.
4. The team approach enables teachers to contrast a student's behavior and ability from class to class, thereby helping them to develop a systematic and consistent approach to helping the child.
5. Allows for closer work with guidance and other specialists.
6. Block scheduling allows teachers greater flexibility in scheduling to accommodate large- and small-group instruction, remedial work, and independent study.
7. Flexible time schedules can be made more conducive to children's developmental needs at this age level than can rigid departmentalized schedules.

---

[4] G. F. Vars, *Common Learnings* (Scranton: International Textbook Co., 1969), p. 91. Used with permission.

8. A number of instructors can lend their individual expertise to a given topic simultaneously.

9. Large time blocks are available for educational field trips, guest speakers, films, etc.; at the same time, scheduling is not disrupted. Less teaching time is lost to repetitious film-showing.

10. Teachers can be more aware of what their students are learning in other classes, what assignments, tests, projects are making demands on their time.

11. Common planning time can lead to more creativity in teaching approaches and to consistency in teaching strategies.

12. Interdisciplinary teaching leads to economy of learning time and transfer among students.

13. Student leadership is distributed among all the teams since each team's students are typical of the total school community.

14. Students are able to identify themselves with a smaller school within a school. With team representation on student council, they are more closely related to student government.

15. Correlated planning of content and project work is more easily carried on.

16. Parent conferences can be arranged by the guidance counselor for times when all students' academic teachers are available.

17. Individual teams may rearrange completely time and period schedules without interference with the overall school program. For example, each team may individually manipulate the time block to provide periods of various length. All students do not move in the hallways at the end of fifty-five minutes.

18. Field trips can now be planned by teams and built-in chaperoning is thus provided. Longer times for such trips are now available without disrupting a multiple number of classes.

19. One of the greatest advantages of team teaching is the assistance provided to the beginning teacher.

20. Building utilization is improved; large- and small-group space is utilized as well as regular classrooms.

21. An interdisciplinary team scheduling arrangement promotes the professional growth of teachers by encouraging the exchange of ideas among members of their teaching team.

Components of Interdisciplinary Teaming

Interdisciplinary team teaching requires the following components.[5]

---

[5] Lorraine Morton, "Effective Interdisciplinary Team Teaching Now: An Approach for the Middle School," Monograph, Austin, TX, 1973, pp. 3–5. Adapted by the authors.

Planning Time

For teachers, planning time during the school day is as essential to team teaching as having pupils to teach; useless one without the other. The very existence of team teaching is predicated upon planning together for the instruction of pupils. Early publications of team teaching efforts reveal that teachers met in homes at night, as well as other times not included in the regular school day, to plan the instructional program. No discussion is needed to point up the weakness of this approach. It is the team approach to teaching which brings out the competencies of teachers, provides teachers with an opportunity to use and enhance their professional skills, and engenders feelings of professionalism so that teachers can receive personal satisfaction from their efforts. Teachers should be given time to plan the job on the job.

Staff Meetings

These meetings are held to discuss the business and routine of team teaching, also to study inservice matters pertaining to aspects of team teaching. It seems wise, however, to separate staff meetings held for general team business from those covering inservice training. Meetings to plan the instruction of pupils should also be held separately. Instructional meetings may be held with all teachers attending, or those of a single discipline, or the several disciplines. *Who* will be meeting will be determined by the type of instructional program being planned and the specific pupils involved.

Scheduling for Instruction

This component provides a structure by which the academic and social needs of the pupils can be met. Team teachers understand that schedules are flexible in time and grouping. No schedule is sacred, but is useful only if it furthers the goals for which it was established. As other goals become evident and old purposes served, it is then time to reschedule to incorporate the more recent needs of the pupils. This is not to suggest there should not be consistency in the schedule. Experience has taught there must be some. For example, the pupil should remain with a particular teacher for most of his basic skills learnings. Obviously, this is an economical procedure for the pupil and teacher.

For other types of activities such as independent study projects, individualized instruction in enrichment areas, guidance, remedial reading, and activities which synthesize the various disciplines, pupils can be rescheduled for instruction with any member of the teaching team. If the activity requires a one-to-one relationship between pupil and teacher, it is preferable that a teacher be assigned who has a harmonious relationship with that pupil.

Large-Group Instruction

In this component, two or more classes are taught together for the purpose of introducing units of work, testing, developing bases for concepts and generalizations, summarizing a section of a major unit or the total unit itself, presenting student projects, and programming other kinds of activities that do not require the pupil-recitation type of response.

Traditional-Size Group Instruction

Pupils are placed in conventional size classes of twenty-five to thirty for routine instruction. The nature of this classwork is conventional and more nearly like that suggested for a large-group instruction. Such a size, in fact, is large-group oriented rather than small-group. Advantages of this size group are that the teacher has the opportunity to further divide into smaller groups, and pupil leaders can be used effectively. The teacher can serve as a resource person to the groups as they work in small discussion or pupil-pupil teaching groups.

Small-Group Instruction and/or Discussion

The number of students involved is ten or less. Discussions of this type enhance learning because pupils have a chance to express their ideas verbally. When held following large group instruction, pupils can respond to the material that was presented in the large group, thus reinforcing learning. It is necessary for the teacher who prepared the large group presentation also to prepare questions which will stimulate discussion in the small group.

Small-group instruction may be used for other clarifications. It is useful for teaching basic skills, remedial work, and general reinforcement; to stimulate thinking, to assess values, behavior, goals, and strengths of pupils. It is an ideal setting in which to observe emerging adolescent growth.

Students as well as teachers can serve as small-group discussion leaders. A successful size for a student leader is five pupils.

Individualized Instruction

In this component, pupils are instructed on a one-to-one basis. Instruction begins after the pupil's needs, strengths, and weaknesses have been assessed, his interests determined, and an appropriate program planned for him. When instruction is individualized, individual differences can be provided for without destroying the pupil's self-image, such as when static academic homogeneous grouping is utilized. Through this type of instruction, pupils can more nearly approach the goals of being independent learners and more responsible persons. It allows the pause to release the mind to inquire and the intellect to be fulfilled.

Independent Study

Here the pupil is given an opportunity to work in depth in any subject discipline of her choosing. The teacher is needed to help the pupil set goals for independent study. The pupil must be given help to achieve competence in basic research.

Group Guidance Sessions

Pupils are divided into groups as small as the team teaching staff will permit for the purpose of discussing topics appropriate to middle school guidance. The group should be small enough to use effective discussion techniques. Topics for discussion can be prepared by the school social worker, guidance counselor, or team teachers. It is during these sessions that pupil values are examined and attempts are made to help pupils understand themselves, their relation to their peer group, their family, and the world.

Use of Specialists

Pupils who have specific learning disabilities or problems of a diversified nature require special attention. That is why specialists like the reading specialist, speech therapist, social worker, guidance counselor, and tutors for pupils who are severely deficient in skill subjects, or those who cannot benefit from a full day in the classroom because of a severe emotional problem, contribute so greatly to team teaching. A team teacher may tutor a student who has been absent or needs additional help. For some pupils, health education sessions of a personal nature with the school nurse are needed. Special learnings, if indicated, can be achieved at the school's resource or material center. Team teachers should individualize pupils' schedules to accommodate specialists during the school day.

Auxiliary Personnel

These include a team clerk, student aides, paraprofessionals, community resource persons, tutorial aides, and, if available, student teachers and substitutes. Though some of this personnel are generally available in a conventional school setting, there are now dimensions for their use in an interdisciplinary team teaching situation.

Pupil-Team Meetings

This component helps plan instruction and deals with group concerns like discipline, student rights, and school-wide activities.

GROUPING IN THE MIDDLE SCHOOL

A flexible organizational pattern in the middle school means that different student grouping patterns are employed in instruction. Such patterns include the following:

1. *Large group*—consists of up to 120–150 students in a team or house. Such a group is used to present introductory material, to hear speakers, or to administer standardized tests.

2. *Medium or class size*—consists of twenty to thirty-five students and is the most common class grouping.

3. *Small group*—operates within a class-size group. It can be easily found when students have common interests or skills.

4. *One-to-one*—this learning situation may be a teacher-to-student or student-to-student. It is an ideal learning situation but one that is not always easy to implement.

5. *Independent study*—may be a part of classwork, homework, or community study.

Figure 5.3 illustrates various student groupings common in the middle school.

Figure 5.3
Various Student Groupings

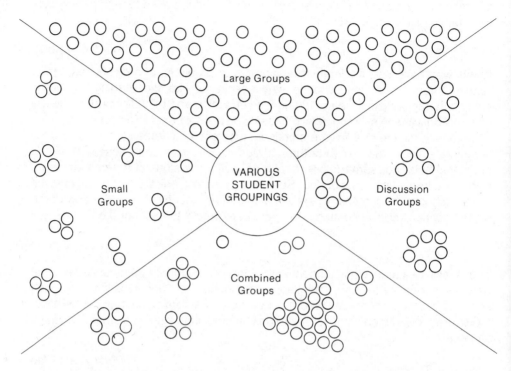

One question that often arises is whether there should be homogeneous or heterogeneous grouping in the middle school. The answer is both. Skills groups should be homogeneous, but should not be static, that is, students should be able to move from group to group as they progress along a skills continuum. Students grouped heterogeneously in teams may be grouped and regrouped according to interests, tasks to be accomplished, and skill levels.

ORGANIZATIONAL PATTERNS OF SELECTED SCHOOLS

The following organizational models are described to illustrate how middle schools operate from unique instructional designs.

Model I—School Management Model[6]

The task force at Fernwood Middle School has designed a shared decision management model (see Figure 5.4) in support of an effective school operation. In this model, directive management and facilitative management work in harmony to

---

[6] Fernwood Middle School, Robert Schuberg, Principal (Portland, Oreg., 1976). Used with permission.

Figure 5.4
Shared Decision Management Model

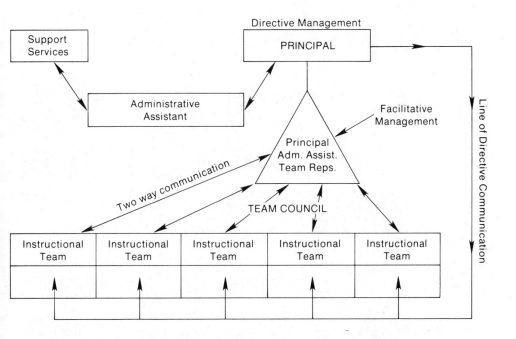

meet the needs of those who provide and receive services in this organization.

The norms of the organization have been stated in the goals, characteristics and expectations as described in other parts of the data.

The basic structure of the organization calls for an instructional team formation with a representative on the facilitative management team. The facilitative management team directs the school's resources in response to program change and development within the organization.

Directive management coordinates the concerns of school law, board policy, and policies from the area office. The staff facilitates directive management and directive management moves into a facilitative role in support of team management.

It is also understood that the staff will require an extensive training program to acquire the necessary process skills to make the model work.

Model II—A Coordinating Team Model

Figure 5.5 illustrates a coordinating team model that consists of a principal and two directors who assume responsibilities of evaluation, curriculum development, budget, and discipline for a designated grade level.

Figure 5.5
Coordinating Team Model—Hadley Middle School

<u>ORGANIZATIONAL PATTERN FOR GRADES 6, 7, and 8</u>

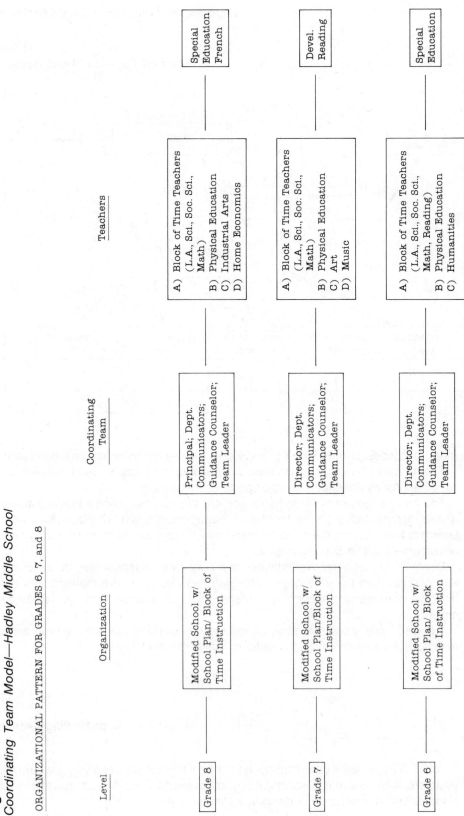

Level	Organization	Coordinating Team	Teachers	
Grade 8	Modified School w/ School Plan/ Block of Time Instruction	Principal; Dept. Communicators; Guidance Counselor; Team Leader	A) Block of Time Teachers (L.A., Sci., Soc. Sci., Math) B) Physical Education C) Industrial Arts D) Home Economics	Special Education French
Grade 7	Modified School w/ School Plan/Block of Time Instruction	Director; Dept. Communicators; Guidance Counselor; Team Leader	A) Block of Time Teachers (L.A., Sci., Soc. Sci., Math) B) Physical Education C) Art D) Music	Devel. Reading
Grade 6	Modified School w/ School Plan/ Block of Time Instruction	Director; Dept. Communicators; Guidance Counselor; Team Leader	A) Block of Time Teachers (L.A., Sci., Soc. Sci., Math, Reading) B) Physical Education C) Humanities	Special Education

Model III—Total School Organizational Plan

The following sample illustrates an organizational plan for a middle school.

Sample 5.1—Program Description—Azalea Middle School

General Characteristics

1. Flexible modular scheduling, which includes twenty-six fifteen-minute mods.
2. Student schedule consists of:
   ...... academic block of time
   ...... ERR (Enrichment, Remediation and Research) 6th grade only
   ...... lunch
   ...... physical education
   ...... related arts block of time
   ...... special interest oriented activity
3. Total student time in school: six hours—thirty minutes
4. Student enrollment: 1,000

6th, 7th, and 8th Grade Academic Block

Characteristics

1. Interdisciplinary team teaching in the 7th and 8th grade consisting of one math teacher, one science teacher, one language arts teacher and one social studies teacher.
2. Interdisciplinary team teaching in the 6th grade with one team consisting of two teachers (one social studies/science and one LA/math) and two teams consisting of four teachers (one social studies, one language arts, one math, and one science teacher).
3. ERR (Enrichment, Remediation and Research) 6th grade only . . . Teacher-Pupil Ratio of twenty students with each 6th and 7th grade academic teacher. Five teachers per 100 students . . . One "period" (45 min.) each day.
4. The manipulation of students, teachers, time, space, and media within the three-hour academic block is determined by the teams in their common planning time.
5. Common planning time is provided for academic and related arts teachers to develop and implement the curriculum, and to diagnose and prescribe for individual student needs.
6. The program in the academic block will focus on:
   ...... basic learning skills
   ...... a curriculum which provides for continuous student progress.
   ...... flexible grouping based on changing needs of pupils with provisions for both large and small groups.
7. Students with learning disabilities are scheduled for assistance from LD teacher.
8. EMR students are scheduled into EMR unit and take many related arts courses and physical education.

6th Grade Related Arts Block

Characteristics

1. Physical education is required.
2. All 6th grade students are required to take the humanities wheel consisting of four nine-week sections.

Sample 5.1—*continued*

9 weeks......exploratory music
9 weeks......communications
9 weeks......exploratory arts and crafts
9 weeks......exploratory world of manufacturing

NOTE: Students may elect to take band or office assistant in place of the wheel.

7th Grade Related Arts Block

Characteristics

1. Physical education is required.
2. Students elect from the following semester courses (take two each semester):

Spanish	Graphic	Business
Band	Communication	Agriculture
American Industry	Home Ec. Cooking	Work Experience
	Home Ec. Sewing	Assistant (office)

8th Grade Related Arts Block

Characteristics

1. Physical education required
2. Students elect from the following: year or semester courses (may take two)

Home Ec. Cooking	Agriculture	World of
Home Ec. Sewing	Band (yr)	Manufacturing
Crafts	Spanish (yr)	Assistant (office)
Business	American Industries	Graphics
		Choral Music

6th Grade RA	7th Grade RA		8th Grade RA	
Mods 1–9	Mods 1–9	Sem.	Mods 14–15–16	Sem.
	Office Assistant		Office Assistant	
	Physical Education		Physical Education	
	Band (yr.)		Band (yr.)	
	Choral Music		Choral Music (yr.)	
Physical	Graphic Communication		Graphic Communication	
	Home Ec. (cooking)		Manufacturing	
Education	Home Ec. (sewing)		Crafts	
	Manufacturing		Business	
	Crafts		American Industries	
	Business		Agriculture	
	American Industries		Spanish (yr.)	
	Agriculture			
	Spanish			
	Work Experience			

Sample 5.1—*continued*

Mods 1–9 6th Grade Wheel	Mods 1–9 Sem.	Mods 17–18–19 Sem.
	Office Assistant	Office Assistant
	Physical Education	Physical Education
9 weeks — 9 weeks	Band (yr.)	Graphic Communication
Communication / World of Manufacturing	Choral Music	Home Ec. (cooking)
Crafts / Choral Music	Graphic Communication	Home Ec. (sewing)
9 weeks — 9 weeks	Home Ec. (cooking)	Manufacturing
	Home Ec. (sewing)	Crafts
	Manufacturing	Business
	Crafts	American Industries
	Business	Agriculture
	American Industries	Spanish (yr.)
	Agriculture	
Band Assistant	Spanish	

Mods 1–9	Mods 1–9 Sem.	Mods 20–21–22–23 Sem.
	Office Assistant	Office Assistant
	Physical Education	Physical Education
	Band (yr.)	Band (yr.)
ERR	Choral Music	Choral Music (yr.)
	Graphic Communication	Graphic Communication
	Home Ec. (cooking)	Home Ec. (cooking)
	Home Ec. (sewing)	Home Ec. (sewing)
	Manufacturing	Manufacturing
	Crafts	Crafts
	Business	Business
	American Industries	Agriculture
	Agriculture	
	Spanish	

Sample 5.2—Special Interest Classes

1. Special interest classes are offered every day during mods 24, 25 and 26.

2. Students may choose one 45-minute special interest class during these three mods. Students change special interest classes every 4 1/2 weeks.

3. Over 50 special interest classes are offered every 4 1/2 weeks.

4. Special interest classes will help students develop interests and explore a wide variety of special areas. Each course will emphasize basic learning skills.

5. Special interest classes will involve all academic and related arts teachers.

6. Listed below are the special interest classes offered during the 1977–78 school year:

Sample 5.2—*continued*

agriculture
band (beg.)
band (adv.)
basic sketching
basketball handling
black history
bridge (beg.)
bridge (adv.)
beautiful burlap
cards, Inc.
camping
chess (beg.)
chess (adv.)
choral reading &
  songs
cinema
co-ed basketball
co-ed volleyball
contemporary music
crazy creweling
creative boutique
creative bulletin bds.
creative wall
  hangings
criminology
crocheting
dance studio
do-your-own-thing
drill team
embroidery
fresh-water fishing
indoor games
gallivanter
golf (beg.)
golf (adv.)
guitar (beg.)

guitar (adv.)
handwriting
hobby club
home crafts
int. morse code
knitting (beg.)
knitting (adv.)
leathercraft I
leathercraft II
lighting crew
macrame I
macrame II
ceramics
creative rhythms
making christmas
  tree orn.
math magic
math enrichment
math study hall
modern music
musical plays
model building
needlepoint
nutty newspaper
pets are people
piano (beg.)
piano (adv.)
pinochle
pocketbooks, Inc.
photography
puppetry
reading for fun
relaxing thru
  exercise
rug hooking
score four
pep squad
student council
sets and scenery
showmanship

slimnastics
liquid embroidery
girls softball
boys softball
spelling made easy
string orch.
string art
supervised study
table tennis
tennis (beg.)
tennis (adv.)
tune in on child care
the play's the thing
T.V. production
girls volleyball
yearbook
your hair, true or
  false
watching your weight
weaving
weightlifting

Source: Azalea Middle School, "Total School Organization Plan" (St. Petersburg, Fla.: 1973). Used with permission.

Model IV—A Nongraded Model of School Organization

The nongraded school makes a suitable provision for each unique student. This means a flexible grouping of pupils, an adaptable, flexible curriculum, and arrangement of materials and instructional approaches. The Riviera model of nongraded organization is presented for the reader's study.

Sample 5.3—Riviera Middle School

Estimated Enrollment
        Grade 6— 300 students
        Grade 7— 420 students
        Grade 8— <u>480</u> students
      TOTAL 1200 students

3 Teams in Team Learning Centers for Basics
(Lang. Arts, Math, Soc. St., Sci., Reading, and Physical Ed.)

      Each Basics Student Center has:
      Grade 6—100 students
      Grade 7—140 students
      Grade 8—<u>160</u> students
     TOTAL   400 students

      Each Basics Teacher Team consists of:
        3-Lang. Arts Teachers
        3-Math Teachers
        3-Social Studies Teachers
       <u>3-Science Teachers</u>
    12
    +2-Physical Education Teachers
     1-Team Assistant (Paraprofessional)

      Related Arts Team Consists of:
        2-Music Teachers
        1-Art Teacher
        1-Humanities, Crafts Teacher
        2-Home Ec. Teachers
        3-Ind. Arts Teachers
        2-Foreign Language Teachers
        1-Business Teacher
        1-Distributive Education Teacher
        1-Health Teacher
       <u>1-Health Occupations Teacher</u>
    15

      Supportive Personnel
        1-Curriculum Assistant
        2-Counselors
        2-Deans
        2-Media Specialist
        1-Work Experience
        1-Enhanced Learning
        1-Learning Disability
        1-E M R
        1-Occupational Spec.

Related Arts Program:

Sample 5.3—*continued*

Grade 6 Exploratory Wheel (3–6 weeks)

Art
Music
Humanities
Explor. Foreign Language
Home Ec.
Ind. Arts
Careers
Health

Grade 7 Exploratory Wheel (9 weeks)

Humanities	*Vocational*
Humanities	Home Ec.
Art	Ind. Arts
Music	Careers
Explor. Foreign Language	Health
	Health Occupations

Grade 8 Electives (equal to 2)

= 1/2	= 1
Amer. Industries	Explor. Foreign Lang.
Art	Band 1, 2 and 3
Business	Orchestra
Crafts	Chorus
Drafting	French
Foods	Spanish
Health	Assistants
Marketing	
Power & Transportation	
Textiles	

Sample 5.4—List of Research, Enrichment and Development Program Offerings (R E D)

Students: During the year you should select a R E D course from each of the three lists below plus one extra which can be from either of the lists. The order is up to you. This means you will take, during the year, one class from the A list, one from the B list, one from the C list, and one which can be from either A, B, or C list.

(A)		(B)		(C)	
3–B	Basketball—Boys	1	Appl. Math	2	Baby Sitting
3–G	Basketball—Girls	11	Creat. Comm.	57	Basic First Aid
		12	Creat. Writing	5	Beginning Typing
4	Beg. Backgammon	14	Debate	18	Emergency
		15	Devel. Math		Treatment
50	Candlemaking	16	Devel. Spanish	23	Gardening
56	Decoupage	17	Dissect. Int. Affrs.	24	Glee Club

Sample 5.4—*continued*

8 Chess—Advanced	20 Everything You've ...	36 Riviera Leader Corps
9 Chess—Beginning	21 Exper. Can Be Fun	40 Sound of Rock
10 Creat. Stitchery	22 Foreign Lang. News	44 Vet. Medicine
26 Leathercraft	54 Globe Making	49 Yearbook & Spec. Eff.
33 Model Building	28 Mass Comm— Advts.	6 Cheerleading
55 Needlepoint	29 Mass Media— Records	7 Cheerleading Clinic
35 Puppet Making	30 Mass Media— Slides	52 Law and You
37 Rocketry	31 Mass Media—T V	38 Safe Boating
53 Softball—Boys	32 Microbiology	
45 Volleyball—Impr.	34 Mysteries of Sea	
43 Tournament Arch.	39 Skinny Books	
	41 Specialized PE	

SOURCE: Riviera Middle School, "A Nongraded Model of School Organization" (St. Petersburg, Fla.: 1977). Used with permission.

The foregoing models illustrate that middle schools can be organized in a variety of configurations and designs. Most often, local resources and levels of instructional sophistication determine the exact school design of the middle school at the local level.

Master Schedules

In Figures 5.6–5.11, the reader will find a number of examples of master building schedules that help organize the instructional day. While schedules, too, come in many forms, they generally tend to be designed to increase flexibility in the use of time. Short duration modules (mods) are used as the basic unit of time.

Figure 5.6

Block Schedule—Enrichment and Remediation Period

6	7	8
8:00–8:10	HR	1976–1977

6		7	8	
8:10		8:10	8:10 A	B
	Basic Studies 90		Related Arts & PE 90	
		Basic Studies 190		
9:40			9:40	
9:40 A B	Related Arts & PE 80		9:40	
11:00			Basic Studies 125	
11:00	Lunch 30	11:20		
11:30		11:20		
11:30		Lunch 30	11:45	
	Basic Studies 45	11:50	11:45	
		11:50 Basic Studies 25	Lunch 30	
12:15		12:15	12:15	
12:15		12:15	12:15	
	45	ENRICHMENT & REMEDIATION		
1:00		1:00	1:00	
1:00	Basic Studies 90	1:00 A Related Arts & PE 90 B	1:00 Basic Studies 90	
2:30		2:30	2:30	

Figure 5.7

Grades 5-8 Middle School Organization

Teacher Day 8:00-3:20
Student Day 8:15-3:10

	8:15-9:11 (1-2)	9:11-10:07 (3-4)	10:07-11:03 (5-6)	11:03-11:31 (7)	11:31-11:59 (8)	11:59-12:27 (9)	12:27-1:21 (10-11)	1:21-2:17 (12-13)	2:17-3:10 (14-15)
Grade 5	Instructional	Instructional	Instructional	LUNCH	Instructional	Instructional	Planning	Planning	Activity Period
6	Instructional	Instructional	Planning	Planning	Instructional	LUNCH	Instructional	Instructional	Activity Period
7	Instructional	Instructional	Planning	Planning	Instructional	LUNCH	Instructional	Instructional	Activity Period
8	Instructional	Instructional	Instructional	LUNCH	Instructional	LUNCH	Planning	Planning	Activity & Planning
Funct. Skills	Instructional	Planning	Planning		Instructional	LUNCH	Instructional	Instructional	Planning
Bi-Ling. Comm. Skills S.L.D. Tutorial	Planning	Planning	Instructional 6th & 7th Grades	Instructional 6th & 7th Grades		LUNCH	Instructional 5th & 8th Grades	Instructional 5th & 8th Grades	Activity Period
R E L A T E D	Planning	R.A. for Special Program Students	6th Grade	7th Grade	7th Grade		5th Grade	8th Grade	
A R T S	Planning	5th & 6th Art, Music & Health; 7th & 8th Pre-Voc. & P.E.	6A Art & Music / 6B Health / 7A—Pre-Voc. / 7B—P.E.	6B Art & Music / 6A Health / 7B Pre-Voc. / 7A—P.E.			5A Art & Music / 5B—Health / 8A—Pre-Voc. / 8B—P.E.	5B Art & Music / 5A—Health / 8B—Pre-Voc. / 8A—P.E.	

Health and P.E. will switch at Semester.

For 1st Semester an Aid will be assigned to Art, Music or Health to balance the classes.

In 2nd Semester 2 P.E. Teachers will balance the 5th and 6th grade classes.

Figure 5.8

Organization Model for 45–15 Year-Round School—Three Tracks in School 45 Days—One Track Out for 15 Days

MASTER SCHEDULE

TIME	MODULE	TRACK A	TRACK B	TRACK C	TRACK D
8:15- 8:30	1	HR	HR	HR	HR
8:30- 8:45	2	ACADEMIC	ACADEMIC	MUSIC ART BAND PRE-VOC PE	ACADEMIC
8:45- 9:00	3				
9:00- 9:15	4				
9:15- 9:30	5			ACADEMIC PLANNING	
9:30- 9:45	6				
9:45-10:00	7		MUSIC ART BAND PRE-VOC PE	ACADEMIC	
10:00-10:15	8				
10:15-10:30	9				
10:30-10:45	10		ACADEMIC PLANNING		
10:45-11:00	11				
11:00-11:15	12		ACADEMIC		
11:15-11:30	13				LUNCH
11:30-11:45	14	LUNCH			
11:45-12:00	15				MUSIC ART BAND PRE-VOC PE
12:00-12:15	16	ACADEMIC	LUNCH		
12:15-12:30	17				
12:30-12:45	18		ACADEMIC	LUNCH	
12:45- 1:00	19				ACADEMIC PLANNING
1:00- 1:15	20	MUSIC ART BAND PRE-VOC PE		ACADEMIC	ACADEMIC
1:15- 1:30	21				
1:30- 1:45	22				
1:45- 2:00	23	ACADEMIC PLANNING			
2:00- 2:15	24				
2:15- 2:30	25	ACTIVITY	ACTIVITY	ACTIVITY	ACTIVITY
2:30- 2:45	26				
2:45- 3:00	27				

Figure 5.9
Riviera Middle School Time Schedule

TEAM 1 TEAM 2 TEAM 3

Time									Time
9:00									9:00
		AID			AID				
9:10	B	1		B	1	P L	1		9:10
9:25		2		A	2	A N	2		9:25
9:40	A	3		S	3	N I	3		9:40
9:55		4		I	4	N G	4		9:55
10:10	S	5		C	5		5		10:10
10:25		6		S	6		6		10:25
10:40	I	7			7	P L		7	B	10:40
10:55		8			8	A N	8	A	10:55
11:10	C	9			9	N I	9	S	11:10
11:25		10			10	N G	10	I	11:25
11:40	S	11			11		11	C	11:40
11:55		12	L U N C H		12		12	S	11:55
12:10		13			13		13		12:10
12:25	B A S I C S	14	L U N C H		14	L U N C H	14		12:25
12:40		15			15	B A S I C S	15		12:40
12:55		16			16		16	B A S I C S	12:55
1:10		17			17		17		1:10
1:25		18	P L A N N I N G		18		18		1:25
1:40		19			19		19		1:40
1:55		20			20		20		1:55
2:10		21			21		21		2:10
2:25		22			22		22		2:25
2:40		23			23		23		2:40
2:55	R E D	24		R E D	24	R E D	24		2:55
3:30									3:30

Figure 5.10
Block Schedule, Wheel Arrangement, Special Interest Classes (ERR)

8:00	8:00 PE R.A 90 Min.	8:00
ACADEMIC 185 Min. (Social Studies, Mathematics, Language Arts, Science)	Band (Year)	ACADEMIC 95 Min. (SS, M, LA, SCI.)
	ACADEMIC 105 Min. (SS, M, LA, SCI.)	9:35 PE R.A 90 Min.
		10:20 PE R.A 95 Min.
11:05 LUNCH 30 Min.	11:20 LUNCH 30 Min.	R.A—45 Min. H. Ec.—2 G. Comm. W. of Mfg. Art Band C Chorus / 11:05 Business Consumer- Math Speech Enrichments
11:35 ACADEMIC 45 Min.	11:50	11:50 LUNCH 30 Min.
12:20 PE R.A 90 Min.	ACADEMIC 120 Min.	12:20
1:05		ACADEMIC 90 Min.
1:50 ERR 40 Min. 2:30	1:50 ERR 40 Min. 2:30	1:50 ERR 40 Min. 2:30

Figure 5.11
Block Schedule, Ten-Minute Modules

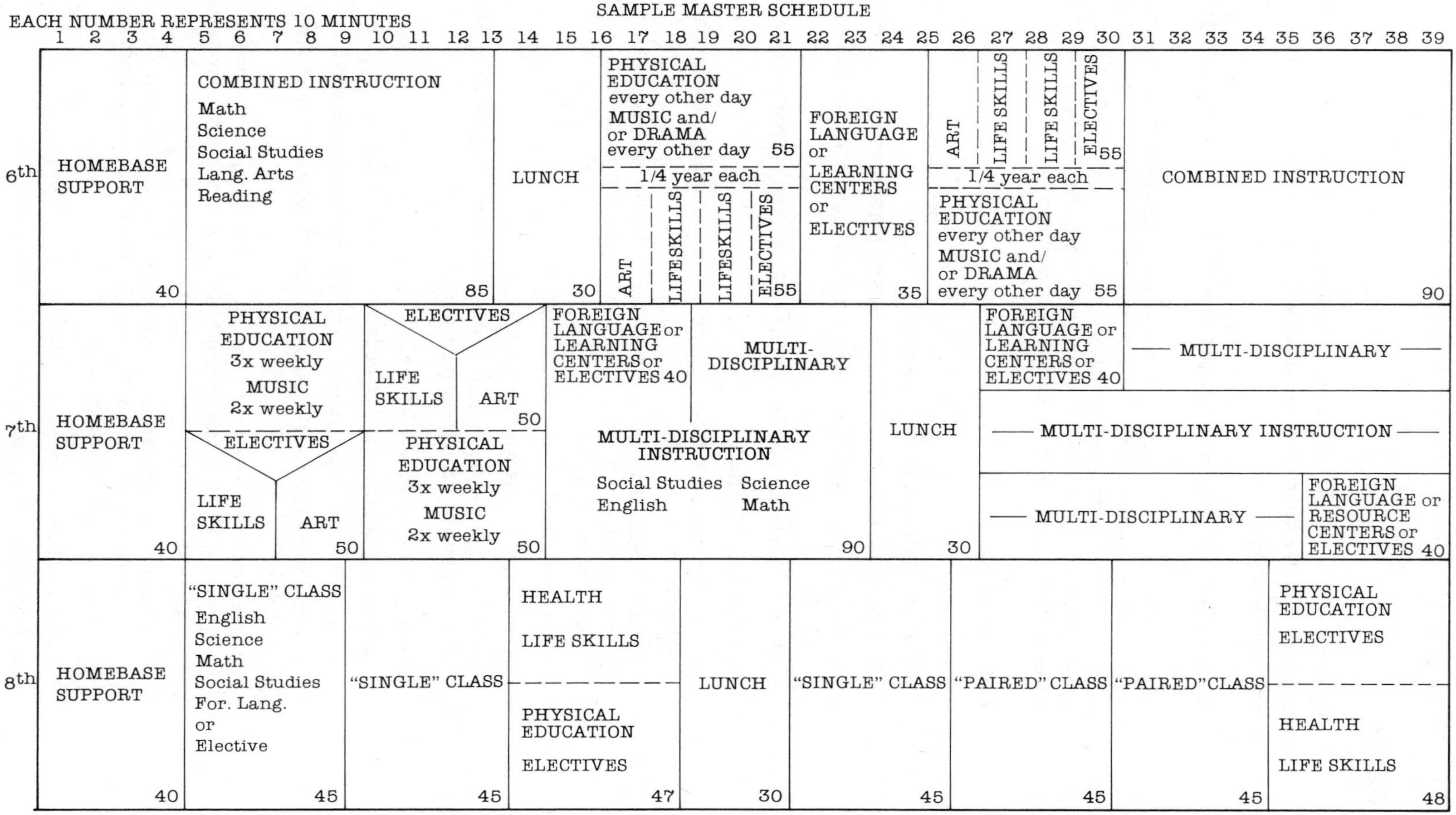

SAMPLE MASTER SCHEDULE

EACH NUMBER REPRESENTS 10 MINUTES

Staffing

Along with organizational design and scheduling, the middle school must staff its program with teachers and other specialists. Below, the reader will find an example of one staffing design.

Sample 5.5—A Possible Model for Staffing a Middle School

Any middle school's staffing is determined by the objectives of the specific school and the restrictions imposed by the local district. For these reasons, there can be no model staffing pattern for all middle schools. In Broward County, Florida, a recommended staffing for middle schools (based on an enrollment of 1,260) was developed. It is outlined below.

Administration... 4

    1 Principal

        a. Curriculum leader of the school

        b. Responsible for staff recruitment and placement

        c. Integrates the school's program with the larger efforts of the overall program

        d. Responsible for the development of the total school program

    1 Curriculum Assistant

        a. Coordinates all the instructional areas to ensure the teaching of basic learning skills

        b. Works with teachers in the places where teaching and learning occur, with emphasis on the instructional and curriculum aspects of the program

        c. Coordinates the work of the master teachers

        d. Assists in student control and discipline

        e. Training, experience, and interest must be in curriculum development, implementation, and evaluation

    1 Student Personnel Administrator

        a. Direct responsibility for welfare of the students

        b. Deals mainly with student problems and student control

        c. Directs the activities of Guidance, Health Education, and attendance assistant

        d. Maintains contact with parents, and coordinates special services provided by the local school board, State, and local governmental agencies

        e. Training, experience, and interest should be in guidance since preventive measures for discipline control will be emphasized, as well as corrective measures

    1 Administrative Assistant in Business

        a. Supervises total school plant maintenance

        b. Serves as central purchasing agent for the school

Sample 5.5—*continued*

    c. Supervises the budget and internal accounts

    d. Further duties involve the transportation system, cafeteria, and operation of the main office

    e. Training, experience, and interest should be in business and school management

Teaching Teams—Basic Skills and General Studies Program.......... 40

    a. Eight teacher teams of 5 members each

    b. The Basic Skills and General Studies Program has as its focal point the development and repair of the basic skills

    c. Team members in the Basic Skills and General Studies Program are responsible for the teaching of:

Language Arts	Reading
Science	Writing
Social Studies	Spelling
Math	Listening
Special Education	

Teaching Teams—Related Program 20

    a. Areas and distribution of teachers in the Related Program:

        2—Basic education for students who experience difficulty and who do not function in a normal classroom situation

        2—Home Economics ⎫

        3—Industrial Arts ⎬   Unified Arts

        2—Art   ⎭

        8—Physical Education

        2—Music

        1—Business Education

    b. The Related Program identifies and utilizes the skills in each area in order to support, magnify, and motivate the individual's progress.

    c. These will be fused with the skills of the Basic Skills Program as an outgrowth of that program by student-motivated undertakings, or by specific assignment of the team.

Reading Clinician 1

    a. Operates learning skills lab

Media Specialists... 3

  2 Librarians

  1 Audio/Visual Specialist

Guidance... 4

  1 Director

  3 Counselors (one trained in testing)

Sample 5.5—*continued*

Master Teachers 2

1 Reading

   a. Responsible for the overall reading program

   b. Ensures implementation of county reading plans

   c. Provides in-service training of all general studies teachers to ensure developmental reading of all children

   d. Correlates the service of the reading clinic to provide maximum remedial reading for those children needing it.

1 Student Activities

   a. Organizes and directs student activity program for entire student body.

   b. Training, experience, and interest must be in the growth and development of the "tween-ager" and an awareness of the activities he likes and needs

Paraprofessionals 12

1 Attendance Assistant

   a. Skilled in case work and family problems

   b. Acts as liaison between the school and other social agencies, enlisting their help in behalf of the student

   c. Concentrates on those outside problems of children which interfere with their learning

1 Health Educator

   a. Provides for the physical well-being of the pupils to minimize problems of school attendance and to help children obtain the health care needed

   b. Provides for services such as:

     Health examinations
     Dental Examinations
     Health Observation and screening
     Health inspection

   c. Serves as resource person in the instruction of health education

10 Aides

   8—General Studies

   2—Related Arts

Secretarial and Clerical 8

5 Administrative secretaries

1 IBM secretary

2 Library Clerks

Source: Broward County Schools, Florida, 1979. Used with permission.

SUMMARY

A flexible organization facilitates the instructional program of the middle school. Middle schools have used a number of organizational patterns to break the lock-step organizational pattern found in many traditional school programs. Some of those flexible patterns include:

Flexible modular scheduling

Team teaching

Nongrading

Interdisciplinary teaming is a major instructional approach in the middle school. The obvious advantages of interrelating subject matter, reinforcing skills from discipline to discipline, and providing affective activities make interdisciplinary teaming attractive to most middle school teachers.

Grouping in the middle school involves many patterns from large group to one-to-one instruction. Homogeneous grouping should be for skill development and special projects only. Students in skill groups should be able to move from group to group as they master skills. Interdisciplinary team groups should be organized as heterogeneous groups.

Organizational patterns, schedules, and staff usage of selected middle schools illustrate the many creative ways time, space, and teacher time have been structured to provide diverse experiences for the diverse group of students in the middle school. It is hoped that the reader will benefit from the many practical examples of school plans presented in this chapter.

Suggested Learning Activities

1. Prepare an organizational plan for your school that would include block scheduling and team teaching.

2. Discuss the advantages and disadvantages of team teaching in the middle school.

3. Prepare a talk to a parent group about flexible scheduling in the middle school.

4. Interdisciplinary instruction has been proposed for your school. What are the subject areas you would include in interdisciplinary teams and why?

5. What is the role of fine arts and practical arts teachers in interdisciplinary instruction? Suggest ways they could work with other academic teams in preparing an Interdisciplinary Unit of Instruction.

Selected References

Bondi, Joseph. *Developing Middle Schools: A Guidebook.* Wheeling, Ill.: Whitehall Publishing Co., 1972.

Eichhorn, Donald. *The Middle School.* New York: The Center for Applied Research in Education, 1966.

Howard, Alvin. *Teaching in Middle Schools.* Scranton, Pa.: International Textbook Co., 1968.

McCarthy, Robert, and Goldman, Samuel. *How to Organize and Operate an Upgraded Middle School.* Englewood Cliffs, N.J.: Prentice-Hall, Inc., 1967.

Moss, Theodore. *Middle School.* New York: Houghton Mifflin Co., 1969.

Stoumbis, George, and Howard, A. W. *Schools for the Middle Years: Readings.* Scranton, Pa.: International Textbook Co., 1969.

Stradley, William. *A Practical Guide to the Middle School.* New York: The Center for Applied Research in Education, 1971.

6

Instructional Leadership in the Middle School

Instructional leadership in the Essential
Middle School is everyone's business

INTRODUCTION

Instructional leadership is a vital link in the middle school and cannot be delegated to others by the principal. We believe the principal is the key instructional leader of the school and he or she must possess the skills necessary to insure that the instructional program is tailored to the diverse needs of emerging adolescent learners (see Figure 6.1 for Instructional Leadership Skills of Principals). The principal is assisted in the instructional leadership process by Assistant Principals, Curriculum Directors, Instructional Associates, Team Leaders, Department Chairpersons, and Classroom Teachers. Together, this group functions as the instructional leadership team in the essential middle school. Under the direction of the principal, the instructional leadership team is responsible for developing, implementing, and evaluating the instructional program; articulating the program within the school and among middle schools; and articulating the instructional program with the elementary and high school. In order to plan an effective instructional program, the instructional leadership team in a middle school must understand patterns of instruction, know how to organize learning experiences, and be able to develop new designs for learning.

THE TEACHER AS AN INSTRUCTIONAL LEADER

It is increasingly evident that instructional leadership is essential to middle school development. Philosophies, goal statements, administrative arrangements, and fiscal support can only facilitate middle school development. Without the creative spark of dynamic classroom teaching, the middle school curriculum will assume the same dull and insipid routine of standard intermediate programs. The essential question in working for a quality middle school is, then, how does one encourage teacher involvement and participation in program development?

The common responses to this inquiry are both predictable and discouraging. A

Figure 6.1
The Principal As an Instructional Leader

To be an effective instructional leader, the principal must—

1. Understand the nature of the transescent learner.
2. Be knowledgeable of new instructional programs in the various disciplines.
3. Understand and be able to develop organizational structures in his or her school such as teaming, interdisciplinary instruction, block scheduling, activity periods, and flexible time arrangements.
4. Be creative, dynamic, and able to communicate well with students, teachers, and parents.
5. Be able to bring in resources to support the instructional program, such as speakers, consultants, district instructional leaders, and materials.
6. Be able to orchestrate the various resources, both human and material, within a school to support the teaching staff and articulate the instructional program within the school.
7. Possess group leadership skills to work with teams and support personnel such as instructional aides, parents, and parent groups such as PTAs and booster groups.
8. Be active in the community and able to tap the community for resource help for the instructional program.
9. Be able to interpret the program to parents, other principals, instructional leaders in the district, and school board members.
10. See the middle school not as an isolated program, but part of the total K–12 curriculum of the school district.
11. Work closely with elementary and senior high school instructional leaders to articulate the total instructional program of the district.
12. Want to get in the classroom and teach at every opportunity.
13. Understand various patterns of instruction and develop new designs for learning.
14. Be able to organize a warm and existing learning environment.
15. Understand thoroughly the teaching/learning process.

few school leaders question the need to involve classroom teachers to a substantial degree in program design, and then proceed to erect administrative sand castles. Other administrators act as if teachers can easily be found who will make the middle school work. Armed with lists of characteristics, they search through the existing staff looking for "profiles." Some school leaders do recognize the need for promoting instructional leadership but encourage staff development without considering why a teacher may or may not respond. In the end, it is assumed that such instructional leadership will "emerge" naturally.

There are some important questions about instructional leadership in middle schools which must be answered before staff development efforts can achieve effectiveness. First, we must know more about who the most likely candidates for leadership are among teachers. We need to know how to encourage those teachers to come forward. We need to be clear on the kinds of teacher involvement which is possible in middle schools. Finally, we need to have some expectations for such involvement. The following thoughts about these topics may prove useful in encouraging instructional leadership in the middle school.

Who Are We Looking For?

Experience over the past decade in middle schools has shown that all kinds of teachers are potential instructional leaders. Age, sex, race, and other social variables appear democratic in their distribution. However, a common denominator among most of those teachers who become influentials in middle schools seems to be their pattern of professional development. Most often, the "take-charge" teachers are those in need of challenge and increased responsibility.

In a major study of teacher professional development, it was found that classroom teachers go through a regular and predictable sequence of development.[1] The first year of teaching, for instance, is an adjustment period where the teacher becomes familiar with routine and environment. The second, third, and fourth years of teaching are devoted to perfecting delivery technique and experimenting with instructional style. Somewhere between the fourth and eighth years, teachers reach a plateau and teaching becomes dominated by routine. At this point, according to the Stinnert study, teachers must find a new challenge or look outside of teaching for personal stimulation. Middle schools must capitalize on this need for professional challenge by identifying and engaging those experienced teachers who are ready for increased responsibility and challenge.

Several signs are helpful in identifying the teacher searching for professional fulfillment. Generally, these teachers have experimented with new techniques in their classrooms over the past several years. They often appear as high-energy individuals whose personal lives may be fulfilled by experiencing activities like art classes or yoga. Many times they have become slightly argumentative in meetings in an attempt to vent their personal frustration. A very important indicator is that they have not yet dichotomized their "school lives" from their "other lives," and that there is still a flow back and forth between these interest areas.

---

[1] T. M. Stinnert, *The Teacher Dropout* (Itasca, Ill.: Peacock Publishers, 1970), pp. 1–80.

How Do We Encourage Teacher Instructional Leadership?

During this century social science research has shown considerable interest in the question, "What motivates individuals to participate in organizations?" A number of recent studies support the idea that people expend their individual energy in situations where they feel their needs will be met. In short, if environments or tasks are perceived as unrewarding or unfulfilling, people will not self-select to be active participants. In searching for teacher involvement in middle schools, we must encourage those who can perceive the middle school instructional format as potentially rewarding.

Three major types of motivation needs might be met by the middle school curriculum: the need for achievement, the need for affiliation, and the need for power.[2] The search for personal achievement can be an outgrowth of the creativity called for in curriculum materials development. The need for affiliation or belonging can be met through counseling roles and interpersonal aspects of team teaching. Power or status needs of individuals can often result by task leadership opportunities or team leadership roles.

It seems certain that the key to involvement of those teachers who are desired is to learn of their needs and match those with middle school development tasks. Often, such a "matching" is merely a perceptual phenomenon whereby the teacher sees the middle school as a personal opportunity.

Involvement Necessary for Instructional Leadership

As instructional leadership in the middle school is identified and encouraged, the type of involvement desired must be clear. While the middle school presents an opportunity for teachers of extraordinary caliber to surface, it would be a disservice to promote involvement without sincerity. The degree of involvement and the opportunities should be spelled out concisely.

In truth, it is necessary to decentralize both decision making and participation in order to have a fully functioning middle school. The flexibility of the program in terms of planning resource allocation, instructional delivery, and evaluation calls for on-the-spot operations. Such irregularity, while troublesome from the administrative vantage point, is also the strength of a highly individualized instructional program.

If we encourage teachers to become involved in instructional leadership, we must be willing to alter traditional administrative patterns to accommodate involvement. To the degree that good classroom teachers can assume additional responsibilities commensurate with their needs for personal growth, the middle school program will be energized and move forward. Such involvement is the key to a quality middle school program.

---

[2] For a treatment of how these needs might be satisfied through work in an organization, see George Litwin and Robert Stringer, *Motivation and Organizational Climate* (Boston: Harvard University Press, 1968).

Benefits from Teacher Leadership in Instruction

In addition to a creative instructional program that is designed, implemented, and evaluated by the same individuals, there are at least two major payoffs that can be anticipated when instructional leadership comes from teachers.

First, energized and involved middle school teachers will teach each other. Rather than a pattern of growth symbolized by scheduled interaction with outside consultants, staff development will occur naturally. The growing, experimenting motif of the individual teacher will be multiplied as teachers "grow on" each other. This interaction of talents and skills will lead to a stronger total staff in the school.

Second, it can be anticipated that the behavior of the teachers will rub off on students in the school. Teacher enthusiasm and energy will encourage student growth. A climate of involvement in organizations is self re-enforcing.

Involved teachers are the key to vibrant middle school programs. Certain teachers are more promising candidates for instructional leadership than others, but they must be encouraged to meet the challenge of leadership. Understanding the needs of good classroom teachers and helping them see the middle school as a means of satisfying those professional needs is the beginning point for involvement. A better instructional program and improved human relations can be anticipated from these acts of encouragement.

INSTRUCTIONAL PATTERNS IN THE MIDDLE SCHOOL

Instructional patterns in middle school education are unique due to the unique goals of the middle school. Teaching in the middle school presents a startling contrast to other, more traditional, intermediate programs. Primary differences in the instructional pattern of the middle school comes more from the orientation of instructional activity than from the substance of instruction. The middle school represents a new way of educating preadolescents as well as a new form of education.[3]

Middle Schools	Traditional
Recognize and respond to the uniqueness of each learner	Treat learners in a uniform manner
Involve the student in the learning process as an active partner	Give the teacher all responsibility for the learning process
Provide an instructional balance in the emphasis given different realms of development	Possess an overriding concern with intellectual capacity
Integrate informational/knowledge bases in instruction	Emphasize the distinctiveness of subjects/disciplines

---

[3] Jon Wiles, *Planning Guidelines for Middle School Education* (Dubuque, Iowa: Kendall/Hunt Publishing Co., 1976), pp. 49–69. Used with permission.

Middle Schools	Traditional
Present learning opportunities in many forms through many medias	Present the learning opportunities in standard didactic forms
Emphasize the application of information and skill development	Provide little opportunity to deal with meaning or application
Teach through student interests and needs	Teach according to predetermined organization of information
Define the purpose of instruction in terms of pupil growth	Define the purpose of instruction according to organizational/administrative criteria such as units of credit and graduation requirements
View teachers as guides or facilitators of the learning process	View teachers as subject matter specialists
Utilize support staff as trainers of instructional personnel	View support staff as specialists in narrowly defined roles
Use an exploratory, inquiry, individualized approach to learning and evaluation	Utilize standardized patterns of instruction and evaluation

From the above comparison it can be seen that instruction in the middle schoo represents a new definition of the teaching/learning process. The new instruction roles are drawn from the philosophy and goals of middle school education ar differ from traditional instructional patterns in the following categories:

1. the purpose of the instructional process itself
2. beliefs about the capacities of students in learning
3. roles of teachers and students in the learning process
4. the way knowledge/information is utilized in formal learning
5. the means by which learning experiences are organized
6. the ways in which pupil progress is to be evaluated

THE ORGANIZATION OF LEARNING

In developing learning experiences in the middle school, two major concepts of importance are the ideas of continuous progress and guaranteed progress. While the ideal condition for any given student is continuous growth and development in a number of dimensions of growth, the middle school also must ascertain that all students grow and develop. The middle school represents the last general education the student will experience.

Previous educational programs in the intermediate grades have been content to pursue learner growth on a plane, being concerned more with rate of development than with order of development. While rate of development in students is a legitimate concern, to assume a sequence of learning based on uniform materials is to totally ignore learner growth patterns. In the middle school, it is believed that the learner growth pattern is a more logical organizer for curricular sequence than for materials.

The middle school seeks to build in continuous instructional progress by focusing on learner developmental growth. The essential thought of a continuous progress plan is that learner development is never static, but always ascending to higher levels of complexity. If the instructional program in the middle school is to keep pace with the learner, and serve all students, the learning design must match learner growth. The learning design must allow for individuality, and must be multidimensional to reflect depth of learning as well as rate of learning.

During the past twenty years, educators have been at work developing "taxonomies" of learning. These taxonomies or hierarchies of learning, have sought to communicate that all modes of learning progress from the simple to the complex. This is true whether the learning is of an intellectual, social-emotional, or physical nature. Learning taxonomies are useful in program planning because they allow us to design learning activities for students at a level which corresponds to their development.

An example of developing a continuous progress learning program based on learner growth patterns can be given using two well-known learning taxonomies and sample objectives from the area of academic adequacy.

Below are found two taxonomies of learning. The Cognitive Domain, developed by Bloom, and the Affective Domain, developed by Krathwohl,[4] are attempts to show a rising complexity of learner responses to stimuli. At the lowest level of response, the learner would possess knowledge after having received it. At the highest level of learning, the learner would evaluate the meaning of the knowledge for himself and internalize that knowledge by acting on it. In between these extremes are various stages of dealing with the stimuli either mentally or emotionally.

Bloom's Cognitive Taxonomy	*Krathwohl's Affective Taxonomy*
Evaluation	Internalizing
Synthesis	Organizing
Analysis	Valuing
Application	Responding
Comprehension	Receiving
Knowledge	

As we look at sample objectives of learning in the area of academic adequacy, it is recognized that the objectives are not of equal complexity on these scales.

---

[4] Benjamin Bloom, ed., *Taxonomy of Educational Objectives: Handbook I* (New York: David McKay Co., Inc., 1956).
David Krathwohl et al., *Taxonomy of Educational Objectives: Handbook II* (New York: David McKay Co., Inc., 1964).

Cognitive		*Affective*
To develop the ability to carefully criticize and examine information (cognitive 6—Bloom Scale)		To develop an appreciation for learning that will stimulate independent and continuous learning (affective 5—Krathwohl Scale)
To develop disciplined and logical thought processes (cognitive 5—Bloom Scale)	Depth of the Concern	To promote and develop one's intellectual curiosity (affective 4) and understand the need for it (affective 2—Krathwohl Scale)
To master computational skills (cognitive 3—Bloom Scale)		
To develop a base of information sources (cognitive 1—Bloom Scale)		

Breadth of the Concern

The value of taxonomies and other indices of learning responses to instructional planners in the middle school is in their demonstration of how learning objectives and activities can be inappropriate. Students have a pattern of readiness for learning, a pattern determined by development in the middle grades, and that pattern is a crucial factor in planning learning experiences. Students can't analyze what they don't comprehend. Students can't internalize what they aren't receiving.

For each student in the middle school there is an optimal sequence of learning and an optimal degree of complexity for any activity. Instructional leaders in the middle school must view their curriculum in terms of its increasing complexity and must order the experiences for each student in terms of her development and readiness for that activity. The sequence of the curriculum is focused on the learner, not upon the material.

It is particularly important that instructional planners in the middle school correlate the cognitive and affective dimensions in school. This correlation can be thought of as a diagonal track (see Figure 6.2).

Continuums of learning in the middle grades can be thought of in terms of information, skills, attitudes, and a host of other concerns of program planners. What is crucial for planning purposes, however, is that the program design recognize the range of learners present and make arrangements for the development of learners within that range.

Because of the immense range of development during the preadolescent period, it is believed that no single standard program can adequately serve all learners. A rule of thumb for the range of intellectual development in school has been said to be one year for each year in school. According to this formula, probably conservative, there may be up to an eight-year range of achievement among students in the middle grades. A comparable range probably exists in terms of physical, social, and emotional development.

Obviously, any responsible program for the middle school must acknowledge and provide for such diversity. One possibility to be considered by instructional leaders is the adoption of a minimum-maximum concept of "acceptable progress." The commitment of an educational program with such a perspective is to insure that all students achieve minimal levels of development, while aspiring to assist all learners in achieving their maximum potential development.

The minimum end of the growth continuum recognizes that not all students entering the middle school will be ready to benefit from its programs. This absence of readiness may be a function of readiness, of environment, or poor previous educational experience.

Regardless of the reason, instructional planners in the middle school can expect to meet incoming students who possess identifiable learning problems—those who do not have primary learning skills and/or basal knowledge; those who have inadequate social maturity; those who possess physical defects; and those who have had severely deprived aesthetic experiences. Such students will be excluded, by an absence of readiness, from full participation in the programs of the middle grades.

The minimum growth expectation for such a student during the middle school would be a curricular experience which would foster a readiness to benefit from later educational experiences. Participation in school experiences is a minimal goal. While each school would have to develop its own expectations, a sample of a minimal commitment to all learners might be the following:

1. Learning deficiencies (sight, hearing, emotion) will be corrected, if possible, and learning problems confronted.

2. Primary learning skills (reading, computation) will be mastered, basal knowledge learned, and primary attitudes toward learning developed.

3. Socially acceptable behavior will be encouraged and rewarded, and each learner will be assisted in forming significant relationships with others.

4. Each learner will be given an opportunity to discover his own personal identity, to explore adult roles, and to develop personal interests.

5. Each learner will be given an opportunity to experience sensory discovery and to uncover latent talents.

While these goals may seem modest for a student emerging from a program of education in the middle school they are, in fact, ambitious. Our present intermediate programs house thousands of preadolescents who possess none of these minimal capacities.

The discrimination of many school curriculums is not limited to those students who are academically or socially delayed in their development. We also often fail to accommodate those pupils who are, because of superior educational preparation, maturity, or environment, far advanced in their development. There are students entering the middle school who are literate, healthy, socially mature, talented, and self-confident. The curriculum in the middle school must also make provision for these students.

Figure 6.2

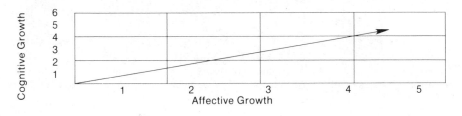

An adequate school program must provide for advanced study opportunities, career exploration, value clarification, talent development, and for the pursuit of individual health-related activity. While each school must assess and develop its own individual commitment to a program of development for learners, sample maximum goals might be these:

1. To allow for advanced study in academic areas of interest, and for the specialization and development of academic talents.

2. To provide opportunities for increasing learner independence and autonomy, and to assist in the exploration of adult roles.

3. To assist learners in the development of skills and interest pursuant to better health.

4. To assist learners in value clarification activities leading to greater self-awareness, career possibilities, and the expansion of interests.

5. To allow for the development and advanced study of aesthetic talents and for the exploration of individual leisure-time activities.

The concept of a minimum and maximum thrust in the middle school curriculum is an attempt to develop learning activities which can benefit all learners. Such a design would span remediation, on the one hand, to expansion of potential on the other.

It would be incorrect for the middle school instructional leader to think of any one student as being completely on either end of such a continuum. Growth and development patterns in this age group are simply too unpredictable for that. It is probable, rather, that an individual student would present a mixed profile of development for any planning of classroom experience. The individual student may be concerned with minimal achievement in one dimension of development and with maximum achievement in another. A hypothetical profile of student growth might resemble the graph in Figure 6.3.

Figure 6.3
Hypothetical Profile of Student Growth

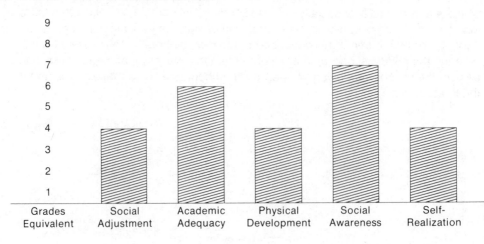

LEARNING DESIGNS

In addition to providing a multidimensional instructional program which will serve all learners in attendance, middle school instructional leaders must develop new designs for learning which will tie the school to the needs of the individual student. Traditional learning designs will not serve the middle school adequately.

In schools throughout the United States, fairly standard learning designs can be found at the classroom level. While many such designs are not the result of conscious planning by teachers, they often are the product of established philosophical positions regarding the purpose of education.

Three exceptionally well-known designs often found in the middle grades are knowledge-based designs. That is, they gain their rationale or order from the assumption that education exists to transmit knowledge. While these designs have been given many names, we can refer to them by their design as "building blocks," "branching," and "spiral" curriculums.

The building blocks design takes a clearly defined body of knowledge and orders it into a pyramidlike arrangement. Students are taught foundational material which leads to more complex and specialized knowledge. Deviations from this prescribed course are not allowed because the end-product of the learning design is known in advance. Equally, activities which do not contribute directly to this directed path are not allowed due to the "efficiency" of the model. Such designs represent the most traditional knowledge-based design.

Another very common learning design found in schools is the branching design. Branching is a variation of the building blocks design but incorporates limited choice in terms of what is to be learned. This plan, too, recognizes the value of foundational material that must be mastered by all but allows choice within prescribed areas beyond that common experience. Like the building-blocks design, branching prescribes the eventual outcomes of the learning experience, although the prescription is multiple rather than uniform. In terms of classroom activities, this design allows for some variation, but again within tightly defined boundaries of acceptance.

Figure 6.4

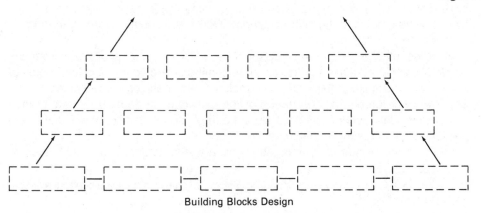

Building Blocks Design

Figure 6.5

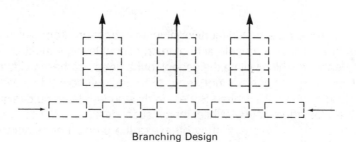

Branching Design

A third common knowledge-based design found in schools is the "spiral" configuration.[5] According to this design, learning in specified areas is continually revisited at higher and higher levels of complexity. While the "tightness" of this design is more difficult to observe, it controls what is taught, and even predetermines the timing of the delivery to the student. Classroom activity is, of course, developed to fit the topics being "uncovered."

Figure 6.6

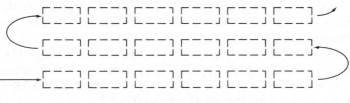

Spiral Design

In visiting a classroom in the middle grades, an observer might see any of the three described designs in operation. In the building blocks design, all students would be experiencing nearly the same program of learning, at the same time, with the same outcome expectations, and with few, if any, distracting extracurricular learning activities. In the branching classroom, students might be grouped according to academic destination and engaged in different activities within the room. The activities, nonetheless, would be predetermined and directed toward future learning experiences. In the spiral classroom, learning would appear like the building blocks design, but would use increasingly diverse and sophisticated "methods" to achieve the planned outcome.

All three of these common intermediate learning designs operate from the assumption that education is the act of becoming schooled in specified bodies of knowledge. Because of this basic assumption, these designs are restricted in their ability to gear learning to the needs of the individual student. They cannot individualize the instructional process because they cannot significantly deviate from predetermined learning expectations.

The knowledge-based learning designs are characterized by set bodies of

---

[5] Robert Gagné. *The Conditions of Learning,* 2nd Ed. (New York: Holt, Rinehart, Winston, Inc., 1970).

knowledge to be mastered, universal experiences for students, standardized learning environments, and tightly defined learning outcome expectations. They do not exist to serve the learner, but rather to serve tradition and the hierarchy of knowledge-based learning.

Throughout this book, the assumption has been made that the curriculum for the middle school should be designed to serve the learner experiencing the program. Because of this assumption, we have looked at philosophic possibilities, ways of assessing common needs of learners, theories of learning which are individual-ized, and arrangements that schools can make at the building level to prepare for such a personalized approach to learning. If we are to develop a program of education that is significant for students in the middle school, we must abandon the knowledge-based designs and refocus our perspective of the learning experience.

The Process-Pattern Design

An alternative design to those traditional knowledge-based designs is what will be called the "process-pattern" learning design. The process-pattern design is, as the name implies, a design which seeks to define education as a process, and school as a medium for learning. *It is a design which attempts to focus learning on each student and her experience, rather than on a predetermined body of information.* It is a design concerned with "how" learning occurs more than "what" knowledge is mastered. As such, the process-pattern design seeks to redefine the purpose of schooling in a philosophical sense by making education serve the learner as an individual.

The essential concept underlying the process-pattern instructional program is that, in terms of ultimate objectives, the purpose of education is to enable each learner to understand herself, to become whatever she is capable of as an individual, and to find ways to allow those capacities and talents to serve society as a whole. Schools, as institutions of society, are mediums for that process.

It is believed that the process of becoming educated, by this definition, must be an individual phenomenon. *To design a learning environment relevant to all students we must have a highly individualized environment, characterized by flexibility and open-ended outcomes.* In terms of design, the process-pattern curriculum seeks to set up learning opportunities, to guide the "delivery" or medium of learning, and to emphasize the meaning of the experience.

In schemata form, the process-pattern design is a series of repeating arrange-ments designed to teach skills, foundational concepts, and meet needs of indi-vidual learners.

Figure 6.7

Process-Pattern Design

The process-pattern design can use data about the learners, such as knowledge of the developmental tasks of preadolescents, to focus learning activity. Such student concerns and needs are linked to school-identified learning skills and processes by carefully designed thematic units.

Figure 6.8

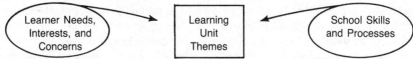

Of course, thematic learning is nothing new. It can be found in many intermediate schools across the country. *What is different about the process-pattern curriculum in the middle school, however, is the rationale for the design.* The thematic approach is used to bring the learning activity closer to the student so that learning may be personalized and, therefore, meaningful to the individual.

Thematic learning which is knowledge-based is generally wasteful in terms of time and resources. If the essential knowledge can be clearly identified, then the efficiency of mastery becomes the only variable in the process of learning design. Many "teaching teams" formed in the middle grades along subject matter lines have made this painful discovery. In the middle school process-pattern design, however, there is no such concern with efficiency; the concern is only with the effectiveness of the design in promoting individual growth, development, and skill acquisition in predetermined ways.

The familiar knowledge bases do, of course, play a role in the process-pattern curriculum of the middle school. These subject disciplines are time-tested ways of ordering perspectives of the surrounding world. The use of these informational frameworks, however, is incidental rather than predetermined. Subjects in the middle school program are perceived as a means rather than an end of learning. As such, they simply represent one more factor to be incorporated into the learning design in the classroom.

It is important to remember that the planning of classroom learning in the middle school should be an extension of previous planning. The middle school philosophy suggests a student-focused learning plan. The arrangements of environmental variables build in planning flexibility. Finally, a classroom level plan is developed which will enable teachers to work with students in many desired ways.

Constructing Process-Pattern Units

The process-pattern unit is similar to units taught in intermediate schools each day except that the primary organizers of the unit are based upon the developmental needs of students and recurrent academic processes rather than on predetermined subject matter.

In the process-pattern design, teachers in the classroom construct units of learning activity by manipulating a number of ever-present variables. Included among these are things known about learner needs and interests, skills and processes identified by the school as essential during this period, and manipulative instructional factors which make up the medium of delivery in the classroom.

Earlier in this book, we presented the needs and interests of the preadolescent under the generic title of "developmental tasks." We found that all students of this age have similar concerns related to "growing up." Among the concerns of late childhood and preadolescence are these:

Late Childhood	**Preadolescence**
Mastering communication skills	Handling major body changes
Building meaningful peer relations	Asserting independence from family
Thinking independently	Establishing sex role identity
Acceptance of self	Dealing with peer group relations
Finding constructive expression outlets	Controlling emotions
Role projection	Construction of a values-foundation
	Pursuing interest expression
	Utilizing new reasoning capacity
	Developing acceptable self-concept

These developmental needs and interests of students in the middle grades were grouped into five broad categories: physical development, academic adequacy, aesthetic expression, social awareness, and self-realization. From these categories, points of intersection by the school can be identified. The instructional program of the middle grades should use the following concerns as organizers for activity:

Physical Development

Promotion of physical and mental health

Physical conditioning and coordination

An understanding of hygiene

An understanding of sexual functioning

An understanding of nutrition

Academic Adequacy

Developing basic literacy

Developing skills for continued learning

An introduction of primary knowledge areas

Development of learning autonomy

Refinement of critical thinking

An exploration of career potential

Aesthetic Expression

Stimulation of aesthetic interests

Development of latent artistic talents

Promotion of aesthetic appreciation

Development of leisure activities

Social Awareness

Refinement of social skills

Acceptance of responsibility

Understanding the interdependence of individuals

An exploration of social values

Promotion of human understandings and relations

Developing interpersonal communication skills

Self-realization

Promoting self-understanding and self-acceptance

Identifying and accentuating personal strengths

Exploration of individual values

Expansion of personal interests

As teachers plan classroom learning activities, these student needs and interests serve as "connectors" or "intersectors" into the lives of the learner. They suggest themes or interests which allow communication with the preadolescent.

Another category of variables essential in planning the learning design in the middle school are those skills and processes that teachers feel must be mastered at this level of schooling. While this category of planning variables is totally dependent upon local educational conditions and expectations, the identification of these items can be best achieved by viewing the educational system as a continuum. By the time the student has reached the middle school what skills does he possess? What skills are essential, and what skills are desired? Beyond the middle school, what skills and processes must the student possess to benefit fully from learning opportunity? Which of these skills and processes are essential and which are desired?

An example of the kinds of skills and processes a teacher might deal with in the middle grades can be extracted from the language arts. Five major skill areas might be reading, speaking, writing, spelling, and listening. These areas might be made up of the following specific skills:

Reading

Developmental—
word analysis
comprehension
structural analysis
phonetic analysis

Functional—
locating information
organizing information
interpreting information
evaluating information

Spelling

Familiarity

Utilization/application

Speaking

Informal

Dramatization

Story-telling

Reporting

Writing

Creative writing

Note-taking

Outlining

Letter-writing

Listening

Appreciation and enjoyment

Critical and evaluative

Application

As teachers or groups of teachers seek to identify and order those skills and processes which they believe need to be encountered and mastered in the middle grades, it is helpful to think initially of them as *isolates* rather than as skills needed for particular experiences in the future. Perceiving the skills in isolation will assist the teacher in planning units in the middle school which are not directed by the specific programs of the high school.

Finally, the teacher engaged in planning units for a process-pattern curriculum must choose among a host of manipulative instructional variables possible in the classroom. Decisions as to which arrangement to employ in a given unit should be made on the basis of the unit's composition. Some of these choices are found in Table 6.1.

Table 6.1

Length of unit

daily

weekly

monthly

quarterly

Unit Location

classroom

learning resource center

school grounds

immediate community

beyond community

Unit Interaction Pattern

LRC research/individual exploration*

question/answer inquiry

group question

team problem-solving

creative projection

Unit Student Evaluation

standardized test/measures

teacher made tests/measures

student "sample work" folders

narrative diaries

student-teacher contract

progress conferences—project products

criterion-referenced demonstrations

*LRC stands for Learning Resource Center.

Unit objective

exposure

familiarity

mastery

analysis

application

Unit Grouping Patterns

individual study

paired study

team study (three to six students)

small group study (seven to twenty students)

large group study (over twenty students)

Unit Medium of Delivery

lecture

individual reading

programmed materials

film, videotape, audio cassette

debate/theatrics

outside speaker

field trip/visitation

simulation

As teachers or teams of teachers ponder these choices and place emphasis in any given unit, a pattern emerges which is unique in composition but uniform in underlying processes. While the format of units avoids monotony, the essence of the learning experience is regular.

According to the schedule and administrative order of the school district, the teacher-planner should arrive at a number of units to be developed for the coming school year. Somewhere between four and nine units is probably a workable number for the middle grades.

The task for the curriculum planners is to weave a design, a multidimensional organizational structure, which is made up of a variety of learning activities, learning approaches, learning skills, learning levels, learning objectives, etc., which will facilitate classroom interaction. It is important, given the need to have a balance among the many expectations of the teacher and the needs of the students, to see that greater emphasis is given to certain areas in different units. One unit, for instance, might be focused on the development of learning skills, be dominated by a mastery orientation, and take place primarily in conventional learning areas. Another unit might be more concerned with the development of individual values and perceptions and could occur outside of the traditional learning spaces.

The essential concept, in planning the year as a whole, is to build in diversity and balance in the design. All of those areas deemed important by the planner should be given sufficient attention sometime during the year. The program in the middle grades should be comprehensive.

In developing units, it will be necessary to identify unifying themes which will give an overall cohesion to the varied activities of the unit. Possibilities for such themes are everywhere. Thinking of the transescent student and observing interaction patterns among students will assist the teacher in identifying the best themes for a particular classroom. Examples are:

advertising	nostalgia
effects of technology	communication
pollution	the future
transportation	comedy

From such a list, and there are extensive possibilities which reflect the varied interests of the preadolescent, the planner selects a manageable number of themes for the coming school year. In the sample calendar shown, five units are conducted during the year using five general themes:

Sept	Oct	Nov	Dec	Jan	Feb	Mar	Apr	May	June
Technology									
		Advertising							
				Pollution					
						Nostalgia			
								The Future	

Once the major themes for the year have been decided upon, the planner begins to construct a learning experience which will achieve both educational objectives and match the needs of the learners. From each major list of variables, the planner seeks key ingredients:

Technology Unit

Developing skills for continued learning

Refinement of critical thinking

An exploration of career potential

Utilization of library resources

Creative writing

Notetaking

Spelling-familiarity

Analysis of data

Hypothesizing

Synthesizing of information

Charting and graphing

Eight-week Unit

Familiarity, analysis, application

Classroom, learning resource center, community

Individual and small group study

Individual reading, simulation, field trips

Inquiry technique, problem-solving

Contracts and project products

Student Needs

Skills & Processes

Instruction

Following the selection of the key ingredients for the unit, the planner then begins to construct the learning activities which will produce the desired outcomes. For each unit there should be a general plan, and then unifying activities which tie all classroom activity together. The following is an example of a technology general plan.

Technology General Plan

For this unit the students will become a community of people during a period of great technological change (mechanization of America 1800–1840), and will assume an occupation or trade which is representative of the period.

Unifying Activity Week I:

All students will investigate life during this period of our national history by attempting to identify an occupation which existed during the era. Attention can be directed to the task of identifying those jobs extending from a previous era, those jobs originating during the era of study due to technological change, and those occupations existing today which date from this period.

Subactivity:

Reading of biographies for overview of period

Limited historical research of period

Writing short descriptive essays about occupations of age

Build list of unusual words discovered in research

Identify occupational counterparts in community

Gather comparative statistical data on era under study

Unifying Activity Week II:

During the second week, each student will participate in the production of a product or the offering of a service which exemplifies a trade of the period of study. The student may wish to choose an early form of the occupation now held by a parent. Occupational activities may be of three kinds: the realistic production of a commodity, the construction of simulated models, or theoretical treatments of technological questions (example: Why was transportation during this era limited to foot, horse, and sail?).

Subactivity:

Discussion about the interrelatedness of work

Students become "reporters" and interview workers about jobs

Field trips to industry altered by technology

Scheduling parents as guest speakers about interesting jobs

Conduct "efficiency studies" of workers

Introduce an assembly line in class—make analysis

Charting and graphing of classroom-generated data

Introduce the computer as a tool of man

Unifying Activity Week III:

During the third week, students will be asked to draw conclusions about life during this age of change and the effects of technology on their own occupational specialty. The objective of the week will be to develop a set of hypotheses (statements) which each student will individually formulate about work and the effects of technology. These hypotheses will assist the student in clarifying his values and feelings about work. Three major relationships are to be emphasized: the effect of technology on work itself, the ways technological developments can affect community development, and the effects of technological change on the worker.

Subactivity:

Set-up assembly line manufacturing, dealing with issues of quality control, over-staffing, strikes within sections, monotony, efficiency, advantages, disadvantages

Develop a list of "vanishing" jobs in America

Ask students to develop a "scale of trade" among their jobs based on analysis of the merits of their work.

Unifying Activity Week IV:

During this week, students will explore the effects of technological life on a worker. Students will look at such things as specialization in work, degrees of education required, independence versus dependence on-the-job, decision-making autonomy, etc. The objective of the week will be to arouse student thinking about the nature of work, its complexity, its moral implications, and the student's personal preferences toward work.

It may be that during this week the teacher will want to introduce some value-clarification material in order to challenge students to personalize their observations. For example:

George Sterns is a master electrician working in Chicago for Local Union 1440. The union has assigned George to work on a two-year project constructing a high-rise apartment on Michigan Avenue.

George has always loved electricity. In high school, he actually constructed a miniature relay station unassisted. After graduation, he became an apprentice electrician and seventeen months later an electrician journeyman. Later, George Sterns was awarded the title of Master Electrician after much study. His wife and family are proud of him.

When George reported to the apartment project, the union representative met him at the gate and walked him to his work station. Located at this site were two small generators run by gasoline engines about the size of a lawn mower's. George was puzzled about what he was supposed to do at the site.

The foreman soon came along to explain the job to George. His sole responsibility, the foreman said, was to start the two small engines and be sure they remained running all day. There must be a mistake, George thought. Why pay a man $15.80 per hour to handle a job a child could do?

Later that afternoon, George stopped the union representative to ask him about the assigned work. The representative, surprised at George's attitude, replied that the position was written into the contract months ago. What's more, he added, an operating engineer and a pipefitter would join George tomorrow at the station.

Seeing that George was still uneasy, the representative smiled and, nudging George, said, "Take it easy, Sterns, the union is looking out for you. After all, where else can you get $15.80 for this kind of work?"

Question:

What do you think is bothering George Sterns?
How would you have felt if this had happened to you?
Is there anything George can do about the job?

Subactivity:

Ask students to interview their parents about their own jobs.

Try to develop categories of things which separate jobs.

Develop a vocabulary list of words relating to work.

The sample unit could be expanded or contracted in its scope to fit the pattern of the school. It is important to note that in the unit, traditional learning skills such as note-taking, graphing, hypothesizing, spelling, and so forth are all taught through the medium of participatory activity. The interest of the student provides the motivational force for more traditional intellectual exercise. Learning ceases to be an artificial product, but rather becomes a process strongly related to the real world.

It can also be noted that in this sample unit on the theme of technology, activities progress through a hierarchy from the simple to the complex. First-week activities were concerned with reading, word building, and gathering simple data, while the last week was concerned with the synthesis, analysis, and applications of learning.

As the teacher-planner looks at a number of thematic units during the school year, balance among objectives is important. A unit-objectives grid can assist in assuring such balance (see Figure 6.9).

Figure 6.9
Unit Objectives Grid

	Unit I	Unit II	Unit III	Unit IV	Unit V	Unit VI	Unit VII
Student Needs							
1	X		X			X	
2		X		X			X
3	X			X	X		
Skills and Processes							
1		X	X			X	
2	X	X		X	X		
3				X		X	X
Instructional Arrangements							
1	X		X		X		
2		X		X			X
3					X	X	

Teachers constructing such units work through a dozen simple steps that become routine with practice:

1. Themes are identified from student interest inventories.

2. Themes are crossed with existing traditional subject areas.

3. Broad goals for the unit are developed.

4. These goals are assessed in terms of general school objectives.

5. Activities for the unit are brainstormed by students and teachers.

6. Activities fitting school objectives and unit goals are selected.

7. Activities are matched with planning variables such as group size.

8. Overall teaching strategies for activities (inquiry approach) are chosen.

9. Activity "outcomes" are projected by teachers and students.

10. Materials and other resources are gathered for activities in unit.

11. Individual learning responsibilities are assigned for activities.

12. Activities are ordered and scheduled. Unit commences.

In summary, the process-pattern design represents a curricular arrangement allowing for flexibility and creativity in teacher planning. Because the design focuses on interaction and on processes rather than on products of learning, it can individualize the instructional process. The process-pattern can incorporate the needs, interests, and tasks of preadolescent development. It is a complex educational design fitted to the learner. It is philosophically aligned with the goals of education in the middle grades.

Instructional Delivery

The process-pattern unit will not be effective as a learning medium until both teachers and students recognize that they each have new roles and responsibilities in the learning process. Instructional leaders can begin to build this awareness and understanding by doing the following:

1. Recognize the crucial role of the affective dimension in learning.

2. Begin learning activities in areas familiar to the learner.

3. Place instructional emphasis on learning patterns which will have academic application at a later time.

4. Actively stimulate intellectual growth through varied experience.

5. Accept many kinds of intelligence, especially creative thought.

6. Recognize the social quality of school motivation and utilize self and peer interests to school ends.

7. Tap ever-present sources of motivation by knowing the needs and interests of individuals.

8. Accept many language patterns, recognizing their cultural emphasis.

9. Place emphasis on "how" to communicate and allow teachers to be seen as people.

10. Realize that groups can aid in the social-emotional growth of students.

11. Realize that values are not easily taught but that value formation is promoted by exposing value alternatives.

12. Understand the importance of out-of-school activity on classroom learning.

13. Acknowledge the power of peer influence and plan accordingly.

14. Capitalize on the potential of media as alternative sources of learning.

SUMMARY

Instructional leadership is essential in the middle school if it is to accomplish its goals. The key instructional leader in the middle school is the principal, and he or she must be able to design an instructional program that will accommodate the diverse group of students found in the middle grades.

The principal is assisted in planning an instructional program by an instructional leadership team consisting of all of the persons in a school charged with carrying out the instructional program. The instructional leadership team is responsible for developing, implementing, and evaluating the instructional plan of a middle school.

Instruction in the middle school seeks to set up learning opportunities, guide the delivery of instruction in meaningful ways, and place emphasis on the meaning of learning experiences. Developmental needs of learners and recurrent academic processes serve as primary organizers for learning. Taxonomies of learning and a minimum-maximum orientation can assist in providing depth and breadth to instructional planning.

Process-pattern learning units should be developed by teachers by weaving an interaction design from student needs, academic processes, instructional variables, and knowledge bases. Since the focus of instruction is on student growth, outcomes for such units are largely open-ended.

Teachers in the middle school must come to perceive the teaching-learning process in different ways if the middle school program is to succeed. Instructional leadership is the key to achieving that goal.

Suggested Learning Activities

1. Develop a position paper on the role of the principal as the key instructional leader in the middle school.

2. Discuss the three learning designs discussed in this chapter.

3. Outline the role of each member of the instructional leadership team in the middle school.

4. Prepare a presentation for your school board on the need for a continuous progress learning program based on learner growth patterns.

5. Design a unit of instruction based on the process-pattern discussed in this chapter.

Selected References

Curtis, Thomas, and Bidwell, Wilma. *Curriculum and Instruction for Emerging Adolescents.* Reading, Mass.: Addison-Wesley Publishing Co., 1977.

Bloom, Benjamin S. *Handbook I: Cognitive Domain.* New York: David McKay Co., 1956.

Howard, Alvin, and Stoumbis, George. *The Junior High and Middle School: Issues and Practices.* Scranton, Pa.: Intext Educational Publishers, 1970.

Howell, Bruce. "Learning Strategies in the Middle School," working paper. Tulsa, Okla.: Tulsa Public Schools, 1974.

Krathwohl, David R. *Handbook II: Affective Domain.* New York: David McKay Co., 1964.

Lounsbury, John, and Vars, Gordon. *A Curriculum for the Middle Years.* New York: Harper and Row, Publishers, 1978.

Riegle, J. "Motivating, Organizing, and Conducting Exploratory Activities." *Dissemination Services on the Middle Grades,* 6 (March 1974).

Stradley, William. *A Practical Guide to the Middle School.* New York: The Center for Applied Research in Education, 1971.

Wiles, Jon. *Planning Guidelines for Middle School Education.* Dubuque, Iowa: Kendall/ Hunt Publishing Co., 1976.

7

Developing Creative Instructional Activities, Materials and Learning Environments in the Middle School

I hear and I Forget;
I see and I Remember;
I do and I Understand.
—Chinese Proverb

INTRODUCTION

The middle school, with its focus on a program designed around developmental characteristics of emerging adolescent youth, suggests instructional activities, materials, and learning environments designed to meet the wide range of achievements and interests of those youth.

Imaginative teachers and support personnel have developed learning activities that embrace a broad range of modes—reading, listening, writing, making, and doing.[1] Learning materials in the middle school represent a wide variety of

---

[1] A.S.C.D. Working Group on the Emerging Adolescent Learner, *The Middle School We Need* (Washington, D.C.: Association for Supervision and Curriculum Development, 1975), p. 13.

media—books, teacher-made and commercial materials, newspapers, wire services, magazines, audio and visual tapes, television, games, maps, and pictures.

To provide for pupils' varying attention and interest spans, arrangements are made in the middle school to provide learning environments that include many opportunities for varied activity-oriented and short- and long-term learning experiences.

In this chapter, we have included a number of examples of creative instructional activities, materials, and learning environments found in innovative middle schools in the United States and Canada.

DESIGNING CREATIVE INSTRUCTIONAL ACTIVITIES

The middle school offers a wide variety of opportunities for learning. Instructional activities are designed to allow students maximum opportunity to interact with peers, teachers, and outside resources in a "real world atmosphere." Activities are centered around the three major programs of the middle school—personal development, education for social competence, and skills for continuous learning. A wide variety of cognitive, psychomotor, and affective learning activities are necessary to account for the full range of students found in the middle grades. The following are examples of creative activities found in middle schools.

Guidance and Affective Activities

Middle school staffs have designed both formal and informal guidance and affective activities for middle school students. The certificate found in Figure 7.1 illustrates a reward system for students used by many middle schools. Such certificates are awarded daily to students who excel in grades, school service, politeness, helping others, etc.

Figure 7.1
Sample of Award Certificate used by Many Middle Schools

CERTIFICATE
OF
APPRECIATION

This is to Certify that

_____

has been Awarded this Certificate in
Recognition of the Excellent Service Rendered
RIVIERA MIDDLE SCHOOL

Given this _____ day of _____ 19 ___   _____
                                                              Principal

Parent messages are another means of teaching parents and students. The messages in Sample 7.1 illustrate an affective approach.

Sample 7.1—How to Help Your Child Succeed in School

1. Send him in a good frame of mind.

2. Build up his confidence. "I am proud of you. I know you will do well. You are a hard worker."

3. Praise him a lot for doing something well, especially if it is not usually his strong point.

4. Do not heap praise on unsatisfactory work, for work not up to par. Do not criticize; just do not praise.

5. Expect to see samples of school work regularly. Ask for it.

6. Support the teacher and the school. If you have a complaint, take it up with the teacher. Don't mention it to the child. (We wouldn't be caught dead criticizing you!)

7. Take what you hear with a grain of salt.

8. Have books around the house, either the library's or your own. Have a dictionary for sure. Other reference books if possible.

9. Keep your child well supplied with school supplies, even if he must go without treats. All workers must have tools. The nicer they are, the better they work—usually.

10. Show real interest in school. Attend PTA meetings, class functions, etc. Teachers take more interest in children whose parents they know personally. It's not "favoritism," it's just that knowing the parent makes the child more "real" to the teacher. The more the teacher knows the child, the more he cares about him.

11. Encourage your child to inquire. Don't put him off. If you don't know the answer, encourage him to look it up or figure it out. Then check to see how he did.

12. Look over your child's homework and encourage him to do it carefully. In the end though, it is his responsibility and not yours or mine. He must remember to do it and to bring the book in each day. Haim Ginott in *Teacher and Child* made some good points. He said, "Homework is the responsibility of the child. When parents take over, they enter a trap. Homework may become a child's weapon to punish, exploit, and worry his parents. Much misery is avoided when parents show little interest in the minute details of their child's assignments and instead convey to him clearly, "Homework is for you what work is for us—a personal responsibility."

Thanks for taking the time to read all this. If you made it all the way through, you are a TERRIFIC PARENT! And if I haven't told you lately, let me tell you now . . . YOU HAVE A REALLY NICE CHILD!

Sample 7.1—*continued*

Dear Parent of _____:

It is very important that your child review during the summer. It is easy for a student to forget math computation skills.

It is possible for me to order workbooks for review purposes. I have the opportunity to purchase these workbooks at a 25% reduction from the retail price.

If you are interested in purchasing one of these workbooks, please send your check by April 6.

The check should be made payable to Morgan Fitzgerald.

Sincerely,

Morgan Fitzgerald
Math Department

(Workbooks and prices listed below this letter.)

The Individual Summer Plan (ISP) illustrated in Sample 7.2 is used to help students continue their learning during summer months. The form includes a student contract, a conference between the teacher, student, and parents, and a packet of materials and activities to be completed during the summer. Materials and activities in the packet are used to reinforce skills, but are also designed to be fun and interesting to students.

Sample 7.2—Individual Summer Plan

I. *TEST RESULTS*

	PRE	**POST**
	Beginning Test Scores	**Ending Test Scores**
Math		
Reading		
Social Studies		
Science		

II. *PROGRESS*

Dear _____ :

_____

_____

_____

_____

_____

To continue your progress your Individual Summer Plan is listed below.

III. *INDIVIDUAL SUMMER PLAN*

1.

2.

3.

Sample 7.2—*continued*

4.

5.

6.

IV. Your summer resource contact persons: Mrs. Jane Hart, ESAA Project Manager and Mrs. Shirley Speakes, Resource Teacher—West Area Office—996-7617

Mr. David R. Campbell, Ass't. Principal, Pahokee Jr. High—924-5241

V. *REVIEW MATERIALS* (Attached)

Learning Units Dealing with Student Interests

Many middle school teachers and teacher teams use learning units to teach concepts. Affective activities can be emphasized in such learning units. Samples include:

"Dating and Etiquette"—students can learn social graces like how to ask for a date, what good manners are in a group, etc.

"Why Don't Teachers"—a unit allowing students a chance to discuss characteristics of teachers.

"Who Am I?"—a unit used at the beginning of school by many teacher teams to examine physical and social characteristics of emerging adolescents. Students often compile a Who's Who booklet which lists students' names, hobbies, phone numbers, and interests.

Discipline Practices

Middle schools have employed many techniques and activities to deal with student discipline. Teacher-advisors, team members, guidance, administrative, and school-support personnel all aid the classroom teacher in solving discipline problems. One innovative technique used by a number of middle schools is the "Time-Out Room." Such rooms are usually staffed by an experienced teacher who accepts those students some teachers feel they can no longer deal with effectively.

Oftentimes, with the guidance and direction given by the teacher in the Time-Out Room, the student can return to the regular classroom without being sent to the office, or worse, suspended from school. Sample 7.3 is an example of a Time-Out Room Referral Form.

Sample 7.3—Time-Out Room Referral Form

Student _____ Teacher _____ Date _____

Time In _____   Time Out _____

Sample 7.3—*continued*

Reason for Referral

_____ 1. Student request (has a problem)   _____ 4. Peer conflict

_____ 2. Classroom disruption   _____ 5. Emotional problem

_____ 3. Refuses to work   _____ 6. Other

Has student completed his work? _____

Have you sent work to be done? _____

Feedback from Time-Out Room if requested _____

_____

_____

Other activities used in middle schools to deal with discipline problems include student-faculty planning committees to discuss discipline problems, behavior modification procedures (like earning free time for good behavior) and parent calls by team members who volunteer on a weekly basis to call parents referred to them.

The Behavior Referral Form illustrated in Sample 7.4 demonstrates the many procedures followed by middle school staff members before a student is referred to a counselor or administrator:

Sample 7.4—Behavior Referral Form

BEHAVIOR REFERRAL	Student's Name	Class-Grade	Date
Fitzgerald Middle School 6410—118th Avenue, N. Largo, Florida, 33540 Phone 541–2611	Date of Incident	Time	Teacher

Notice to Parents

1. The purpose of this report is to inform you of a behavior incident involving the student.
2. You are urged both to appreciate the action taken by the teacher and to cooperate with the corrective action initiated today.

REFERRING TEACHER HAS EXPLORED AT LEAST THREE OF BELOW ITEMS:

__ Held team conference   __ Telephoned parent

__ Change in curriculum   __ Held conference with parent

__ Checked student's folder   __ Sent previous report home

__ Held conference with student   __ Other _____

__ Consulted counselor   _____

__ Changed student's seat   _____

REASON(S) FOR REFERRAL:

__ Five or more tardies   __ Rude, discourteous behavior

__ Continuous annoyance to   __ Destructive to school property

    classmates   _____

__ Inappropriate dress

Sample 7.4—*continued*

PRESENT ACTION AND RECOMMENDATION(S):

___ Time out—isolation   ___ Student placed on probation
___ Referral to Guidance Counselor   ___ Student suspended
___ Student will make up time   ___ Parents notified
___ Student regrets incident,   _____
cooperative

COMMENTS

_____

_____

_____

Parent's Signature   Office Signature

Source: Fitzgerald Middle School, "Behavior Referral Form" (Largo, Florida, 1978). Used with permission.

Guidance counselors can assist teachers in developing a system of finding out about student behaviors. Sample 7.5 is an example of such a system:

Sample 7.5—Classroom Learning-Behavior Inventory

CONFIDENTIAL

Student_____ Grade_____ Semester 1 2
Subject_____ Teacher_____
Counselor_____ Information needed for:
                                        _____ Staffing
Return to_____   _____ Parent
    by_____   _____ Other
                                        _____

Please rate the learning-behavior characteristics of the above student on a scale of 1–4. Please circle the appropriate number.

Scale Code: 1—Always applies
             2—Frequently applies
             3—Sometimes applies
             4—Never applies

Rating	Behavior	Description
1 2 3 4	Hyperactive	Restless, unable to sit still
1 2 3 4	Impulsivity	Reacts without thinking, demands immediate attention
1 2 3 4	Excessive reaction	Responds too quickly and too much to stimuli

Sample 7.5—*continued*

1	2	3	4	Anxiety	Overly worried, upset by failures
1	2	3	4	Excitability	Another type of over-response; extreme reaction to normal situations
1	2	3	4	Daydreaming	Withdraws from reality and problem situations
1	2	3	4	Irritability	Touchy, cross, out of sorts
1	2	3	4	Insecurity	Constantly in need of attention, encouragement
1	2	3	4	Emotional instability	Reactions unpredictable, inconsistent
1	2	3	4	Distractibility	All items have equal value; cannot concentrate on one thing
1	2	3	4	Short attention span	Cannot work at anything for long; often does not finish tasks
1	2	3	4	High motivation	Tries very hard in spite of failure
1	2	3	4	Confusion	Misses total concepts; often cannot figure out what is wanted or needed
1	2	3	4	Retention	Poor memory
1	2	3	4	Perseveration	Tendency to repeat activity or phrase after meaning and purpose have ceased
1	2	3	4	Perceptual-Visual	Cannot see wholes against a distracting background
1	2	3	4	Perception-Auditory	Cannot distinguish sounds against background noises
1	2	3	4	Speech	Hesitant, slow, stuttering, substitution of gestures
1	2	3	4	Reading & Writing	Reversal of letters and words
1	2	3	4	Talkativeness	Constant chattering, irrelevant conversations
1	2	3	4	Flightiness	Lack of steadiness
1	2	3	4	Explosive laughter	Sudden, loud, uncontrollable
1	2	3	4	Annoying, teasing	Disturbing others to gain attention

Describe the Student's Attitude Toward the Subject you Teach

ATTENDANCE: Cumulative number of days present this semester_____

Cumulative number of days absent this semester_____

Sample 7.5—*continued*

ADDITIONAL COMMENTS:

Teacher_____ date_____

SOURCE: Boca Raton Middle School, "Classroom Learning—Behavior Inventory" (Palm Beach County, Florida, 1976). Used with permission.

Other instructional guidance and affective activities in the middle school include student governments, student assistant projects, and work-study programs.

Student government in the middle school differs from the junior high model in that a few select students are not the only ones elected to school or class offices. Often teams or houses elect their own officers. School offices are frequently made up of a panel of students instead of a class president, a vice-president and a secretary.

Student-assistant programs include such activities as a "meeters and greeters" group involved in the school's public relations, team assistants, peer tutors, and office assistants.

Work-study programs in many middle schools allow students to work outside or within the school for a class period or more a day and earn a salary while also receiving class credit for their work. Students learn to fill out job applications and to participate in real job interviews. Vocational guidance is also provided.

Gaming and Simulation

The middle school has become a place where gaming and simulation activities enjoy widespread use. Such activities have been used to stimulate interest in all subject areas.

Games are based on the belief that learning ought to be fun and through the conviction that allowing middle school students find joy in learning will bear fruit throughout their lives.

The attitude of a learner towards an activity is important because it crucially affects how well she will learn that activity. The use of gaming and simulation devices and activities provides the student with an opportunity to learn by doing and, further, emphasizes the maximum of self-discovery through her activity. In the appendixes, the reader can find an extensive list of academic games and simulations used in the middle school.

Learning Unit Activities

The following list of activities extracted from learning units in the middle school illustrates the rich variety of learning experiences made available to middle school students. Such activities may be structured in Learning Activity Packages (LAPS), interdisciplinary units, content units, or other curriculum units.

1. Administer a carefully devised questionnaire to a selected sample of 200

students, being sure to balance such variables as race, sex, creed, age; survey their attitudes about questions of belief. Compare your findings with those of professional pollsters; draw conclusions about the beliefs of young people.

2. Survey students at school as to what school rule they would most like to have changed. Survey twenty other selected schools on how they handle a similar problem. Survey the faculty and administration on their attitudes. Draw up a proposal which you can present to student council and administration on the basis of your study.

3. Make a study of war songs which were popular during our country's major wars, beginning with the Revolutionary War. What conclusions can you draw about changing styles in war songs? Write the lyrics to a song which you think would be appropriate to the conflict in Vietnam.

4. Write and produce a radio script entitled "On the Nature of the Good Life." Select readings from the great philosophers of the past and present. Write narrative bridges between these passages and record appropriate musical background. Record on tape for later presentation.

5. Make an 8mm sound movie illustrating a consistent theme. Select a subject which can be handled in a relatively short segment—film is expensive. This project would require careful preparation.

6. Study the lyrics of the fifty most popular recordings of the past year. What do these lyrics reflect about our culture and our times? Write lyrics which you think have the same ingredients as the popular songs.

7. Make a study of "beauty in art." Prepare a program directed to a large audience; include slides and prints to illustrate how artists have felt about beauty from earliest times.

8. Make a historical study of American automotive design for the past thirty years. What does our taste in cars reveal about us? Predict what design changes will take place in the next ten years, and design the car for 1990.

9. Study the historical development of the Justice of Peace as a local administrator of justice. Read what contemporary authorities have said about the pros and cons of the JP system. Interview selected JPs from the surrounding area. Correspond with judges in the higher courts. Draw some tentative conclusions about the strengths and weaknesses of the JP system and offer recommendations for its improvement.

10. Trace the development of the sports hero from the time of the Greek Olympics to the present day. Talk with local professional athletes. Draw some tentative conclusions about the changing nature of the sports hero and what this change reflects about our own times.

11. By using primary sources—interviews, minute books, original documents, local materials—write a history of your community or school.

12. Prepare a tourist's guide to your town. Illustrate it with maps and photographs.

13. Prepare a 35mm slide program featuring your community or school. Write a script for use in presenting it.

14. Prepare a visitor's guide to your school which takes the visitor through a typical day in a student's life. Illustrate it with maps and photographs.

15. Take any short story that we have read in class, or one we did not read, and turn it into a radio script. Tape-record your script with appropriate musical and sound effects.

16. Study magazine advertisements from three decades: 1950, 1960, and 1970. What do they reveal about changing taste and moods? Draw up a series of ads for a selected product you think would appeal to young people.

17. Create, select, and arrange a series of paintings and photographs in essay format to reveal the effects of the machine in American culture.

18. Develop a project entitled, "Improving the Community." Talk with civic planners, local civic leaders; read what other communities have done. Draw up a blueprint for improving your own community.

19. If our school ever needed additional space, what kinds of facilities and what new ideas should be incorporated into the planning? Illustrate your ideas with sketches.

20. Take a recording of classical or contemporary music and create your own dance for it. Combine your dance with a reading of selected poems either by yourself or by another student.

21. Study the history of protest movements and minority opinions in America. Attempt to draw conclusions about the people involved and the times in which various movements occurred. If possible, make comparisons or contrasts with current events.

Independent Study

Independent study is a learning activity that becomes an integral part of the middle school program.[2] Independent study may be an individual project undertaken by some members of a class or a plan of study developed for exceptional children judged by a teacher as needing a broader knowledge of a particular area.

Many middle schools are using contracts between student and teacher (see Samples 7.6 and 7.7).

Sample 7.6—Language Contract

I, _____, agree to meet commitments outlined on the reverse side of this contract to the best of my ability.

---

[2] Joseph Bondi, *Developing Middle Schools: A Guidebook* (Wheeling, Ill.: Whitehall Publishing Co., 1972), pp. 67–68.

Sample 7.6—*continued*

DATE _____   _____
                                       Pupil's Signature
Comments Upon Completion of Contract: Date_____

                                       _____
                                              Pupil

                                       _____
                                          Subject Advisor

                                       _____
                                           House Advisor

                                       _____
                                              Parent

Sample 7.7—Independent Study Contract

I, _____, agree under the advisement of _____ subject advisor in _____, to complete the tasks outlined on the Progress Form to as high a degree of mastery as I am capable of attaining. In addition, I agree to undergo constant self-evaluation as part of my personal responsibility for learning. Class activities on this contract will be concluded _____.

                                       _____
                                        Signature of student

COMMENTS:
COMPLETION OF CONTRACT:
DATE: SIGNATURE:

_____   _____
                                          Of Student

_____   _____
                                       Of Subject Advisor

Creative Instructional Activities—Examples

As the middle school has evolved, many creative instructional activities have been developed for emerging adolescent learners. The authors have selected *teaching basic reading skills through the use of the newspaper, telephone directory, T.V. Guide and merchandise catalogs* as examples of such activities for review.

Sample 7.8 illustrates the use of such everyday references to teach basic reading skills to middle school students.

Sample 7.8

MATERIAL	ACTIVITY	SKILL
TELEPHONE BOOK Look on the inside cover . . .	Circle a star Underline a Put a square around a Circle a	Pre-reading Following directions Recognizing symbols for various emergency numbers Auditory and/or visual discrimination
Look at the area code map of the U.S.	What state would you live in if your area code was 208, 913, 703, etc.? What time zone would you live in if your area code was 808, 303, 913, 304, 506?	Decoding Word recognition of the various states Map reading Number recognition
NEWS-PAPERS Advertise-ments Select similar ads from different stores	You want to purchase a stereo radio and record player. Where will you get the most for your money? There are five grocery stores near you: (select five ads) Plan a meal for five people. You have $10 to spend. What will you purchase? Where will you purchase it? Why? List your items. Where can you buy one dozen oranges for the lowest price?	Comprehension Reading for detail Compare and contrast Compare and contrast Math skill Nutritional ability
T.V. GUIDE Entire Guide	On what day would you be able to watch the "Partridge Family"? On what channel could you see the "Doris Day" show? If Sally turned on her TV at 9 PM on Saturday, how many different movies would be playing? Joe has to be in bed by 9 PM on Thursdays. Can he watch "Truth or Consequences"? The "Dean Martin" show?	Locating skills Reading for detail Problem solving

Sample 7.8—*continued*

MATERIAL	ACTIVITY	SKILL

CATALOGS
Sears
	Fill out an order form. Print your name, address and phone number. Order the following items:
	  2 pairs boys' slacks
	  1 ski parka
	  1 shower curtain rod
	  3 records
	
	Indicate on the order form the page you found each item on; the price of each item; the combined price; and the catalog number of each.
		Decoding
		Using the table of contents
		Math skills
		Number sequence

A Week of Special Activities

All students and teachers participate in a special week of activities. Language fairs, art displays, student-faculty basketball games, gymnastics, plans, family team, cookouts, are some of the activities found in such activity weeks. Sample 7.9 illustrates a typical activity week.

Outdoor Classroom Activities

As many middle schools develop or utilize outdoor education areas, middle school teachers have devised a number of creative instructional activities designed to show how each content or subject area can be reinforced in the study of nature. The following are examples:

Math

Do scale drawings in form of maps.

Figure percentage of slopes.

Do shadow ratios.

Pace distance in hiking.

Estimate and check distance or height of trees.

Average temperature readings.

Construct geometric figures with magnetic compasses.

Measure diameters of specific areas.

Measure circumference of ten round natural objects.

Find examples of different geometric shapes in nature.

Sample 7.9—Sixteenth Street Star Spangled Spectacular—Schedule of Events, Week of May 2–5, 1979

Following are week long activities:

Horticulture Display—Library Open 9–3 each day and Wednesday evening (Sign-up to visit—2 classes/period)
Science Displays—Science Wing Open all week (school hours)
Subject Area Displays—Guidance Conference Room—All week
Stage Performances—Gymnasium as follows:

Pd	Monday	Pd	Tuesday	Pd	Wednesday	Pd	Thursday	Pd	Friday
3rd	*Fillyau*—	7th	*Savelle*—2 One	1st	*Ethridge*—	3rd	*Igney*—"It's		DANCE ? ?
4th	Majorette	2nd	Act Plays	2nd	Gymnastics	4th	Music"		
	Drill Tm,			Evening	*Igney* "It's				
	and Dance				Music"				

Performances in Ms. Savell's room—Rm 9

Pd		Pd		Pd		Pd	
4th	*Irwin*—Drop In	3rd	*Clayton*—Choral			4th	*Bowers*—Play
5th	Players		Reading			5th	

Sign-Up Activities—You may sign up for any of the following activities to visit your room 1 period during the week. The number of students involved is listed plus other requirements. Sign up with J. Birge.

Video Tape Presentation (Savell)—1 student (Sign for equipment)
Irwin's Drop-In Players (Irwin)—15 students
Choral Reading (Clayton)—30 students (Class coverage for Clayton)
Play performance (Bowers)—25 students (Class coverage for Bowers)

Language Arts

Keep field notes.

Categorize various specimens in nature.

Improve listening skills through night hiking.

Create ecology commercials.

Write an imaginative story about a drop of water's journey through the water cycle.

Write myths to explain natural phenomena.

Dramatize an event in nature.

Debate hunting.

List adjectives describing a specific specimen.

Arts and Crafts

Reproduce a spider's web with string art.

Prepare cork boats for floating in stream currents.

Make a collage of natural objects.

Prepare leaf rubbings.

In addition to the foregoing examples, the following activities are listed by title and short description:

Fostering Oral Expression—Twenty ways of getting shy students in a middle school to express themselves. Examples include impromptu skits, TV show productions, carrying out a political campaign, paired activity learning, and cumulative stories.

Values-Clarification in Social Studies—"Bringing the Puritans up to Date." Students compare modern day events such as World War II internment camps for Japanese-Americans and Joe McCarthy hearings to Salem witch trials.

Moon Survival or Desert Survival Problems—Students must make "life or death" choices for survival as individuals and as small groups.

Grave Rubbings—Graven Images—Students reproduce gravestone designs and epitaphs by rubbing charcoal over light paper on the surface of the gravestone. Students learn history and also study various art forms found in early burial grounds.[3]

Teaching With Newspapers—Teachers use newspapers to teach a variety of skills as well as current events. Students can also use the newspaper to compare feelings and actions of others with their own behavior.

Wire Service Machines in the School—Wire services have instituted programs placing wire service machines in middle schools. Such machines pro-

---

[3] Evelyn Alexander, "Graven Images," *The Teachers' Arts and Crafts Guide* (June 1976), pp. 17–19.

vide students with up-to-the-minute news; print sheets produced by the machines are used to teach reading skills as well as to provide content material for the various subject areas.

Although the descriptions of foregoing activities are but a few of the hundreds of such activities found in innovative middle schools, they do illustrate the imagination and creativity of middle school teachers in planning instructional programs for emerging adolescent learners. Sample 7.10 lists a number of teaching techniques associated with the creative activities found in the middle school.

Sample 7.10—Teaching Techniques

Learning Centers	Role-playing
Collages	Resource people
Models	Field trips
Films	Interviews
Bulletin Boards	Debates
Small group discussion	Newspaper articles (want ads)
Exhibits or displays	Brainstorming
Games	Research projects
Scrapbooks	Simulated work activities
Notebooks	Writing letters
Speeches	VTR (Videotaping)
Plays or skits	Unipacs or LAPS
Large group discussion	Committee work
Filmstrips	Overhead and/or opaque projections
Observations	
Panel discussions	Demonstrations
Assigned readings	Problem-solving
Slides	Decision-making problems
Puppets	Radio and TV programs

DEVELOPING CREATIVE MATERIALS

Instructional materials in the middle school reflect a wide variety of media including books, teacher-made materials, visuals, audio- and videotapes, and television. Most of the materials are generally included in units of instruction designed especially for middle school students. The diversity of achievement, background, and interests of emerging adolescent learners creates a demand for diversified learning materials.

A Model for an Instructional Unit

An instructional unit can be illustrated through the following model:

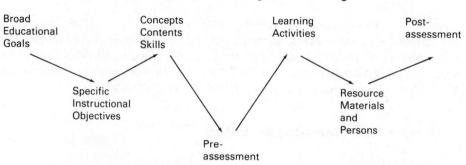

Broad Educational Goals → Specific Instructional Objectives → Concepts Contents Skills → Pre-assessment → Learning Activities → Resource Materials and Persons → Post-assessment

An Explication of the Model

a. The relationship of the instructional unit to the broad goals of society and to the school's total curriculum must be clearly defined.

b. Instructional objectives must be delineated in unambiguous behavioral terms.

c. The instructional unit must include the concepts to be developed, the content to be assimilated and the skills to be mastered. A continuous progress prescription is essential.

d. Performance criteria must be established in order to preassess the learner's degree of success in understanding of concepts or proficiency in skills.

e. The learning activities must be tailored to several levels of difficulty in order to challenge the individual learner. Most learning will occur in small groups or independently.

f. Resource materials and persons (teachers and aides) are needed to facilitate learning.

g. Post-assessment is administered in order to measure the degree of proficiency to which the learner can perform the skills, understand the content and demonstrate observable changes in behavior.[4]

An Explication of an Instructional Unit

A. The Nature of the Learner

1. Sets his own pace.

2. Has unique abilities, variegated interests and unfulfilled needs.

3. Is assiduously striving to improve his image.

4. Is inextricably entangled in "self;" (self-esteem; self-direction; self-fulfillment and self-actualization).

---

[4] James F. Garvey, "Outline of Instructional Objectives Usage," La Canada, Calif., Unpublished paper, 1972.

B. The Imperatives of the School

1. Nurture sequential concept development (spiral learning rather than fragmented learning).

2. Maintain a balance between convergent and divergent thinking.

3. Maintain a balance between the cognitive and affective domains.

4. Cultivate critical judgment.

5. Imbue values.

6. Inculcate the spirit of inquiry.

C. The Instructional Unit

1. It must be purposeful to each learner.

2. It must be at the learner's level of understanding, that is, his or her expectancy level and not his or her frustration level.

3. It must remove hurdles that stultify the learner's progress in moving from concept to concept.

4. It must be sequential in order to be efficacious.

5. It must have a salutary effect upon the learner.

Self-pacing Materials

Unit Packages (Uni-Pacs), Learning Activity Packages (LAPS), Mini-Pacs, and Pacer-Pacs have become a part of the vocabulary of middle school students and teachers. These names refer to self-pacing materials developed to individualize instruction in the middle school. Such materials are usually found in school settings where the following features are typically found:

Concept-Centered Curriculum

Some Type of Provision for Flexible Scheduling

Continuous Progress

Team Teaching

Independent Study

Self-pacing materials are designed to teach a single idea or concept and are structured for independent use in a continuous progress school program. Such materials generally include a statement of a major concept, subconcepts, behavioral objectives, a pretest, sequential and diversified learning activities, multilevel content, quest study, post-test, evaluation of materials, teaching suggestions, and identifying information. Behavioral objectives are written at all levels of the cognitive, affective, and psychomotor domains.

We have selected excerpts from several "Uni-Pacs" and "Mini-Pacs" to illustrate various facets of self-pacing learning materials. (See Samples 7.11–7.14.)

Sample 7.11—A Uni-Pac Excerpt
"Charlie Brown, You're Not Listening to Me"

What is a good listener?
A good listener is:

1. Mom, who lets Dad gripe after work, no matter how hard her day has been.

2. Your dog. He can't out-argue you, and never talks back.

3. Your best friend. (The one who listens for hours to your moans and groans about that "certain someone.")

4. Your teacher, who listens to *ALL* your problems . . . if you can get her attention!

5. That smart aleck in the next row who gets all the main points of even the most boring lecture!

What have you noticed about these good listeners? _____
_____

What ways of listening do they have in common? _____
_____

If these very same people were in a room together and *all started talking at once,* would they still be good listeners? _____
_____

How does a good listener act? What does he do? Write at least three things.
_____
_____
_____

Now let's see if we can decide what a good listener does NOT do:

1. He doesn't let his attention wander out the window or over to the next group of kids while you're talking.

2. He doesn't tune out a speaker just because he doesn't agree with the speaker's ideas. That's prejudice! (Look it up, silly!)

3. He doesn't get all involved in just one of the speaker's ideas and forget to listen to the rest. He catches all of it.

4. He doesn't interrupt before the other speaker has finished what he has to say.

Now that you have a good idea of what a good listener is, you should be thinking of some ways that you could develop these good listening habits.

Sample 7.12—Single-Concept Exercises

A. RECOGNIZING SENTENCES: Drill Sheet I

Name_____   Date_____

A SENTENCE is a group of words expressing a complete thought: Airplanes fly.
Every sentence must have a *subject* and a *predicate.*

Sample 7.12—*continued*

The subject names what the sentence is about: AIRPLANES FLY. (Airplanes is the subject.)

Jet AIRPLANES FLY AT HIGH SPEEDS. (Airplanes is the subject; fly is the predicate.)

Some of the words below are complete sentences and some are not. On the line before each complete sentence write S; before each incomplete sentence write F for fragment.

EXAMPLES: ____ A. Fall is the best time of the year.
     ____ B. Starting to school in September.

____ 1. We are beginning a new school year.

____ 2. Making grades is only one of our goals.

____ 3. All the students in my class.

____ 4. Want to learn to get along with people.

____ 5. The popular students considerate of others.

____ 6. He always has a pleasant smile.

____ 7. An opportunity for many new friends.

____ 8. This year can be very pleasant for all of us.

____ 9. No student who loafs in school.

____ 10. We hope to enjoy our English work this semester.

Activities:

 I. On a separate sheet make complete sentences out of the word groups in the above exercises that are not already complete sentences.

 II. Write ten sentences about school.

Sample 7.13—Uni-Pac Excerpt

MAN ATTEMPTS TO SOLVE HIS PROBLEMS
       NAME _____
       Date _____

Introduction:
In this Mini-pac we shall learn how men through the ages have tried to overcome and solve their problems and of those of their fellow men. In many instances the family of man has made great steps in overcoming problems of disease, in humane treatment of the less fortunate, social conflict, government of men, and world conflict. We will study some social reforms and reformers who have contributed to making man's life more comfortable.

Objectives:
 1. Given a list of social reformers, be able with 80% accuracy to state the contribution made by each to the betterment of man.

Sample 7.13—*continued*

2. Select one social reform to use in writing a paragraph describing the condition which brought about the reform and the condition after the reform came into existence.

Skills:

1. Be prepared to follow printed and oral directions carefully.

2. Be prepared to use the basic skill of research effectively.

Reading Assignment:

You will read all or parts of the references listed below. It may be a good idea to look at other interesting books on the topic. You may find it helpful to make a list of possible books and pages which would be helpful to you in doing the activities in this mini-pac. Be sure to read before starting the activities.

1. Eibling, King, and Harlow, *World Background*, Chapter 22.

Sample 7.14—Mini-Pac Excerpt—Newspapers— A Point of View

Lesson I

Component Part:

A news article is made up of facts.

Behavioral Objective:

1. Given five articles from the newspaper, you will pick out the news stories and underline the facts in each.

2. You will define in writing the following terms:
   a) fact _____   b) opinion _____

3. Given a list of statements, you will identify which statements are fact.

Directions:

All work done must be put in the assignment box. Choose one or more of the activities listed below. When you *know* you can do the objectives, then turn to the self-test for Lesson I. (It is suggested that most students do three activities in order to understand the lesson.)

Activities:

1. Read the handout "Fact vs. Opinion" which is found on the materials table. After reading both sides, then answer the 4 questions on the back (page 8). Find three news articles in the papers on the materials table. Underline the facts in the article. Clip it to your first paper and put it in the assignment box.

2. View the film on Comparisons. Read the bulletin board to find out *when* and *where* you can watch it. Then answer the questions on the film that are next to the projector.

   Put your paper in the assignment box.

3. Read the handout on newspaper writing and paragraphs, then do the required work at the end of the handout.

Sample 7.14—*continued*

    4. Report to the learning center on political cartoons.

    5. Stage a skit for the whole class in which something happens like a robbery or beating. Then see if each member of the class can write a paragraph stating only the facts. Check with Mrs. Rubeck or Miss Jones to get specific directions.

Interdisciplinary Units of Instruction

Although we have included interdisciplinary units of instruction under the heading of "materials," such units represent more than just the use of creative materials. They include creative learning activities and a variety of learning environments.

Interdisciplinary or family teams represent a combination of teachers from different subject areas who plan and correlate the instruction for particular groups of students. The aim of the team is to promote cooperation among subject specialists qualified to help students solve real-world problems through unified problem-solving techniques.

As outlined in Chapter 6, the interdisciplinary team utilizes a block of time for instruction during the school day. Although most interdisciplinary teams in middle schools are organized around language arts, mathematics, social studies, and science, other specialists, including related arts teachers, are found on interdisciplinary teams. Many middle schools employ a core curriculum in which two disciplines are correlated, usually social studies and English.

The following are five basic premises of interdisciplinary teaming:

1. The interdisciplinary approach is a way of organizing the school in terms of curriculum, instruction, and resources, both human and material.

2. Disciplines do not lose their integrity through a team approach. Rather, the interdisciplinary approach clearly demonstrates the uniqueness of each discipline's contribution to the solution of problems.

3. The interdisciplinary approach is compatible with team teaching, individualization of learning, nongradedness, and flexible scheduling.

4. The interdisciplinary approach is ideally suited to the middle school student because it provides many and varied opportunities for success, exploration, and growth.

5. All disciplines need not combine for all interdisciplinary teaming. Teachers of complimentary skills may combine. Moreover, there are areas of instruction which may best be taught in the discipline to which they belong.

In order for interdisciplinary units of instruction to be developed, there are four essential requirements:

1. A staff committed to the interdisciplinary approach as a means of serving the needs of students.

2. Positive interpersonal and professional relationships among all members of the staff.

3. Common team planning time.

4. Sufficient planning time.

Figure 7.2 illustrates the steps necessary in the development of interdisciplinary units of instruction. Figure 7.3 lists examples of interdisciplinary topics.

Figure 7.2
Steps in Developing an Interdisciplinary Unit of Instruction

STAGE I. CONCEPTUALIZATION OF THE PURPOSES OF THE INTERDISCIPLINARY APPROACH TO INSTRUCTION

    A. Having Informal Dialogue about the Needs of Students

    B. Organizing Student Needs into Goal Statements—Expected Outcomes

    C. Selecting a Unifying Statement, Theme, or Concept

    D. Identifying Some Objectives Based on Goals—Particularly Objectives in the *Affective Domain*

STAGE II. RESEARCH

    A. Selecting Curricular Options and Activities

    B. Identifying and Selecting Resources

STAGE III. FUSION (DISCIPLINE)

    A. Organizing the Curriculum

        1. Developing Specific Learning Objectives

        2. Determining the Sequence of Learning Experiences

        3. Determining Entry-Level Skills Along a Continuum of Learning Experiences

        4. Selecting and/or Developing Evaluative Criteria

        5. Categorizing Resource Materials

        6. Developing Units, etc.

    B. Developing Prototypes in the Form of Flow Charts that Clearly Determine How Students Will Move

STAGE IV. PROGRAMMING

    A. Organizing Learning Centers

    B. Developing Team Schedules to Include:

        1. Small Groups

        2. Large Groups

        3. Independent Learners

        4. Individuals in Need of Special Help

    C. Scheduling Off-campus Visits, Guests, etc.

STAGE V. IMPLEMENTATION

    A. Pretesting

    B. Monitoring

    C. Post-testing

    D. Recycling

Figure 7.2—*continued*

STAGE VI. EVALUATION

          A. Professionals

          B. Students

Figure 7.3
Sample Interdisciplinary Topics

Imagination and Discovery
Bicentennial
Sports and You
Careers in Transportation
The Concrete Jungle
Man Accepts the Challenge of City Living
The Law and You
International Trade
Rural Life
Communications
Temporary Living: Camps and Camping
Greece
You Are What You Eat
Let's Get Personal
Foreseeing the Unforeseeable
Be It Ever So Humble
Cities—What You Always Wanted to Know
Shock: A Serious and Dangerous Condition
Elections
M.A.N.—Minorities Are the Nation
Of Mice and Men: An Interdisciplinary Unit
Sports and Your Identity
Changing Sex Roles in the Twentieth Century
The Wheel in the Social Development of Man
Animal and Human Interdependence and the Necessity for Cooperation
Feeding the Population
Evolution: Process of Change
America: The First Two Hundred Years
How Environmental Factors Affect Shelter
The Civil War and Reconstruction
Anchors Away to a New World
The World Series
Sports in America
The Pollution Problem
Man as a Consumer
Then and Now
The Westward Movement
Westward Expansion
Take Me Out to the Ball Game

In addition to the examples of creative instructional materials illustrated in this chapter, we have included numerous examples of similar materials in the appendixes. The variety and number of teacher-made and commercial materials found in most middle schools are helping instruction come alive for middle school students.

Modern-day technology has resulted in the use of computers, television systems, and learning machines to help students learn better. The Essential Middle School is a school where all such learning materials and devices are employed.

STRUCTURING CREATIVE LEARNING ENVIRONMENTS

It is clear that environments, both real and perceived, set a tone for learning.[5] Traditional intermediate schools have been characterized by solitary, sedate, and ordered environments. That atmosphere has resulted from many forces: a narrow definition of formal education, a limited public access to knowledge, and a didactic (telling-listening) format for learning.

By contrast, the Essential Middle School is an innovative school that is the organizational opposite of the traditional, tightly structured school. The atmosphere is open and sometimes noisy. Although there is structure, there are numerous activity centers planned by teachers and students that exist within the structure.

A new understanding of the environmental conditions that enhance learning has resulted in the establishment of creative learning environments for middle school students. In the following pages, you will review growth conditions in the classroom affecting pupil attitudes toward self (see Table 7.1), examine an example of creative learning instructional centers found in dynamic middle schools, and examine types of school rooms and buildings found in middle schools.

Table 7.1
Learning Environments—Growth Conditions Self-concept

High Growth Conditions	Low Growth Conditions
High acceptance/respect of pupil's ideas	Low acceptance/respect of pupil's ideas
1. Pupil ideas are frequently accepted. The teacher listens to and incorporates pupil ideas in discussion and other learning situations.	1. Pupil ideas are rarely encouraged or accepted. There is little opportunity for discussion. When discussion occurs, it is highly controlled and seeks *recall* of previously learned information. Pupil contributions are frequently criticized.

---

[5] Jon Wiles and Joseph Bondi, *Curriculum Development: A Guide to Practice* (Columbus, Ohio: Charles E. Merrill Publishing Co., 1979), p. 357.

High acceptance/respect
of pupil's affect

2. Pupil feelings and emotions
   are accepted by the teacher
   as long as harm to others
   is avoided.

Low acceptance/respect
of pupil's affect

2. Pupil feelings are avoided
   or discouraged. The
   teacher is unwilling to
   recognize expressions and
   discussions of feelings.

High encouragement/support
of pupils

3. Pupils are encouraged to
   explore, make suggestions,
   etc. An atmosphere of
   "try it and tell us what
   happens" pervades the
   classroom.

Low encouragement/support
of pupils

3. Pupils are discouraged
   from exploration. The
   teacher has the one right
   way of doing things and
   only that way is accepted.
   Alternatives are not
   discussed or tested.

4. The teacher is willing to
   "get off the subject" when
   an interesting event or
   question is raised. At
   times the question
   becomes the actual topic.

4. The teacher controls the
   subject at all times.
   Penetrating philosophical
   questions are discouraged.
   The principal aim is to
   teach the lesson and complete
   it.

High pupil individualization

5. The teacher attempts to understand and respond to each
   child's psychological needs.
   The teacher recognizes that
   some children may need more
   direction and control while
   others may need the opportunity
   to exercise greater choice. The
   teacher, therefore, encourages
   children to learn and explore
   in ways that each child is
   comfortable with.

Low pupil individualization

5. The teacher denies individual
   differences and needs and demands
   conformity. The teacher who
   demands that every child participate
   in an "open" classroom may produce
   the same low growth conditions as
   the teacher who provides a "lock-
   step" classroom atmosphere. Both
   strategies are authoritarian, and
   demand conformity at the possible
   expense of pupil feelings of
   esteem, control and connectedness.

High pupil involvement

6. A continuing dialogue with
   pupils is maintained to involve
   children in making decisions
   about their learning (e.g.,
   individual and small group
   projects, work contracts, etc.),
   and to help children further
   clarify what they are learning.

Low pupil involvement

6. The teacher always tells pupils
   what and how they are to learn.
   Little room is left for pupil
   choice and expression.

High teacher genuiness/realness	Low teacher genuiness/realness
7. The teacher is genuine, willing to express ideas, feelings, experiences and be a real person rather than play a role. Where appropriate, the teacher allows students entry into his/her private world of feelings, ideas, needs, and concerns.	7. The teacher plays a role and presents a facade that conceals feelings. The teacher acts in a confined, prescribed manner revealing little of own uniqueness and inner thoughts. A wide emotional gap is maintained between teacher and pupil and little of the common bonds, needs and feelings that the two may actually possess is explored.

SOURCE: J. D. Wiggins and Dori English, "Affective Education: A Manual for Growth" (Dover, Del.: Del. Department of Public Instruction, 1975), pp. 4–6. Used with permission.

Learning Centers

A learning center or station is a means of organizing instruction so that middle school pupils can be responsible for much of their own learning. A learning *station* implies the way a student learns (auditory, visual, kinesthetic) while a learning *center* implies what a student will be learning (grammar, fractions). A learning center/station is generally characterized by the following:

1. Clear directions that help a student proceed through a learning activity without constant reliance on the teacher.

2. Clearly stated objectives.

3. Choice of activities so students can use a variety of learning modes.

4. Multilevel activities so that learning activities are appropriate for each student.

5. Evaluation activities that allow students to check their work at the center.

6. Opportunities to work in small groups so that students can assist each other and learn together.

Every learning center/station should contain multimedia materials to support the topic, theme, concept or skill. These include slides, filmstrips, audio- and videotapes, books, records, self-pacing materials, and manipulative materials for exploration and discovery.

Every learning center/station needs the reinforcement of a teacher's introduction to what the center contains and how it can be used. A flexible organizational pattern in the classroom and school must be planned so that pupils can have easy access to learning centers or stations.[6] Sample 7.15 shows an example of a plan for a learning center in an art class.

Sample 7.15—Color Me Happy!

A Learning Center, Involving Middle-School Students in the Joy-of-Experimentation with Color

---

[6] Sandra Kaplan et al., *Change for Children: Ideas, and Activities for Individual Learning* (Palisades Park, Calif.: Goodyear Publishing Co., 1970), pp. 21–22.

Sample 7.15—*continued*

I. Skills Covered

    1. Following written directions.

    2. Correct use of liquid and solid tempera paints.

    3. Correct use of glue, scissors, brushes.

    4. Abstract reasoning in the development of choice of color for various purposes.

    5. Logical reasoning in the development of choice of color for specific purposes.

    6. The development of an esthetic appreciation of color.

II. Behavioral Objectives

    1. Students will distinguish between primary, secondary, and tertiary colors.

    2. Students will define warm colors, cool colors, shade and tint.

    3. Students will demonstrate knowledge of mixing secondary and tertiary colors, shades and tints.

    4. Students will demonstrate correct working procedures using liquid and cake tempera paints.

    5. Students will develop a rationale for the use of selected colors, shades, or tints.

III. Materials Needed:

1. egg cartons	10. crayons
2. white paper	11. rubber cement
3. newspaper	12. brilliants
4. brushes	13. folder for each child
5. rulers	14. water cans
6. paper	15. liquid tempera
7. tissue papers	blue red
8. glue-water	orange yellow
9. compasses	green white
	purple black

IV. Procedures in the Use of the Center

    1. Entire class/group will take the pretest. Students are placed into the proper *Color Corner*, according to pretest scores:

        Color Corner 1—Primary and secondary colors
                    Warm and cool colors
        Color Corner 2—Tertiary colors
        Color Corner 3—Shades and tints
                    Value

    2. Students proceed with activities in their Color Corners. After post-tests are graded, a satisfactory score (80 or above), moves students to the next group.

V. Teacher-evaluation is achieved through post-test scores and objective criticism of work produced. Student-evaluation is obtained from teacher who encourages self-criticism of student's work.

In middle schools, learning centers or stations are housed in classrooms, in media areas, or in specially designed rooms. Learning Resource Rooms for reading or mathematics are often structured around teaching machines that include computer terminals and a variety of learning stations containing both hard- and software materials. Middle schools with a number of learning centers can utilize parent and community volunteers to assist in those centers. For instance, a parent with an interest in arts and crafts could assist in an art center such as illustrated in the "Color Me Happy" plan in Sample 7.15.

Classroom Climate

Once an instructional learning area has been established, its effectiveness is dependent on a number of factors. The "set" of the instructional learning environment, commonly referred to as classroom climate, directly affects learning. In Table 7.2, we have identified some of the important variables affecting classroom climate.

Table 7.2

Variables Affecting Classroom Climate

Structure	the feeling students have about constraints on the group: rules, regulations, "red tape."
Responsibility	the feeling of being your own boss, not having to double-check all decisions, freedom to do the job.
Reward	feeling of being rewarded for a job well done, an emphasis on positive reward rather than punishment, perceived fairness in rewards given.
Risk	the feeling that taking calculated risks (asking a "foolish" question) is all right, that you don't have to play it safe to succeed.
Warmth	the feeling of general good fellowship, the prevalence of friendly and informal social groups.
Support	the perceived helpfulness of the teacher, emphasis on support from both above and below.
Standards	the perceived importance of performance standards, the emphasis on doing a good job.
Conflict	the feeling that the teacher and other students want to hear different opinions, the emphasis placed on getting problems out in the open.
Identity	the feeling that you belong and are a valuable member of a working team, the importance of team spirit.

SOURCE: Adapted from G. H. Litwin and R. A. Stringer, *Motivation and Organizational Climate* (Boston: Harvard University Press, 1968), pp. 67–68. Reprinted by permission.

Students in the middle school are acutely cognizant of non-verbal communication.

It seems clear that a distinct classroom climate can be created by varying teacher leadership style. Once created, these climates have a significant effect on motivation and performance.

Climate determines motivation

Teachers determine climate

Teachers can determine motivation

Management of classroom motivation involves four key variables: (1) individual student needs, (2) organizational tasks, (3) work climate, (4) teacher-leadership style.

School Buildings

The physical nature of middle school buildings and school grounds are subtle indicators of the school's perceived mission and, therefore, are useful measures for a visitor or interested observer. Features such as access points, building warmth, traffic control inside the building, and space priorities tend to reflect the school's program.[7]

Architects have observed that buildings are a physical expression of content. A dull, drab, unexciting school building may reflect a dull, drab, unexciting educational process. On the other hand, an exciting, stimulating, dynamic building may mirror an active, creative, total learning center. A building not only expresses its

---

[7] Jon Wiles and Joseph Bondi, *Curriculum Development: A Guide to Practice* (Columbus, Ohio: Charles E. Merrill Publishing Co., 1979), pp. 360–65.

interior activity, but may also affect and even control the success of these functions. If school corridors, for example, are colorful, well-lighted, and visually expansive, the resulting excitement and stimulation controls or guides the behavior of the individual in such a space. It is for this reason that most new airports are built with extremely wide and brightly colored corridors.

Architecturally, school buildings have been altered greatly during the seventy-year history of junior high schools and middle schools. (See Figures 7.4–7.8.) This transformation has reflected the more subtle changes in school programs. A stereotypic evolution of junior high and middle school buildings in the United States

Figure 7.4

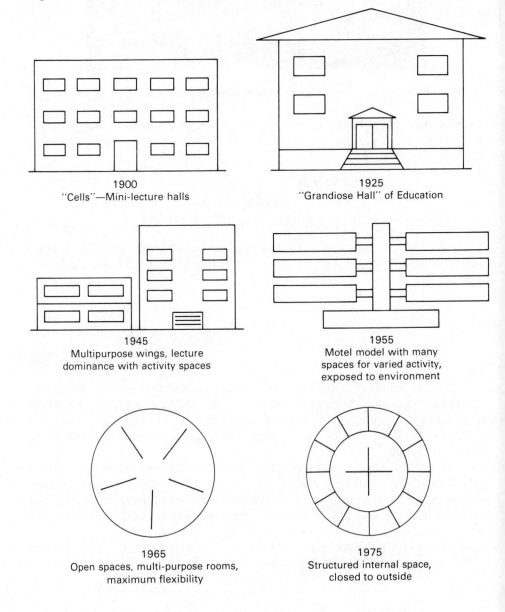

1900
"Cells"—Mini-lecture halls

1925
"Grandiose Hall" of Education

1945
Multipurpose wings, lecture
dominance with activity spaces

1955
Motel model with many
spaces for varied activity,
exposed to environment

1965
Open spaces, multi-purpose rooms,
maximum flexibility

1975
Structured internal space,
closed to outside

Figure 7.5

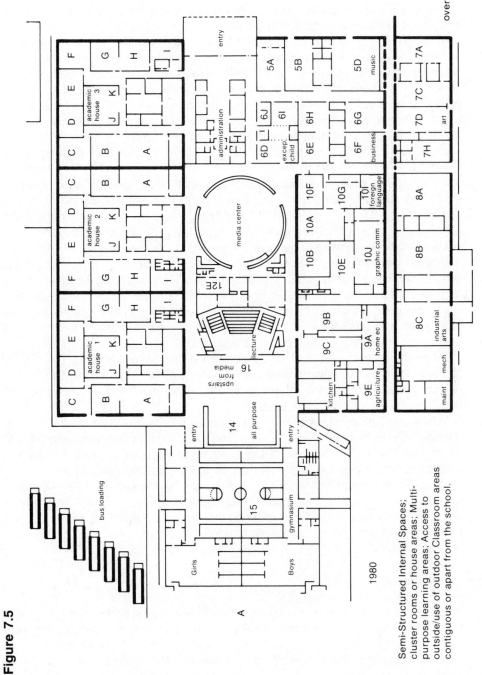

Semi-Structured Internal Spaces;
cluster rooms or house areas; Multipurpose learning areas; Access to
outside/use of outdoor Classroom areas
contiguous or apart from the school.

1980

overall floor plan

219

would show a progression from a cellular lecture hall (many one-room school houses together) to an open and largely unstructured space.

In the 1980s school buildings are a unique combination of previous designs. In the floor plan in Figure 7.5, we find semi-structured spaces with clusters of rooms (houses) and multipurpose learning areas. Access to the outside is multiple to encourage learning beyond the building.

Although many of these changes might be explained by evolutions in architecture and cost-effectiveness demands, a primary force behind the diminishing structure in school buildings has been the dissemination of knowledge through other mediums. As the narrow curriculum of the early junior high school gave way to a more broadly focused program in modern junior high schools and middle schools, buildings were designed to incorporate diversity. Because spaces had multiple uses, the construction was necessarily flexible in design.

Just because a middle school school building is traditional or open-space in design, however, tells the visitor little about the current philosophy of the school. Many flexible programs are found in old "egg crate" buildings and, equally, highly structured programs are sometimes found in modern open-space schools. The degree of access, the "warmth of the building," traffic control patterns inside the building, and space priorities give meaning to the program in the building.

Many schools, because of genuine danger (drugs, crime, etc.) in the immediate neighborhood, limit the number of access points to the school building. Other schools deliberately limit public access as a means of controlling the environment and personnel in the building. Signs of extreme control in school buildings are a single entrance for all entering the building, constantly locked spaces such as bathrooms and auxiliary spaces, and purposeful physical barriers to movement such as long unbroken counters in school offices.

Related to physical access is the concept of "building warmth." The size of spaces, scale of the environment (relationship between size of the people and objects in the environment), shape of spaces, coloration, and use of lighting all affect the warmth of a school building.

In the past, small classrooms with oversized furniture, drab coloration, and square walls were used purposefully to control environmental stimulation and to direct attention to the teacher. Such a discomforting setting presupposed that teacher behavior was the significant action in the learning environment.

More recently, middle schools have used bright colors, curved walls, expansive spaces, and acoustical treatments to encourage student mobility and mental freedom. Such an environment assumes that education is an act which is highly individual and one that is conducted through exploration.

Classroom Spaces

Just as the school learning environment may be revealed in school dimensions like community involvement and building use, the organization, movement, and ownership of physical space in the classroom is often indicative of the intentions of the school. In viewing these classroom characteristics, it is again obvious that all schools are not alike.

One way of viewing classroom spaces is in terms of the organization for

Figure 7.6

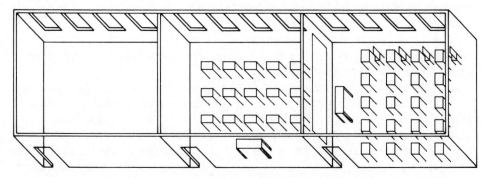

instructional effectiveness. The traditional pattern would be to lay out the room so that all vision and attention would be on the teacher. The example in Figure 7.6 shows there is little opportunity for lateral communication in such an arrangement. Activity is "fixed" by the placement of furniture. The conditions are perfect for teacher lecture, but little else.

Another possibility in organization of classroom spaces is to create multipurpose spaces with the focus of attention generally in the center of the classroom. (See Figure 7.7.) This style permits increased student involvement, mobility, and varied

Figure 7.7

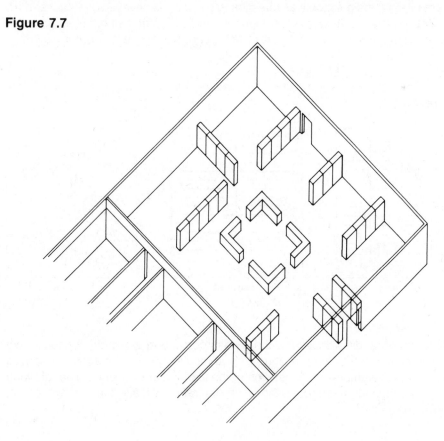

learning activities simultaneously. It does not focus attention solely on the teacher and yet can easily be controlled in terms of noise or lateral communication among students.

Pupil movement within the classroom is a strong indicator of the structure or flexibility present in the learning environment. Movement in some classrooms is totally dependent upon the teacher.

Students in this type of classroom must request permission to talk, go to the washroom, or approach the teacher. Such structure usually minimizes noise and confusion but restricts activity to verbal exchange only. Movement in such classrooms, when it occurs, is generally forward and aft from the teacher's locale.

In a less stationary classroom, movement is possible within controlled patterns monitored by the teacher. Movement is usually contextual depending upon the activity being engaged in. During teacher talk, for instance, movement may not be allowed, whereas, at other times students may be able to sharpen pencils, get supplies, or leave the room for a drink of water without complete dependence on teacher approval.

Pupil movement is sometimes left to the complete discretion of the student. Even during a lesson or a teacher explanation a student may leave to use the washroom. In open-space buildings with high degrees of program flexibility, students are often seen moving unsupervised from one learning area to the next. Parents who have attended more structured, traditional programs often view such movements in middle schools as questionable since it is believed the teacher must be in direct contact with students for learning to occur. Yet, self-directed, unsupervised movement is an integral part of any open, activity-centered curriculum.

Figure 7.8

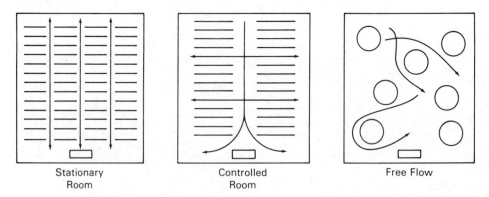

| Stationary Room | Controlled Room | Free Flow |

There are great differences in school classrooms, and these differences reflect the intentions of the school in educating students. As such, classroom spaces represent another important dimension of the learning environment. The following descriptive continuum suggest the potential range of alternatives present in schools.

Classroom Organization

Uniform seating arrangement dominates room	Classroom furniture uniform but not symmetrical	Furniture arranged for each activity	Multipurpose spaces in room	Space out of classroom used for instruction

S— — —|— — — — — — — —+— — — — — —+— — — — — —|— — — — — — — —+— — —F

Classroom Movement

Movement totally restricted by teacher	Total teacher control with noted exception	Pupil movement contextual	Pupil has freedom of movement within limit	Pupil movement at pupil discretion

S— — —|— — — — — — — — — —+— — — — — — — —|— — — — — —+— — — — — —|— —F

Classroom Ownership

Classroom space is dominated by teacher	Teacher dominates, some student zones	Classroom has areas of mutual free access	Territory only at symbolic level—open to all	All classroom spaces totally accessible to all persons

S— —|— — — — — — — —|— — — — — — — —+— — — — — — — —|— — — — — — — —+— —F

SUMMARY

The middle school, with its focus on a program designed around the developmental characteristics of emerging adolescent learners, must provide instructional activities, materials, and learning environments that are as diverse as the group of studies utilizing them.

In this chapter, you have been able to study both the rationale for development of creative instructional activities and the many examples of such activities in present middle schools. You have also been able to examine creative instructional materials used in many middle schools and to review ways creative learning environments have been developed and used in schools for emerging adolescent youth. Key elements in the development of activities, materials, and learning environments are creativeness, imagination, and flexibility.

In the Essential Middle School, there has to be a commitment to making provisions for each learner. Through a wide use of learning activities and materials as well as the development of warm, exciting, learning environments, curriculum and instruction can be tailored to individual needs and be relevant and exciting.

Suggested Learning Activities

1. With a group of colleagues, develop a catalog of creative activities found in middle schools. List each activity with a short description of how it is carried out. Also list sources for finding out more information about an activity.

2. Develop outlines for a series of workshops on building self-pacing materials, setting up learning centers, and writing interdisciplinary units.

3. Develop an outline for an interdisciplinary unit utilizing at least four disciplines, including a related arts subject.

4. Design a learning center for your classroom. List the materials and activities you would include in such a center and the processes by which students would move in and out of the center.

5. The school board has decided to make improvements in the building in which your middle school is housed. Develop a position paper outlining the rationale for a variety of learning areas in the school including learning centers/stations, learning resource rooms, and flexible space for groups of students.

Selected References

Bondi, Joseph. *Developing Middle Schools: A Guidebook.* Wheeling, Ill.: Whitehall Publishing Co., 1972.

Lounsbury, John, and Vars, Gordon. *A Curriculum for the Middle Years.* New York: Harper and Row, Publishers, 1978.

Schein, Bernard, and Schein, Martha. *Open Classrooms in the Middle School.* West Nyack, N. Y.: Parker Publishing Co., 1975.

Timmermann, Tim. *Growing Up Alive.* Amhurst, Mass.: Mandala, 1975.

Wiles, Jon, and Bondi, Joseph. *Curriculum Development: A Guide to Practice.* Columbus, Ohio: Charles Merrill Publishing Co., 1979.

Wiggins, J. D., and English, Dori. *Affective Education: A Manual for Growth.* Dover, Del.: Delaware Department of Public Instruction, 1975.

In addition to the above references, we would like to suggest a review of the following materials:

Self-Incorporated Films—Fifteen 15–minute color films designed to help 11–13 year-olds cope with emotional, physical, and social problems. Agency for Instructional Television, Bloomington, Ind.

Teacher and *Instructor Magazines*—These two publications are excellent sources of free materials and readings about developing creative activities and learning environments.

McDonald's Corporation—Oak Brook, Ill., and other commercial firms publish a variety of materials relevant to middle school students.

Druthers—A publication of the New York State Department of Education contains a collection of creative ideas from rural schools in New York. This publication was developed through ESEA Title III funds.

American Newspaper Publishers Association Foundation—Box 17407, Dulles Airport, Washington, D. C.; furnishes numerous ideas and materials for using the newspaper in the classroom.

An Interdisciplinary Approach to Teaching in the Middle School—Contains model interdisciplinary units developed by teachers in Oklahoma City.

8

Planning Considerations for Middle Schools

The establishment of a middle school is a complex activity
that requires planning as well as ambition

INTRODUCTION

The curriculum of the middle school, with its concern for the special needs of preadolescents, with its comprehensive definition of education, with its promotion of continuity in learning and development, is more than a series of catch phrases and educational innovations. The middle school is, in fact, a highly complex plan for educating a special learner. Due to the complexity of the educational design, successful implementation of the program calls for a significant degree of advanced planning.

During the 1970s the middle school movement entered a new era of maturity. A decade of practical application of middle school concepts brought new insights for planning the middle school. In this chapter these planning considerations are outlined, and examples of school and district-wide plans are included to help the reader understand the complex processes involved in developing middle schools.

Many understandings and decisions are necessary to initiate and promote the middle school concept. The type and size of the community, the amount of funding, the availability and resourcefulness of trained personnel are but a few of the primary concerns.

In assisting a number of middle schools during the establishment stage, we have noted that planning often determines the fine line between success and failure. Such planning is necessary at the district, school, and classroom level if the program of the middle school is to succeed. This chapter seeks to provide guidelines which will assist middle schools in avoiding problems which can be overcome by good planning.

DISTRICT LEVEL PLANNING

As often as not, middle schools come into being because dedicated intermediate educators are seeking a better way to serve their students. If programs originate at the school level, however, their development is sometimes delayed by a lack of planning at the school district level. The system which constructs a building without understanding the middle school concept, for instance, is going to handicap the program somewhere in the future. District-level planning must be conducted if the middle school concept is to succeed in one of its schools.

It is our further observation that the *sequence* of district-level planning is particularly important to the smooth implementation of programs. The following district-level planning steps, in sequence, are recommended in the establishment of a middle school.

Analysis

The middle school should arise from need. Although it is ideal to hope that school systems and communities will proceed through value-clarification processes which reveal the logic of the middle school design, it is hoped that programs will be initiated based on what is known about their students. Overcrowding, integration, or building availability are poor reasons for choosing the concept.

An important point in making such an analysis is not to allow the search to be focused only on problems. It should also be projective—what kind of an educational experience do we want for students during this period of development?

Involvement

Preliminary investigations of the middle school should involve all parties with vested interests in intermediate education. A step often taken in planning the middle school is to explore the concept without involving those who will be most directly affected by its activation: students, teachers, parents, and the community. At a superficial level, the elimination of this stage will probably lead to future confrontations over both programs and policy (interscholastic athletics, social events, grading policies, community-based learning). More important from the planning standpoint, however, is the dedication and support that will be needed to put such a program into practice in the first place. *The middle school cannot be implemented and maintained unless it is believed in by those involved.*

Of the constituencies mentioned above, particular attention must be given to the community in which the middle school will reside. Not being accustomed to educational jargon, and being unfamiliar with national trends in educational programs, many citizens will resist the middle school because of misunderstandings about the academic nature of the program and the necessary organizational arrangements. Without a clear understanding of the rationale of the program and the reason for these arrangements, community resistance will be high.

Involvement of community members representing all segments of the population in the initial analysis of student needs, in the investigation of the middle school concept, in the drafting of documents, and in the planning of implementation stages will build in a means of communicating with the community at later times.

Commitment

Philosophical commitments to the middle school definition of education should be secured prior to activating the program. This book has repeatedly underscored the necessity of understanding and accepting the middle school's philosophic position on education as a prerequisite for successful implementation of such a program. *An understanding or lack of understanding of the middle school concept represents the largest potential stumbling block to successful implementation.* Without such understanding and a basic philosophic acceptance of the middle school concept, there can be no substantial rationale for practices and programs found in the middle school.

It is important to note that this understanding and acceptance must go beyond school board approval and superintendent acquiescence—although both are consequential. Such an understanding and commitment must be held by the building principal, the involved teachers, and the parents of involved students.

Funding

Appropriate monies must be earmarked for activation of the plan. An observable phenomenon in American education is that finance is the "fuel" of progress. Few major innovations of the past twenty years (middle schools being a notable exception) have really succeeded without substantial financial support.

Although it is not impossible for a building faculty to implement the middle school concept with sheer dedication, two simple facts about middle schools are worth noting: *Middle schools are a more complex form of education than traditional programs and as such, they require more energy and money to operate.*

Every deviation from standardized patterns of educating, such as the uniform textbooks, the classroom-confined learning experience, and the single-dimension instruction will require effort and expense. As school districts do commit themselves to the middle school concept, a pledge equal to their commitment for financing building conversion, materials acquisition, staff development and so forth is called for.

Resources

Resources commensurate with the task must be allocated. One of the common pitfalls in establishment of middle schools is to assume they can operate on the same resource base as the traditional intermediate school. To rely on teacher-made materials exclusively, to overlook a consumable materials budget, to fail to allocate materials to build up the instructional resource center, to make no provision for off-campus experiences and so forth is to doom in advance the programs of the middle school. *Middle schools, if properly operated, require substantial resources for instruction.*

Personnel

There must be an attempt to staff middle schools with dedicated and enthusiastic teachers. There are several appropriate comments to note regarding the selection, training, and use of middle school staff. The middle school will be only as effective as its personnel in succeeding at new roles. With only several colleges in the nation training teachers and staff members exclusively for middle school positions, most teachers and support personnel will enter the middle school from other more traditional educational designs. Such persons, regardless of their belief in and allegiance to the middle school philosophy of educating, will need special assistance in adjusting to their new roles. *It can be expected that the middle school staff will need extensive assistance in assuming new roles.*

A problem witnessed in many school districts is that middle school teacher behaviors are prone to return to traditional patterns if sufficient support is not maintained. Many middle schools open under the so-called Hawthorne Effect (a term coming from the Hawthorne Studies in which workers were found to be more productive regardless of work conditions if they first received sufficient attention as being special), and with such a condition, teacher enthusiasm and energy is understandably high. However, as program development slows or resource bases erode with the gradual lessening of attention, it is not unusual for old patterns of teacher-pupil interaction and learning to creep in. Such a condition would warn against a one-shot summer treatment for the middle school staff and would call, instead, for long-term, systematic training opportunities.

Detailed Planning

Prior to the development of a middle school it is essential that detailed planning be conducted. From an administrative/organizational perspective, it is crucial that schools conduct detailed planning to smoothly implement the middle school concept. The past experience of many middle schools suggests that a "broken front" approach to this concept does not work. The middle school concept does not easily emerge because there are prerequisites for implementation. There must be an understanding of objectives; there must be a commitment to this definition of educating; there must be an involvement of those who support the school; there must be money and resources to implement its components; there must be personnel capable of and willing to assume the required roles. *The time frame for opening a middle school must allow for the magnitude of the process proposed.*

While the amount of preparation time required to open a real middle school is dependent upon environmental conditions in the community, a minimum period appears to be eighteen to twenty-four months. This estimate is based on several definable steps of planning:

1. Awareness and study phases.
2. Educating community and gaining commitments.
3. Budgeting for development.
4. Selection of staff, site.
5. Construction of detailed implementation plan.
6. Intensive training of staff.
7. Development of curriculum.
8. Construction or conversion of site.
9. Opening of middle school.

It is recognized that in some communities and school districts it would be possible to accomplish the above steps in six months or less due to central office organization and support from the community leaders. The experience of many middle schools, however, would suggest that to hasten through steps 2, 6, and 7, or to proceed with step 8 prior to step 7 leads to significant problems later on. *Eroding community support, an ill-prepared staff, a superficially constructed curriculum, and a dysfunctional site all are causes of middle school failure.*

Determining the Odds for Success

Not all communities are ready for a middle school. As with its predecessor, the junior high school, the middle school has achieved tremendous numerical growth in a relatively short period of time. The rush of this "bandwagon" effect has caused many communities to plan and construct middle schools without due consideration of the implications of their actions. When the true nature of the middle school program is first made known to parents and to teachers not involved in decision making, misunderstandings and conflict can result.

The implementation of educational change is always a relatively unpredictable phenomenon due to the immense number of variables involved. One research project sponsored by the State of Florida, and directed by the authors, sought, through study and on-site observation, to identify the crucial variables which indicate the probability of an educational innovation being accepted at the building level. (See Figure 8.1.) While the profile on the following page in no way promises success for those attempting to open a middle school, it can provide a rough

Figure 8.1
Educational Innovations Probability Chart

High Risk ◄———► Lower Risk

Category					
Source of Innovation	Superimposed from outside	Outside agent brought in	Developed internally with aid	External idea modified	Locally conceived, developed, implemented
Impact of Innovation	Challenges sacrosanct beliefs	Calls for major value shifts	Requires substantial change	Modifies existing values of programs	Does not substantially alter existing values, beliefs or programs
Official Support	Official leaders active opposition	Officials on record as opposing	Officials uncommitted	Officials voice support of change	Enthusiastically supported by the official leaders
Planning of Innovation	Completely external	Most planning external	Planning processes balanced	Most of planning done locally	All planning for change done on local site
Means of Adoption	By superiors	By local leaders	By Reps	By most of the clients	By group consensus
History of Change	History of failures	No accurate records on	Some success with innovation	A history of successful innovations	Known as school where things regularly succeed
Possibility of Revision	No turning back	Final evaluation before committee	Periodic evaluations	Possibility of abandoning at conclusion	Possible to abort the effort at any time
Role of Teachers	Largely bypassed	Minor role	Regular role in implementing	Heavy role in implementation	Primary actor in the classroom effort
Teacher Expectation	Fatalistic	Feel little chance	Are willing to give a try	Confident of success	Wildly enthusiastic about chance of success
Work Load Measure	Substantially increased	Heavier but rewarding	Slightly increased	Unchanged	Work load lessened by the innovation
Threat Measure	Definitely threatens some clients	Probably threatening to some	Mild threat resulting from the change	Very remote threat to some	Does not threaten the security or autonomy
Community Factor	Hostile to innovations	Suspicious and uninformed	Indifferent	Ready for a change	Wholeheartedly supports the school

Shade the response in each category which most accurately reflects the condition surrounding the implementations of the middle school. If the "profile" of your school is predominately in the high risk side of the matrix, substantial work must be done to prepare your school for change.

SOURCE: Jon Wiles, *Planning Guidelines for Middle School Education* (Dubuque, Iowa: Kendall/Hunt Publishing Company, 1976), p. 30. Used by permission.

pattern for study. Such a device is also helpful in directing energies to increase the changes of successful implementation.

Building-Level Planning

Beyond district-level planning for middle school programs is the preparation at the building level. If substantial and lasting curriculum change is to occur in schools, the planning of such change must be both comprehensive and coordinated. Existing literature on change in school environments suggests that curricular alterations of school programs are both complex and difficult to control. Changes dealing with programs are rarely isolated and comprise, intentionally or otherwise, a series of interrelated and interdependent events. The challenge to building-level planners is to develop a comprehensive monitoring device to observe and direct the numerous on-going changes. One such "building blueprint" is the *developmental staging concept.*

Developmental staging is basically a construct using a form of "discrepancy analysis." It consists of outlining anticipated change steps in program development which are intermediate conditions between what currently exists and what is desired. In a sense, developmental staging attempts to break down the sometimes enormous gaps between the "real" and "ideal" while at the same time displaying the comprehensive nature of the change being planned.

The utility of the "staging" concept to promote desired curricular change is dependent upon several essential conditions. First, it is assumed that some sort of philosophical consensus is present among those engaged in the change process so that terminal goals can be described and progress toward those goals accurately assessed. Stated simply, it is impossible to construct a chart of progression toward desired goals in the middle school program if such ends are not clearly identified and agreed upon.

Second, it is vital that the staging plans leading toward desired goals begin with an accurate portrait of present realities. A staff must use its best judgment to distinguish between educational intentions and day-to-day practices. Often the only accurate means of testing such potential discrepancies is to view the condition or practice through the eyes of a single randomly selected middle-school student. What is read, what is desired?

Finally, the use of developmental staging should always be preceded by an acceptance of the fact that lasting change of a curricular nature is almost always a tedious process. A predisposition toward patience and a long view of progress will assist a staff in a thoughtful identification of stages of progress.

Continuums of Progress

In global reorientations of school programs, such as in the design of a middle school, monitoring categories of school change can provide more accurate indicators of progress toward desired ends. In one city, for instance, a planning team identified fourteen areas (see Table 8.1) in which they felt progress should be monitored.

Table 8.1
Present and Desired Conditions: A Contrast

Moving From	Moving Toward
1. *Philosophy* A written document on file in the school office, defining the school in terms of knowledge areas and administrative concerns.	An active, working philosophy which is known by all teachers and which serves as the basis of day-to-day decision making. Defines the school in terms of expected learner growth.
2. *School Plant* Using only standard classroom spaces for instructional purposes.	Encompassing varied learning environments, using all available building spaces for instructional purposes (school yard, corridors).
3. *Staffing Patterns* Isolated teachers in self-contained classes.	Teachers grouped in cooperative arrangements, dealing with large numbers of learners collectively. Planning time and home-base teaching function built-in organizationally.
4. *Instructional Materials* Classrooms dominated by a basic grade-level text. Libraries usually study halls for large class groups.	Diversified learning materials within any given classroom setting, "something for everybody." Multiple texts, supplemental software, integrated and cross-subject materials. Heavy use of multimedia learning resource centers for independent exploration.
5. *Organization of Students* Basic pattern of one teacher and thirty students in standardized room spaces. Students in the same sized groups all day.	Greater variability in the sizes of learning groups ranging from individualized study to large group (120 students) instruction. Grouped according to the objective of the instruction.
6. *Teaching Strategies* Variety of approaches found, but most classes dominated by lecture, single text, question-answer format.	Greater variety of patterns of teacher-pupil interchange. Teaming when advantageous, greater use of media, possible peer teaching, counseling, more hands-on experiences.
7. *Role of the Teacher* Defined in terms of subject(s) taught. Teacher perceived as source of knowledge and responsible for order.	Greater concern with students. A planned teacher-counselor role. More group work (projects, issues). Teacher role an organizer, facilitator of learning experiences. Teacher monitoring "contracts" with students. Shared responsibility for order.
8. *Role of Student* Passive recipient of knowledge. Most instruction paced to group. A reactive posture.	Greater input and chance for expression. Involved in planning. Goal to become self-directed. Emphasis on self-conduct and "success." Use of contracts for student goal setting.

Table 8.1—*continued*

Moving From	Moving Toward
9. *Role of Parents* Limited access to the schools. Few parents involved at meaningful level. Involvement in only administrative concerns.	Greater involvement of all parents in school activities. Opportunities for more direct involvement in instructional roles in classroom and curriculum planning. Greater flow of information to parents about school objectives and program.
10. *Role of Community* Limited interface with schools. Some strong foundational ties with social services in the city.	School becoming more outwardly oriented; seeing the community as a learning environment and source of instructional resources. Systematizing the connections with social services in the community.
11. *School Rules and Regulations* High degree of regimentation through rules and regulation. Little student input into process. High degree of student dependence on adults for direction.	Greater involvement of students in the design of regulatory policies. Identifying the really essential rules. Aiming toward minimum acceptable level of control. Goal to foster increased student independence and self-control.
12. *Discipline* Reactive pattern of discipline, ranging from admonishment and parent conferences to paddling and expulsion.	Designing an active program to deter potential disciplinary problems. Greater involvement of pupils in process. Insured degrees of success for all students, seeking to curtail frustration and boredom.
13. *Reporting of Student Progress* Letter grades assigned, concern with only narrowly defined academic progress.	Striving for varied student evaluation using a more descriptive medium (conferences, student folders, etc.). Focused on all dimensions of student growth. Sometimes reported as student competencies.
14. *Staff Development* Global, not closely tied to building-level needs of teachers and students.	Designed to attack building-level problems identified by teachers and students. Development of a monitoring process to measure achievement of predetermined goals.

Taking the foregoing areas of concern for middle school development, and grouping them under headings such as the school environment, participant roles, instructional arrangements, and administrative conditions will allow middle school planners to begin to see connected "areas" of concern.

In the model of developmental staging on pages 238–41, areas within each of the four large categories are followed through five major stages of development. Stage one in each of the categories describes in a few words the realities of present conditions. Stage two reflects an awareness of the directions of change and possibly some "tinkering" with the status quo. Stage three is generally an experimentation stage during which the desired changes are auditioned. Stage four represents an adoption stage during which the change is institutionalized or supported by administrative acts. Stage five is a brief description of the ideal condition or stage being pursued.

Regardless of the nature of the change or of the value system such change represents or reflects, it is crucial that a description of the stages be derived from the statement of philosophic purpose. Such "guidance" will promote consistency among the stages and, therefore, support continuous progress toward the desired changes.

The present condition of the school described in stage 1 is not unlike that of many schools across the nation. There is either no philosophic statement of purposes or such a statement is left over from the last accreditation visit and remains locked in the principal's desk drawer.

The environment of the school shows "learning" occurring only in the standard classroom spaces, and those spaces are characterized by meager materials. There is little or no interchange between the school and the immediate neighborhood and community about it.

Roles at the school are highly traditional. The principal is the "boss," the broker of rights and favors, the enforcer of rules. Teachers represent units of subject-matter specialization. Students are passive and without individual academic identity.[1]

The instructional organization of the school causes the teachers to be cut off and isolated from each other. Teaching is chiefly by lecture method, and the instructional team is receiving random doses of "help" from periodic district staff development efforts.

Administrative conditions find students regimented for convenience and economy. Student progress is reported in abbreviated letter or number symbols in five or six arbitrarily selected areas of growth. The school is dominated by a plethora of rules—rules for any and all occasions—and by a reactive and repetitive program of discipline.

The ideal or desired condition (stage 5), on the other hand, represents a very different portrait for the developing middle school. Such a school aspires to a tailor-made learning environment, for a logical allocation of available resources, an individualized curriculum for students, and instructional contact with the community beyond its walls.

The desired roles for this transitional middle school would feature involved and self-reliant students, facilitating and creative teachers, and supportive administrators who themselves are instructional leaders within the building.

The desired instructional program would have organizational arrangements which reflect the intent of the curricular components. There would be a variety of instructional patterns present at any given moment, and problems would be resolved with the aid of specific staff development assistance.

Administrative conditions, ideally, would be supportive of the curricular program and, therefore, flexible to change as program focus and intentions change. Report of student progress would be comprehensive, individualized, and descriptive. Rules and regulations would be minimal. Discipline, when needed, would be efficient and effective in changing behavior.

The usefulness of the developmental staging concept in the planning of a middle

---

[1] Jon Wiles, "Developmental Staging—In Pursuit of Comprehensive Curriculum Planning," *Middle School Journal*, 6, no. 1 (Spring 1975): 7–10.

school program is multifaceted.[2] Such a technique can provide a ready profile of a school and its educational program and also display areas of concern. Using a staged format, discrepancies, inconsistencies, and severe problem areas can be identified and confronted.

Developmental staging also serves as a master blueprint for comprehensive change and, where stages are defined and described in behavioral terms, a tool for periodic evaluation. As a display of reality and a picture of progress, it can serve as a medium for in-house communication. (See Figure 8.2.)

Most important for emerging middle schools, however, is the usefulness of the staging concept in overcoming feelings of "powerlessness." Such feelings result from being overwhelmed by the many dimensions of the change process in school environments. In dealing with the sometimes wide gulf between real conditions and ideal conditions, those involved in planning and development of the middle school can "witness" progress in the many continuums and experience the "pace" or momentum of the changes occurring.

The ends to be pursued, the categories to be monitored, and the proofs of progress in stages should all be developed internally by those persons involved in planning and implementing the middle school. Developmental staging as outlined is a useful concept in serving as a curricular blueprint for development.

It should be noted that the staging concept outlined here can be valuably linked with management devices, such as PERT/CPM, to give an even clearer picture of progress toward desired ends. It is felt that the development of the middle school concept, without such an effort to perceive and control the complexities of change, can cause the permanent division of theory and practice, thereby undermining the credibility of middle school potential.

EXAMPLES OF STATE DISTRICT SCHOOL PLANNING FOR MIDDLE SCHOOLS

A growing number of states have established guidelines for development of middle schools. Those guidelines include programmatic and organizational definitions, inservice and preservice education standards, and certification requirements. School districts and individual schools have also established planning guidelines for middle school development.

State Planning for Middle Schools

Florida was a pioneer in developing a plan for middle schools in that state. In 1970, following the First State Conference on the middle school at the University of South Florida, the State Board of Education appointed the Special State Committee on the middle school to develop guidelines for identifying middle schools and certifying pre- and inservice middle school teachers in the state.

---

[2] Jon Wiles, *Planning Guidelines for Middle School Education* (Dubuque, Iowa: Kendall/ Hunt Publishing Company, 1978), pp. 5–11, 25–40.

Figure 8.2
Developmental Staging—Middle Schools

SOURCE: From "Developmental Staging—In Pursuit of Comprehensive Curriculum Planning" by Jon Wiles, *Middle School Journal* 6 (September 1975): 7–10. Used by permission.

	Present Condition	Awareness Stage	Experimentation Stage	Adoption Stage	Desired Condition
	Stage 1	Stage 2	Stage 3	Stage 4	Stage 5
The School Philosophy	Either no formal statement or a written document on file in the school office.	School staff share beliefs, look for consensus, restate philosophy and objectives in terms of expected behavior.	Staff begins use of goals as guide to evaluating school practices. Begin to involve students and community in planning.	Philosophy and goals used to shape the program. Formal mechanism established to monitor program and decision making.	Philosophy a living document. Guides daily decisions. The program a tool for achieving desired educational ends.

The Learning Environment

	Present Condition	Awareness Stage	Experimentation Stage	Adoption Stage	Desired Condition
Use of the Building	Only uniform instructional spaces. Little use of the building spaces for educational purposes.	Some deviation from traditional space utilization (classroom learning center). Possibly a complete demonstration class for bright ideas.	Limited building conversion (knock out walls). Begin to identify unused spaces. Planning for large learning spaces.	Development of a comprehensive plan for use of grounds and building. Total remodeling of spaces.	Tailor-made learning environment—all spaces used to educate. Building facilitates the learning intention.
Use of Materials	Classrooms are dominated by a grade-level text. Library with a limited offering. Used as a study hall for large groups.	Use of multi-level texts within classroom. Materials selected after an analysis of student achievement levels. Supplemental resources made available to students.	Diverse materials developed for the students. Resource centers established. Cross-discipline selection of materials. More multi-media used. Some independent study.	Materials purchasing policies realigned. Common learning areas established as resource centers. More self-directed study built in.	Diversified materials. Something for each student. Integrated subject materials. Portable curriculum units (on carts). Heavy multi-media. Active learning centers.

Figure 8.2—*continued*

Use of Community	Little or no access to school. Information about programs scanty. Trust low.	Some school program ties to community. Token access via PTA and media. School perceived as island in neighborhood.	Preliminary uses of community as learning environment. Identification of nearby resources. Use of building for community functions.	Regular interchange between school and community. Systematic communication. A network of services and resources established.	School programs outwardly oriented. Community seen as a teaching resource. Systematic ties with services and resources around school.

Instructional Organization

Staffing Patterns	Building teachers isolated in self-contained classrooms. Little or no lateral communication or planning present.	Limited sharing of resources. Some division of labor and small-scale cooperation in teaching. Informal communication about student progress.	Regular cooperative planning sessions. Some curricular integration via themes. Students rotate through subject areas. Problems of cooperation identified.	Interdepartmental organization. Use of common planning time. Administrative support such as in scheduling. Use of philosophy as curricular decision-making criteria.	Teaching staff a "team" working toward common ends. Staff patterns reflect instructional intentions. Administration in support of curricular design. Coursework integrated for students.
Teaching Strategy	Some variety but lecture and teacher-dominated Q-A session the norm. Homework used to promote day-to-day continuity.	Observation of other teaching models. Skill development via workshops. An identification of staff strengths and weaknesses. Some new patterns.	Building level experiments by willing staff members. "Modeling" of ideas. On-site consultant help made available for skill development.	School day divided according to the teaching strategy employed. Faculty evaluation of the effectiveness of new ways after a trial period.	Great variety of methods used in teaching, uses of media, dealing with students. The curricular plans determine strategy.
Staff Development	Staff development is global, rarely used to attack local needs and problems. Occurs as needed.	Staff identifies in-service needs and priorities. Philosophy assists in this process. Local staff skills and strengths are recognized.	Staff development realigned to serve needs of teachers. Opportunities for personal growth are made available.	Formal procedures for directing staff development to needs established. Staff development seen as problem-solving mechanism.	Staff development an on-going process using available resources. An attempt to close theory-practice gaps.

Figure 8.2—_continued_

Administrative Conditions

	Present Condition	Awareness Stage	Experimentation Stage	Adoption Stage	Desired Condition
	Stage 1	Stage 2	Stage 3	Stage 4	Stage 5
Organization of Student	Uniform patterns. One teacher, 30 students in six rows of five in each row in each period of each school day.	Understanding that organization of students should match curricular intentions. Some initial variation of group sizes in classroom.	Limited organization to facilitate the grouping of the students. Begin use of aides and parents to increase organizational flexibility.	Full administrative support for a reorganization of students. Building restructed where necessary. An increase in planning for effectiveness.	Group sizes vary according to the activity planned. Full support given to eliminate any problem areas.
Report of Student Progress	"Progress" is defined narrowly. Letter grades or simple numerals represent student learning in the subject areas.	Recognition of broader growth goals for students. Use of philosophy to evaluate the existing practices.	Experimentation with supplemental reporting procedures. Involvement of student and parents in the process.	Development of a diverse and comprehensive reporting procedure for student progress.	Descriptive medium used to monitor individual student progress. Broadly focused evaluation. Team of teacher, student, and parents involved.
Rules and Regulations	High degree of regimentation. Many rules, most inherited over the years. The emphasis on the enforcement and on control.	Staff and students identify essential rules. Regulations matched against the school philosophy.	Rules and regulations streamlined. Used as a teaching device about life outside of school. Increased student self-control.	Greater use of student and staff input into the regulation of the school environment. Rewards built-in for desirable performance.	Moving toward minimal regulation and an increased student self-control. Regulations a positive teaching device.
Discipline	Reactive pattern ranging from verbal admonishment to paddling and expulsion. Reoccurring offenders.	Staff analysis of school policies. Shift of emphasis to causes of the problems. Some brainstorming of possible solutions.	Establishment of a hierarchy of discipline activity. Begin implementing preventive strategies.	Design of curriculum programs to deter discipline problems. High intensity program for regular offenders.	Program of the school eliminates most sources of discipline problems. The procedure for residual problems clear to all.

Figure 8.2—*continued*

Roles of Participants

Student Roles	Passive recipient of knowledge. Instruction is geared to average student. Reactive communication with the teacher.	Investigation of new student roles by teacher. Limited hierarchy of trust established in the classroom. Needs and interests of student investigated.	Groundrules for increased student independence set. Student involvement in planning. Role of student connected to philosophy of the school.	Periodic staff review of student roles. Roles linked to school-wide rules and regulations. Philosophy guides role possibilities.	Students involved in planning and conducting the program. Increased independence *and* responsibility. Use of "contracts" to maintain new understandings.
Teacher Roles	Defined by the subjects taught. Perceived as the source of all knowledge. Other roles peripheral.	Perceiving roles suggested by the philosophy. Roles accepted at verbal level. Limited experimentation with new roles.	Investigation of new roles—trying on new relationship. Goal-setting for individual teacher. Skill development through in-service.	Administrative reorganization for role support. A sharpened planning and action skills needed to serve the student according to the philosophy.	Teacher role is defined by student needs. Teacher the organizer of the learning activities. Teacher talents used more effectively.
Principal Roles	Solely responsible for school operation. The "boss". Enforcer of all rules. The linkage to all outside information and resources.	Awareness of role limitations. An awareness of real leadership potential. A setting of role priorities.	Limited sharing of decision-making in area of curriculum. Limited joint planning with the faculty. Review of existing policy according to the philosophy.	Role perception changes to manager of resources. Emphasis on development (active) rather than on order (static). Increase in curriculum leadership functions.	An instructional leader. Administrative acts support the curriculum program. Philosophy guiding decision-making. Built-in monitoring system for evaluating building level progress.

The middle school was defined by the state as "a school providing a program planned for a range of older children, preadolescents and early adolescents, that builds upon the elementary school program for earlier childhood and, in turn, is built upon by the high school's program for adolescents. The school's program should be designed for children, usually ages ten through fourteen, heretofore classified in grades 5 or 6 through 8. Schools temporarily having only two of these grades may be classified as middle schools if their program reflects middle school goals. Schools having a different organizational pattern could, upon justification to the commissioner, apply for a waiver of this definition in the same manner as for a waiver of a regulation under the provision of the State Board of Education Regulation 6A–1.011.[3]

Florida's certification of inservice middle school teachers required that teachers participate in staff development programs as outlined in district master plans for inservice, teach in one of the areas of science, mathematics, English, or social studies, and teach successfully for a year (certified by the principal and district superintendent) in a state-identified middle school program. Preservice teacher education programs were also approved to prepare teachers for the middle school. The checklist suggested in Figure 8.3 was also developed by the Florida Special Committee.

The West Virginia State Department of Education has done the most extensive work in recent years in establishing guidelines for middle school development. *The Programmatic Definition of Middle Schools in West Virginia* is a comprehensive document which outlines in detail program expectations for West Virginia middle schools. The State Department also sponsored a series of successful State Conferences on the middle school in 1978, 1979, and 1980.

Many states have organized Leagues of Middle Schools that sponsor conferences, publish monographs, and share information about middle schools. The 1970s saw a rapid growth of Leagues of Middle Schools and the birth of the National Middle School Association.

District Planning for Middle Schools

School districts often include planning committees that are appointed by school boards to develop middle school programs. Such committees are often charged with establishing a timetable and identifying responsible agents for converting junior high schools to middle schools or organizing a new middle school from an elementary or secondary school.

Development of a District Curriculum Plan:
A Case Study

The following Comprehensive Plan was developed as a result of the "felt need" of many parents, teachers, and students for a better program for pre- and early

---

[3] Special State Committee on the Middle School, *Development of Middle Schools in Florida,* (Tallahassee, Fla.: State Dept. of Education, 1972), p. 1.

Figure 8.3

A Checklist for Districts Moving to the Middle School Plan

Although there is no one correct way to move to the middle school plan, any district considering this change might use the following checklist as a guide to determine whether adequate planning has taken place:

The Basic Issues   Yes   No

1. Are the needs of the child between childhood and adolescence being met?

2. Is a different organization needed?

3. Has the school board, with the superintendent's recommendation, considered a change in the existing organization?

4. Is the middle school the organization to provide the best education for this aged child?

5. Have planning groups been formed?

6. Have the following groups been included in planning committees:
    a. administration of district and school?
    b. faculty?
    c. parents?
    d. community?

The Problem of Feasibility

1. Has the proposed move to the middle school plan been accepted by:
    a. the school board?
    b. superintendent and district administrative personnel?
    c. the total school staff?
    d. parents?
    e. students?
    f. community?

2. Has the school board set a realistic date allowing a minimum of 12–18 months?

3. Has the planning committee designed a timetable which provides adequate time?

4. What will the present facilities and/or contemplated facilities permit in reorganization as a middle school?
    a. Is there money to build new facilities?
    b. Do existing facilities permit the kind of program desired?
    c. If the existing facilities are to be utilized, what changes in the physical plant are to be considered and is money available?

5. Has the school board made a total commitment to the program?

Planning the New Program

1. Have the characteristics and needs of the middle school learner been reviewed by the faculty?

2. Has the faculty compiled and reviewed information on the student population to be served?

3. Has there been an evaluation of existing programs for children of middle school age?

4. Has the evaluation determined which programs are appropriate or relevant for this age group and which programs are lacking or inappropriate?

5. Have representatives from the senior high school and the elementary school been involved?

Figure 8.3—*continued*

Yes   Nc

6. Have other middle schools been invited?

7. Have teachers been included in all visits?

8. Have personnel from exemplary middle schools in other districts and instructors from colleges and universities been invited to act as consultants?

9. Has the faculty reviewed alternate methods of classifying children for administrative and instructional purposes?

10. Have specific program plans been developed which take into account the following:

    a. instruction in the organized knowledge or common learning components of the curriculum, including a description of the scope of instruction in each major area?

    b. instruction and guidance in the personal development curriculum area?

    c. instruction, including self-instruction, in the learning skills area?

    d. operation of the special interest program?

    e. staff utilization with reference to instructional organization?

    f. individual pupil evaluation and progress?

    g. scheduling arrangements for the program of the school?

    h. arrangements for the use of learning resources and centers?

    i. articulation with levels above and below?

    j. responsibilities of administrators and other special school personnel?

    k. plans for the evaluation of the school program?

Securing Community Cooperation

1. Has a strong information plan for readying the community for the change been undertaken by the staff, selected laymen, and parents, if all groups have been involved from the outset? Does this plan include the involvement of each of the above groups?

2. Are there plans for the maintenance of a continuous orientation plan after the school opens?

3. Have resource people been involved in the community relations program?

4. Are plans developed so that the community relations program will be an on-going program?

Designing a New Facility

1. Has adequate time for planning been provided?

2. Have teachers, students, parents, and members of the community been involved in the planning?

3. Have educational specifications been developed to ensure that the new facility will meet the demands of the program?

Recruiting the Staff

1. Were volunteers accepted from other schools?

2. If a staff existed, were persons permitted to transfer if they were not committed to the middle school concept?

3. In a personal interview, were members of the staff, in addition to the principal, involved in the selection?

Figure 8.3—*continued*

Orienting Those Concerned   **Yes**   **No**

1. Has time been provided for a preschool workshop for the entire staff?
2. Have the following effective means of communication been used with parents:
   a. written materials, such as newsletters?
   b. PTA meetings?
   c. discussion sessions?
   d. school visitation?
   e. lay membership on planning committee?

Maintaining Changes After a Program Has Been Implemented

1. Has an evaluation design been developed which can be the basis for continuous change?
2. Is the faculty permitted to make changes on the basis of an evaluation?
3. Is provision made for consultants and outside resources to continue?
4. Are public information programs to be continuous to keep parents and students informed?
5. Does the staff recognize that mistakes will be made and adjustments must be made?

adolescent learners in a Stamford, Connecticut school district. Although the plan is not a complete plan (specific objectives are not listed), it does illustrate a process that resulted in the development of a dynamic new middle school program.

COMPREHENSIVE PLAN FOR MIDDLE SCHOOL DEVELOPMENT

Preface:

In 1969, the Board of Education accepted a document entitled *"A Master Plan for Implementation of the Middle School in Stamford."* This master plan was the result of committee work involving professional individuals from the school system.

The middle schools of Stamford have made steady progress in implementing the organizational patterns detailed in the master plan. Also, at the direction of the Board of Education, a middle school committee composed of lay and professional individuals was formed to study the middle school program. The report of this committee has been submitted to the Board of Education.

In the spring of 1975, at the conclusion of a workshop directed by Dr. Joseph Bondi, the middle school principals decided to assume the responsibility themselves of forming a central committee to further the implementation of the middle school concept in Stamford. Subsequently, a workshop was held during early summer 1975, to review the initial master plan. What follows is the report of that review in a form of philosophy, recommendations and time frames for the accomplishment of specific objectives as established by the Middle School Coordinating Committee.

Philosophy:

The middle school in Stamford shall be organized to provide an educational environment suited to the unique needs, interests and abilities of the early adolescents as it helps them develop to their maximum potential.

In an effort to promote quality education, each student should be accepted as an individual. The middle school should provide a unique program for the diverse age group which it serves—youngsters who are in the transition from childhood to adolescence. Each student shall have the opportunity to grow in self-awareness, in personal discipline, in citizenship, and in academic and social skills through diversified educational experiences.

This middle school program is presented as a dynamic, humanistic approach capable of utilizing the findings of ongoing research and educational innovation.

Goals:

The middle school must do the following:

1. Meet the wide range of needs and abilities of the early adolescent.
2. Emphasize the learning process and the joy of learning.
3. Focus attention on the unique development stage of each child, the need for personal responsibility and independence, the identification of a positive self-image and the necessity of experiencing success.
4. Be staffed with personnel who respond to the unique needs of the middle school child.
5. Be a place in which students develop positive relationships with and among the school community.

Needs Identification:

The following needs have been identified:

1. Better communication lines to be established between district personnel, principals, and staffs of the middle schools concerning goals and purposes of the middle school in Stamford.
2. A comprehensive plan developed to fully implement the middle school as originally proposed in 1969 and revised in 1975.
3. Teachers to become more aware of the unique needs of the middle school child.
4. Better ways of diagnosing and monitoring skills in the subject areas, especially the three Rs, must be established.
5. The middle school program be better articulated in the subject areas to provide more continuity between grade levels.
6. Classroom instruction to be reviewed and updated as appropriate in all subject areas. Teachers to make use of varied and current methods of instruction for middle school youngsters.
7. An expanded program (including special interest courses) to be fully

implemented in all schools in balance with a strong academic program including the basics and the unified arts.

8. The interrelationship of subject matter to be emphasized.
9. Students to have close identification with teachers, a more flexible schedule and program.
10. Better continuity of programs, sharing of materials, and curriculum articulation to be developed between the middle schools.
11. The middle school program to be better articulated with the elementary and senior high school programs.
12. Long range goals to be set for middle schools in Stamford and a system developed to sustain positive curriculum changes in the middle school.

Recommendations:

1. The establishment of a middle school coordinating committee.
2. The development of a comprehensive plan for middle school development in Stamford.
3. Preparation of a district plan for full implementation of the middle school concept in Stamford.
4. Conduct workshop sessions dealing with the characteristics and pre- and early adolescent children for all teachers in the middle schools.
5. Provide for vertical articulation, scope, and sequence in all subject areas.
6. District-wide workshop sessions conducted by coordinators with teachers from the four middle schools in all subject areas leading toward a better defined and articulated program in the middle grades.
7. To provide an expanded program (including special interest courses) in balance with a strong academic program.
8. Provide for better correlation of applied sciences, physical education, foreign languages, fine arts and music programs.
9. Workshop sessions conducted during released time and planning periods for the teachers of various disciplines to identify and plan for implementation of interdisciplinary units—objectives and activities—as well as content.
10. A comprehensive evaluation procedure be established to assess the ongoing efforts and programs of the middle school plan.
11. Develop objectives which will clearly define the strategies to be employed.

Evaluation:

A detailed plan for evaluating the Middle School Program for Stamford will be prepared by the Research Office. The plan will provide for the following:

1. Developing specific, measurable objectives by those persons responsible for project activities.
2. Measuring the extent to which project objectives are met.

Table 8.2
Timetable for a Comprehensive Plan

PERT Chart

Task	Responsible Agent	1975 June	July	Aug.	Sept.	Oct.	Nov.	Dec.	1976 Jan.	Feb.	March	April	May	June
Middle School Design Review Workshop	MSCC**	6/30 – 7/2												
Middle School Coordinating Committee: Sub Groups—														
1. PERT Chart	G. Roman			8/27										
2. Philosophy	C. Robinson				9/10									
3. Design	J. Markiewicz				9/14									
Comprehensive Middle School Plan: final review	MSCC				9/24									
Comprehensive Middle School Plan: to Superintendent	C. Robinson				2:30pm 9/30									
Middle School Project Inservice Workshop	SDC & Dr. Bondi			8/26 –29										
1. Awareness of middle school child														
2. Orientation of staff														
3. Curriculum develop.														
4. Team building														
Middle School Project Workshop (1–3 p.m.)*	SDC & Dr. Bondi					10/14 10/15								
1. Awareness of middle school child														
2. Orientation of remaining staff														
3. Curriculum needs														
4. Team building														

Table 8.3
Continuum for Development

Components	→	→	→	→
Organization for Instruction	COGS—four academic disciplines per 100 shared students. Other disciplines—independent units serving all students. Individual teacher in self-contained classroom.	COGS—four academic disciplines per 100 students. Other disciplines—independent units serving all students. Teams representing at least two disciplines* responsible for planning for common group of students (CORE).	COGS—related arts teams & special service teams. Four COGS teachers responsible for planning and teaching common group of students and/or related arts teams or LSP (special service teams)* working to plan for common group of students.	Teams representing all disciplines (COGS, related arts, special service)—working together to plan for common group of students.*
Learning Support Programs	Evaluation Crisis Referrals	Evaluation Crisis Referrals Diagnostic Counseling-Therapy Planning	Evaluation Crisis Referrals Diagnostic Counseling-Therapy Planning Preventive	Evaluation Crisis Referrals Diagnostic Counseling-Therapy Planning Preventive Consulting Developmental Therapeutic
Curriculum	Following one text with system continuum. Teacher—directed group instruction.	Interrelating scope & sequence in at least 2 content areas.* Teacher-directed group instruction. Small group organization.	Interrelating 4 content areas. Include special services for areas of self-awareness (values, study skills, career education)—interdisciplinary instruction. Teacher-directed group instruction—small groups, some teacher-pupil negotiation—individualized & independent work.	Interdisciplinary planning including all areas of curriculum.* Some teacher-directed group work. Some small group work. Independent work. Some pupil-directed work.

Table 8.3—continued

	→	→	→
Materials	One adopted text at grade level.	Multi-level texts. Media Center as Resource Center.	Supplemental texts, kits, and manipulatives. Media Center as an extension of classroom (teaming center). Production of media.	Manipulative, audio-visual, programmed kits. Community as classroom. Media Center as Learning Center.
Grouping	Programmed by guidance counselors for entire year.	Proficiency & interest groups formed by evaluation & diagnosis.	Formation of sub-groups through more complete diagnosis.	Program planned cooperatively by students & teacher. Small group work. Individualization
Scheduling	Set time periods on an administrative developed schedule.	Block of time scheduled to provide common instructional and team planning time.	Larger blocks of time to provide common instruction & planning for 4 disciplines. Flexible size of groups. Flexible time blocks.	Larger blocks of time to provide common instruction & planning for all content areas. Flexible size of groups. Flexible time blocks.
Physical Plant Organization	Separate self-contained classrooms Library	COG classrooms clustered together. Media Center	Flexible use of clustered space. Media Production Area	Flexible working space which may be adapted by teams to fit specific needs.
Articulation	Permanent records transfer Textbook & guide hierarchy	Permanent records —— Text hierarchy Communication at building level	—— (continues)	Totally integrated, articulated program.

Table 8.3—*continued*

Parent Communication	Individual report cards sent home. Open house	Parent conference with teachers → Report cards → Newsletters → Open house → Progress reports → Group activities for parents (seminars, parents' night, open house).→ COG meeting attendance → Profile sheets K-12 → Communication between elementary, middle, and high schools. → All previous involvement & participation in school.
Staff Development	Optional workshops & inservice courses offered for credit.	Mandatory workshops directed by Staff Development Center. Half days & optional inservice courses. → Workshops requested by staff & supported by Staff Development Center. Optional inservice courses. Mandatory workshops → Teachers structure activities according to their own needs—assume responsibility for constructing plans for professional growth. Mandatory workshops & inservice

*While maintaining the integrity of individual disciplines.

SOURCE: Stamford Public Schools, "Comprehensive Plan for Middle School Development," Stamford, Connecticut, 1969. Used with permission.

Attention will be given to measuring intermediate and long-range objectives, as well as short-range objectives. Thus, for example, we will attempt to determine whether increases in teacher knowledge about the characteristics of preadolescents, gained through workshops, result in expected improvements in the teaching process and the student outcomes.

The timetable in Table 8.2 and continuum for development in Table 8.3 are part of the comprehensive plan.

SCHOOL PLANNING FOR MIDDLE SCHOOLS

Planning at the school level must include teachers, students, parents, and administrators if it is to result in the development of a dynamic middle school program focused on the individual student. Those planning a middle school should participate in a middle school study such as the one outlined below. The authors have used this study format in working with numerous middle school groups:

Middle School Study

I. Purpose

The purpose of the middle school study is to explore the organization, curriculum and instruction within the middle school with special emphasis on the following:

- A. The rationale of the middle school
- B. The nature of the middle school child
- C. The middle school teacher
- D. Program of the middle school
- E. Organization of the middle school
- F. Implementing and evaluating the middle school

The study will acquaint the personnel who staff a middle school in the philosophy and skills needed to function in the middle school program. The study is designed to meet the specific needs of middle school teachers, children, and the communities middle schools serve. It will provide time to develop a total middle school program by participants.

II. Objectives

Major objectives of the study are these:

1. To examine the rationale of the middle school and to identify its goals and purposes.
2. To study the nature of the middle school child.

3. To study certain organizational plans that have been identified with the concept of the emergent middle school.

   a. Flexible scheduling

   b. Cooperative teaching

   c. Non-gradeness

   d. Independent study

   e. Programmed learning

4. To establish curricular aims that include:

   a. A basic core of subject matter (discipline)

   b. Personal skills of an independent nature

   c. A concept of personal valuing

   d. Teacher-pupil counseling

   e. Evaluative procedures

5. To develop a procedure for preparing the elementary child to function effectively in the middle school environment.

6. To develop a series of units, or projects, to be used in each learning area.

7. Development of scope and sequence in each disciplinary area.

8. Preparation of self-pacing materials.

9. Interdisciplinary team teaching (planning).

10. Visits to other middle schools.

11. Development of exploratory program.

12. Planning for flexible use of academic block.

13. Examination of methods of diagnosis and prescription to prepare a totally individualized program of instruction.

III. Evaluation

A. Since the study will concentrate on orienting a faculty to the middle school concept with emphasis on innovative use of human resources, self-evaluation to measure change will be a significant part of the evaluation.

B. Informal evaluations will take place on a continuous basis throughout the study.

C. A subjective study will be made of comments and summarizations of the participating teachers before, during, and at the close of the study.

IV. Expectations of Participants

A. It is expected that each staff member will participate in the study and workshop sessions, and exercise initiative and intellectual curiosity in regard to reading, reflective thinking, discussion, and writing.

B. A written Middle School Guide will result from the study that will outline in detail a program that can be implemented in a middle school. Major sections of the Guide will be the six areas listed under A–F Section I. Staff members will be expected to work on one or more committees in addition to participating in horizontal and vertical team planning.

C. Workshop sessions for participants dealing with carrying out the objectives listed under Part II will be scheduled during the study.

An example of a school plan with a focus on the individual follows.

Suggested Plan for Any School Whose Purpose is to Focus on the Individual—Meadowbrook Middle School

Assumptions Related to the Learning Process:
—that learning is evidenced by a change in perception and behavior, and that the most meaningful learning takes place through the process of inquiry and discovery for oneself.

—that relationships are uniquely drawn from an experience by each individual.

—that there are similarities among individuals and differences among individuals.

—that learning can best take place when the individual has freedom of choice.

—that the individual reacts to a stimulus, initiates action and progresses at a rate and depth which may be independent from other members of a group.

—that learning takes place best when an individual makes a personal commitment to and becomes involved in his own education and its selective use.

The Child:
—that the child is in the continual process of individual growth and learns in a transactional process between his own goals and the goals set by society.

—that there is a direct relationship between meaningful learning and the amount of personal, dynamic involvement.

—that the child has rights and responsibilities as an individual and as a member of groups.

The Teacher:
—that the teacher has the primary task of contributing to a change in the perception and behavior of the student.

—that by providing opportunities for freedom of choice, the teacher helps the student accept the responsibility for his own education.

—that in fulfilling this task, the relationship between the teacher and pupil should be viewed as a transactional one where the teacher acts as a resource person.

—that learning situations must be provided at many levels, in different groupings, and enhanced by a variety of approaches to meet the varying individual needs.

The Environment:

—that the environment must be one which provides for integration of experiences, offering a daily opportunity to meet in a situation which encourages a feeling of belonging and security.

—that the student must have the chance to think and work as an individual and as a member of a small group composed of various age levels in a situation which is free from the pressures of subject content.

Goals:

Meadowbrook believes it should develop each student's ability to

1. Take responsibility for his own actions. This involves purposeful, responsible decision-making behavior. (AGENCY)

2. Initiate action on his own rather than depend primarily on teacher or authority-initiated action. (MOTIVATION)

3. Think in terms of many alternatives rather than in set, stereotyped patterns. (CREATIVITY)

4. Use the school resources to develop the academic skills, concepts, and understandings necessary for high-level functioning in a changing world. (SCHOLARSHIP)

Philosophical and Goal Statements from Selected Middle Schools

Berea Middle School—Berea, South Carolina

We believe that Berea Middle School should provide successful experiences for every child. Each child is a unique being and should be given opportunities to develop to his or her potential mentally, physically, and socially so he or she may become a productive, creative, responsible member of society in a changing world.

Hebron Middle School—Bullitt County, Kentucky

We believe that every person is of worth, is endowed with human dignity, is unique and has a right to the opportunity to realize his own potential.

Northside–Blodgett Middle School—Corning, New York

The middle school is a completely different educational structure from the elementary or senior high school. The middle school's uniqueness is not primarily that of the organization of courses, grouping, schedules, staffing, or materials; it is a matter of the focus and spirit of the whole operation.

Anne Arundel County, Maryland, Middle School

The purpose of the middle school is to provide a school setting which takes into consideration the transition period between childhood and adolescence. The middle school should encourage students to become increasingly self-directing.

Monsignor Wegner Middle School—Boys Town, Nebraska

It is the responsibility of the schools to offer students the opportunity to experience success while conveying that knowledge which is basic to the understanding of the world.

Grosse Point, Michigan, Middle School

A middle school program is designed to foster the intellectual, social, and emotional growth of children without snatching their childhood from them.

SUMMARY

Establishing a school in the middle grades that will truly serve preadolescent youth requires extensive planning on the part of school faculties. State departments of education, school districts, leagues of middle schools, and national professional organizations are providing leadership for the middle school movement.

An examination of the goal statements from middle schools in the United States reveals a commitment to emerging adolescent youth and the ideals of the middle school. An examination of the comprehensive planning required to implement a middle school illustrates the sincerity of middle schools in moving to achieve their avowed goals. The middle school is a real and dominant force today in American education.

Suggested Learning Activities

1. Prepare an outline of a district plan for organizing a middle school.

2. Organize a panel discussion on the topic "Why we need a middle school." What type of persons might contribute to your panel?

3. Prepare an outline of a school study designed to prepare a faculty for the middle school.

4. Develop your own goal statement for a middle school program. From this statement, extract the essential components of a middle school program and curriculum.

Selected References

Bondi, Joseph. *Developing Middle Schools: A Guidebook.* Wheeling, Ill.: Whitehall Publishing Company, 1972.

Lounsbury, John, and Vars, Gordon. *A Curriculum for the Middle School Years.* New York: Harper and Row, Publishers, 1978.

Vars, Gordon, editor. *Guidelines for Junior High School and Middle School Education.* Washington, D.C.: National Association of Secondary School Principals, 1966.

West Virginia Department of Education. *The Programmatic Definition of Middle Schools in West Virginia.* Charleston, W. V., 1978.

Wiles, Jon. *Planning Guidelines for Middle School Education.* Dubuque, Iowa: Kendall/ Hunt Publishing Company, 1976.

Wiles, Jon, and Bondi, Joseph. *Curriculum Development: A Guide To Practice.* Columbus, Ohio: Charles E. Merrill Publishing Company, 1979.

Wiles, Jon, and Bondi, Joseph. *Supervision: A Guide To Practice.* Columbus, Ohio: Charles E. Merrill Publishing Company, 1980.

9

Implementing the Middle School

Where there is a will, there is a way

INTRODUCTION

Once a school faculty has developed a rationale for a middle school and designed a program and organization to fit the needs of the emerging adolescent learners it serves, it must develop a plan for implementing the middle school structure. The implementation of a middle school involves communication at the highest possible level. Students, parents, school board members, elementary and high school staffs, and the supporting community must be informed as to the goals and purposes of the middle school and possible changes in program, organization, and school buildings. In addition, a continuous inservice training program for teachers, administrators, and support personnel must be developed.

Since few middle schools have "arrived" when they open their doors, a plan for phasing in the middle school should be developed. Examples of developmental plans were presented in Chapter two, and guidelines were established for district and school planning for middle schools. Figure 9.1 proposes an example of a middle school implementation schedule that moves from a conventional junior high program to a model middle school program. Middle schools might be at one level of curriculum and at another in learning. By designing an implementation schedule

Figure 9.1
Moving Toward a Model Middle School Program

Conventional Junior High School Program ————————————————→ Model Middle School Program

Category	Conventional Junior High School Program			Model Middle School Program
Curriculum	Single text county course guides	Interrelated scope/s sequence in at least 2 content areas	Interrelation of 4 content areas—include scope & sequence for self-awareness	Interdisciplinary instruction at maximum level—skill development	High interest curriculum interdisciplinary program—skill, etc.
Staff	One certified teacher—300 minutes—pupil-teacher ratio	Clerical assistance to teams	Use of para-professionals classroom duties	Differentiated certified personnel—task assignment	Utilization of varied personnel—task assignment
Schedule	Administrative decision is conventional	Block Schedule common instruction common plan	Larger blocks of time—flexible time blocks	Block schedule—flexible instructional planning time	Demand schedule—flexible—individualized
Grouping	Lock-step	Proficiency interest groups	Specific diagnosis sub-groups, flexible groups	Cooperative planning between students & teachers	Ind. Student planned program—teacher & child
Materials	State adopted text at grade level	Multi-level texts	Supplemental texts, kits	Manipulative audiovisuals programmed texts peer prod. of materials	Use of community as classroom
Teaming	None	Team representating 2 disciplines	Teaming representing 4 disciplines	Include at least one exploratory	Differential use of total staff

Conventional Junior High School Program ————————————————→ Model Middle School Program

such as the one found in Figure 9.1, realistic goals can be set for full implementation of the middle school concept.

The following guidelines for developing and sustaining middle schools should be kept in mind as an implementation plan is developed for the essential middle school:

1. Involve as many individuals as possible within a school or school district in the planning process. Make sure the involvement is both systematic and meaningful. Involve students, parents, teachers, administrators, and community persons from the very beginning.

2. Determine through a needs assessment what the needs are in your school or school district. Start with a thorough study of the children to be served in your middle school(s).

3. Develop a set of objectives to meet the needs you have identified.

4. Identify the responsible agents for carrying out the objectives you have formulated.

5. Set up a reasonable timetable for achieving your objectives.

6. Develop an evaluation design to determine the success of your program. Make sure the evaluation process is continual and that the program is monitored over a three to four-year period.

7. Develop inservice training that will include all faculty members and administrators in your middle schools. Effective staff development can be carried out at both the district and school levels, but staff development at the school level is more effective.

8. If a consultant is to be utilized, make sure the consultant will stay with you over a two or three-year period. Creditability and accountability for consultants result when inservice training is measured over a two-three year period. The program of the middle school should be constantly evolving.

9. Sustain inservice training. New teachers need inservice training each year, but returning teachers also need constant reinforcement.

10. Provide adequate time for inservice training. Many districts are not only scheduling traditional summer workshops, but also providing time during the school year for teachers to participate in inservice training. A promising trend found in school districts is the early dismissal of students several days a month to free teachers for inservice training during the day.

11. In developing new middle school programs teachers and administrators should be provided with as much lead time for planning as possible. A year of planning is preferable to a summer of planning for a middle school.

12. "Don't bite off more than you can chew." If your school is undergoing the transition to a middle school, do the things your faculty can do well the first year. Trying to do too much too soon often results in a disillusioned faculty and the failure of your middle school program. Don't hesitate to continue the planning process during the first year of partial implementation of a middle school program, especially where there has been little lead time in planning a total program.[1]

---

[1] Joseph Bondi, "Addressing the Issues: The Middle School—A Positive Change in American Education," in *The Middle School—A Look Ahead,* published by The National Middle School Association, 1977.

EFFECTIVELY COMMUNICATING GOALS AND PURPOSES OF THE MIDDLE SCHOOL

All groups concerned with the middle school must be informed with pertinent data so they will be aware of the uniqueness, appropriateness, and importance of having a middle school in their community. Even though students, teachers, parents, school board members, representatives from other school levels, and community persons have been involved in the planning of a middle school, the full implications of having such a school are not realized until the middle school is implemented. Often critics emerge after a program is implemented and they must be presented with accurate information about the middle school. Change alone is enough to precipitate criticism. "It simply isn't what I'm used to," is a comment often heard when new middle school programs and organizational structures are implemented.

A continuous presentation of information via school and newsletters, handbooks, press releases, radio and television programs, open houses, and community meetings will overcome doubts and antagonisms and facilitate the implementation process.

The following are examples by which information about the middle school has been effectively communicated.

1. Handbooks for Students and Parents

Many schools have developed handbooks that are both interesting and informative. The following proposed Table of Contents for a middle school handbook was developed by a faculty undergoing inservice training in preparation for the transition of their junior high school to the middle school.

Proposed Table of Contents for Parents Handbook on the Middle School

I. Introduction	This section would include the meaning and purpose of a middle school; and when and where it will begin.
II. Goals and Philosophy	A simple summary of our school's goals and philosophy to explain what the middle school will try to accomplish.
III. Middle School Child	This section should include a brief statement from the middle school child group showing how this new system would create a more motivated student because of much more individualized instruction.
IV. Curriculum— Organization	A short description of the three phases of our middle school program—skills, education for social competence, and personal development. Include an example of the student's schedule in a middle school on a particular day.
V. Team Teaching— Interdisciplinary Instruction	A page summary about teaming. Also included here. Could be a simple statement about interdisciplinary instruction.

VI. Enrichment Courses	This section would include a list of activities that would demonstrate how the activities program is designed to inspire, motivate, and enrich the student in school.
VII. Middle School Questions	A list of general and most-often-asked parent questions with the answers.
VIII. Conclusion	A personal letter from our principal stating assurances of the success of the middle school plan.

Another suggestion for a booklet for parents follows:

Booklet for Parents

The booklet will be prepared in "layered" form with the description of the student on one page, the school on another.

1. The middle school student is enthusiastic.
2. The middle school student must be motivated to learn.
3. The middle school student's objectives (and attention span) are short term.
4. The middle school student differs widely in physical attributes and maturity. He is growing rapidly, inclined toward overexertion.
5. The middle school student is activity-minded.
6. The middle school student desires freedom but fears a loss of security.
7. The middle school student needs communication with his peers and adults outside of his home.

1. _____ Middle School has a team of specialists ready to challenge him, to capitalize on and support his enthusiasm.
2. Nothing succeeds like success. The student will progress at his own rate, motivated by repeated success in an individualized program.
3. _____ Middle School will have flexible scheduling. Classes will be arranged for students, will vary in length to avoid boring them or interrupting them before they finish a task.
4. _____ Middle School offers a wide range of activities designed for this age student. Some will be instituted at student's request.
5. Physical education classes are carefully planned for the middle school student. Intramural sports provide an outlet for competitive feelings, yet protect the rapidly growing youngster from serious injury.
6. _____ Middle School allows students to create their own schedules and select areas of interest to them. Counselors and teachers support and encourage them.
7. At _____ Middle School students will meet their peers in small groups and activities. They will meet and learn to know teachers and counselors.

2. *Letters to Parents*

Jefferson Davis Middle School

May 1979

Dear Parents:

Jefferson Davis Middle School is now experiencing its first year in the philosophy and concepts of the middle school program. Our staff has been involved for the past eight weeks in an inservice study evaluating our present curriculum and making new plans for changing and improving our total program for next year. All three grades will be included in the middle school program starting in August.

Our schedule will be organized in the "School within a School" concept. This means that each grade level will function as a unit within certain designated areas of our school, thus increasing the supervision, guidance and security of each child. We feel this is important as our predicted enrollment is approximately 2100 for next fall. Periods of block time will be assigned to academic and related arts courses. Greater concern will be given to individualized instruction (child centered) based upon achievement levels and student needs. We are adding three additional teachers, one at each grade level, to concentrate on helping our students improve their reading skills.

Today your child has filled out the registration forms for next year. A copy of these forms he/she has also brought home along with this letter for you to see. Please note there are two sheets, one for academic and related arts and the other for the activities period.

These activity experiences are for a length of six weeks, making six experiences during the year. These classes come at the close of the day when students are somewhat tired and their attention is hard to hold. These activities are designed to be pressure-free, somewhat unstructured, with a high-interest level, hopefully to give each child a pleasant learning experience before leaving school. Many good things have happened this year, and we are hoping to continue these activities next year.

If for some reason you do not agree with his/her selections, will you please make the necessary changes, sign the forms and return them to the Guidance Department by May 9. If we do not receive your forms, the ones we have will be used for his/her program, and we will assume they meet with your approval.

May your summer vacation be pleasant and may your child be refreshed and ready to meet the challenge of education when school opens in August.

Sincerely,

_____

Principal

A Message From Your Principal

Dear Students:

Beaumont Middle School will be a new experience for you and for us. Instruction will be somewhat different in that your academic classes (Mathematics, Science, Social Studies and English), will be taught in a block of time, approximately three and one-half hours. Day-to-day time for each subject will be scheduled each week so that some days you will meet longer in an area of instruction than others. This flexibility is one example of methods used to allow the instruction to be more varied, one way of creating interest.

The program will give students an opportunity to explore areas of their interest due to wider electives or special interest offerings. This booklet will give you more detailed information.

We are looking forward to a very exciting school year. We feel you will enjoy your years in Beaumont Middle School. See you in September.

Sincerely yours,

E. E. Ramone
Principal

TO: Fifth Grade Students
      Parents of Fifth Grade Students

FROM: Guidance Center

The faculty and staff at _____ Middle School would like to take this opportunity to give a brief explanation of your child's program for next year and express our welcome and desire to work with you and your child.

Students will have the opportunity to explore some subject fields which should help in their preparation for more advanced studies in academic and vocational areas.

The sixth grade student will be assigned to a team of academic teachers (Math, Science, Social Studies, and Language Arts), for a large portion of the day. The remaining portion of the day the student will be in the exploratory and enrichment areas.

All sixth grade students will be required to take the following exploratory subjects sometime during the school year: Physical Education, Home Economics or Industrial Arts, Business Education, and Health. Other enrichment possibilities will include Spanish, Art, Music, and special interest classes.

3. Illustration of Booklet Provided by a School District

QUESTIONS PARENTS ASK—
A Question-Answer Interpretation of
the Philosophy and Program of the Middle School

Introduction:

During the school year of 1979–80, the _____ Board of Public Instruction embarked upon a building construction and renovation plan to meet the demands of a changing school population. Two facilities were renovated and a new school constructed in _____. Plans include provisions for a middle school. Although it was recognized that a junior high school would meet the demands of growth, it was not certain that it would adequately serve the changing characteristics of our emerging adolescent youth.

The decision to provide a "middle school," housing grades six, seven, and eight, was based upon three major factors:

1. The middle age child (11–14) was responding to his environmental factors with differing levels of maturation.

2. A regrouping of children might provide a better transitional period between childhood and adolescence. Hence, a new educational approach would be needed if consideration were to be given to the intellectual, social, physical, and emotional growth of the child. The high school curriculum could be revised to provide a comprehensive sequence for grades nine through twelve.

3. The elementary schools could accommodate the greater pupil load in grades one through five if the sixth grade students were moved to a middle school.

Research into the philosophy of the middle school; information from various school systems that had experience with the middle school; attendance and participation in conferences on the middle school concept; visitations to selected middle schools; and other means of research and information were carried out. The conclusion was reached that this move to reorganize the _____ County Schools into a one through five, six through eight, and nine through twelve grade pattern was and is within the philosophy of education and the development of the educational system of the county.

The Board of Public Instruction, by official action, reorganized the schools into the new pattern that included the middle school concept.

Forward:

The decision to reorganize the _____ County Schools to include grades six, seven, and eight in middle school has caused many questions to be asked concerning this new concept. These questions were asked by teachers, by students, and by parents. This booklet has been prepared in the attempt to answer many of those questions and to promote interest in the educational patterns of _____ School district.

Hopefully, the questions answered herein will lead to a better understanding not only of the middle schools, but of the total educational program of _____ County.

Questions Parents Ask About the Middle Schools:
1. Why a middle school?
   The school is exactly what the name suggests—a school between
   the elementary and the high school. The program has been designed to meet the needs of students who are changing rapidly in
   all aspects of physical, social, and academic growth. Thus, the
   middle school has been created especially for these children and it
   will not follow the pattern of the traditional junior high, which
   imitated the high school.

2. Why were grades 6, 7, and 8 selected for these schools?
   Research has shown that sixth graders of today are ready for
   greater depth and breadth of exploration in subject matter than
   the traditional elementary school offers. The middle school offers
   opportunities in language arts, home economics, industrial arts,
   and guidance, in addition to greater resources in academic subjects. Ninth graders of this generation have reached a point in
   maturity where they are socially and academically ready to be
   with senior high school students. Many colleges require four
   years of high school credit as an entrance requirement and many
   vocational areas need two years of basic background experience plus
   two years of special area training. Thus, grades 6, 7, and 8 are
   a more appropriate grouping of students.

3. Is this an experimental program?
   No. Prior to making the decision on reorganization, research was
   conducted in organization, team teaching, grouping, open space
   classrooms, and flexible scheduling. These are not experimental
   areas but have been tried and proven worthwhile throughout
   many areas for many years.

4. May parents visit the schools?
   Yes, and parents are encouraged to do so. Visits may be arranged
   through the school office. Visitations will be arranged in order to
   present the least disruption of normal educational procedures.
   The education of the students will always be foremost.

Questions Parents Ask About the Buildings:
1. *How will _____ Middle School differ from conventional*
   schools?
   The _____ Middle School was designed and constructed
   from educational specifications written specifically for the middle
   school. It will be completely air-conditioned and of "open-space"
   construction. Classrooms will not be separated by wall but by
   sight barriers. There will be freedom of movement and flexibility
   of programming. Since there are no hallways, all spaces are learning areas. The learning resource center, or library, is centrally located and instantly available for use by pupils and teachers.

2. *Why is the building completely carpeted?*
   The open space design demands acoustical treatment of the entire area. It has been proven that carpeting is no more expensive
   than upkeep and maintenance on other type floors, and the learning environment advantage is tremendous.

3. *Why aren't there walls between classes? How does anyone concentrate?*

   Flexibility is the key. The building was designed to permit easy adjustment to teaching needs and programs. Groups of various sizes may meet in any area at any time. Where sight dividers are needed, teachers may arrange them to suit the need. Students who feel it necessary to study individually or separate themselves from a group may use individual study carrels, conference rooms, and project rooms. Thus, space has been provided for every need.

4. *How does the cost compare to a conventional building?*

   The _____ Middle School was constructed for the same cost per square foot as a conventional building. Savings from hallways and corridors were returned to the building in improved acoustics, carpeting, air conditioning, paneling, and general interior improvement over traditional buildings. However, this does not mean the building contains superfluous design, equipment, or "gingerbread." It is functional, flexible, and designed entirely to meet the needs of the middle school concept in education.

5. *How does _____ Middle School differ from*
   _____ Middle School?

   _____ will be housed in a traditional building. However, the middle school concept is as applicable to the traditional design as it is to the open space design. The philosophy is the important ingredient, not design. Although open space design provides a more flexible and more rapid movement and grouping, the facilities at _____ can and will be used in the middle school philosophy.

6. *How will _____ Middle School differ?*

   _____ Middle School will also operate on the middle school philosophy within a traditional facility. However, it should be understood that the philosophy of the middle school is based upon the needs of the student. Therefore, no two schools will be identical in program due to the difference in student body, community, and environmental factors that affect the program.

7. *How will _____ use the middle school concept in a*
   grades 1–12 school?

   _____, and indeed, all other schools in the county, and all teachers in the county will study and apply those techniques and educational methods appropriate to the particular school, the particular teacher, and the particular phase of education involved. The philosophy and approach to teaching used in the middle school program can be adapted to education regardless of where the middle grades are housed.

Questions Parents Ask About the Program:

1. *Why team teaching?*

   The combined skills, talents, interests, and training of three or four teachers in a subject offers more to the student than one teacher is able to offer. Team teaching also enables the teachers to adjust the group to an appropriate size depending upon the activity. For example, ninety students may be grouped together for the viewing of a film one day while another day these same students will be divided into smaller groups with one teacher helping those students who need individual help, two or three teachers helping those students who request help, and another teacher supervising students who are working on self-directed projects. Also, the schedule permits teachers to plan together, learn new skills and techniques, and upgrade their overall professional level.

2. *Are teachers prepared for this program?*
   _____ has had a modified program of flexible scheduling and team teaching for the past two years, giving those teachers valuable experience in the program. Prior to the 1978–1979 school year, a three-week workshop was held for middle school teachers where they were involved in planning, discussion, curriculum development, scheduling, and other problems of middle school organization. This inservice training for teachers will continue throughout the year and for the years to follow. Consultant service and inservice programs have been and will continue to be provided through long-range planning and development of education in the _____ County schools.

3. *How does the program provide for the gifted and the slow learner?*
   Individualization is the key. The broad range of experience program will provide a broad basic background, while the individualized program will provide the opportunity for the gifted child to study in depth and the slow learner to receive individual assistance, each progressing at a rate commensurate with his ability and guided by counselors and teachers.

4. *Are classes nongraded?*
   The middle schools will progress toward a nongraded program. This term is often misinterpreted and should be referred to as "individualized instruction." Some students will be working on more advanced materials while others may be receiving remedial help. However, all will be progressing at different rates. It should be clearly understood that nongradedness is not to be confused with giving of grades or reports to parents, nor of a complete disregard of levels of achievement and preparation for advancement into high school.

5. *What is the function of the teacher aide?*
   Teacher aides do the typing and stenciling of teaching materials, record grades, check attendance, assist teachers whenever and wherever possible. The teacher, relieved of clerical tasks, may turn full attention to planning, and preparation of educational duties. Teacher aides will not instruct students but will be available to assist students in obtaining materials, equipment, and other such services.

6. *What is the program of unified arts?*
   Unified arts are the areas of physical education, art, music, home economics, and industrial arts. These areas will not stress specialized skills but provide an exploratory program. The experience in unified arts is important for both boys and girls and all students will be required to enroll in some phase of each program.

7. *What other programs are available?*
Personal typing and foreign language will be available to students. Typing will introduce the student to the touch system and encourage the use of the typewriter on a personal basis. It will not be the intent to teach typing in depth, only for personal use. Spanish will be available on an elective basis. The number of language teachers limits the number of students in this area. Students will be selected according to their aptitude and elementary school experience in Spanish. As the program develops, it will be possible for Spanish students to complete one level before entering high school. This will provide the opportunity for the student to select a second language in the high school program.

Questions Parents Ask About the Students:

1. *After being in the middle school how will my child adjust to high school or another school system?*
The flexibility of youth will probably take care of such adjustment in case of transfer to another system. In high school, the broad experience background provided in the middle school, the study habits and patterns developed, and the greater responsibility placed on the individual student will better enable the student to meet the requirements at the high school level. Many methods of instruction used in the middle school are already in use at the high school and more changes will come about as the middle school student continues his educational growth in the high school.

2. *How does the program prepare the middle school student for high school?*
Success in the world of work depends upon self-motivation and self-discipline. By establishing acceptable patterns of behavior in the middle school, the student will be better prepared for the responsibilities of high school. Middle school teachers will check closely to see that such patterns are developed. The guidance program will be directed toward better self-discipline on the part of the student.

3. *Will there be too much freedom in the middle schools?*
Self-discipline is one of the aims of the middle school. Students who have shown themselves to be capable and responsible will be granted more self-directed time. Others will be under direction. Conduct which is detrimental to learning or unacceptable behavior in any other school will not be condoned in the middle schools.

4. *What extracurricular activities will be available to the students?*
Intramural sports will be available to every student wishing to play. The music department will offer band and chorus as well as individual instruction. Clubs such as drama, art, science, photography, chess, and a variety of others will be available depending upon the interest of the students. Social activities will be of the general social party variety rather than the typical boy-girl dances of the high school. The extracurricular activities follow the general philosophy of the middle school; that of meeting the needs

of the students rather than an imitation of the high school. No interscholastic activities on a competitive basis will be planned.

In conclusion, the middle school program is designed to meet the needs of the student. Total emphasis will be given to the objective.

The middle schools need the understanding and cooperation of the entire community. Our program is not new, our philosophy is not new, but our techniques, methods, and approach will be under constant evaluation and revision in order to better serve the youth of our communities.

We invite your participation and urge your cooperation in making _____ County the outstanding educational system in the state and in the nation.

4. Samples of Team and School Newsletters

Team Newsletter

January, 1980

Dear Team F parents,

Team F is a four subject interdisciplinary team involving Language Arts, Social Studies, Math and Science. In order to keep you informed as to what your child is doing in these areas, we will begin sending a newsletter home with your child at the end of each report period.

Following is a description of what has taken place these past six weeks.

Social Studies this past grading period was assigned the concept of exploration and discovery. We grouped the students in sections so that poor readers and those students with above average reading ability could move at their own speed.

Using skill kits designed to help both groups, the average students were given task sheets to work from, designed as to teach inquiry and concepts. We tried to have task sheets made up so that the student would use outside resources and the media center.

Science classes have been involved in a study of physiology. We have studied various body processes and also reviewed briefly, various systems of the human body.

Some students have been reading from a selected text which covers various scientific topics from geology to biology. There are selected groups which are working in packets made from the Steck-Vaughn series which includes various biological topics. Students have been allowed to proceed in their work on an individualized basis within a time framework. Extra credit reports were submitted those who desired to upgrade their work. Students are allowed to complete or submit extra credit work on any scientific topic throughout the six weeks period.

Various students were assigned book reports on science-related books.

The entire team was moved from a class type situation to the lab. We will begin the new semester with various laboratory experience.

In *Mathematics* students have been grouped according to their ability.

The different topics being studied at this time include whole numbers, fractions, integers, rational numbers, and algebra. The groups are exposed to a variety of teaching techniques including skills kits, cassette tapes, worksheets, workbooks, textbooks, and lectures.

In *Language Arts* the students have been working on two skills kits and a six-weeks literature and creative writing unit. The skills kits covered usage, vocabulary, punctuation and spelling. Each student worked at his own rate.

The literature unit centered around a book called *Imagination, the World of Inner Space.* At the beginning of the unit students contracted for their grade, different amounts of work being required for each grade. The book contained short stories, poems, and plays. After reading the material students did creative writing assignments from a logbook. Students were also assigned a group project for completion of the contract. At the end of the six weeks the Imagination notebook and group project were handed in. I enjoyed reading them! Many students did good work.

School Newsletter

One of the highlights of the _____ Middle School program is the Humanities exposure. The students are encouraged to have encounters in Art, Music and foreign language. Such experiences could be playing a musical instrument, singing songs, dancing, designing a leather disc, making a clay object and learning to speak either Spanish or French. The general goal of the Humanities program is to provide myriad opportunities for the student to gainfully use his or her leisure time. This knowledge could become invaluable later on when these people become involved in the world of work.

ATTENTION PARENTS—You must see to believe. Our Agriculture program headed by Mr. _____ has developed faster than expected. His students are growing about anything you can name and have a hot house 2nd to none in the county. There are now 72 boys and girls learning to plant and grow things and appreciate the effort put forth by the farmers of America in growing what we eat. These kids are doing an outstanding job and enjoying what they are doing.

The academics are also being introduced to the vocational world. Many fine people from the local business and industrial community have come to the school to lecture and show through slides on how their particular business operates. We have recently had Mr. _____ from the _____ *Times* who had a slide presentation on "How to make a newspaper". This was a field trip which was brought to the school to give the students an insight into something most people take for granted, that is our daily paper. Mrs. _____ a writer for the *Times* also talked to many students about writing and the importance of getting as much English as possible out of school.

Midshipman _____ also visited us. He is a second classman at the United States Naval Academy at Annapolis, Maryland. He is a Math major, aspiring to be either a jet pilot or be stationed aboard nuclear subs. He told many of our students the importance of attaining as much proficiency in this area as possible and to be continually thinking about making a career choice. He emphasized that our students should make a few selections of possible careers now and then explore them as much as possible before making a final choice of one or possibly two.

Including the people now attending, we have 18 boys and girls involved at the Work Evaluation Center in _____. Here they are observed by several evaluators who assist them and test them in performance tasks. An example is taking a telephone apart and putting it back together correctly. The student is given directions and must learn to follow them. They are graded on time and quality of work. All tasks require a certain amount of reading and math to be able to perform. This 9 day series of work related tests tells the boy or girl in which area they are proficient in and a lot of time motivates them to stay in school and study harder as they have more of a meaning of their academics. Several of our _____ students have also been given either the Ohio Vocational Interest Survey test or the Kudex Interest test. These tests are given to the students on a voluntary basis and are many times a motivating factor in that they show the student where his or her interests lie.

WE WOULD AT THIS TIME LIKE TO EXTEND AN OPEN INVITATION TO ALL YOU PARENTS TO VISIT US AT _____ MIDDLE SCHOOL AND OBSERVE OUR STUDENTS IN ACTION.

5. *Advisory Groups*

Many schools have set up lay advisory committees to keep parents and the community aware of educational changes. Such committees can be extremely valuable in informing the public of the benefits of the middle school. This group can choose members to appear before various organizations in the community and assist the middle school staff in interpreting the middle school program.

6. *News Releases to Newspapers, Radio, and TV*

Frequent releases can be given the news media by middle school staffs as they undergo studies leading to the transition from the junior high school to the middle school. The public is interested in educational changes the middle school brings and is much more receptive to those changes when they are kept aware of what is going on in the schools.

7. *Orientation Programs for Students*

Students must be familiarized with the middle school program. Informative booklets have been developed for students which help in this process. Small group guidance sessions have also been successful in preparing students for the middle school. Once students are convinced that the middle school is best for them and begin to enjoy individual successes, they will sell the program to parents. The best public relations possible for middle schools is for their students to like school.

Several school districts have set aside days prior to the opening of school where new middle school students could visit their school and run through a day's schedule on a shortened time basis. Positive attitudes of teachers and students at the beginning of school are extremely important to a new middle school.

Figures 9.2 and 9.3 illustrate school-developed information sheets designed to acquaint parents, teachers at other levels, and the public about the middle school.

Figure 9.2
Change to the Middle School—Why?

C—*Challenge*   Space-age technology demands that children be taught to adapt to its complex requirements. Teaching methods must keep pace with these demands in order to provide our children with educational experiences which will help them live a successful life in the environment we have created for them.

H—*Habits*   We need to get rid of many of our old habits and approaches. Too long we have been laboring under the misconception of structure based on conformity. It's time we developed creativity.

A—*Achievement*   Our children are not achieving as they should. We need to teach critical thinking and problem solving techniques.

N—*Needs*   Our children have many needs (physical, social, emotional, as well as intellectual) and we must provide for them through a program that will create a desire to reach the ultimate goals in education.

G—*Grouping*   The self-contained classroom with the graded curriculum organization is not the only avenue to success. We need flexibility to provide for the individual needs and rates of development. Oftentimes it becomes necessary to have a self-contained classroom when students have been identified as needing more structure than a flexible approach can offer.

E—*Evaluation*   Grade standards and expectations are unrealistic. We need continuous evaluation of each child's progress.

CHANGE—Ingredients?

C—*Child*   Our program of education must be child centered to meet the unique needs of the transescent child.

H—*Helpers*   We need the cooperative effort of a professional staff, clerical personnel, aides, cafeteria personnel, custodians, parents, and the community to provide an effective educational program.

A—*Attitude*   We as teachers, must be sincerely concerned for the welfare of each child and accept him for what he is. We must give the same respect to our students as we expect them to give us.

N—*Nongrading*   The philosophy of nongrading is spreading rapidly. Its great success is in meeting individual needs through an academic as well as Special Interest approach.

G—*Growth*   We must permit each child to reach his ultimate goals and to progress continuously at his own rate.

E—*Enthusiasm*   Become enthusiastic for a change! Due to the many changes in the emerging middle school, teachers selected must be enthusiastic.

Figure 9.3

Characteristics of Middle School Children and Their Implications for Instruction

Characteristics	Implications for Instruction

1. Physically active; short attention span; rapidly changing interests; many projects left undone.
 	
Differ widely in physical maturity, temperament, ability, and achievement.
	1. Wide variety of opportunities for learning. Many ways afforded for pupils to come up with understandings:
	a. Explanation
	b. Group discussion h. Drawing, painting
	c. Demonstration i. Constructing
	d. Reporting j. Experimenting
	e. Movies, slides, and k. Decorating
	   filmstrips l. Role playing
	f. Workbooks and practice m. Quizzes and contests
	   sheets n. Field trips
	g. Charts and maps o. Texts, other books—in
	   class and library

2. Curious, spontaneous, and enthusiastic; talents and giftedness, if present, appear and become pronounced.	2. Classroom is a "laboratory of life." Learn by doing. Units of instruction cannot be bound to a textbook or a teacher lecture of even a predominantly teacher-directed discussion. Actual real-life experiences form the basis for instructional activities:
	a. Experimenters, investigators e. Builders; models, etc.
	b. News reporters f. Independent projects or
	c. Story tellers and writers: study
	   fiction and non-fiction g. Student Officers,
	d. Poets, artists, musicians managers
	   h. Committees, small-group
	   work, tutoring

3. Shifting from adult influences and standards to peer-group standards. Gregarious—form clubs and small cliques. Developing self-awareness; seeking identification; evaluating selves. Becoming interested in money-making activities.	3. Increased responsibility in management of student affairs: a. Active student government helps in development of own standards of behavior and guidelines for interpersonal relations. b. In classroom, students help determine operating procedures, standards of achievement, and distribution of responsibilities. Opportunities for pupils to read about and discuss outstanding people in many walks of life: a. Pupils analyze and determine qualities of greatness. b. Models help pupils formulate personal goals and values. Opportunities for pupils to join clubs or special interest groups: a. Function as an integral part of the school day. b. All who wish may participate—no arbitrary exclusions.

GUIDELINES FOR PLANNING AND USING SCHOOL FACILITIES

Physical facilities are important in implementing the middle school program. Unfortunately, as with junior high schools, most middle schools have inherited old buildings in school districts. Where there has been an opportunity to build a new facility for a middle school, warm, flexible, and exciting spaces have been provided for emerging adolescent learners. School buildings are means and not ends to facilitating middle school programs, and because flexible space exists does not mean that the space will result in a flexible program.

Whether the middle school student is to attend school in a traditional building or in an open space modern facility, there are guidelines that are important in planning and using school facilities:

1. The school should be a pleasant place for students to work and play—the middle school child likes the school.

2. The total staff should be involved in taking a close look at the school program and objectives to assure that the needs of the middle school child at the school are being met. The staff then has the responsibility of preparing educational specifications or suggesting renovations for the old plant to accommodate the program. Districts should consider utilizing the resources of the Department of Education which are available.

3. The middle school philosophy mandates some form of teaming approach which, in turn, will affect the planning or utilization of the physical plant.

   a. Adequate space for the team to meet should be provided.

   b. Students on each team should be housed in the same general area. In the newer facilities, a team may be housed in a pod or quad; in an older facility, four classrooms adjacent to one another may be utilized. The team arrangement also facilitates flexibility of time, and by housing the students in close proximity, they may move freely from one activity to another without disturbing others.

   c. The teaming arrangement facilitates large and small group instruction, so there can be provided a facility to house more than the traditional 30 students in a classroom. In addition, each team should be provided a place where the child can work independently or in small groups.

   d. Because the team member many times functions as the adult "closest to the child" in school, space should be provided where the teacher and child may converse in privacy.

4. The school counselors should have space where they can meet students to discuss problems privately.

5. The learning resource center should be in close proximity to all other instructional areas. The center should provide suitable space for systemized storing of learning resources and audio/visual resources, and the space to use such materials. The facility must provide room for independent or individual work, but also should be arranged to permit small groups of students to work together when appropriate.

6. Furniture should be carefully selected to be appropriate for each specific learning area.

7. The physical plant should include ample space out-of-doors so the middle school child may be able to interact with the environment beyond the usual four walls of the classroom. Facilities and equipment for physical education should be provided in such quantities and quality to permit maximum activity by all students. A developed turf area is needed as is a hard surface area to accommodate basketball, tennis, volleyball, and other related activities. A

physical development area, consisting of challenging and safety implanted apparatus, is also of high priority.

8. There should be a continuing review of new and better ways to utilize the school plant. Students, staff, and parents may be effectively used in evaluating the strengths and weaknesses of the school building.[2]

SUSTAINING INSERVICE TRAINING

After implementing a middle school program, the training of teachers, administrators, and support personnel must continue if the middle school is to carry out its goals. A major problem in the middle school movement has been the lack of sustained inservice training for teachers. Too often, we see a marked decline in the quality of middle school programs because a faculty originally trained for the middle school fails to implement follow-up inservice training. Also, new teachers coming into middle schools are not provided with the training the original faculty experienced during their first year. Unless there is a sustained inservice training for teachers, the middle school will suffer the same fate as the junior high school and become a miniature high school.

Many school districts are setting up teacher renewal centers where inservice training for new and old teachers is offered on a continued basis throughout the year. Such programs lead to an increased interest in the middle school and help sustain and improve existing middle school programs. Examples of such centers are found at the end of this chapter.

It is unfortunate, but the elementary-secondary syndrome of training intermediate teachers has prevailed in colleges of education. As was the case with the junior high school, very few universities are providing special undergraduate training programs for middle school teachers. Consequently, the major emphasis in the years ahead will continue to be inservice training. Declining enrollments and a tight job market have leveled off the constant turnover of teachers. As a result, we are finding experienced teachers teaching for longer periods of time in our middle schools. Our focus, then, in the future, will be the grading of present staffs. The renewal center concept for constant inservice training offers an attractive alternative to the hit-and-miss system of college courses or isolated workshops.

Developing Competent Principals for the Middle School

What do we mean by competent middle school principals? *Competent* means many things. First, a middle school principal has to understand and love the age group found in the middle grades. Second, he or she has to be an instructional leader and not just a manager.

The middle school principal must understand organizational structures like teaming, interdisciplinary teaching, flexible scheduling, and block scheduling, and

---

[2] Special State Committee on the Middle School, *Development of Middle Schools in Florida,* Florida State Dept. of Education, 1974, pp. 83–84. Used with permission.

be able to develop those organizational patterns in his school. He or she has to be creative, dynamic, and communicate well with kids, parents, and teachers alike. Last, the middle school principal has to be strong enough to stand up in the system when the middle school comes under attack from those who don't understand it. A strong middle school leader will be able to communicate with the elementary and high school administrators and work towards an articulated K–12 curriculum. He or she must not see the middle school as an isolated structure, but as part of a total system of education.

Where are these administrators trained? In very few places. Our universities and school districts need to get busy to train good middle school principals. A promising trend in many school districts is the implementation at the school level of curriculum assistants who hold administrative lines, but who work directly with teachers in the classroom. Many of these individuals are advancing into principalships and good results have been experienced from such appointments. Perhaps the day will come when positions like Deans of Boys or Girls and Assistant Principals in charge of discipline can be eliminated. How much more productive the middle school could be if administrative lines could be converted into additional guidance and curriculum positions.

Competent middle school principals are indeed a key element in the success of the middle school movement. School districts should develop special programs for identifying promising middle school administrators and provide them with inservice training necessary to work with emerging adolescent learners.

Team Building

Since most middle schools employ an organizational approach of teaming, it is important in the implementation process that teachers receive help in team building. Most training in team teaching comes before teachers actually implement a new middle school program. The authors have found there must be a continuous means of evaluating team progress and a program of sustained team building if teaming is to succeed.

Team building is a process by which persons learn to work together in an effective manner to:

1. Build a spirit of trust and collaboration with each other.
2. Set and achieve shared goals.

Here are characteristics each team member must possess:

1. *Flexibility in Planning*—team members must be able to make schedule changes at short notice and not isolate themselves from the group process. Meetings must be frequent and time cannot be wasted on trivial matters.

2. *Flexibility in Working with Others*—it is essential that a team member be able to give and take—to compromise. A team situation is a learning situation and in a learning situation new things have to be tried, new methods attempted, and new approaches taken.

3. *Ideas Must Be Examined Vis-a-Vis Personalities*—team members must be objective and examine ideas rather than the personalities involved. Often alternatives must be examined in problem-solving and members must modify stated positions. Team leaders must help members stay on topics under discussion. Listening skills are very important in facilitating communication among team members.

Ways of building team identity for teachers and students include:

1. Interdisciplinary Units—teachers and students working on a common concept.
2. Special Events in which the team participates together.
   a. speakers
   b. field trips
   c. sitting as a team at school events
   d. team meetings for decision making, movies, team awards day, library orientation, etc.
   e. team birthday party after school
3. Intramural Competition by Teams
4. Team Newsletter
   a. informs students and parents of team activities
   b. should be used to reinforce learning by summarizing concepts taught in each discipline (this reinforces student learning and informs parents of current work). It can also communicate the team's philosophy
   c. builds team morale by recording events
   d. builds student morale by mentioning names of students who:
      1. help others
      2. have birthdays
      3. do special projects
      4. improve their work
      5. participate in intramurals and other school activities
      6. make the honor roll
      7. encourage their parents to visit the team, come to Back-to-School night, etc.
      8. read extra books
   e. students help to write the newsletter

Making Teaming Work—Some Helpful Hints

A. Helping the Situation to Become Comfortable

1. Sit in a circle where everyone is easily seen and heard by everyone else. Introduce yourselves
2. Check the physical setting so that it is as comfortable as possible (chairs on floor, temperature, lighting, ventilation)
3. Use newsprint (ask different *volunteers* to record on the newsprint at different times)

4. Team-brainstorm an agenda on newsprint
—then decide in what order to discuss each item
—begin with sharing answers to questions in "B"

B. Developing a Climate of Openness

1. For New Teams: Getting Acquainted so that *trust can emerge.* Ask *each person* to share his or her answers to the questions below. Do not debate the accuracy of comments, rather *try real listening, seeking clarity,* and *showing acceptance of each other's comments.*
   a. What are my hopes and fears about our task as a team?
   b. What are my hopes and fears about being a member of this team?
   c. What personal resources do I bring this team?
   d. What support do I want from this team?
   e. What assumptions have I made about the other members of the team?

2. For teams that have worked together previously: Getting Better Acquainted so that *more trust* can emerge. Ask *each person* to share his or her answers to the questions below. Do not debate the accuracy of each other's comments, but try real listening, seeking clarity, and showing acceptance of each other's answers.
   a. What are my hopes and fears about our task as a team?
   b. What are my hopes and fears about being a member of this team?
   c. What personal resources do I bring this team?
   d. What support do I want from this team?
   e. What assumptions have I made about the other members of the team?
   f. In what ways have we as a team worked well together?
   g. What in my relationships to other team members hinders me from working well with the team?

C. Establishing Clear Contracts in the team helps trust to continue and goals to become accomplished.

1. What do we expect of each other as team members? *Develop a clear newsprint contract:*
   a. Attendance, tardiness, leaving early, absenteeism, letting someone know when you can't come
   b. Schedule of meetings—length, starting and ending on time
   c. Leadership—Team Leader
   d. Participation in meetings
   e. How decision will be made—*record team decisions on newsprint*
   f. How records of meetings will be kept
   g. How team will communicate with absentees and others who need to know what team is doing
   h. How team will give and receive feedback from each other and evaluate themselves as a team on task accomplishment and team cohesiveness

2. What do we expect of persons with special responsibilities? *Develop a clear newsprint contract between team members and any persons with special responsibilities,* e.g., team leader.

Step 1: Team members as a group work separately from team leader, etc. List on newsprint: How we would like (name) to function as (*person's special responsibility*) for our team. At same time team leader, working alone, lists on newsprint "How I would like to function as _____ of this team."

Step 2: Hang newsprint lists side-by-side and negotiate the difference

An example of a list of team leader responsibilities negotiated by a team and team leader follows:

1. Provide leadership in conducting team business.
   a. grouping and scheduling students
   b. planning and conducting team meetings
   c. planning team activities
   d. planning for use of resource personnel
   e. developing guidelines for student discipline within the team
   f. planning parent conferences
   g. organizing record keeping

2. Oversee the curriculum in all four academic areas and work closely with the department chairpersons to assure adherence to state, county, and course objectives.

3. Act as a representative of the team in communicating on team matters.

4. Encourage those practices which implement middle school philosophy.

D. Setting Goals for the Team facilitates the team moving together in the same direction.

   1. Set team goals using *brainstorming* and priority setting

   2. Use subgroups (a subgroup can be one or more persons) to expedite work
      a. Ask team members to *volunteer* for subgroups
      b. Put newsprint subgroup *tasks* before team divides
      c. Set *time* for subgroup work and decide how you will negotiate for more or less time
      d. When subgroups report on *newsprint,* agree before giving reports how reports are to be responded to—will rest of team make suggestions *or* will whole team make changes in the report

Before ending a session ask each member to state—

   3. The jobs I am going to do for the team as (specific jobs) by _____ (dates) . (Record these on newsprint and send out right after meeting)

E. Assessing the progress of the team-building process.

   1. You need to compare continually *what is happening* in the team with *contract statement* and *team goals* and the hopes for the group. As you perceive the team "on-the-track" or "off-track"—SAY SO AND SAY WHAT YOU SEE THAT LEADS YOU TO YOUR CONCLUSION

   2. Set a time at the end of each meeting to evaluate the meeting and *do it*

Staff Development Centers—A Promising Trend

To sustain inservice training of middle school teachers, a growing number of school districts are developing teacher renewal or staff development centers. Some of the centers are classified as teacher education centers while others are extensions of the regular staff development program of the school district.

The purpose of such centers is to provide practical, hands-on types of inservice workshops for middle school teachers. The authors have participated in the development of a number of these centers and also have conducted numerous workshops at such centers. Teachers have been extremely positive about their participation in staff development centers. The follow-up help they receive in their own classroom from instructional associates and curriculum specialists attached to the centers makes the centers even more popular with middle school teachers.

An excellent example of a middle school staff development center is the Pinellas County, Florida, TORC model. A description of the TORC model follows.

T.O.R.C. (Teacher Orientation/Renewal Center)

In recent years the emergence of middle schools has been, in many cases, in name only. The purpose of TORC is to provide a practical approach to providing teachers with additional methods of classroom management and skills development to assist them in meeting the needs of the middle school learner. One way to involve teachers in the development and implementation of a learner-oriented classroom is to establish a center at which they can experience modeling of teacher behaviors and can explore a variety of techniques of classroom management.

TORC objectives for participants are: individualization, behavior modification, behavioral objectives, diagnosing and prescribing, classroom organization, classroom management systems, flexible scheduling, and student participation in planning, for these areas can be related to content in the various disciplines.

RATIONALE:

TORC is based on the educational principle "learn by doing." The way to involve teachers in the development and implementation of a learner-centered classroom is to be sure teachers experience a learner-centered classroom as a learner. Teachers learn varied classroom management systems and teaching strategies by experiencing them. The trainer models the teacher's role.

DESIGN:

Teachers may volunteer to attend a three-day training session in a center designed to model various management systems. Teachers may then sign a contract with a resource teacher and their principal to continue study of the content of TORC or to implement TORC ideas in their classrooms. They may earn component points for this work. Resource teachers provide follow-up support which includes:

1. keeping the TORC center open Wednesdays from 3 to 9 P.M.
2. helping teachers obtain instructional materials, supplies, and equipment

3. pooling materials and ideas from various schools and making them available for sharing

4. writing a newsletter to TORC graduates offering suggestions and encouragement

5. working in classrooms to help teachers introduce students to new classroom procedures

6. helping teachers make instructional materials, such as audio tapes, kits, and games

7. helping teachers redesign their classrooms, and

8. serving as a contact person with content supervisors

TORC can be used by teachers to fulfill part of the requirements for middle school certification. Participation would be on a voluntary basis and teachers interested in a learner-center classroom can receive direct help and support to put their ideas into operation. Materials would be pooled and shared among schools so that successful programs throughout the county can be shared by all Pinellas County middle school students.

TORC RESULTS:

These proposals and alternatives offer a way to put the learner-oriented school into practice. They give the teacher concrete methods and support in implementing the middle school program. Teachers working together and sharing ideas and materials, with follow-up support from curriculum assistants and supervisors, will improve morale as well as enhance students' educational experiences. Following their attendance at the center, teachers can better determine which style, or combination of styles, the classroom management and techniques best suit them and their students.

Stamford Staff Development Center

A second innovative model of a staff development center for middle school teachers is the Stamford, Connecticut, Staff Development Center. The Stamford Center provides inservice training for all teachers in the district. It played a big part in carrying out the district's Comprehensive Plan for Middle School Development (see Chapter Two for a description of the Stamford Comprehensive Plan).

The Stamford Staff Development Center plans all staff development activities *with* middle school teachers. A variety of delivery systems for inservice training are utilized including two Wednesday afternoons a month at which time students are released early so that teachers can participate in inservice workshops. Other activities include workshops in the staff development center (an old converted elementary building), pre- and postschool workshops, and contracted inservice workshop time where groups of teachers work in their own schools on projects of their choosing. Eight instructional associates work with the Director of Staff Development in planning and conducting workshops and working directly with teachers in the classroom. Although the Comprehensive Plan for Middle School Development has been carried out, the Staff Development Center continues to provide sustaining inservice activities for middle school teachers.

Inservice Workshops—Sample Topics

After a needs-assessment is conducted with middle school teachers to determine inservice needs, workshops and other activities must be developed to help teachers develop and refine the kinds of skills necessary for teaching in the middle school. Two areas of need that are often identified by middle school teachers are "Skills of Teaming" and "Interdisciplinary Teaming and Unit Building." To assist you in understanding the types of topics dealt with in inservice workshops, we have selected excerpts from an announcement and outline of two of the many such workshops they have conducted with middle school staffs.

Fresno, California

To assist interested middle school teachers in the development of interdisciplinary teaming skills before the 1978–79 school year begins, a special five-day summer workshop has been planned. The workshop is scheduled to be held at the Staff Development Academy during the week of 19–23 June. Participants would include three-to-four person teacher-teams who have indicated an interest in becoming a part of an interdisciplinary team in their assigned middle schools. The workshop content will be very practical and structured to promote the development of necessary team skills. A required product from each team will be the development of an interdisciplinary unit which can be used in the middle school during the 1978–1979 school year.

To assure the best instruction available in the United States, the services of highly competent and experienced middle school educators will be utilized. The following outline provides information of value to interested teachers.

Dates/Times:	19–23 June, 8–4 p.m.
Place:	Staff Development Academy, Rooms C–1, C–5, & C–6
Participants:	One interdisciplinary team (3-4 teachers) from each of the ten middle schools
Credit:	Arrangements are being made to get 2–3 semester units through Pacific College and C.S.U.F. The fee per-unit will be $12 and must be paid by each participant desiring college credit.
Stipend:	Each teacher-participant will be reimbursed at the rate of $50 per-day for each of the five workshop days.
Workshop Staff:	Jon Wiles, University of Montana Joseph Bondi, University of South Florida Pegoty Johansen, Fitzgerald Middle School, Largo, Florida.

Middle School Workshop
Interdisciplinary Teaming and Unit-Building

Killeen, Texas, August 7–11

Workshop Goal: Designing Strategies for Implementing Interdisciplinary Teaming and Unit-Building

Objectives:
1. To identify elements of the middle school curriculum.
2. To explore the concept of "team" and to practice the team-building process.
3. To facilitate development of leadership skills.
4. To develop interdisciplinary teaching skills and develop interdisciplinary units.
5. To examine materials on the following topics:
   a. Setting up Learning Centers
   b. Designing Creative Instructional Activities
   c. Examining Skill-Building Techniques
   d. Dealing with Reluctant Learners
   e. Reviewing Grouping Techniques
   f. Ways of Using Audio-Visual Materials
   g. Overview of the middle school

ARTICULATION

In modern middle schools there has been an increased emphasis on articulation of the middle school with feeder elementary schools and receiving high schools.

Efforts should be made at all three levels of schooling to establish and implement a well-defined plan of articulation to help students make the transition from one level to the next.[3] Such a plan might include visitation or exchange days for elementary students that will allow them to spend a day in the middle school they will enter the next year. Middle school students, in their last year, might spend a day visiting the high school they will enter. They could meet and talk with future schoolmates and teachers and get acquainted with the physical plant. Students could proceed through a simulated day in the high school. Many school districts have implemented teacher exchange days between schools in the three levels to give teachers a better understanding of the programs that precede or follow their own programs.

District committees of teachers with representatives from all three levels have developed articulated skills programs, content programs, and guidance activities. The organizational chart and time schedule found in Figure 9.4 illustrates such a process. The middle school, with its emphasis on a continuous progress plan of learning, has done much to precipitate articulation activities leading to a breakdown of lock-step-graded patterns of instruction. Recent reforms in the high school

---

[3] *An Overview of the Philosophy, Rationale, Objectives, and Program for Middle Schools in Broward County, Florida,* (Fort Lauderdale, Fla.: Broward County Board of Public Instruction, 1974), pp. 9–10.

Figure 9.4
Process for Curriculum Decisions—Reorganization

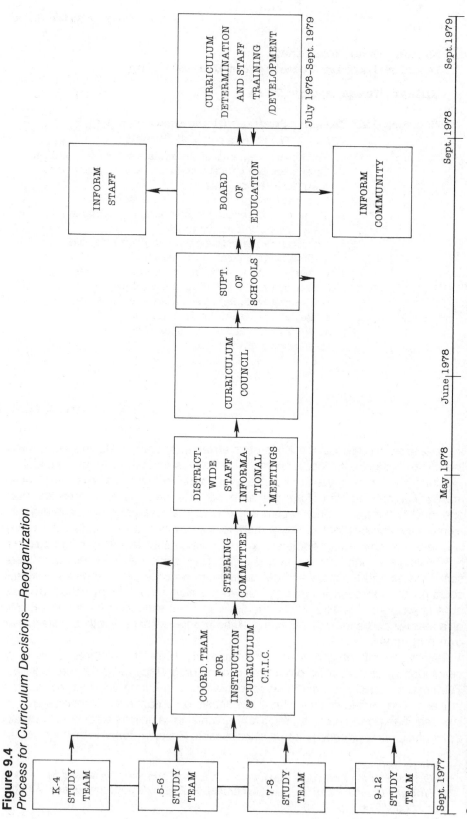

SOURCE: White Plains Public Schools, "Process for Curriculum Decisions—Reorganization," White Plains, New York, 1969. Used with permission.

286

have seen a carrying forward of interdisciplinary teams to the ninth grade and a continued emphasis on skill building and effective activities.

Elementary schools have implemented additional guidance experiences and core programs in the upper elementary grades and developed special interest classes as a result of the influence of middle schools.

Articulation among middle schools in a district or geographic area has been facilitated by the establishment of curriculum data banks that include samples of interdisciplinary units and teacher-made materials; consortiums that provide studies of grading and instructional practices; and leagues of middle schools which share ideas about successful practice in middle schools.

K–12 curriculum studies have resulted in district curriculum guides in all subject areas.[4] Such guides have helped middle schools structure programs in the various disciplines. They have also helped all three levels to communicate better with students, parents, and the general public about the interrelationships of the various levels.

Interschool faculty meetings and shared student programs such as science and math fairs, art exhibits, and dramatic and musical performances have helped foster better relationships between school levels.

SUMMARY

Successfully implementing the middle school requires that the goals and purposes of the middle school be clearly understood by students, teachers, parents, and the supporting community. A number of practical examples of communicating goals and purposes of the middle school are included in this chapter.

Along with planning a middle school program and organizational structure, a plan for phasing in the middle school should be developed. An implementation schedule should include provisions for sustained inservice training of teachers, administrators, and support personnel.

Included in any implementation plan is a discussion of the types and uses of facilities available to house middle schools. Most middle schools have had to use buildings designed for high schools, junior high schools, or elementary programs. In many cases, the buildings have had to be renovated to accommodate modern middle school programs.

Sustaining inservice training of teachers, principals, and other middle school staff members has been a major problem in the middle school movement. Team building and interdisciplinary teaming have become major inservice areas as middle school programs have been implemented. A major stumbling block to implementing effective middle school programs and organizational structures has been that of getting middle school teachers to work together in team settings. In this chapter, the authors have identified a number of processes available for making the team concept work.

Successful delivery systems for carrying out inservice programs have been

---

[4] An excellent example of a K–12 curriculum plan is the *SAVVY Plan,* a series of subject-area curriculum guides developed by the Memphis City Schools in 1976.

developed, including the Teacher Renewal or Staff Development Center Model. Two successful models are discussed in Chapter Nine.

In implementing a middle school program, that program should be a part of the total grades K–12 structure of the school district. Articulation among middle schools, as well as with feeder elementary and receiving high schools, must be initiated and sustained by middle school staffs if the middle school is to be understood and accepted.

Suggested Learning Activitie

1. Write a handbook for students and parents outlining the goals and purposes of the middle school.

2. Select a school facility not designed for a middle school and outline the changes you would make in the building to accommodate a middle school program.

3. Conduct a needs-assessment for your faculty on types of inservice desired and delivery systems needed to carry out those activities.

4. Design a team-building workshop for an interdisciplinary team in a middle school.

5. You have been asked to chair a committee on articulating the middle school program with the elementary and high school programs. Outline an assignment for the committee with whom you work. Assume the committee will include representatives from all three levels of schooling.

Selected Reference

Bondi, Joseph. *Developing Middle Schools: A Guidebook.* Wheeling, Ill.: Whitehall Publishing Company, 1972.

George, Paul, ed. *The Middle School: A Look Ahead.* National Middle School Association, 1977.

Hansen, John, and Hearn, Arthur. *The Middle School Program.* Chicago: Rand McNally and Company, 1971.

Hertling, James, and Getz, Howard. *Education for the Middle Years: Readings.* Glenview, Ill.: Scott, Foresman, and Company, 1971.

Kindred, Leslie et al. *The Middle School Curriculum: A Practitioner's Handbook.* Boston: Allyn and Bacon, Inc., 1976.

Leeper, Robert, ed. *Middle School in the Making.* Washington, D.C.: Association for Supervision and Curriculum Development, 1974.

10

Evaluating the Middle School

There is no greater burden
than a great potential

INTRODUCTION

Evaluation of the middle school should be a continuous process involving pupils attending the middle school, professional staff, consultants, school district personnel, and members of the community.[1]

This book has stressed the belief that the existing programs and organizations found in most upper elementary and junior high levels do not provide the best possible learning situation for the pupils who attend. The middle school has been proposed as being more appropriate for pupils between childhood and adolescence.

To test a middle school program and organization, we should look at the following objectives which the middle school purports to serve:

1. Facilitate a smoother articulation and more continuous progression between the separate components of the educational system.

---

[1] Joseph Bondi, *Developing Middle Schools: A Guidebook* (Wheeling, Ill.: Whitehall Publishing Company, 1972), pp. 118–19.

2. Create a plan of staff utilization that will maximize the personal and professional development of teachers.

3. Facilitate new teacher education programs based on career opportunities in this special area.

4. Facilitate the introduction of needed specialization in the upper elementary years by using team teaching and special instructional centers.

5. Provide for more realistic and effective guidance through the use of teacher counselors and planned guidance sessions.

6. Create a social and physical environment free from the pressures of competitive athletic programs and highly organized social activities typical of junior high programs, and one that requires less dependence upon adults than typical elementary programs.

7. Promote a greater degree of individualization through encouraging pupils to progress at different rates through different programs by using independent study plans and self-pacing materials as well as newer media of instruction.

The following hypotheses might be tested in the evaluation of a middle school:

1. The middle school will provide a rich program of exploratory experiences.

2. There will be fewer and/or less intense social and psychological problems found in middle school students than age-mates in other types of schools.

3. Middle school students will develop more adequate self-concepts than age-mates in other types of schools.

4. Pupils in middle schools will become more self-directed learners.

5. Middle school graduates will succeed better in high school.

6. There will be less teacher turnover in the middle school.

7. Teacher morale will be higher in the middle school.

8. The organization of the middle school will facilitate more effective use of special competencies and interests of the teaching staff.

9. The average daily attendance record of middle school students will exceed that of pupils in conventional schools.

10. Teachers in the middle school will use a greater variety of learning media than teachers in conventional schools.

11. Patrons of the middle school will hold more positive attitudes toward objectives and procedures of the middle school than patrons of conventional schools.

12. Achievement of middle school students on standardized tests will equal or exceed that of pupils in conventional schools.

Each middle school, because of unique conditions and programs, must develop its own carefully designed evaluation component. To ignore or fail to emphasize evaluation in a middle school will have inevitable consequences for this complex educational design. To survive, middle schools must be able to identify, justify, and document their achievements.

EVALUATION AS A SYSTEM

Like the instructional program for students, the evaluation program in a middle school must be comprehensive if it is to achieve its objective—*promote better learning.* Like the curriculum, the instructional pattern, and the operation of the school, evaluation should be a product of the objectives of middle school education. Middle school evaluation must be systematic if it is to assess truly the effectiveness of the program.[2]

The primary question in designing systematic evaluation in the middle school is "education for what?" The middle school has been identified as a school "designed to promote personal growth and development in preadolescent learners." That single purpose defines the parameters of middle school evaluation. Evaluation serves to answer this question: Is preadolescent development being promoted?

As we seek to answer the above question, our evaluative focus shifts to the learning design created to achieve this end, and to the arrangements for learning which have been made. In doing so, middle school evaluation goes beyond the areas of student growth, identified in Chapter Three, to include a much broader range of concerns. Personnel, facilities, learning materials, rules and regulations, and all other program planning considerations become concerns of evaluation. Evaluation in the middle school is defined by the purposes and activities of the middle school program.

One way of viewing evaluation is as a feedback or corrective mechanism. Here the goals of the school are translated into objectives which in turn create a program design. Student learning, for instance, is structured into activity which have distinct foci. As evidence is gathered and analyzed, discrepancies between desired outcomes and real outcomes are discovered and adjustments in program are made. Goals are refocused and the feedback cycle is renewed:

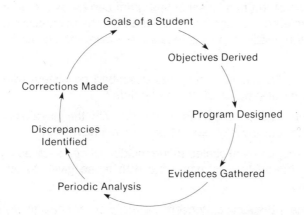

Another way to approach middle school evaluation would be to use evaluation as a means of "validating" program goals and objectives. In this approach, evidences are gathered to justify specific facets of the program and these facets or

[2] Jon Wiles, *Planning Guidelines for Middle School Education* (Dubuque, Iowa: Kendall/Hunt Publishing Company, 1976), pp. 71–79.

subsystems collectively comprise the evaluation program. Examples of such subsystems are student performance, teacher effectiveness, program design, resource utilization, facilities usage, policies and regulation, parent and community feedback, and staff development programs.

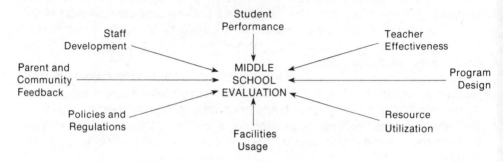

An example of how this approach might work can be drawn from the middle school's concern with teaching academic processes. If, for instance, students were not demonstrating growth in study skills, each area or subsystem could be analyzed for probable cause: i.e., materials for teaching skills are inadequate, teachers need additional training in teaching reading, etc.

By combining these two approaches to evaluation, a school can develop a means of regularly assessing its programs and taking corrective actions where findings are not satisfactory. Some guiding questions in each of the above mentioned areas are provided for study.

Program Design

The overall design of the middle school program can be assessed from both an external and an internal vantage point. Viewed from the perspective of the school district in which the middle school is located, the following questions seem pertinent:

1. Is the middle school concept as described consistent with the overall philosophy of the district and its leaders?

2. Does the middle school articulate (fit) with the preceding elementary programs and the high school programs which follow?

3. Are the resources allocated to the middle school, such as building, staff, monies, materials, commensurate with those given to other levels of schooling?

From an internal perspective, concern for the program design would focus on the structure of the curriculum and the learning opportunities for students. The following questions might guide such an analysis:

4. In what ways does the curriculum actually provide for the intellectual, physical, social, and emotional differences of students?

5. What materials and equipment contribute to the development of skills, interests, abilities, and special talents of students?

6. By what means are all of the learning experiences in the school integrated with one another?

7. What provisions are made for student growth and development in health, personality, and character?

8. How are learning activities individualized to meet student needs and interests?

9. What special provisions have been made to insure the mastery of basic learning skills?

10. What adjustments in the organization of the school have been made to promote a "climate" for exploration?

Facilities Usage

Regardless of the age or condition of the facility in which a middle school program is operated, much can be done with a facility to support the advancement of activities. Schools should be built or converted in anticipation of program needs.

Although some facility concerns in the middle school are more obvious than others (such as using a building that promotes flexibility and physical movement, that allows for variable grouping of students, and that encourages cooperative planning and teaching), others are subtle. The following questions may assist in illuminating facility-usage evaluation in the middle school:

1. Does the allocation of space in the facility, both in location and in volume, reflect program priorities?

2. Is space utilization in the facility flexible enough to allow for individualized instructional activities?

3. Is the instructional resource center (IRC) centrally located and readily accessible to teaching spaces?

4. Are there noisy spaces relatively isolated from needed quiet areas?

5. Is the entire building stimulating in its spatial and color orientation?

6. Are all available spaces like stairwell corners and foyers being used to educate and communicate with students?

7. Is there a sufficient number of special focus areas in the facility like darkened projection areas, storage areas for projects, commons areas, and areas for private conversations to promote program objectives?

8. Is the administrative area accessible to students, teachers, parents, and visitors?

9. Are provisions made for the display of students' work, such as tackboards and cork strips in the hallways?

Resource Utilization

The allocation and utilization of resources, both human and material, is a problem area for many middle schools. An all too familiar pattern is seen in territorial rights established in buildings, or available resources allocated to favored segments of a program. Middle schools must use all available resources judiciously to promote their programs. The following questions suggest some areas worth analyzing:

1. Is there a clear relationship between the allocation of funds and materials in the school, and the curricular objectives of the program?
2. Are staff members assigned to positions in the program according to function and talent rather than by credential?
3. Are high-priority areas like skill buildings given sufficient support in the form of staff and consumable materials?
4. Are immediate resources available to support innovative instructional techniques?
5. Is there an established means of assessing future resource needs and planning for their acquisition?

Policies and Regulations

Few middle schools regularly view administrative policy and regulation from a program objectives standpoint. Yet, no other single area in a middle school is so important in setting the tone or climate for learning. It is important in evaluation that the following questions be asked:

1. What policies and regulations are absolutely essential to the operation of a middle school?
2. What existing rules or policies might contradict the "spirit" of the middle school concept?
3. How might policy-setting and regulation enforcement best be handled to promote the objectives of the school?

Student Performance

Since the terminal objectives of the educative process, in any school at any level, are concerned with student performance or behavior, this area of evaluation is generally given more attention by parents, teachers, and administrators than any other phase of schooling. In the middle school, as students are evaluated, the folly of redefining the purpose of education must be avoided while still retaining the old yardsticks of measurement.

Middle schools must evaluate student performance in areas that are truly important; areas suggested by the conceptual image of the middle school design. A comprehensive evaluative approach is needed to match the comprehensive educational program. The following questions may assist in the development of such an approach:

1. Is student evaluation perceived and conducted as a measure of personal development for each student?

2. Is student evaluation both systematic and continuous in nature?

3. Is the student fully involved in the evaluation and measurement of his own growth and development?

4. Is the reported student evaluation social-personal as well as academic?

5. Is the evaluation of student progress related to his own ability and previous performance?

6. Are parents actively involved in the evaluation of their children?

7. Is the gathering of evaluative data comprehensive in nature, such as a combination of periodic testing, student self-report files, teacher-pupil conferences, observations, etc.?

8. Is student progress reporting directional in nature, indicating where improvement is needed?

9. Is student progress reported to parents in a positive manner with emphasis on growth as shown in the following scheme?
   C = Commendable Achievement
   S = Satisfactory Achievement
   I = Improving
   N = Needing more work
   NA = Not Applying

Teacher Effectiveness

Teachers in the middle school are more than simply a resource, they are in fact the medium or delivery system through which the middle school sends its message. Without the full support of the teaching staff, the middle school will falter under the weight of ambition. Full effectiveness from each member of the instructional staff is needed. Evaluation of teacher effectiveness might center around the following questions:

1. Have the talents and abilities of all staff members been fully explored and cataloged?

2. Are members of the instructional and support staffs working where they believe they can be most effective?

3. Are there organizational and administrative constraints on teaching styles in the school?

4. Is there an active mechanism by which teachers can share ideas and activities with other teachers?

5. Is there an established means for program-improvement input by the instructional staff?

6. Does the administration use a mechanism for reviewing teacher growth?

Team Effectiveness

Teachers in middle schools are often organized into teams. Procedures must be developed to analyze the strengths and weaknesses of the team approach. Evaluation must include the role of the team leader. Evaluation of team-effectiveness might center around the following concerns:

1. Team climate—does the team display cooperation and teamwork?

2. Team goals—does the team use integrative, constructive methods in problem solving rather than a competitive approach? Are team goals understood by all teachers in the team?

3. Team contract—has the team put into writing the expectations of its members regarding meeting times, reviewing performance, and building agendas?

4. Team leadership—does the team leader provide leadership in facilitating communication within the team and with other teams? Does the team leader coordinate curriculum planning by the team and provide resources, both human and material, for the team?

Staff Development

In the middle school evaluation schemata shown earlier, staff development was seen as a corrective device for program improvement. Rather than a regularly scheduled or unfocused treatment which characterizes many inservice programs, staff development efforts in the middle school attack real problems faced by educators. The following questions suggest a possible evaluative focus:

1. Are there monies budgeted for staff development efforts during the school year?

2. Do staff development needs arise from analysis of other areas of evaluation such as student performance and teacher effectiveness?

3. Can staff development efforts be conducted on short notice during the school year?

4. Do teachers regularly have a chance to critique staff development activities and suggest areas of future need?

Parent-Community Feedback

Perhaps the most important dimension in the middle school evaluation system is that which monitors the reactions and interest of parents and the community in which the middle school is located. Without support from both of these groups—at a minimum, tacit support—the programs of the middle school cannot fully succeed.

Involvement of the community, like involvement of parents, is a matter of degree as well as frequency. The following questions may assist in evaluation of this part of the middle school program:

1. Were members of the community involved in the original study of the middle school concept and the drafting of formative documents?

2. Is there presently in existence a citizens committee at the school whose major function is to communicate to parents and to the community about programs at the school?

3. Are members of the community regularly kept informed, through school dissemination efforts, of changing programs or changes in operation?

4. Can citizens actively participate in school functions at a meaningful level of involvement?

Each of these components of the evaluation "system" is important in terms of program improvement and increased performance by those actively engaged in the operation of the school. All components are interrelated and crucial to other areas.

STUDENT EVALUATION

Perhaps the greatest challenge to middle school education is developing a program of student evaluation equal to the goals of middle school education. If the goals of the middle school are comprehensive, then it is equally important that the evaluation of student performance be broad.

A useful distinction in attempting to develop a comprehensive student evaluation plan is to differentiate between "evaluation" and "validation" of performance. Evaluation generally refers to a judgmental process where decisions are made about the qualitative nature of events. Validation, a more recently developed process used to evaluate many federal programs, is an evidence-gathering and assessment activity. The key difference between evaluation and validation is that in validation evidences are selected prior to activity so that the determination of progress is a result of objective analysis.

A survey of middle schools by the authors has determined a number of student outcomes regularly assessed and measured:

work habits and academic skills

social attitudes and evidences of adjustment

physical and mental health

knowledge acquisition and achievement

creativity—interest expansion—aesthetic appreciations

self-concept and personal philosophy

aspects of critical thinking

These categories, and others, suggest that the middle school should evaluate student development in a variety of areas and that the emphasis of the evaluation program be placed on individual growth rather than on comparison to norm-referenced standards. Comparisons to norms, of course, would not make sense in a program seeking individual development.

Finally, it should be noted that student evaluation plays three specific roles in the instructional process. It is a diagnostic device which allows the instructional staff to determine current student growth patterns. It is a descriptive device that allows teachers and parents and students to communicate about the growth and development of the individual student. Finally, evaluation of the student serves to give direction to future learning activity by pinpointing needs. Because student evaluation is diagnostic, descriptive, and directional, it serves the learner and the middle school program.

SUMMARY

While middle schools are student-focused in their orientation, there is nonetheless a pressing need for specificity in the evaluation of programs. If this complex learning design is to survive, it must be able to document its achievements.

The middle school can best demonstrate its value as an educational design by focusing on the effects of its highly coordinated program. A systematic assessment of school operations using a validation procedure will provide a better justification for activities than a judgmental process.

In building an evaluation system, each school must select its own criteria for analysis. The philosophy and objectives of middle school education will suggest the parameters of such a system.

Middle schools must pay particular attention to student evaluation since this is the area historically viewed most closely by the public. Within student evaluation, a broad spectrum of evidences is gathered which, collectively, represents a pattern of individual growth on the student's part. Such evidences should be used as diagnostic, descriptive, and directional tools in providing feedback about the program being experienced by the student.

The reader is invited to review Appendix Eleven for samples of evaluation and reporting instruments used in the middle school.

Suggested Learning Activities

1. Develop a list of objectives for the middle school that could serve as a basis for structuring an evaluation of the middle school program.

2. You have been asked to chair a committee to evaluate middle school facilities in your district. What questions would you and your committee devise to study existing facilities?

3. Design a checklist for evaluating team effectiveness.

4. Develop an instrument for evaluating parent and community support of the middle school.

5. Review various reporting systems used by middle schools to report student performance. What areas of student performance would you evaluate?

Selected References

Bondi, Joseph. *Developing Middle Schools: A Guidebook.* Wheeling, Ill.: Whitehall Publishing Company, 1972.

Bondi, Joseph, and Tocco, Thomas. "The Nature of the Transescent as it Affects Middle School Evaluation." A paper presented at the 1974 annual conference of the American Educational Research Association, April 16, 1974.

Broward County Middle School Study, 1975–76. A study conducted by the Broward County, Florida, County Council Parent-Teacher Association.

Committee's Report on Visitation of Eisenhower Middle School. Albuquerque, N. M., Public Schools, December 1976.

George, Paul, and Erb, Thomas. *A Comparative Study of Middle Schools and Junior High Schools in the State of Florida.* Florida League of Middle Schools, Spring 1975.

Gordon, Jeffrey; Johnston, J. Howard; Markle, Glenn; and Strahan, David. "A Delphi Study to Determine Needed Middle School Research." Paper, University of Cincinnati, 1978.

McGee, Jerry; Krajewski, Robert; and Keese, Earl. *A Three Year Study of Brown Middle School, 1974–77.* Middle Tennessee State University, 1977.

Morrison, William. *Good Schools for Middle Grade Youngsters: Characteristics, Practices, and Recommendations.* National Middle School Association, 1978.

Robinson, Glenn. *Summary of Research on Middle Schools.* Educational Research Service, Inc., 1975.

Tocco, Thomas. *Preliminary Evaluation of Azalea Middle School, 1973–74.* Pinellas County, Florida, School District, 1974.

Webster Transitional School—Three Year Progress Report. Cedarburg, Wis., School District, 1977.

Weld County School District Middle School Evaluation, 1979. Weld County, Colo., 1979.

Standards for Evaluation of Middle Childhood Programs in West Virginia, West Virginia Department of Education, 1978.

Wiles, Jon. *Planning Guidelines for Middle School Education.* Dubuque, Iowa: Kendall/ Hunt Publishing Company, 1976.

Wiles, Jon, and Thomason, J. "Middle School Research 1968–74: A Review of Substantial Studies." *Educational Leadership,* March, 1975, pp. 421–23.

11

Future Directions of the Middle School

The future of tomorrow's society
can be found in today's middle school youth

INTRODUCTION

The emergence of the middle school in the United States has represented a dramatic break from the past. Much progress has been made in developing and implementing new programs for pre- and early adolescents, yet there is still much to be done. As with other changes in American education, the middle school has met with varying degrees of understanding and acceptance. Issues have been identified that hold continued significance for the middle school movement and they must be addressed. Beginning with the processes involved in developing good middle schools—and to sustain good programs once they are developed—we must provide the leadership necessary to insure that the middle school will continue as a positive force in American education.

THE CHALLENGE OF THE MIDDLE SCHOOL

As the number of middle schools reach and surpass the number of junior high schools during the eighties, educational leaders must not lose sight of the purposes of the middle school. They must not let the middle school revert to the kind of school it purported to succeed. Below are some comparisons of past shortcomings of the junior high school with possible weaknesses of the present middle school. Consider the following:

Junior High School Movement	Middle School Movement
Reasons for Organization:	
Building needs brought on by increasing or declining enrollments; integration purposes; bandwagon effect.	Building needs brought on by increasing or declining enrollments; integration purposes; bandwagon effect.
Teacher Preparation:	
Few undergraduate programs designed for middle grades preparation. Teacher preparation program usually part of elementary or secondary degree program.	Few undergraduate programs designed for middle grades preparation. Teacher preparation program usually part of elementary or secondary degree program.
Certification:	
Attached to existing certification program. Failed to recognize need for a difference in teacher preparation programs for middle grades teachers.	Attached to existing certification program. Failed to recognize the need for a difference in teacher preparation programs for middle grades teachers.
Teaching Methods Emulated:	
Lecture, recitation, static grouping, reliance on textbook.	Lecture, recitation, static grouping, reliance on textbook.
Implementation:	
Usually implemented in name only with little understanding of basic underlying theory and intent.	Usually implemented in name only with little understanding of basic underlying theory and intent.

The early years of the middle school movement were characterized by excitement, innovation, experimentation, and a sense of urgency to develop and implement a better program for emerging adolescent learners. As the middle school reaches maturity in the eighties, its challenge is not to let those qualities become lost in a sea of complacency and retrenchment.

SUSTAINING MIDDLE SCHOOLS—PREVENTING A REGRESSION TO STANDARDIZATION

Middle schools have grown in number in the United States and have resulted in positive changes in American education. Many middle schools in the sixties and seventies resulted from changing enrollment patterns, integration efforts, and the "bandwagon" effect. Nonetheless, many intermediate level educators saw these "wrong reasons" for establishing a middle school as the "right opportunity" to improve school programs for an age group long ignored in our schools. At the time of this writing, declining enrollments, limited budgets, and a lack of sustained inservice training are causing some school districts to re-examine the middle school structure. These developments are encouraging those not really committed to the education of preadolescents to take the easy way out by returning to an inexpensive, highly structured, standardized intermediate school. It is hoped that these pressures will not overcome two decades of good work at the intermediate level.

The middle school is a structure which must be constantly reviewed and reaffirmed. The subtle but momentous change in the purpose of educating, suggested by the middle school design, is easily lost in the day-to-day tasks of operating a school. To focus an entire curriculum on the learner, rather than on content mastery, calls for a commitment to serving each learner in a personal and individual manner. Given the diversity of the preadolescent population, this can only be done through careful planning and execution of school programming. The middle school is a special design for learning.

The authors have introduced a number of social statistics in this book to communicate the open fact that many of the traditional support systems for growing up seem to be dissolving. At a time in our history when the emerging adolescent needs the kind of guidance and personal development activities that a middle school can provide, there are some who say it is time to return to the impersonal grades 7 through 9 junior high school structure that had seventy years to develop a program for preadolescents. Because the junior high school continued to model itself after the high school program, its curriculum was arrested in serving adolescents rather than those in transition.

Sustaining middle schools means we must go back and re-examine some of our existing middle school programs. Our faculties need to restudy the nature of the age group they are serving and re-establish the philosophy of the middle school. New inservice training programs must be established to help new and old teachers cope with the program of today's middle school youngster.

Those committed to the middle school program must set up an effective communications network to convince the public and colleagues that the middle school is still the best alternative to the junior high school. The middle school has produced a positive change in American education and it must not fail.

SUMMARY

Although the middle school can be defined by goals, purposes, and characteristics, there is no exact blueprint for the development of a successful middle school. Each school must consider the characteristics of its students and develop an instructional program that takes into consideration the unique needs of those students it serves.

The middle school must never be static. It must be constantly *evolving* if it is to respond to a changing society. The middle school offers an exciting challenge to those seeking a more relevant educational experience for youth emerging from late childhood into early adolescence. Our energies in the eighties must be expended to make the middle school truly something special, something significant, something stimulating in American education. If we are to provide for tomorrow's society, we have no other choice. The middle school must be THE ESSENTIAL MIDDLE SCHOOL.

Suggested Learning Activities

1. Develop a "renewal plan" for your middle school faculty to help your staff review the goals and purposes of its existence.

2. Prepare a report to the community outlining the rationale for the continued existence of the middle school in your district.

3. Develop a position paper on the need for a middle school teacher preparation program that has its own identity apart from the elementary or secondary program.

4. Organize a parents' committee to study your middle school program. Outline the charge you would give that committee.

5. Prepare a report on "The Middle School of the Eighties" to be presented to a citizen's group.

Selected References

Bondi, Joseph, and Gourluck, Russ. "Is There a Middle School in Your Future?" Paper presented at the First Congress on Education, Canadian School Trustees Association, June 18, 1978.

Bondi, Joseph, and Wiles, Jon. "What Do Middle School Students Really Value?" *Middle School Journal* 10, no. 2 (May 1979): 4, 29.

George, Paul, ed. *The Middle School: A Look Ahead.* Gainesville, Fla.: National Middle School Association, 1977. See Joseph Bondi's "Addressing the Issues: The Middle School—A Positive Change in American Education," Chapter Four, and Jon Wiles, "The Middle School: Issues and Action Plans," Chapter Seven.

Lounsbury, John, and Vars, Gordon. *A Curriculum for the Middle School Years.* New York: Harper and Row, Publishers.

McGlasson, Maurice. *The Middle School: Whence? What? Whither?* Fastback, Bloomington, Ind.: Phi Delta Kappa, 1973.

Wiles, Jon, and Bondi, Joseph. *Curriculum Development: A Guide to Practice.* Columbus, Ohio: Charles E. Merrill Publishing Company, 1979.

Wiles, Jon, and Bondi, Joseph. *Supervision: A Guide to Practice.* Columbus, Ohio: Charles
E. Merrill Publishing Company, 1980.

The authors also suggest a continual review of publications from The National Middle
School Association; Leagues of Middle Schools in the States; Consortiums such as the
A-O-K Middle School Consortium, University of Tulsa; and the National Middle School
Resource Center, Indianapolis, Indiana.

Statements of Goals, Definitions, and Characteristics of Middle Schools

HASTINGS PUBLIC SCHOOLS
Second Draft, Revised Educational Goals
and Goal Indicators*

GOAL: Competency in skills essential to live a full and productive life.

INDICATORS: The student will demonstrate:

    (a) Skill in reading, writing, speaking, listening and viewing;

    (b) the ability to express an idea or feeling visually, verbally, physically (in writing), or in any combination of these;

    (c) skill in computational operations, such as mathematical conceptualization, problem–solving, data collection;

    (d) skill in the logical process of thinking creatively and critically;

    (e) the acquisition of skills and interests for constructive leisure and continued learning;

    (f) an ability to structure and balance work, study, and recreation;

    (g) the development of individual creative talents.

GOAL: The ability to maintain one's mental, physical, and emotional health.

INDICATORS: The student will demonstrate:

    (a) The acquisition of knowledge about good health habits and the conditions required for physical and emotional well-being;

---

* Not listed in order of importance

Revised Educational Goals and Goal Indicators—*continued*

> (b)   the development of his/her physical potential to the fullest extent possible;
>
> (c)   the acquisition of essential understanding of her/his bodily functions.

GOAL: *Competency necessary to secure employment or further training.*

INDICATORS: The student will demonstrate:

> (a)   The acquisition of useful work skills and work habits;
>
> (b)   awareness of career and educational opportunities;
>
> (c)   ability to discriminate among a variety of occupational opportunities;
>
> (d)   acquisition of an attitude to enhance one's ability to be employable in the future.

GOAL: *Understanding of the process of effective citizenship and the ability to participate in and contribute to our society.*

INDICATORS: The student will demonstrate:

> (a)   Understanding about political, economic and legal systems, particularly democratic institutions and the global interdependence of these systems:
>
> (b)   understanding of the American political process at the national, state and local levels;
>
> (c)   understanding of taxation and fiscal policy;
>
> (d)   acquisition of citizenship skills
> (1) decision–making
> (2) group participation
> (3) leadership and "followership"
>
> (e)   understanding of alternative life styles;
>
> (f)   understanding of contemporary society;
>
> (g)   understanding of alternative futures.

GOAL: *The acquisition of a positive self-concept.*

INDICATORS: The student will demonstrate:

(a)   Possession of a sense of self in relationship to others;

(b)   acceptance of himself/herself as a worthwhile person;

(c)   contributes to setting his/her own goals;

(d)   confidence in making choices;

(e)   willingness to venture into new fields;

(f)   freedom to formulate and express his/her own convictions;

(g)   acceptance of criticism;

(h)   respect, sharing and cooperation with others without being possessive or feeling threatened;

(i)   awareness of the joy of learning and inquiry for its own sake;

(j)   the assumption of responsibilities appropriate to his/her level of maturity;

Revised Educational Goals and Goal Indicators—*continued*

(k)   the ability to cope realistically with his/her own strengths and weaknesses;

(l)   the ability to use his/her successes and failures as learning experiences;

(m)   the ability to deal with situations new to one's personal experience.

GOAL: Competency in the processes of developing values leading to an understanding of human relations—respect for and ability to relate to other people in our own and other nations—including those of different sex, origins, cultures and aspirations.

INDICATORS: The student will demonstrate:

(a)   Knowledge and acceptance of a variety of value systems;

(b)   the ability to analyze what he/she thinks, feels, says and does and thinks of others on a continuing basis;

(c)   skill in making value-based judgments;

(d)   the ability to form a value system for himself/herself based on the principles of individual dignity and humane treatment of others;

(e)   respect for other social, cultural and ethnic groups;

(f)   understanding the responsibilities inherent in family life.

GOAL: Knowledge and appreciation of our culture.

INDICATORS   The student will demonstrate:

(a)   A general knowledge of art, musical, literary and drama forms;

(b)   appreciation of the diversity of mankind's historic and cultural heritage;

(c)   development of aesthetic sensitivities;

(d)   knowledge, appreciation and use of such resources as museums, historic sites, performing arts, groups, etc., that reflect our cultural heritage and achievement as a people.

GOAL: Knowledge of the humanities, social sciences, natural sciences and environment and the relationship between one's own acts and the quality of the environment at a level required to participate in an ever more complex world.

INDICATORS: The student will demonstrate:

(a)   Knowledge of the basic methods of inquiry in each field;

(b)   interdisciplinary efforts to focus knowledge on contemporary and future problems;

(c)   awareness of one's relationship to the environment;

(d)   an attitude towards preservation and wise use of natural and human resources;

(e)   understanding the effects on the environment of man's activities and values, lifestyles, technologies, population growth, energy utilization, etc.

SOURCE: Hastings Public Schools, "Revised Educational Goals and Goal Indicators" (Hastings–on–Hudson, N. Y., 1974.) Used with permission.

A PROGRAMMATIC DEFINITION FOR MIDDLE SCHOOLS IN WEST VIRGINIA

1.0 Rationale

The middle school has been erroneously equated by many as another name for the junior high school. In reality, it is an alternative to the traditional junior high.

1.1 The Learner

Research through the State-County Testing Program of the West Virginia Department of Education indicates that the middle childhood period (ages 10 to 14) is characterized in the following ways:

1. Achievement rates are slowed considerably during this age range, particularly in the basic skills, although verbal and nonverbal ability scores remain relatively constant.

2. Interest levels related to school and school subjects show a gradual decline.

3. The inclination to drop out of school among eventual dropouts surfaces during this developmental period.

A review of other research on the preadolescent stage of development indicates:

1. A rapid change in physical growth, development, and maturation resulting in restlessness, frequent movement, and the desire for constant physical activity.

2. A period in which the learner attempts to seek an appropriate balance between dependence and independence. Emotional turmoil is caused by striving for independence while maintaining acceptance by peers and parents.

3. A self-analysis period, demonstrated by the learner seeking to redefine his/her role and identify as an individual. While moving from child to adult patterns of behavior, the learner experiments with behavior patterns which cause erratic responses during this formative stage of identity and value formation.

4. An unusual attentiveness to self-appearance.

5. A great need for peer acceptance.

It is the intention of the middle school concept of school organization to develop a program to encourage maximum intellectual, physical, and social-psychological growth to the full extent of the learner's abilities. Growth in each of the three areas does not occur in isolation but in relation to the other two. Thus, the middle school attempts to create an organizational and instructional pattern that is based on data about growth and development in the preadolescent child and in this way responds to intellectual, social-psychological, and physical needs.

1.2 Philosophy

The philosophy of the middle school derives from the earlier and increased rate of change that is occurring in the preadolescent learner (ages 10–14). Since this increased rate occurs at the same time the preadolescent is expected to discard childhood behaviors and adopt those of adulthood, this growth period becomes unique. Thus, the educational environment should be sensitive to this uniqueness. The preadolescent learner should be valued for what he/she is: awkward and sometimes insecure, sensitive, self-conscious, restless, in need of exploratory opportunities (where appropriate), and frequently in need of opportunities for trial and error.

Data on growth patterns in preadolescents support the organizational pattern of the middle school in which the traditional ninth grade is placed into the high school while the sixth grade (and sometimes the fifth grade) is taken from the elementary school setting and placed into the middle school setting.

Three basic assumptions are at the heart of the middle school approach:

1. Preadolescents have special needs which identify them as a unique group within the K–12 learning continuum.

2. Transition from childhood to adolescence requires an environment with an organization that is designed to meet these special needs.

3. Transition from the elementary school to the high school should be a gradual and personalized process.

Education helps people to change and, by changing, to grow. It is imperative that educators and learners communicate to each other the changes that are feasible and desirable. Parents, school boards, and the community have important roles to play in effecting educational growth and change. The development of goals and objectives for the middle school should be a cooperative effort of the educational community, the local community, and the learners. Those participating in the decision-making process of planning curriculum have the responsibility to state goals and objectives in clear, simple, and explicit terms.

In establishing a middle school program, the following components should be included:

1. Establish goals and objectives for a middle school program.

2. Establish instructional procedures and materials that are appropriate to the instructional objectives and to the preadolescent learner.

3. Establish evaluation methodologies.

4. Implement a system which provides continuous information relative to program objectives and standards.

1.3 Educational Goals

Because of the unique nature of this age group, the educational program should include the following goals which are ranked in order of priority:

1. Provide a developmental, comprehensive program in the basic skills of communicative and mathematical competencies through a variety of learning experiences.

2. Provide a program to help students achieve understanding and awareness of aesthetic, social, multicultural, scientific, health, and physical areas of knowledge.

3. Provide enrichment and advisory programs to assist learners in their quests for personal identity and self-expression and to prepare them to make appropriate educational, career, and recreational decisions in the future.

4. Provide experiences designed to develop attitudes and beliefs necessary for functioning as part of a democratic society.

5. Provide processes whereby learners receive multiple services designed to enable them to acquire and apply the skills and attitudes necessary to make a successful transition from the elementary to the secondary school as well as from childhood to adolescence and to develop positive self-concepts, self-disciplines, and reliable judgments.

6. Provide experiences designed to develop skills in interpersonal relationships.

7. Provide personalized instruction which offers an equal educational opportunity for all learners.

8. Provide specific programs needed by teachers to meet the needs of learners, and emphasize the goals, objectives, instructional processes, and evaluation procedures necessary to implement an effective middle school.

9. Provide cocurricular activities, including intramural, as an instructional vehicle while deemphasizing interscholastic competition in athletics.

2.0 Needs Assessment

Needs assessment involves specifying the goals and objectives a program should achieve and determining how well those goals and objectives are being achieved. In middle school program development, the basic purpose of a needs assessment is to identify discrepancies that exist between desired goals and objectives and existing programs for each of the eight components of the middle school programmatic definition. Each discrepancy identifies a need.

A needs assessment process should include the following four-part strategy:

1. Specify desirable goals and objectives for each component that might be involved in middle school needs assessment. The following sources should be contacted to ensure a wide range of goals which reflect the broad spectrum of the educational community:
    a. State and federal mandates and legislation.
    b. Local and national concerns identified in editorials, articles, and legislation.
    c. Parental concerns as voiced in letters, PTA meetings, and conferences with parents.
    d. Community concerns voiced by unions, business organizations, and other special interest groups.
    e. School records and reports.
    f. Curriculum guides, program descriptions, and recommendations of educational institutions and organizations.

   g. College requirements.
   h. Teacher reports and comments.
   i. Learner requests and comments.
   j. Prepared composite sets of goals and objectives.

2. Determine the relative importance of the goals and objectives. The involvement of teachers, parents, learners, school board members, curriculum experts, consultants, community groups, principals, and administrators should be ensured in a rater process. These individual raters should be selected on the basis of the scope of the needs assessment and of each rater's educational expertise, involvement in implementing the program, and participation in the program. The relative importance to be attached to the rating given by each type of rater should be determined by the persons responsible for implementing the goals and objectives.

3. Assess the degree of discrepancy between the important goals and objectives and their achievement by existing or nonexisting programs. The objectives on which data are collected should be determined by their importance rating and feasibility of data collection. Particular attention in the data collection process should be directed toward objectives receiving high ratings and reflecting high priorities and on which present achievement is substantially below the desired level. This process will lessen the discrepancy between "what is" and "what is desired" in the middle school learning system.

4. Decide which of the discrepancies between present performance and goals and objectives are the most important to correct. The purpose of this step is to determine which of the highest rated objectives should receive priority. This is the final step in identifying and selecting the major program thrusts. This step requires two types of information: the rated importance of the objective and the discrepancy between present and desired performance levels on each objective. Once possible goals are specified, the school system should maintain a continuous needs assessment process.

3.0 Curriculum

Curricular patterns should be designed to be compatible with the needs, interests, and developmental levels represented by the preadolescent age group as well as relevant to the needs of learners in a specific locale.

The following concepts and implementation approaches, ranked in order of priority, should be considered in developing the middle school curriculum:

1. The middle school is for competence in basic skills.
   a. Basic Skills and Extension: The middle school curriculum should extend the basic education program fostered in the elementary school and should provide opportunities for learners to receive clinical help. Improvement and utilization of basic skills by learners should receive top priority in the middle school curriculum.
   b. Continuous Progress: The middle school curriculum should offer a program for continuous progress for each learner in the basic skills and feature an organization that allows learners to progress toward goals regardless of chronological age.

   c. Personalized Instruction: The middle school curriculum should provide instruction in the basic skills based upon learner needs and abilities and should provide learning experiences conducive to different learning styles, learning rates, and learner interests.

2. The middle school is for self-understanding, self-knowledge, independence, and interdependence.

   a. Creative Experiences: The middle school curriculum should include opportunities for learners to express themselves in a creative manner.

   b. Evaluation: The middle school curriculum should provide an opportunity for the evaluation of a learner's work that is personal, positive in nature, and individualized. Parent-teacher-learner conferences on a scheduled and unscheduled basis should be a basic reporting method. Reports of student progress should be based on open and honest pupil-teacher-parent communications.

   c. Planned Gradualism: The middle school curriculum should provide experiences that assist learners in making the transition from childhood dependence to adult independence, thereby helping to ease the transition between elementary school and senior high school.

   d. Social Education: The middle school curriculum should provide social experiences appropriate for the preadolescent youth which contribute to personal and self-concept development, assist each learner in classifying his/her values and those of others, contribute to responsible citizenship, and permit wide exploration of personal interests.

   e. Interpersonal Skills: The middle school curriculum should provide experiences that promote the development of interpersonal relationships.

   f. Security Factor: The middle school curriculum should provide every learner with a peer group that meets regularly and a teacher who knows learners well and to whom learners relate in a positive manner.

   g. Physical and Health Development: The middle school curriculum and the extension of classroom activities should provide physical activities for all learners. A broad range of intramural experiences should be provided to supplement the physical education classes. These experiences should center activities upon helping learners understand, develop, and use their own bodies.

   h. Intramural Activities: The middle school curriculum should feature extensive intramural activities rather than interscholastic activities.

3. The middle school is for exploration.

   a. Exploratory and Enrichment Studies: At the preadolescent stage, the curriculum should offer alternative learning opportunities in addition to strong general education areas which should be explored by all learners. These exploratory areas should widen the range of educational alternatives learners experience rather than specialize their education. Elective courses and objectives should be a part of the program of every learner during his/her years in the middle school. These experiences should help to develop self-discipline, self-motivation, and self-evaluation in the preadolescent.

   b. Multimaterials/Multimedia Approach: The middle school curriculum should offer to learners a wide range of easily accessible instructional materials. Classroom activities should be planned around a multimaterials approach referenced to learning objectives rather than a basic "chapter-by-chapter" textbook approach.

Curriculum development specialists in the content areas of art, foreign language, health, home economics, industrial arts, language arts, mathematics, music, physical education, reading, science, and social studies should develop specific philosophies, goals, objectives, learning alternatives, and evaluation techniques that are consistent with the Educational Goals for West Virginia and the philosophy and guidelines of this document.

4.0 Instruction

Instruction is the process of delivering content and process skills in order to facilitate a learner's abilities to act and interact within his/her society and environment. If instruction is to be successful in the middle school, the learner must be the focal point of instructional planning.

Goals and Objectives

The middle school instructional system should arrange human and material resources in such a way as to facilitate the physical, intellectual, and social-psychological growth of each learner.

1. A variety of strategies, techniques, materials, and resources should be included in the instructional process. To some extent, the content or process skill being fostered will determine the strategy. Likewise, the specific instructional objectives and the level of cognition of the objectives will influence the strategies chosen.

2. The learning style of the learner should be a key factor in the selection of instructional strategies.

3. Learner instruction and evaluation should be individualized and personalized in order to facilitate maximum instructional effectiveness.

4. An instructional model which facilitates the learner's mastery of skills along an educational continuum should be utilized. The instructional process, is, therefore, viewed as a sequential movement through necessary instructional components.

An instructional plan to meet these criteria requires a systematic process of diagnosing learner needs, developing optimal strategies for instruction, determining through student evaluation the degree to which mastery of instructional objectives has occurred, and developing recycling or remediating strategies to achieve the objectives which are not mastered. This process requires optimal communication between teacher and learner if effective results are to be expected.

5.0 Staffing

The needs of preadolescent learners require that middle schools be staffed with personnel who possess special competencies. It is necessary that staff members have training designed to enable them to properly function in the middle school setting. Such training will include:

1. The growth and development of preadolescents.

2. The middle school philosophy.

3. The middle school curriculum.

4. The instructional strategies for preadolescents.

5. The teaching of basic communication skills.

Teacher training institutions, in cooperation with the West Virginia Department of Education, should develop specific programs at the undergraduate level to train personnel in these areas. Programs should be designed for further middle school specialization at the graduate level. The local education agency should assume responsibility for offering staff development activities specifically designed to support middle school programs.

Professional personnel should be selected for employment on the basis of their ability and competence to carry out the goals and objectives of the middle school. Their philosophy and attitude toward education should be compatible with the **Educational Goals for West Virginia** and the middle school rationale contained in this document. The professional education staff should include administrators, counselors, teachers, and media personnel. Support and services staff should be available for the areas of instruction, health, secretarial, social services, food services, transportation, and building maintenance.

6.0 Program Management

Management has been defined as a distinct process consisting of planning, organizing, coordinating, controlling, and evaluating. Program management for middle school is the application of these functions to the teaching/learning system.

Effective management of the middle school teaching/learning system is the primary responsibility of the building principal. In effectively fulfilling this role, the principal works with the central office staff, especially supervisors of instruction, and the total staff at the building level. Learners, support personnel, parents, and others have a major interest in the school. Program management philosophy promotes relationships among these groups as decisions are made.

An effective program management system gives consideration to the following component areas:

1. A Statement of Mission for the School: The mission statement addresses the unique function of the middle school in terms of the needs of preadolescents and the needs of a particular learner population.

2. A Continuous Needs Assessment: Effective program management is dependent upon data provided through attempts to determine the needs of learners. Attention should be given to the aspects of cultural pluralism, academic achievement, and socio-economic status.

3. The Identification of Goals for the School: Goals are generated by the mission statement and data from the needs assessment. As such, they are philosophy-based general statements which guide the management of the teaching/learning program.

4. A Listing of Implementation Objectives: Implementation objectives serve to operationalize the goals. Objectives should attend to the identification of content emphasis, the support services to be provided learners, the cocurricu-

lar activities to be offered, and the provision for appropriate evaluation. In addition, responsibility for particular objectives should be assigned, and time-lines for achieving objectives should be specified.

5. An Evaluation System: The evaluation system should yield data that are sufficient for making teaching/learning decisions.

The heart of the middle school is the learner. Effective program management generates from the intellectual, physical, and social-psychological needs of learners. The program management system should serve as the framework within which decisions of an administrative and supervisory nature are made. Decisions based on data from the management system ensure that learner needs are properly addressed.

7.0 Evaluation

Curriculum evaluation is a systematic process of collecting and analyzing information to determine the degree of goal achievement as well as to determine the worth or value of the curriculum. Some of the questions that are answered during this process are:

1. Is the curriculum fulfilling the purposes for which it was designed?
2. Are these purposes valid?
3. Is the curriculum appropriate for the group of learners with which it is used?
4. Are the instructional materials that are used appropriate to the instructional objectives?

An evaluation model should be designed which provides school personnel with the framework for logical and systematic decision-making to ensure accountable and efficient expenditure of school funds.

The following components should be included:

1. Needs Assessment: This involves stating the goals and objectives of the entire programmatic definition as well as each related component to be met and determining how the existing middle school program is meeting these objectives. This information is used to identify middle school program needs.
2. Program Design: This is the planning and development of the program tools (techniques & instruments) to aid planning decisions. It includes the proce-dures needed for assessing whether or not the program is operating as planned and how well it is achieving its objectives.
3. Implementation Evaluation: This is a monitoring process to determine the extent to which the specified components of the programmatic definition have been implemented as planned.
4. Progress Evaluation: This provides information about the progress of the program's components in meeting the program's objectives. The information is used to modify the program when and where necessary.
5. Outcome Evaluation: This provides information about the success of the entire middle school program, programmatic definition, and individual compo-nents. This information can support a decision to maintain, modify, expand, or discontinue the program, programmatic definition, and individual compo-nents.

8.0 Communication

Communication is the process of giving and/or sharing information. Effective communication involves a two-way flow of information, both formal and informal as well as internal and external. A formal communication system generally identifies the person or persons charged with specific responsibilities relating to decisions about the information to be communicated, to whom it is to be communicated, the content of the communication, and the best medium for transmitting the information. Informal communication is largely face-to-face contact, verbal in nature, and unplanned.

The primary objective of a school communication system is to develop cohesive and harmonious interpersonal relationships within the school as well as with individuals and groups outside the school. Clearly defined, efficient channels of communication are necessary. Effective communication usually results in the following:

1. Improved work performance.

2. Healthy attitudes.

3. Understanding among administrators, staff, learners, school, and community.

4. Concern for the attainment of the educational goals of the school.

Management plans for middle schools should give attention to the need for effective communication. Since most communication occurs within the school, the middle school principal should organize and implement communication channels through which output and feedback may flow and which attend to both formal and informal means. These channels should include links with the community, parents, learners, support personnel, the central office, other governmental agencies, and the internal school communication systems.

SOURCE: West Virginia Dept. of Education, "A Programmatic Definition for Middle Schools in West Virginia" (Charleston, W. V.: 1977.) Used with permission.

CHARACTERISTICS OF AN ESSENTIAL MIDDLE SCHOOL

1. A philosophy and objectives cooperatively developed by community and staff that are based on the uniqueness of the middle school student and which express their convictions on the purposes of the school, how students learn, the content and methods of instruction, desirable types of student activities, and the outcomes to be attained.

2. Staff members, including administrators, teachers, and non-certificated personnel, who recognize and understand the uniqueness of the middle school student—their emotional, physical, and social problems and their fears and frustrations in trying to cope with all the changes facing them.

3. Auxiliary staffing: teacher aides, clerical aides, student and parent volunteers, community helpers.

4. An environment that assures opportunities for all students to succeed.

5. A curriculum that offers a general education with major emphasis placed on learning how to learn, with provisions for developing social and intellectual skills, and with opportunities for an extension of basic skills.

6. Learning experiences that assure articulation from elementary to high school by avoiding repetition and by providing for continuous progress that allows each individual to progress at his/her individual rate of learning.

7. Cooperative teaching that might include team teaching, team planning, interdisciplinary team planning and teaching.

8. An open climate that encourages students to develop abilities in problem solving, to determine values, and to be receptive to new facts that might alter their conclusions.

9. A broad exploratory or personal interest program that supplements the art, music, home economics and industrial arts programs. Many electives should be open to transescent students to help them discover more about themselves, their interests, and the world around them.

10. Provisions for independent study with an available teacher who acts as a resource person and who assists the student in planning.

11. Opportunities for the expression of creative talents: music and dramatic programs, student newspapers, art, and other means of student expression in which students do most of the planning and carrying out of activities.

12. A multimaterial approach as an integral part of all classes. If the needs and interests of the individuals within a class are met, a wide range of instructional materials are needed to care for the differences in progress. A single textbook does not recognize the wide physiological and intellectual range of middle school age students.

13. An attractive media center that not only offers a wide range of materials and guidance in using these materials, but provides opportunities for students to learn how to produce media for their own use in their classes.

14. Flexible class schedules that are based on the instructional needs of students for the various activities provided.

15. A strong intramural program that replaces the traditional highly competitive athletic programs that are inappropriate for transescent students. Stress should be placed on helping students understand and use their bodies.

16. Appropriate social experiences that provide for the unique needs of this age group and act as an extension of the formal curriculum—small and large group activities, clubs, "mixer" type dancing, and other such activities.

17. Appropriate guidance services that include teacher-pupil counseling and counseling from trained guidance counselors. Group counseling, as well as individual counseling, is highly effective and very important to a guidance program in the middle school.

18. Facilities that allow for a diversity of grouping patterns and for student activities related to art, health and physical education, music, drama, and occupational exploration.

19. Continuous inservice education that stresses the unique personality development of the transcecent student and the implications implied for learning.

20. A planned program of community relations that not only provides information about school program and activities, but constantly involves parents and other community leaders in the decision-making process.

Samples of Long-Range Plans for Development of Middle Schools

Preliminary Plan for the Development of a Long-Range Plan for the Middle School

1. *What are the questions that a long-range plan answers?*

   A long range plan:

   a. Identifies where the school would like to be ultimately, i.e., it identifies in fairly concrete terms the "ideal" condition or state;
   b. identifies where the school is now and how it might arrive at the "ideal" condition or state over orderly steps;
   c. presents criteria for validating the ideal state as best under the existing conditions;
   d. identifies a time line for the orderly progression or growth of the school (and its parts) toward the ideal state (here it takes into consideration peculiar local conditions, funding, enrollment, etc.);
   e. identifies the ways and means and time for determining if sufficient progress has been made toward the desired ideal state;
   f. identifies the work to be done to meet the orderly steps identified;
   g. identifies crucial decision-making points and alternatives to be considered at those decision-making points.

2. *How can the "ideal" or "desired" future middle school be described?*

   One way is to break the "school" into identifiable parts. One scheme is to use the following criteria:

   a. Overall approach or philosophy
   b. Curriculum
   c. Organization
   d. Staffing
   e. Administration
   f. Instruction

   To answer these questions the following must be described:

   a. Approach: what unique thing is the middle school trying to attain?

    b. Curriculum: what will be offered (statement of general scope and depth)?

    c. Organization: how will the school be configured or shaped to achieve its objectives?

    d. Staffing: what kinds of people resources must be obtained and how shall they be deployed?

    e. Administration: under what principles and procedures will the school be run?

    f. Instruction: what will be the dominant modes of instruction, suggested scope of such modes?

3. *How is such a plan validated?*

Validation consists of identifying the criteria to be applied to the plan and having the necessary groups indicate their agreement with the criteria and the plan.

The criteria can be both item #1 (validation of what a long range plan is) and #2, (the indices of breaking the school into identifiable parts). Do these parts cover the major aspect of a school?

After the criteria the plan can be validated by:

    a. Securing staff reaction and approval as to the "ideal" or "desired" state; (what constitutes "approval" should be defined);

    b. Securing expert opinion and reaction to the plan (Bondi-Wiles, etc.);

    c. Securing Board/Superintendent reaction to the future desired state;

    d. Other; (the literature, etc.).

The end product is a plan to which all parties have agreed is desirable (not necessarily immediately practical or economical).

4. *How is the future desired condition related to the present?*

One approach is to work out a simple format and fill in the blanks. A sample is shown below:

Area	Where We Want To Be	Where We Are Now	Where We Were in the Past
Curriculum			
Staffing			
Organization			
Instruction			
Administration			

5. *How is the future desired condition of the school related to desired pupil learning?*

Several approaches can be used. The first might be to examine the proposed district goals and work back into desired exit skills, knowledges and attitudes for eighth-grade students. These then can be broken into disciplines of the curriculum, i.e., art, physical education, music, etc. These become the future desired learner conditions. A sample follows.

SAMPLE

DESIRED DISTRICT EXIT EDUCATIONAL GOAL	DESIRED MIDDLE SCHOOL EDUCATIONAL GOAL	PRESENT STATUS OF GOAL(S) (The extent to which the goal is being achieved)
Twelfth Grade	Eighth Grade	

6. *How will the actual plan for next year be developed?*

Once the future desired condition is described and the present condition fixed, then a series of logical steps is developed for each area given time, personnel and funds to proceed towards the ultimate desired end. These can be broken into smaller steps within the confines of annual units. Following this, various procedures can be developed by which the tasks get accomplished.

PROJECTED TWO-DAY WORK SESSION

Individual preparation
1. Reread original middle school specifications.
2. Read Bondi-Wiles—*Curriculum Development: A Guide to Practice.*
3. Look over attached plan (as amended) and schedule.

FIRST DAY

1. Review total tasks.
2. Develop future desired and ideal middle school.
3. Validate minimally the desired state.
4. Develop list of current conditions and past conditions. (Farm out to work groups.)
5. Joint-critique each step after period of work.
6. Begin statement of desired learner skills, knowledges, and attitudes. (Interpolate from draft of district goals.)
7. Develop comparison to actual status (where known).

SECOND DAY

1. Develop statement of desired condition for 1980–1981.
2. Lay out major steps for remainder of 1979–80 and summer of 1980 and then for 1980–81 to arrive at desired end.
3. Identifies what alternatives will be considered.
4. Joint-critique each step.
5. Develop ways to expand known data base and who will be involved in collecting data for description of status quo.
6. Decision as to format and dates of presentation to staff, Board, Administrative/Instructional Council, parents, etc.

Peggy—A Middle Schooler Affective Materials for Middle School Students

Peggy is a beautiful person. Everybody told me that when she was born, and though I was brought up not to praise my children (Puritans believe that is akin to praising yourself), still I must admit she is beautiful. People still today tell me she's beautiful. Strangers talk about her face and friends talk about much more. She is what she is.

As I write these words, though, my instinctive reaction is to add—*but*—(why is it that mothers must always qualify praise?). Perhaps it's because thirteen years ago she was an extension of me and there is, in me, a continuing need to explore the complexities and contradictions (the good and the evil, if you wish, to go back to my Puritan ancestral terminology) and by extension (or is it projection?) to explore the same complexities that must exist in her. She *is* beautiful; I have to work hard sometimes to keep that truth in front of me because I am constantly, like Mrs. Darling in *Peter Pan,* pulling out the drawers of her being and sorting through the contents, attempting to "tidy" them up. Of course, as all mothers know, tidiness is a concept totally foreign to children. Peggy may be, on the surface, beautiful and ordered, but inside things are somewhat rumpled.

Since I spend a good amount of time thinking about Peggy, I may as well try to put her complexities on paper. I hope it will give the word *beautiful* some meaning, but then one must take the chance that it won't.

Peggy is thirteen years old. I began to think that specifically because a book I looked at recently had pictures of three girls, all thirteen years old, all in totally different stages of physical development. What struck me was that Peggy doesn't look remotely like any of them. She's been growing like the proverbial weed for at least a year, but I only realized it when the usual trip to the shoe store proved not only that her feet had grown two sizes in four months, but that they were bigger than mine. Since that time she's grown from a child to a child-woman who is only one-half inch shorter than I am and weighs more. The first scraggles of hair that appeared last summer are now darker, but her breasts are still "buds" only noticeable under a tight shirt.

Despite those pictures it would seem that Peggy is "average" or "normal" almost to the month. Yet Peggy perceives all kinds of abnormalities.

"I'm too fat."

"When am I going to lose this pot?"

"Why do other girls have waists?"

Trips to the pediatrician and looks at height and weight charts seem to do nothing to alleviate her view of her imperfections. Instead she is dieting and into yoga. She even quit gymnastics because she was tired of folding her arms over her "pot" in between exercises.

The possibility of a growth in sexual sensitivity is even more incomprehensible in Peggy. Last week it was: "This thing is huge, Mommy, and it's *bothering* me." Repression on my part, plus a rather total silence in the numerous books, left me unable to deal with that one. Thank heavens for pediatricians. A call there (after a surreptitious glance at the dictionary to make sure I was pronouncing clitoris properly) assured me (I'm not sure about Peggy) that enlargement and sensitivity are absolutely normal at age thirteen. Peggy *is* very attractive but my feeling is that she's lost sense of it for the moment. She's lost the global vision and is immersed in the details:

"I hate the color of *that* hair. Why can't it be blond like the rest of my hair?"

(Why are words like pubic and vagina absent from both her mother's and her vocabulary?)

Anyone who knows Peggy will tell you that she's very mature for her age; adults have always related well to her. She's good, responsive and fun to be with. Yet at age six she was so immature, both physically and in her reaction to institutionalization, that I kept her an extra year in kindergarten. Then and now I would question whether outward expression, particularly for girls, necessarily indicates inner abilities to act. Too often the adult definition of maturity is so close to the stereotyped adult female role (passivity, sensitivity, neatness, etc.) that we label a docile child "mature" when, in fact, she is withdrawing in a very childlike way from too fast an entry into adulthood. (Perhaps again I'm the mother who is forever saying *but* in the face of all the testimony to the contrary that Peggy is indeed a very adult, together person.)

There is no doubt that intellectually Peggy is over the divide between childhood and adulthood. I see her intelligence working most clearly in our talks about human relations. Her sensitive analysis of her relationships with other people, her mother's and her father's relationship to each other, her own relationship to each of them, reflect complex abilities to dissect many facets of complicated situations which have changed gradually over time. Her sense of history is in place, not just her own which is of prime importance to her, but of civilization's. She absorbs quantities of historical fiction along with an equal diet of Nancy Drews (whose analytical talents, by the way, should not be demeaned). Though Peggy will deny it through tears of frustration, she can even diagram sentences. Her values tell her that pure intellectual exercises like grammar are useless, and perhaps she's right. But she can do it, and that's a very advanced type of analytical task. Perhaps most telling is her ability to be introspective. She thinks about her thinking, and the results are sometimes rebellion, sometimes withdrawal, and sometimes very good poetry.

A poem by Peggy:

The Blues

Blue is a color
A most irregular color
A color of wondrous shadows.

A misty blue,
Firely blue, warm blue,
Life climbing to the sky endless.

Climbing blue,
Misty strong country.

Socially, she's a child-woman who at the moment is feeling a need to cultivate the child. She's never been a member of a crowd and somehow I doubt that that "normal" part of adolescence will ever be significant to her. Instead she has three close friends. Their sleepovers are the quintessence of growing up. Each child arrives with suitcases full of dressups which range from old filmy nightgowns to ancient bridesmaids gowns. Then there are the makeup kits, some borrowed and the rest bought out of hoarded allowances. They spend hours in the bathroom and then pose as sophisticates, amid spasms of giggles, for my camera. The memory of Peggy at three in those same dressups, and the vision of her five years from now with that glamorous tinge, is bittersweetness at its essence.

At the same time she's very much into boys. Despite her "crushes," she seems to have a real sense of how to attract a boy, and silliness doesn't seem to be part of it. She's got a string of boys who during the summer will climb mountains with her during the day and square dance with her at night. During the school year, she sees boys at a children's theater group. Again, she is involved in meaningful activity with them. She is impatient with moody, "false" boy-girl parties and was totally relieved when her class decided to substitute a roller skating party for the traditional sixth-grade Valentine's Day dance. (I wonder if it is the child in her that is still relating to boys in the usual way, or the woman in her that intuitively knows that shared activities are the only basis for a long-term relationship.)

Very few people would call Peggy rebellious; one has to be tuned to subtleties and relationships that are low-keyed. She is a poet, a writer and a dramatist and is fascinated with astrology and E.S.P. Her mother, in contrast, is a pragmatic social scientist. (Peggy consistently insists on getting "Bs" in social studies.) She's not dramatic but she is very definite about her separation.

She's up and down about her rebellion about being a woman and responsible to the family. Last fall she was the epitome of helpfulness. She cooked family meals twice a week, baby-sat for her brother and neighborhood children, kept her room immaculate, and loved earning extra money cleaning the car or the basement. Today, issues are at a much more fundamental level. Waking her up in the morning is an issue; getting her to make her bed is an issue; insuring that the laundry is in the hamper and not in a heap on her floor is an issue. Cooking and doing extra jobs have all but disappeared, and baby-sitting is under protest. It's all very subtle—no raging scenes—but no, she won't be put into the mother-cleaning lady-good girl role right now. It's hard for me because I've come to depend on her, but I'm not sure that she isn't right to confront the role expectations now rather than twenty years from now.

Her conflicts over values are intense, particularly now that her parents are entering what might most kindly be expressed as a relative stance towards moral truths. In this case the normal parent-adolescent value struggle is reversed. Peggy has very firm notions of right and wrong and her parents are waffling. Her rebellion is rather strange, but it is nonetheless real. She dogs us with her truths, and it is hard to refute her in any absolute sense. One must hope that she will grow (and I hope not too soon because her values are atuned to her own needs right now) to see beyond dogmatism and rule to a more humanistic morality.

Perhaps, though, if I could abstract my own needs (to have household help and to be understood), maybe I'd get closer to the "real" Peggy. She sees herself on stage. Six times she has tried out for leads in theater productions and each failure has been a major crisis. She is always a finalist but never chosen. Yet she persists and has a vision of herself as a star. She sees herself also as deeply sensitive, able to communicate in extrasensory ways. I can't tune into that part of her but I read her poetry and see her ability to sustain deep relationships. To Peggy all things are possible. Mothers are mainly useful as cushions when society says, "No, they aren't."

A letter from Peggy to the Director of her Children's Theater production:

> Jim,
>
> For the two years I've worked with you, you have given me some of the most valuable lessons I could ever have. You were made for acting and directing. Your firmness and kindness are perfect for directing and your ability to make yourself into anything is incredible. I am really going to miss you, but you will always be in my heart. And I mean that.
>
> Someday I will be on Broadway.
>
> I believe
> it
> or
> not.
>
> > Much love,
> >
> > Peggy
>
> Roses are red
> Violets are blue
> You are the best actor
> And some day I might be too.

The problem with this description, which I began a week ago, is that it is already outdated. I stated that Peggy was in full-scale rebellion against the mother-housekeeper image. Yet at this moment she is baking and decorating a "patriotic cake" for her brother so he can hold his head up at tomorrow's Cub Scout cake auction. (Her mother has her priorities fairly firmly in order, and completing a master's program comes ahead of Cub Scout cakes.) The problem is that one can't ever describe Peggy at thirteen years of age because she's constantly changing. For several weeks she will need me; we'll have incredible discussions on all kinds of topics. Then two weeks later she's gone from me:

"How's school?"

"Good."

"Did you have fun at Claire's party?"

"Of course."

Then I'll be walking down the corridor at her school and see her "bugging" her male gym teacher in that outrageously silly, flirtatious sixth-grade way. Next I'll be sitting at the top of the stairs listening to the four friends riotously "settle down" to a sleepover. Or I'll be watching her, as I am right now, curled up in the chair opposite me, absorbed in a novel called *Peggy*, waiting for her cake to get done.

I don't know Peggy. I love her and believe she's a beautiful person. I just can't capture her either physically or in words. Perhaps that's both a definition of her as a "pre-adolescent" and for the best in any case. I doubt if any of us really wants to be captured.

The authors express their appreciation to Elizabeth Loughren for sharing this personal description with our readers.

GROWING UP:

AN AFFECTIVE ACTIVITY FOR STUDENTS

Nova Middle School
Language Arts

Mr. Richard Hoffman

Growing Up

All of us, at least once in our lives, have been asked, "Why don't you grow up?" Grow up! Two simple words which cover some of the most exciting years of our youth and, on the other hand, our most *formative* years. These are the years in which we develop our *values,* opinions, ethics, mores, and in a general sense, the way we shall conduct our adult life. In other words, these "growing up" years, or our *formative years*, produce a finished "product"—a life style.

Growing up isn't easy. Challenges must be met; mistakes will be made— some major and some insignificant; responsibility must be learned; and a sense of reliability must be earned. This process takes time and great effort. In fact, if we were to compare it to a race at a track-meet we'd have to have *endurance.*

This unit will help to provide some *insight* or *perspective* to the progress you have already made and what you can expect from the future. You will read about other young students who have already "grown up" and have met their challenges. You will not only read about successful adventures but also some failures, for growing up means *both.*

Resource materials for this unit include the instructor, textbooks, library books, periodicals, television, and *you.* Your life experiences are important and *significant* and can help you to better understand yourself.

At the conclusion of this unit you will have an *appreciation* for the progress you have already made, and a sense of awareness of the experiences that are still ahead in the future as you grow up.

PRELIMINARY ACTIVITY:

Think about each of the following words after researching them in the dictionary:

formative	perspective
values	responsibility
mores	awareness
insight	decision

Elect a recorder to take notes. How do these words relate to you? Discuss in *groups* (minimum 4) how you have encountered or have not encountered situations relating to these words.

GROUP DISCUSSION ACTIVITY

When have you been told to grow up? What were the circumstances? How did you respond? Did you learn anything from the experience?

1. Prepare a list of circumstances that might help a student to grow up. This list will be reported to the class by an elected member of each group.

*2. What are values? Where do we get them? Make a list of values. As a group, prepare a *collage* of pictures, sketches, words, photographs that reflect the values discussed by the group. These, too, will be reported to the class after discussion with the teacher.
    *See the teacher before starting any art work.

3. Have you ever had to make a difficult decision? Discuss your individual circumstances with the group. Perhaps another member of the group has had a similar situation. Have any of your decisions greatly affected your life? Each member of the group is to write a story describing his decision and the results of that decision. Exchange stories and discuss as to whether you made the right decision.

4.A. What is a challenge? Have you ever been challenged? Your group is to define the term and make a list of challenges that students face both in and out of school. The group recorder should keep notes for a class presentation.

4.B. What challenges do your parents face?
What challenges does Broward County face?
What challenges does the State of Florida face?
What challenges does the United States face?
*See the teacher before starting this group activity.

4.C. After completing 4-B prepare reports describing some of the decisions that must be reached in order to meet the challenges from 4-B. You may use library materials, magazines, newspapers for this assignment. Your reports must include charts, drawings, posters, taped interviews, etc.
*See your teacher before starting this group activity.

Source: Richard Hoffman, "Growing Up: An Affective Activity for Students," (Plantation, Fla.: Nova Middle School, 1978). Used with permission.

Examples of a State Certification Program

State of Florida Requirements for
Middle School Teacher Certification

I. *Definition of Middle School*—The middle school is defined as a school providing a program planned for a range of older children, preadolescents, and early adolescents that builds upon the elementary school program for earlier childhood, and in turn is built upon by the high school's program for adolescence. The school shall include twelve (12) year olds and/or thirteen (13) year olds (or grades 6 and/or 7).

The upper limit of the range of students includes students normally considered eighth (8th) graders and the lower limit of the range of students includes students normally considered fifth (5th) graders. The middle school may, in unusual situations, include students normally considered ninth (9th) graders as a secondary appendage or students normally considered fourth (4th) graders as an elementary appendage.

A. Each district shall submit annually to the designated representative of the Elementary-Secondary Division of the Department of Education the following:

1. A letter of application for middle school identification, by December 1, 1971, which will include the following: (Reapplication may be made by fulfilling a–dl prior to September 15, of each year.)

   (a) Superintendent's signature
   (b) Verification that the school(s) meets District School Board approved standards and Regulations for classifying and standardizing schools Section 230.23 (4)(e)
   (c) Verification that the school(s) meets state definition of middle school
   (d) Attachments to the letter shall be: Suggested limit of four (4) pages for (1)–(4)
       (1) Name and number of each school covered by application

(2) Range of students enrolled (age-grade)

(3) Goals of middle school(s)

(4) Brief description of program of middle school(s) (include curriculum, organization and staffing)

B. The designated representative of the Elementary-Secondary Division shall:

1. Receipt the letters of application

2. Evaluate the letters of application and attached materials on the following criteria:

(a) All items and specifications in II A are on file in the Department of Education.

3. Issue annually an official list of identified middle schools in Florida.

II. Change *Accreditator,* Volume 10, 11 and 12, Number 3 for three years (1971–72 through 1973–74) in the following manner:

A. Identify courses presently identified for grades five (5) through eight (8)

B. Make Section 3 of the *Accreditator*—"Junior High or Middle School" Section

C. List courses in item A above in Section 3

D. Re-number elementary courses 5 and 6

E. List required certification as a combination of the present certification required for elementary and junior high courses.

Recommended Middle School Teacher Certification

Specialization requirements for certification in Middle School:

Certification may be given in separate subjects of Middle School English, Middle School Mathematics, Middle School Science, or Middle School Social Studies as specified below:

1. Middle School English—

(a) At least a Bachelor's degree with a major in Middle School English

OR

(b) At least a Bachelor's degree and Rank 3 certification in Junior High School, Junior High School English, Secondary English or Elementary Education *and* verification by a Florida district superintendent of at least one year of *successful teaching experience* of English, grades 5–8, in a department of education approved Florida middle school *and* successful performance in prescribed middle school components of an approved inservice master plan for teachers.

2. Middle School Mathematics—

(a) At least a Bachelor's degree with a major in Middle School Mathematics

OR

(b) At least a Bachelor's degree and Rank 3 certification in Junior High School, Junior High School Mathematics, Secondary Mathematics or Elementary Education *and* verification by a Florida district superintendent of at least one year of *successful teaching experience* of mathematics, grades 5–8, in a department of education approved Florida middle school *and* successful performance in prescribed middle school components of an approved inservice master plan for teachers.

3. Middle School Science—

(a) At least a Bachelor's degree with a major in Middle School Science

OR

(b) At least a Bachelor's degree and Rank 3 certification in Junior High School, Junior High School Science, Secondary Physics, Secondary Chemistry, Secondary Biology, Secondary Earth Science, or Elementary Education *and* verification by a Florida district superintendent of at least one year of *successful teaching experience* of science, grades 5–8, in a department of education approved Florida middle school *and* successful performance in prescribed middle school components of an approved inservice master plan for teachers.

4. Middle School Social Studies—

(a) At least a Bachelor's degree with a major in Middle School Social Studies

OR

(b) At least a Bachelor's degree and Rank 3 certification in Junior High School, Junior High School Social Studies, Secondary Social Studies or Elementary Education *and* verification by a Florida district superintendent of at least one year of *successful teaching experience* of Social Studies, grades 5–8, in a department of education approved Florida middle school *and* successful performance in prescribed middle school components of an approved inservice master plan for teachers.

SOURCE: Florida State Department of Education, "State of Florida Requirements for Middle School Teacher Certification" (Tallahassee, Florida, 1975). Used with permission.

Samples of Middle School Program Activities

Social Studies Curriculum—Seminole Middle School

American History Data—Grade 7
American Institutions Data—Grade 8

Unit Themes	Concepts	Generalization

YOURSELF	1. Human needs
	  a. need gratifica-
	    tion
	  b. belief system
	  c. human be-
	    havior
		1. Understanding one's self helps in trying to understand others

	2. Value commit-
	  ment
	  a. Openmindedness
	  b. Tolerance
		2. To be open-minded is advantageous to learning.

	3. Inquiry	3. Being tolerant of varying beliefs is necessary in a free society.
	4. Personality	4. An individual's environment helps shape his personality.
	5. Conscience (value conflict)	5. A culture's "behavior pattern" is learned by children and their conscience, therefore one's conscience will be in conflict when change is encountered.
BETWEEN YOU AND YOUR TEACHERS	1. Responsibility	1. Because humans are part of the ecosystem, they are interdependent on each other and must be responsible for survival.
	2. Ethnic relations	2. There are physical differences among humans, but humans are more alike than different.

Unit Themes	Concepts	Generalization
	3. Alienation	3. Differences in groups of humans may cause alienation from group to group.
	4. Variability (Human Traits Race)	4. Humans vary in physical traits and are sometimes categorized into "races."
	5. Human needs	5. All humans have certain basic needs.
	6. Empathy	6. Conflicts can be resolved easier if humans would "look through others' eyes."
	7. Intelligence	7. No significant differences exist in the innate intelligence and capabilities of people from varying racial & ethnic backgrounds.
EXPLORATION/ DISCOVERY	1. Spatial Relation (location)	1. Geographic skills are essential in gaining knowledge about earth.
	2. Exploration	2. Exploration, both physical & mental many times leads to change.
	3. Discovery	3. Societies draw upon ideas from other cultures.
	4. Conquest	4. Conquest is one means of acquiring newly discovered lands.
	5. Technology	5. Increased technology causes cultural changes.
	6. Inventions	6. Inventions are usually the resulting discovery of creative exploration.
SURVIVAL	1. Needs	1. Needs of humans must be satisfied for survival, the process used is secondary.
	2. Wants	2. Relative scarcity demands resources allocated to best satisfy people's wants.
	3. Problem-solving	3. Humans are constantly meeting problems to solve, and must become skilled at the task in order to survive.
CONFLICT	1. Conflict	1. Humans encounter conflicts of many types continuously; conflicts must be identified before being resolved.
	2. Accommodation	2. Sometimes conflicts are resolved by simply "one side" giving up.
	3. Choices	3. Humans have alternatives for conflict-solution.
	4. Decision-making	4. Decision-making skills are essential.
	5. War	5. Sometimes violence is used to resolve conflicts.
	6. Compromise	6. Compromise is a valuable ability in solving conflicts.
	7. Revolution	7. Sudden overthrow of authority by force or persuasion sometimes happens when conflicts are not resolved to the satisfaction of certain groups of people.

Unit Themes	Concepts	Generalization
	8. Reform	8. Conflict resolution tends to bring reform in varying degrees.
GOVERNMENT	1. Freedom	1. Man's freedom
	2. Anarchy	2. Freedom is best obtained by granting individual freedom and rule by laws and not of men.
	3. Systems	3. Organized groups are the vehicles through which society does its work.
	4. Responsibility	4. Responsibility and freedom are basic tenets of democracy.
	5. Security	5. Governments are established to provide security for people.
	6. Rights	6. Humans are "born" with certain rights, such as life, liberty, and the pursuit of happiness.
	7. Ideology	7. A nation determines its policies and actions according to its *ideology,* and a nation's ideology can be discovered by evaluating its actions and policies.
	8. Power	8. Nations exercise their authority over their people by use of police powers.
	9. Politics	9. Government officials gain power and keep it through the use of "politics."
	10. Structure	10. The structure of government is not constant, but changes with a tendency to become more complex.
	11. Government	11. Through government, the ruler and laws for community living are developed, interpreted and enforced.
ENVIRONMENT	1. Resources	1. Humans use natural resources to effect changes which facilitate the way they make a living
	2. Conservation	2. The wise use of resources is necessary for the survival of all living things.
	3. Pollution	3. Humans are able to change their environment; and the environment may change humans.
	4. Conflict	4. Geographic factors are often the source of conflict between cultures.
	5. Technology	5. Humans are constantly re-examining their environment according to their developing technical skills.
	6. Responsibility	6. The use of resources carries individual and group responsibilities.
TRAILBLAZING	1. Exploration	1. Humans at various times seek to explore the unknown.
	2. Conquest	2. Humans at various times seek to conquer other humans.

Unit Themes	Concepts	Generalization
	3. Technology	3. Technological improvements have sometimes solved problems and caused more problems.
	4. Transportation	4. Transportation determines the rapidity of cultural exchange.
LOYALTY	1. Ideology	1. A person's beliefs tend to define him.
	2. Conflict	2. When two or more loyalties are contradictory a serious personal conflict results.
	3. Patriotism	3. Different people have varied beliefs about what patriotism means and each tends to become dogmatic with his own form.
	4. Responsibility	4. Loyalties cause responsibility in varying degrees.
	5. Value Commitment	5. Because loyalties cause value commitment, people seldom change loyalties.
CHANGE	1. Sectionalism	1. Various cultures do co-exist; culture influences people's thought, values, and actions.
	2. Sovereignty	2. a. The concept of state sovereignty intensified sectionalism in America during the 1850–60s. b. State sovereignty was used to justify the actions of Southern states against the union.
	3. Change a. Social b. Political c. Economics	3. Societies vary in culture and rate of cultural change.
	4. Progress	4. a. Progress is not necessarily the result of change. b. Without change progress would be non-existent.
	5. Historical Analysis (generalizing, application and verification)	5. History basically is the recorded data concerning changes that have taken place in any society and the results of these changes on that respective society.
	6. Innovation	6. Cultures change technologically and communication skills improve.
ECONOMICS	1. Poverty	1. Even in a wealthy nation, economic situations cause some parts of society to remain in poverty.
	2. Wealth	2. The wealth of a nation is in its resources (human and natural), and when this wealth is not totally recognized, "poverty" can result.
	3. Systems (economic)	3. Societies have some kind of economic system to control the production, distribution, and use of goods and services.

Unit Themes	Concepts	Generalization
	4. Needs and wants	4. Needs and wants are sometimes difficult to ascertain.
	5. Resources	5. Resources are not evenly distributed, thereby causing allocation problems.
	6. Allocation	6. Economic systems' ways of allocating resources characterized.
	7. Scarcity	7. Because resources are limited, a scarcity problem is constantly reoccuring.
	8. Consumer	8. Consumers tend to choose goods and services which satisfy them.
	9. Conflict	9. Conflict results over the uses of a nation's resources.
	10. Choices	10. Consumers make choices by buying or not buying goods and services.
	11. Goods & Services	11. In a free economic system, goods and services are tied to what consumers want and to maximum profit.
	12. Interdependence	12. Because of resource scarcity, societies are interdependent and must seek cooperation for survival.
URBANIZATION	1. Density	1. Density of population in most urban areas has caused a need for increased urban planning.
	2. Growth	2. The trend in population migration in America has caused ultrarapid growth of urban areas.
	3. Conflict	3. The rapid growth of urban areas has caused conflict to develop over best uses of limited land resources.
	4. Overpopulation	4. Cities become overpopulated because that's where jobs are found.
	5. Spatial Relation	5. Cities begin where there are natural geographical features which aid in commerce or are planned to meet specific needs.
	6. Stability	6. Mobility rather than stability is the trend of urban populations.
	7. Change	7. A drastic change in life style will be necessary to promote healthy urban living.
TRADITIONS	1. Institutional Structure	1. Traditions of a society are preserved and perpetuated by its institutions.
	2. Language	2. Perhaps the most outstanding characteristic of a particular culture is its language.
	3. Socialization	3. The teaching of traditions is an important part of the socialization process of a society.
	4. Belief System	4. Societal belief systems are strongly influenced by the traditions of that society.

Unit Themes	Concepts	Generalization
	5. Value System	5. Value systems developed around cultural tradition are not easily changed.
	6. Ritualism	6. a. The overt form used to express a culture's traditions are rituals. b. Ritualism is used by societies to teach traditions and values to their youth.
CULTURE	1. Behavior	1. A man's behavior is determined to a great extent by the values of his culture.
	2. Norms	2. All societies have acceptable behavior patterns for individuals in that society, and these are called norms.
	3. Deviancy	3. Some cultures are so different that peaceful interrelations are almost impossible.
	4. Conformity	4. To gain acceptance in a culture, members must conform to some extent to the society's norms.
	5. Incultivation	5. From birth, individuals in a culture are indoctrinated about society through institutions, both formal and informal (school, church, family).
	6. Institutions	6. Institutions are developed in a society to preserve, protect, perpetuate the values of that society.
	7. Language	7. Language is among the strongest ties between the people of a particular culture.
	8. Beliefs	8. An individual's beliefs are influenced by his culture.
	9. Ritualism	9. Cultures act out unique rituals to reenforce and teach the beliefs and values of that culture for its people.
	10. Value System	10. Values systems of individuals within a culture are usually not as divergent as value systems of individuals living in different cultures.
	11. Diversion	11. Cultural change may occur when people from one culture are exposed by one means or another to people and ideas of another culture.
	12. Family	12. The family is the basic social unit common to most cultures.
	13. Role	13. Roles the individual plays in his life are determined by cultural standards.
	14. Status	14. Status is a person's rank in relation to others in his society.
	15. Class	15. Most cultures fall into one of three class categories: open, closed, or classless.
	16. Mobility	16. Mobility between classes in the American Culture is very flexible in relation to many other cultures.
	17. Objective	17. The desire of the people to establish objectives in a culture that was developed in a democratic political system.

HISTORIOGRAPHY (Social Science) (Skills)		SEE SKILLS CONTINUUM
JUSTICE	1. Equality	1. Equality is a characteristic of democracy to which people constantly must strive for in order to obtain it.
	2. Freedom	2. Because of the desire for freedom, humans, from time to time, seek to gain it through various ways.
	3. Rights	3. The protection of the rights of all individuals is the major concern of the American judicial system. This includes the accused as well as the accusor.
	4. Democracy	4. The concept *democracy* implies equal opportunity and treatment for all people of society, not necessarily majority rule.
	5. Civil Liberty	5. In a democracy, the government does not have the right to curtail the civil liberties of the population.
	6. Responsibility	6. In a democratic society, it is the responsibility of each person to preserve the right of his fellow citizens.
	7. Individualism	7. Pure democracies preserve a person's right to be different.
GEOGRAPHICAL ENVIRONMENT	1. Location	1. Physical location determines land use.
	2. Resources	2. All natural resources are limited.
	3. Conversation	3. Preservation of more environment on earth depends on how well resources are managed and conserved.
	4. Pollution	4. Pollution of home resources has a chain-reaction effect.
	5. Conflict	5. Technological advancement and ecological preservation may be conflicting goals.
	6. Density	6. Population density in urban areas has endangered life because of the many types of pollution that have developed.
	7. Population	7. The standard of living of a population is in part determined by its geographical environment.
POLITICS	1. Political Behavior	1. A nation's leaders determine, to a great extent, its political image and behavior to its citizens and to other world nations.
	2. Ideology	2. Oftentimes the attitudes of leaders reflect the ideology of their respective organizations or groups.
	3. Action	3. A characteristic of leadership is the willingness to take action on the desires and goals of a group or on one's self.

	4. Conflict	4. A major role of a leader is to minimize conflict between members or factions within a group.
	5. Persuasion	5. An attribute of leadership is the ability to convince people to act in a desirable way.
	6. Reform	6. Sometimes reform can be brought to a group or society by a change in its leadership.
FUTURE	1. Change	1. Preparation for survival in the future requires many changes in the way we live today.
	2. Discovery	2. Discovery and creativity are the hope for a better future for all mankind.
	3. Technology	3. Increased technology may result in both desirable and undesirable effects on our future.
REFORM	1. Generalization	1. Man's attitudes and beliefs are affected by the generalizations he accepts as true.
	2. Social Systems	2. The world is made up of many different societies, and a system of organization that may be good for one may not be good for the others.
	3. Institutions	3. A society's institutions are designed by the values of that society and serve to perfect and perpetuate those values.
	4. Change	4. Reform usually is viewed as change for the better.
	5. Stability	5. When the stability of a society is upset, people attempt to reform the institutions causing the problem.
	6. Tradition	6. Traditions many times act as blocks to needed reform within a society.
	7. Conflict	7. When large numbers of a population conflict with one or more of its institutions, reform may be forthcoming.
	8. Power	8. The power to bring about social reform usually depends on the effectiveness of the people to organize.
	9. Action	9. Reform may be a result when men take action on their beliefs and values.
	10. Involvement	10. Individual involvement in special interest groups helps to bring reform to inefficient institutions.

SOURCE: Seminole Middle School, "Social Studies Curriculum" (Seminole, Fla.: 1974). Used with permission.

Agreement Form for a Student Work Experience Program

SCHOOL _____ DATE _____

WORK EXPERIENCE PROGRAM TRAINING AGREEMENT

STUDENT _____ SOCIAL SECURITY NO. _____
EMPLOYER _____ EMPLOYER'S ADDRESS _____
JOB TITLE _____ INDUSTRY _____
WORKING HOURS, DAILY ____ TO ____; SAT. ____ TO ____.
WAGES PER HOUR ____

In order to carry on an effective Work Experience Program, it is advisable that all parties concerned agree to the following responsibilities:

Employer's Responsibilities:
The student will be placed on the above named job for the purpose of providing work experience and will be given work of instructional value. The student's work activity will be under the close supervision of an experienced and qualified person. The work will be performed under safe conditions. The student, when possible, will receive the same consideration given employees in regard to safety, health, social security, general work conditions and other regulations of the firm.

Coordinator's Responsibilities:
The coordinator will visit each student at least once per-month at the work station and will become acquainted with the person to whom the student is responsible while on the job.

The coordinator shall endeavor to adjust all complaints with the cooperation of all parties concerned, and shall have the authority to transfer or withdraw a student.

The coordinator will make plans to contact each student's parents or guardian several times during the school year.

Parents' Responsibilities:
Parents' (or guardians') responsibilities include an agreement to allow the student to participate in the Work Experience Program, and to encourage the student to abide by his own responsibilities in the program.

Student's Responsibilities:
I agree whenever possible to follow the rules set up by school, employer, and coordinator.

When I am absent I will call the school office by 10 A.M. I will also call my employer well in advance to let him know I will be absent.

I understand that on days when I miss school, I will not be able to work.

Student Signature _____ Parent Sig. _____

Employer Signature _____ Coord. Signature _____

Employer should keep his copy on file, attached to the student's work permit. Coordinator should keep an extra copy for his file.

A Teacher Advisor System

Rationale: In order to help meet the social and personal needs of our students we should:
1. Provide an opportunity for positive student interaction in a multi-grade group.
2. Provide a more suitable school contact for the parents of every student.
3. Provide a better opportunity for staff to relate to all students beyond the regular teaching program.

Guidelines for Organization
1. Each teacher advisor group to be as small as possible.
2. Total staff involvement.
3. Schedule time for T.A. to meet goals of program, and not jeopardize the accepted teacher preparation time that we presently have.
4. Flexibility for T.A. to use T.A. time for large groups, small groups, or individual sessions with T.A. students.
5. Regular contact with T.A. and his/her students.
6. Provide T.A. with discretionary authority to call T.A. meeting during scheduled times.
7. Administration of T.A. program to be in hands of Administration and Guidance personnel.
8. T.A. groups to be as heterogeneous as possible.
9. Suggested structure for use of T.A. time to be organized by Administration and Guidance and given to every T.A.

Teacher Advisor Proposal
1. Groups of 16–18 per Teacher Advisor. All teachers take a group (includes Administration).
2. A teacher has 2–3 T.A. periods per cycle. To be used to see individual students or groups of students. This is at the discretion of the Teacher Advisor.
3. Teacher Advisor groups to be formed from various teaching units. No more than 2–3 students and a Teacher Advisor from one Teaching Unit.
4. Students meet with Teacher Advisor for registration and announcements every day.
5. Teacher Advisor meets with each student every three weeks (individually or in a group).
6. All Teacher Advisor time spent in contact with students.
7. Teacher Advisor can call students from Teaching Units at his/her discretion.

Aims of Teacher Advisor System

1. To provide an opportunity for positive student interaction in a multi-grade group.
2. To develop a positive relationship between parent and school.
3. To bring together staff and students.
4. To provide consistent guidance for all students.

5. To make the school a more humane place.
6. To help students develop a stronger self-concept.
7. To develop a confiding atmosphere between students and staff.

Distribution Chart for Individualized Student Mathematics Skills Program

LEVELS

LEVELS	NUMERATION	PLACE VALUE	ADDITION	SUBTRACTION	MULTIPLICATION	DIVISION	COMBINATION OF PROCESSES	FRACTIONS	MONEY	TIME	SYSTEM OF MEASUREMENT
H											
G			G.C.								
F	C.S.		S.Q. M.Y. M.K.	G.C.			C.S. M.Y. G.C.		P.S. M.Y. G.C. M.K.	P.S.	
E	G.C.	S.Q. P.S. C.S. M.Y. G.C. M.K.	P.S. C.S. K.M.	S.Q. P.S. C.S. M.Y. K.M. M.K.	M.K. C.S. M.Y. G.C. K.M.	K.M. P.S. C.S. M.Y. G.C. M.K.	P.S. M.K.	G.C.	S.Q. C.S.		P.S. G.C. M.K.
D	P.S. M.Y. K.M.	K.M.					C.S. P.S. M.Y. M.K.	K.M.			M.Y. K.M.
C	S.Q. M.K.			S.Q.	S.Q.		S.Q. K.M.	K.M.		S.Q.	C.S.
B								S.Q.			S.Q.
A											

A Sample Math Skill Card for Grades 6–8

MATH SKILL CARD

LAST NAME   FIRST

SIXTH GRADE TEACHER

SEVENTH GRADE TEACHER

EIGHTH GRADE TEACHER

School	Group
Year	
Sixth Grade	
Seventh Grade	
Eighth Grade	

FARRAGUT MIDDLE SCHOOL

School	Group
Year	
Sixth Grade	
Seventh Grade	
Eighth Grade	

WHOLE NUMBERS

Add	Sum of 3 digits—regrouping
	Horizontal to vertical form
Subt.	Difference—3 digits—regrouping
	Horizontal to vertical form
Division	Single digit divisor
	2-digit divisor
	Zero in the quotient
Mult.	Single multiplier
	2-digit multiplier
	3-digit multiplier—regrouping
	Multiplier with zero
General	Place value to millions
	Round to thousands
	Prime factors of whole numbers
	Operation of denominate numbers

FRACTIONS

General	Name the reciprocal of a whole
	Name the reciprocal of proper fraction
	Name the reciprocal of improper frac.
	Name the reciprocal of mixed number
	Name equivalent fractions
Add	Sum—like denominators
	Sum—unlike denominators
	Difference—like denominators
	Difference—unlike denominators
	Difference—whole—fraction
Division	Proper ÷ Proper
	Proper ÷ Improper
	Proper ÷ Mixed
	Proper ÷ Whole
	Improper ÷ Proper
	Mixed ÷ Mixed
	Whole ÷ Proper
Mult.	Product—Simple fractions
	Product—Mixed numbers
General	Convert mixed no. to improper fraction
	Convert whole to fraction
	Simplify fraction to lowest terms
	Measurement

DECIMALS

- Addition involving decimals
- Subtraction involving decimals
- Multiplication of decimals
- Decimal ÷ whole
- Whole ÷ decimal
- Decimal ÷ decimal
- Identify place value of decimal
- Round decimal as indicated
- Rename decimal as fraction
- Rename fraction as decimal

PERCENT

- Rename fraction as percent
- Rename decimal as percent
- Rename percent as decimal
- Find missing element in proportion

GENERAL

- Recognize terminating decimals
- Recognize repeating decimals
- Expanded notation
- Operations of exponents
- Find square roots

SIGNED NOS.

- Addition
- Subtraction
- Multiplication
- Division

Source: Farragut Middle School, Hastings-on-Hudson, N. Y., 1972.

345

Suggested Activities in a Middle School Guidance Program

COUNSELING

Objectives for Counselors:

To identify the special needs of students and to work through counseling and the utilization of other resources to help meet the needs of these students so that they may become more effective learners.

Implementation:

The counselors counsel with students who have special needs. This is done with individual and groups of students. The school staff usually refers these students, but some are self-referred to the counselors. These students may have emotional, social, or personal problems.

PARENT INVOLVEMENT

Objectives for Parents:

To become knowledgeable about good child rearing practices.

To be aware of the social and emotional needs of their children.

To become knowledgeable about providing an atmosphere that is conducive to good mental health and therefore better school achievement.

Implementation:

The counselors are available for individual or team conferences with parents. They serve as liaison between parents and Lee County Student Services personnel (visiting teacher, etc.). The counselors provide multi-cultural understanding activities for parents and students.

CLASSROOM GUIDANCE

Objectives for Students:

To have positive personal interaction with others including peers, school staff and parents.

To be able to define values and understand how values are formed and changed.

Implementation:

The counselors conduct guidance activities in all classes on a scheduled basis. Guidance is for all students.

SCHOOL STAFF

Objectives for School Staff:

To identify and provide for the emotional, social, physical and academic needs of students.

To provide for exceptional child education.

OTHER GUIDANCE ACTIVITIES

Consults with school staff and individual parents about students with special needs.

Orients new students to the school.

Works with the school's staff to promote on-going guidance activities.

Helps students plan for the entrance into the next grade level.

Coordinates the school's testing program and interprets results.

CAREER EDUCATION

Objectives for Students:

To become aware of the world of work.

To become aware of the personal and educational requirements for a variety of careers.

To relate personal values to career requirements.

Implementation:

The counselors coordinate career education lessons on a scheduled basis and are the school's resource persons on career education.

Guidance is for All Students

Implementation:

The counselors serve as resource persons to the teachers and the administration in identifying and providing for special needs of students. The counselors coordinate health programs (hearing, speech, vision, etc.).

Organization of Special Interest Activity Period

Sample Activity Period Curriculum

ENRICHMENT, RESEARCH, REMEDIATION

Choose *one* year course, *one* nine-week course, or *two* 4 1/2-week courses.

Year Courses

1. Band—beginning band.
2. Chorus—sing for enjoyment as well as for performances, such as Christmas programs, caroling and the spring concert.
3. 4–H—students in this class will work with four teachers during the year. You will choose projects and study topics, such as: crafts, dog care, gardening, care of horses, public speaking, indoor plants, and other 4–H projects. You will be able to compete in the county fair and are eligible for all 4–H club activities, including summer camps. You will also have the opportunity to get help with your academic subjects from your teachers. Extra help in math will be stressed.
4. Guitar—learn to string and tune a guitar, read music, learn chords and sing. You must have your own guitar.
5. World of manufacturing—learn to use hand tools and power equipment. Make projects in wood, leather, plastics and plaster. You may also choose to work with the wood lathe.

Semester Courses

6. Careers in art—students will cover six major career areas in art:

graphic design, photography, advertising design, printing, ceramics and crafts.

7. Media production—students will learn how to use media, such as slide pictures, movies, videotapes, recorded music and readings to prepare programs.

9—Week Courses

8. Eagle's Cry—school newspaper. Write news, sports, and feature stories. You must be able to work after school occasionally. You must possess good writing skills.

9. Needlepoint—students will learn fundamentals of needlepoint. They will create pictures, pillow tops, belts, etc. Students must bring their own materials.

10. Sewing—students will learn pattern selection, fabrics, pattern lay-out, application of zipper, garment decoration, etc. Students must purchase fabric and other materials.

11. Tennis—learn to play tennis at Northwest Youth Center. You must bring a racket and tennis balls. *You must have a signed permission form from your parents to register.*

4 1/2—Week Courses

12. Appreciation of literature—interesting stories and poems will be read and presented dramatically. Even students who don't like to read will enjoy the class.

13. Art of listening—discover the world of music and learn to hear as you never have before. This is a course to teach listening skills which will not only teach you how to listen to music, but how to use listening to help you in many ways in life.

14. Body building with weights—to develop all the body muscles more fully through a weightlifting program. *You must have a signed permission form from your parents to register.*

15. Body mechanics—conditioning exercises, weight control, increased endurance.

16. Brain teasers—mind benders—exercises in math and science.

17. Chess—learn the basic moves and strategy of chess. Games are played daily.

18. Cooking—continue to learn about cooking. This class is for students who are in Mrs. Pike's class this nine weeks.

19. Decorating clothing—fabric painting, batiking, tie-dyeing, quilting. Students will provide fabric or clothing plus a fee of $1.50 for paint and dye.

20. French—learn greetings, common vocabulary, names, days of the week, months, counting, etc.

21. Handwriting—develop good cursive writing which is easily read and easily written.

22. Horticulture—grow vegetables and flowers in cans.

23. Knitting, crochet, and macrame—learn one or more of these skills. Students must provide materials.

24. Magic—learn magic tricks. Practice the tricks on videotape and prepare for a magic show.

25. Model building—each student will provide his or her own model kit and necessary materials.

26. Needlepoint—students will learn the fundamentals of needlepoint. They will create pictures, pillowtops, belts, etc. Students must bring their own materials.

27. Puzzles, riddles and games—a variety of mind-teasers.

28. Recreational reading—a quiet place to read.

29. Rug Hooking—decorate your room or make a gift for mom. Students must bring their own kits. (Kits cost about $6.95.)

30. Science enrichment—use this time to get extra help in science or to work ahead on special projects.

31. String design and weaving—use string, yarn, or leather to do string designs and weaving. Students must bring materials.

32. Supervised study—a chance to do homework with a teacher on hand to help.

33. Typing—learn correct touch typing. Type work for teachers, business forms and letters.

A Sample Activity Period Schedule

Teacher Day 8:00–3:20
Student Day 8:15–3:10

Grades 5–8 Middle School Organization

	1–2 8:15–9:11	3–4 9:11–10:07	5–6 10:07–11:03	7 11:03–11:31	8 11:31–11:59	9 11:59–12:27	10–11 12:27–1:21	12–13 1:21–2:17	14–15 2:17–3:10
Grade 5	Instructional	Instructional	Instructional	LUNCH	Instructional	Instructional	Planning	Planning	Activity Period
6	Instructional	Instructional	Planning	Planning	Planning	LUNCH	Instructional	Instructional	Activity Period
7	Instructional	Instructional	Planning	Planning	Planning	LUNCH	Instructional	Instructional	Activity Period
8	Instructional	Instructional	Instructional	LUNCH	Instructional	Instructional	Planning	Planning	
Funct. Skills	Instructional	Planning	Instructional	Instructional	Instructional	LUNCH	Instructional	Instructional	Planning
Bi-Ling. Comm. Skills S.L.D. Tutorial	Planning	Planning	Instructional 6th & 7th Grades	Instructional 6th & 7th Grades	Instructional 6th & 7th Grades	LUNCH	Instructional 5th & 8th Grades	Instructional 5th & 8th Grades	Activity Period

RELATED ARTS

	1–2	3	4	5–6 (6th Grade)	7 (7th Grade)	10–11 (5th Grade)	12–13 (8th Grade)	14–15
R E L A T E D / A R T S	Planning	R.A. for Special Program Students	5th & 6th Art, Music & Health; 7th & 8th Pre-Voc. & P.E.	6A Art & Music / 6B Health / 7A—Pre-Voc. / 7B—P.E.	6B Art & Music / 6A Health / 7B Pre-Voc. / 7A—P.E.	5A Art & Music / 5B—Health / 8A—Pre-Voc. / 8B—P.E.	5B Art & Music / 5A—Health / 8B—Pre-Voc. / 8A—P.E.	Activity & Planning

Health and P.E. will switch at Semester.

For 1st Semester an Aid will be assigned to Art, Music or Health to balance the classes.

In 2nd Semester 2 P.E. Teachers will balance the 5th and 6th grade classes.

351

Sample of Team Leader Communication and Team Planning Form

Sample—Team Leader Communication

1. Monday—short team meeting at 9:30 concerning scheduling. Please bring the file folder I put in your P.O. box with you since we will be discussing 9th unified scheduling and 9th condensed English scheduling. Roger Oakley will attend to answer questions.

2. Tuesday—9:30 meeting with Language Arts Consultant—all team members attend. Will be held in far end of teachers' room. Topic: Progress Report on Transformational Grammar.

3. Team Meeting Wednesday 9:30.
   1) Next year's team operation
   2) Scheduling
   3) New literature groupings—how to organize. Please have grades ready for next week's meeting
   4) Team evaluation
   5) New grammar
   6)

4. Agenda for Thursday's team meeting 9:30.
   1) leftovers
   2) history unit
   3) lesson plan
   4)

5. The lesson plan this week does not completely explain the history schedule. Please note that a good portion of Monday and Tuesday's history period should be devoted to the minipace on notetaking and that the outlining section should probably be completed by the end of next week. Chapter II test will come about Friday of next week.

6. Scheduling—information will be handed out to the students on Tuesday,

February 24th. Scheduling will be the next day. We are to complete scheduling by March 2nd so plan your parent conferences accordingly. Remember we must contact all parents of students recommended for condensed English and students recommended for 9th unified.

7. Independent study rules for students:
   1) Go to and from independent study areas with no talking and no stopping along the way.
   2) No talking without Supervisor's permission in I.S. areas. Must use conversation areas.
   3) Any breaking of behavior rules will "immediately" eliminate a student from I.S. areas and he will have to complete the project on his own time.
   4) Revolutionary War projects are in the learning center and Constitution projects are in the library.

8. Whew! I think we will be sick of each other after all these meetings. When are we going to see parents?

Team Planning Form

TEAM _____

WEEK _____

AGENDA

DECISIONS MADE

   ORGANIZATIONAL

   EVALUATION

   CURRICULUM

   OTHER

Interdisciplinary Unit

THE LAW AND YOU

I. GOAL

At the conclusion of this unit, students will have an understanding of how different aspects of the law apply to them.

II. UNIT OBJECTIVES

A. Students will understand and develop a working knowledge of:

1. Civil Law—the private rights and obligations, not public or political rights and obligations.
    a. Buying and selling contracts—a legal agreement between two or more people involving a purchase.
        1. Evictions
        2. Acceptance
        3. Repossessions
    b. Small Claims Court
        1. Examples
        2. Definitions
    c. Loans
        1. Liens on property, etc.
        2. Finance charge
        3. Simple interest
        4. Compound interest
    d. Nonverbal Contracts
        1. Responsible for any child you beget regardless of marital status

2. Criminal Law.
    a. Misdemeanor
        1. Vocabulary

          2. Types of cases

          3. Cases as examples

      b. Felony

          1. Vocabulary

          2. Types of crimes

          3. Cases as examples

      c. Quasi cases (treated as a crime but not recorded on your record as a crime)

          1. Some traffic cases

          2. Some support cases

      d. Drug laws

          1. What they are

          2. Why they were made

          3. What happens when they are broken and persons are caught

   3. Bill of Rights—First ten amendments to Constitution.

      a. Implications of the Constitution

          1. Freedom of speech, press, religion, assembly, fair trial

          2. Accustomed liberties enjoyed shall be continued

          3. Powers not given to the federal government belong to the state or people

      b. Examples

          1. Newspaper articles, Watergate

          2. Rallies, taxes

          3. Schools, trials

          4. Using Fifth in court

          5. Given amendments, students will give examples

      c. Responsibilities associated with Bill of Rights

          1. Voting

          2. Infringing your rights on others

          3. Not using Bill of Rights as lever against "Law and Order"

      d. Comparison

          1. Government of the United States vs. other countries

          2. Governments (Bill of Rights vs. none)

B. Students will explore their own values, and the relationship of those values and feelings to the laws examined.

C. Skills.

   1. Language Arts

      a. Listening

      b. Reading

      c. Writing

      d. Spelling

      e. Speaking

   2. Social Studies

      a. Define Bill of Rights

      b. Illustrate at least one example of each

      c. Compare life of people living under written Bill of Rights and those without

      d. Illustrate three implications of the preamble to the Constitution

3. Mathematics
   a. Place value
   b. Decimals
   c. Fractions
   d. Percents

4. Science
   a. Drug groups
   b. Effects (short and long term)
   c. Drug laws
   d. Consequences of breaking those laws

5. Career Education
   a. Need for occupations
   b. Changing roles
   c. Job opportunities in law enforcement

6. Guidance
   a. Exposure to values exercises
   b. Group interaction
   c. Forced choice situation
   d. Rank order situation

D. These objectives will be accomplished by:

1. Speakers

2. Field trips

3. Role playing

4. Films

5. Examination of printed and audio-visual material

6. Small group discussion

7. Research in the classroom and media center

8. Classroom discussion

9. Values-clarification session

10. Structured lessons in texts and teacher-made materials, etc.

11. Any other related methods

Source: Moore—Mickens Middle School, "The Law and You—Interdisciplinary Unit" (Dade City, Fla.: 1975). Used with permission.

Anthropology Unit

Student Guide to the *DIG*

Prepare to get your hands dirty! You and your fellow students are about to go on an archeological excavation, or dig. Using the techniques of modern archeology, you will unearth and bring back to the classroom strange and mysterious artifacts for reconstruction and analysis. But this dig will be unusual. The cultures you excavate will be the result of your imagination and construction and knowledge concerning the nature of culture.

During the next few weeks this team will become four cultures (red, yellow, blue, and green) that create cultures and artifacts in complete secrecy from each other. YOU will create a geographic setting. YOU will decide on the time, past, present or future. YOU will decide the beliefs of the people. Each culture will bury its artifacts for the other culture to excavate and reconstruct. Red culture will dig up yellow culture, yellow will dig up red, blue will dig up green culture, and green will dig up blue culture. After reconstruction and analysis, each culture will meet in a final confrontation to reveal the accuracy of each team's analysis.

What will be expected of you? The challenge to your imagination and abilities is unlimited, for throughout Dig, tasks will require individual effort and creativity.

After your culture has decided the setting, time, and theme of itself, we will divide into smaller groups that will work on religion, language, government, recreation, etc. You must convince your fellow group members that your fantastic ideas fit the theme of the culture and do not conflict or cancel out *their* fantastic ideas!!

Once approval has been given to your ideas, you must design an artifact that reflects your cultural universal accurately. Constructing this artifact requires imagination, skill, and hard work. Those prehistoric objects you have seen in museums will seem quite amazing to you by the time you have constructed your own artifact. You may wish to help create your culture's language or number system. How tricky can you be in composing an alphabet for the other culture to decipher? Or you may give most of your attention to making a secret tomb that will confuse and trick the "grave robbers." If you enjoy art, you may decide to construct a large mural on plaster of paris. Some of you may make tools or screens to help at the Big Dig. This is only a partial list of the activities ahead of you.

On the actual excavation, known as the Big Dig, you will discover the importance of careful measurements and record keeping. You must plan where to place or "salt" the broken artifacts that the opposing culture must unearth. Which of your relics should be found at the lowest level of the pits, which should be at the surface? Will putting two artifacts close to another one provide important clues for the opposing culture???

As you excavate each other's strange cultures, you may find yourself working as a cryptographer, a cartographer, washer-bagger, recorder, photographer, digger, measurer, or another job. You may even be a co-crew chief. Whatever your job, you will work as any professional archeologist works on a scientific dig.

Back in the classroom you will have the responsibility of reconstructing and restoring at least one artifact. One of your most challenging assignments will be analyzing what the artifact represents in the unknown culture. And even if you are certain of its function, can you convince your fellow culture members that you are correct? The work of the entire culture will be brought together to reconstruct the excavated culture. During the final confrontation, your team's views will be presented and then answered by the other culture. How close will your analysis be? How valid will the opposing culture's artifacts be? Which culture will be the most creative? Which will have made the best artifacts? Answers to many of these questions will come during the confrontation. (If there is time at the end of the

Dig Calendar

Monday	Tuesday	Wednesday	Thursday	Friday
April 17	April 18	April 19	April 20	April 21
SOCIAL SCIENCE INTRODUCTION TO ANTHROPOLOGY MATH INTRODUCTION (History of Math's Gridding) SCIENCE INTRODUCTION ON PRIMITIVE MAN AND PREHISTORIC ANIMALS LANGUAGE ARTS INTRODUCTION ON HIEROGLYPHICS AND CRYPTOGRAPHY				
April 24 Classes begin rotating by home room	April 25 8:30 speaker Judge Perry (Mastodon)	April 26 Rental films: "How we learn about the past" "The archeologist and how he works"	April 27 Decide themes for cultures and universals	April 28 8:30 speaker Mr. Dlugopolski (cave art) hour 2 theme and universals decided upon; title of culture
(Two-week display of African artifacts by N. Robson)				
May 1 Development of artifacts to fit universals	May 2 Development of artifacts continued	May 3 ARBS—go over artifact blueprint sheets	May 4 Give TGBD explaining tools and tasks for BIG DIG. P.M. speaker Charles Ellenbaum (archeologist) "What is culture?"	May 5 8:30 speaker Mr. Wramly (archeologist). Catch-up day. P.M. speaker Mrs. May, art demonstration using plaster
May 8 Make artifacts. Mr. Don Storey's help	May 9 Make artifacts. Digs pits for burial (Wed.) P.M. speaker Mr. Ellenbaum	May 10 Burial (outside)	May 11 Dig (outside)	May 12 Dig (outside)
(Two-week display of skulls and "Rosetta stone" replica)				
May 15 Analysis of culture found	May 16 Analysis of culture found	May 17 Confrontation	May 18 3 field trips 1) Braidwood coal fields fossils 2) Oriental Inst. 3) St. Charles, Ill. dig site	May 19 Museum open house for parents and students

year, we will have a Museum Open House where we will display many of
the artifacts made and reconstructed during the DIG.)

By the time you have finished participating in DIG, you will have lived with
the intricacies of human culture and will have gained first-hand knowledge
of how people past and present have shaped their beliefs and behavior in
the face of universal human problems and needs. You should have a new
respect and admiration for the individual who is capable of creative thinking, a type of activity that must be maintained if we are to have a truly
democratic and open society.

SOURCE: From Hadley Junior High School, Glen Ellyn, Ill., 1975.

Brief Outline of a Student-Created Culture

I.   Culture Background

    A. Time is 2002 AD.

    B. Setting is a few miles outside of what used to be Houston,
        Texas, North America.

    C. Due to mutations, the inhabitants appear to be 20th century
        Homo sapiens except for very small heads and very large mus-
        cles.

    D. Two cultural phases are represented at the site:

        1. Remains from before the Great War that destroyed most of
            the world in 1934, represented by artifacts common to the
            United States of today.

        2. Remains from the culture that developed after the Great War
            that date from the year 2002.

II.   Themes

    A. These people believe man is good and machines are bad.
        Machines and the intellectual activities that created machines
        led to the Great War. As a reaction against this, mental activity
        is frowned upon, while physical activity is the highest good.

    B. Anything that leads to physical exertion is good; anything that
        hints of intellectual activity is evil.

    C. The central symbol of this culture is man over machine as
        shown at right. Note the small head and large extremities,
        which stand over a gear, symbol of machines.

III. Economics

    A. Two types of technology are represented:

        1. the machines and gadgets of before the Great War.

2. the simple devices which require physical exertion of the year 2002.

B. Due to the desire for physical exertion, both sexes engage in hard work. Young children demand a chance to cut wood and dig ditches at an early age.

C. Since this is the only group that survived the Great War, there is trade with no outside group. Money consists of extremely heavy stones; the heavier the stone the greater the value.

IV.   Food, Clothing, and Shelter

A. Foods requiring great amounts of work are in high demand. In fact, the easier a crop is to raise, the higher the price! The only animals allowed for domestication are those which show the least intelligence, such as the dodo bird and donkey.

B. Clothing consists of skins that have weights attached.

C. These people live in the ruins of the machine culture that was destroyed. But instead of using elevators, long ropes are climbed to reach the upper floors which, because of the exertion required, are in great demand. Transportation is by foot power only with the added delight of attaching heavy weights to the legs when going for a pleasant Sunday afternoon walk. Of course Sunday is the hardest workday.

V.   Family and Kin

A. Your mate is chosen according to physical strength, which is the only criteria of beauty.

B. Child training revolves around physical exercises. Rites of passage consist of reading books and engaging in intellectual activity, which is the worst pain in this culture.

VI.   Political Organization

A. The government is a dictatorship in which the leader is chosen by a yearly physical contest, something like Indian wrestling.

B. Since no outside cultures exist, war is unknown. Conflicts between individuals are usually resolved by a contest of strength. When convicted of breaking a law, such as not working on Sunday, you are sent to jail which is the library of the pre-Great War culture. The worst punishment is being sentenced to read books and play with computers.

VII.   Attitude Towards the Unknown

A. Religion in this culture revolves around hatred of machines and intellectual activity. For example, once a week groups gather and smash machines with primitive clubs. When you die, you go to the Great Rock Pile in the sky.

B. Death rituals involve placing as many examples of physical exertion as possible in the tomb. To die from multiple hernias is the highest honor you can bestow on your survivors.

VIII.   Communications

A. The language appears to have a very limited number of letters and a small vocabulary consisting of words of few syllables.

B. The number system consists of scratching crude lines in the soil. A very intricate system is found only in the cells of those sentenced to confinement for breaking laws.

IX.   Arts and Esthetic Values

    A.   The only musical instruments are those that require great exertion to play. The greatest and most loved compositions are rhythmic sounds that add to one's ability to work hard. Jogging is the most popular of dances. Beauty is found in all work. The largest selling perfume has the aroma of body odor.

X.   Recreation

    A.   Leisure time in this culture consists of working harder than is usually done on the job. Games of physical strength abound.

The name of this culture is The Specibians, derived from spelling "biceps" backwards and adding "-ians."

"Dig"

AN INTRODUCTION TO THE HISTORY OF MATHEMATICS

Basic Information

8th grade level
1 (one) week unit (five 55-min. class periods)
primary objective—better understanding of our number system

Specific Information Covered

tally systems
repetitive principle
additive systems
    Egyptian
    Roman
    Greek-ancient
    Greek-Ionic
multiplicative systems
    Chinese-Japanese
place value systems
    Babylonian
    Mayan
    Hindu-Arabic

Terms To Be Understood

tally	subtractive principle
system of numeration	place value principle
repetitive principle	concept of order
hieroglyphics	abacus
additive principle	prime
Hindu-Arabic numerals	multiplicative principle

Activities

role-playing
compare systems of numeration
construct own system of numeration

"Dig"

Materials Needed for "Dig" in Social Science

1. similar problems
   Family of Man by E. Steichen
   The Big Wave by Pearl Buck
   Beginnings: Earth, Sky, Life, Death by Sophia Fahs

2. learned not born
   pictures of: sleeping people of all ages, races, countries
   eating
   list of foreign and domestic foods

3. predict how to act
   pictures of: christening, Greek national dress, kilts, Samoan dress
   Alice in Wonderland by L. Carroll (record in library)
   Gulliver's Travels by J. Swift

4. my way is best
   My Mother Is the Most Beautiful Woman in the World (tape) folk tale
   Anna and the King of Siam (King and I)
   My Fair Lady (record) "Why Can't the English"

5. logical culture
   pictures of: snow blizzard, gentle snowfall, packed, drifts, etc.

6. use other's ideas
   "A Majority of One" (play)
   List of words in English with foreign derivation

7. culture's change
   "Rip Van Winkle" (see *Stories to Remember*—7th grade)
   list of inventions—tell intellectual, economic political, aesthetic, social effects
   Human Problems in Technological Change by E. Spicer
   The Pearl by J. Steinbeck
   "The Million Pound Note" by Mark Twain

8. hard for man to study man
   visual sequence of behavior to be interpreted by class

9. to illustrate and dramatize
   "The Castaways"
   "The Admirable Crichton" by Barrie

"Dig"

Introduction to Anthropology

The following are the eight fundamentals of Anthropology that we will be studying as an introduction to the DIG.

1. hard for man to study man
2. cultures change
3. cultures have similar needs and problems
4. "my way is best"
5. cultural differences are learned not born

6. cultures are logical to themselves
7. knowledge of culture lets man predict how to act
8. cultures use others' ideas, beliefs and inventions

Example from Anthropology Study

Beside the following articles below put a "B" if you think the article is mostly for boys and a "G" if the article is for girls.

football helmet	jump rope
purse	baseball
model car	hair ribbon
pet snake	kitten
stuffed animal	doll
go-cart	dress
roller skates	

Put "yes" beside the following foods that you like and "no" beside the foods that you do not like. Answer all below.

apple pie	okra
fried chicken	paolla (tomatoes, clams, chicken, etc,)
gazpacho (cold soup)	ice cream
chocolate chip cookies	coke
eggplant	7-up
black olives	octopus
hamburgers	grits
sauerkraut	caviar
frog legs	hot dogs
squid	black-eyed peas

Comic Book Making and Reporting the News

1. Read one of the stories in Action Comics or in another comic. Pretend that the story you read has a chapter that is missing. Write this chapter and illustrate it. Why not get a friend to do this with you?

or

2. Make a comic book story using just pictures. Try to say what you want to say using pictures.

or

3. Look around you. Observe for a few minutes just what's going on in this room because this is the "News." You are a radio news reporter. Write up the news as you see it, record it over the tape recorder as if it were a radio, and play it for me and a few of your friends. Remember that the radio program should last five minutes. So carefully select the material you think you should report. Don't report stuff that you think people might not care about hearing.

or

4. Do number 3 except you need not write it.

or

Do number 3. Talk it over the recorder while someone else writes it.

or

5. Pick an object in your home or classroom. You are going to be on television for three minutes advertising this object. Sell it, as best you can, to the public. The public, since no television is available, is me and your friends. Write it, or talk it, or both. Let me know when you're ready.

Individualized Task Sheet: a Unit Contract

1. use a soft voice.
2. Select a partner.
3. Do your work without disturbing others.
4. Finish one task, go on to another.

Name_____ Section _____ Week _____

Check the correct space when the task is finished.

	Mon.	Tues.	Wed.	Thurs.	Fri.
1. Read a story (small books)					
2. Write the title					
3. Draw a picture about the story					
4. Do four lessons (practice readers)					
5. Practice instant words or phrases (filmstrip)					
6. Study phonics lesson (record player and filmstrip)					
7. Read a story (controlled reader)					
8. Listen to record or tape					
9. Study 10 new words (language master)					
10. Read a poem					
11. Study a skill (overhead projector)					
12. Play a skill game					
13. Talk to me					

An Effective Procedure for Handling
Homework in the Classroom

This procedure works toward the following *objectives* for the individual student:

1. To place the responsibility for completing homework assignments on the student.

2. To provide the student with motivation and opportunity to improve his homework performance.

3. To provide the student a chance to make meaningful personal decisions about work habits without being forced to dream up believable excuses or convincing lies.

4. To build the classroom atmosphere of honesty and trust.

5. To reinforce the idea of natural consequences and avoidance of punishment.

6. To provide the student with a written record in his own handwriting of missing assignments.

The following are some of the beneficial *results* of the procedure for the teacher:

1. Avoids judgments and decisions regarding excuses.

2. Avoids recording each assignment for each student in the grade book.

3. Provides you with a written record of make-up work needed for absent students.

4. Provides you with a record of deficiencies in the student's own handwriting for use at parent/student conferences.

The following materials are necessary to implement the idea in the classroom:

1. A supply of Missing Assignment Sheets with the following information printed on them:

   Student's Name_____ Date_____ Period_____

   I have not turned in the following assignment:

   _____

   _____

2. A folder for each class of students you meet each day—for example, one might be labeled "1st Period Social Studies"

3. The will power to stick by the "no excuses, please" rule for the first week!!!

Procedure:
Whenever a homework assignment is to be collected or checked, students are expected to turn in either the assignment *or* a Missing Assignment Sheet. No excuses are asked for or listened to. You convey to the student that you understand that there are sometimes good reasons for not doing an assignment as planned, and that you have confidence in their ability to complete the work as soon as possible. Students are told that they may

makeup the work at their convenience, *without penalty*. Emphasis is placed on the need for each student to be honest. Reassurances must be given that either the sheet or the assignment is equally acceptable.

Sheets and assignments are counted when collected to verify that everyone has participated. Discrepancies are handled first by letting the class know that someone has not turned in the necessary sheet or assignment and asking for the class's cooperation to make the count correct. Only after this has failed to produce the missing papers should the assignments and sheets be checked by name.

Missing assignment sheets are then filed in the folder for that class and period. The folder should be placed where students have easy access to it. When a student does a missing assignment, he pulls the sheet from the folder, shows the assignment to the teacher, and tears up the missing assignment sheet, usually with a great deal of enjoyment!!

No records are necessarily kept in the grade book for homework. At midpoint in the grading period and again at the end of the grading period, the folders are checked by the teacher. If a student has no papers in the folder, he/she has a perfect record for completing homework assignments. At those times, and only at those times, are missing assignments counted against the student.

Students may make up the assignments at any time during the grading period. An assignment is just as acceptable whether turned in on time or three weeks late. Students soon realize the importance of doing the assignments when due so that they can be prepared for class discussions and tests.

Absent students are required to fill out sheets for all work turned in while they were absent or collected on the day they return. This ensures that they have a clear understanding of make-up work that is needed to keep up with the rest of the class.

Comments:

The procedure sounds much more complicated on paper than it is. Students really respond to the idea that homework assignments are their problem, not the teacher's and they have the responsibility for handling that problem. I have seen good peer pressure exerted in the classroom to make sure the procedure is an honest and effective one. Even students who have failed to keep up, experience a fresh start with the folder empty at the beginning of each new grading period. I especially like not having to record each assignment in the grade book. Students usually receive their homework back the same day, once the count has been verified. The entire procedure could be handled by the students themselves.

Submitted by:

Carolyn A. More
Hoover Junior High School
Washington Avenue
Indialantic, Florida 32903

Source: Carolyn A. More, Hoover Junior High School, Indialantic, Florida, 1979: Used with permission.
Source: An adaptation of an idea discussed in Haim Ginott, *Teacher and Child* (New York: Avon, 1972), p. 167.

School Newspaper Report—"The Reel Thing"

Advertising by Sue Anderson

Mrs. Child had a unit in her social science class that was a lot of fun—advertising.

After studying advertising and the work of advertising agencies, we all chose a product that we wanted to make our own commercials on—a TV commercial, a newspaper and a magazine ad, a radio ad, and a billboard. Each student was the member of a group of from 4–6 people and each group made up a product within a certain category—gum, car, candy, soft drink, cosmetics, equipment, etc.

Each group made up its commercials and ads and project book and presented them to the class. All the billboards were displayed around the school. The project book for each group was a book on all different kinds of real-life magazine and newspaper ads. We cut them out according to the kind of article they were and what kind of appeal they made to the readers. Examples of these appeals are: brand loyalty, feminine attractiveness, luxury, and vanity. To close this part of the unit, we videotaped our TV commercials so that we could see what they would really look like on TV.

French Advertising by Kathy LaPietra

In French class, three days were set aside for a French mini-unit in advertising. In this unit students were supposed to make one project book and an original advertisement in a small group. This was an extension of our study of advertising in social science class. Our projects were graded by Madame Dilday and Mrs. Child, who gave us criticism—good and bad—on our projects.

Videotaping by Micky Hartman

If you've never done videotaping, believe me it isn't easy. Mrs. Child's social science class, after making up their own commercials during our study of advertising, videotaped them. The kids did a good job and the commercials turned out well. Each class period had its own cameramen and technicians to tape the commercials.

The cameramen did a good job with the taping and they had a lot of fun, too. Mrs. Fish, in the library, spent two days training them on how to run the videotape machines. The cameramen/technicians were: fifth period—Tom Garite, Bruce Douglas, Hal Linde; sixth period—Wally Page, Dave Tripp, Karl Lange; seventh period—Mark Besore, Joe Berdych, Martin Seifert; and eighth period they were Barb Andres, Maria Pum, and Peter Reniche.

After all the commercials were videotaped, the classes got to see all the commercials. Some examples of the original products and commercials were: Ali Punch, Sparklemint Gum, Push-and-Brush Mascara, Cyclo-Sound radios, and Mean Jeans. Everyone loved doing and looking at the commercials. The costumes and props were great, and we all hope that next year's social science class will get to do it!

A Visit From Mr. Page by Tom Lysaught

This quarter we had a visitor from the Chicago-Tokyo bank, Mr. Frank Page. He came to our math classes to talk about how companies pay for products that are imported, and he explained the foreign line of credit. He told us how companies buy goods from other countries and the procedures for getting a "letter of credit." He explained this to us clearly, answered all of our

School Newspaper Report—*continued*

The Kiosk by Roxy Schmidt
            Carolyn Colson
            Cathy Jordan

The kiosk is a cylindrical structure with a pointed umbrella-like top. In Paris you may see them in the parts of town to advertise operas, musical programs, shows, etc. Some kiosks may have postcards for sale.

Team 8A French students, under the direction of Madame Dilday, made a kiosk. It is similar to the French kiosk—or news-stand—with posters and advertisements on it. The posters and advertisements on our kiosk were made by Team 8A French students as part of their advertising study in French. The kiosk may be seen on display in the junior high library.

Mr. Nicpon and Peter Pan by Chuck Cote

Mr. Stanley Nicpon of the Leo J. Burnett Advertising Agency came to speak to us. He showed us many commercials and told us facts about them.

There is one important rule of advertising that he told us—"Always choose one main subject to emphasize and stick to it throughout the commercial."

Mr. Nicpon is in charge of the Peter Pan account at Leo J. Burnett and he brought with him uncut footage of the new Peter Pan commercials. The new theme for Peter Pan Peanut Butter is "If you believe in peanut butter, you gotta believe in Peter Pan." He also gave us Peter Pan Peanut Butter buttons and showed us a reel of commercials made by his agency.

Mr. Faulkner by Don Sowers

Mr. John Faulkner is a very good artist. He draws "Tony the Tiger" for the Leo J. Burnett Advertising Agency, which handles the Kellogg account.

Mr. Faulkner came to speak to us. Dave Ladik introduced him to us. Mr. Faulk-

questions and gave us each a yen, Japanese money.

Peanut Butter Taste-Testing by Maria Pum

As we walked into the classroom, we noticed two things: the overwhelming smell of peanuts and the four large jars of peanut butter (their labels covered) on a table at the front of the classroom. Each jar was numbered—2, 3, or 4.

Prior to this, we had been doing research in teenage consumerism and foods. The preceding day, we had received a few pages of background on peanut butter to introduce us to the qualities of peanut butter—what to look for in the peanut butter. This was part of our closing activities of the Com-Com advertising unit in social science.

As soon as we were seated, a type of ballot was passed out with a list of categories to rate the peanut butters. The categories included rating such qualities as flavor, aroma, texture, and appearance and taste. We also got two tongue depressors—to taste with—and a cup of water, to drink between tastes.

We took turns going up to the table and taking a sample of each peanut butter. There were exclamations of how good or how bad some were. We rated the peanut butters on a range of 1–5.

The votes were counted, and it turned out that two classes chose *Peter Pan* and two chose *Skippy* as the best. Of course, this cannot be accepted as the standard for the kind of peanut butter you should buy. First of all, we did not test every brand of peanut butter on the market, and the two brands chosen—*Peter Pan* and *Skippy*—were not unanimously voted for by the tasters. Each purchaser must understand what makes up a good peanut butter and then make his or her own choice.

School Newspaper Report—*continued*

ner is a free lance artist who works for art directors of several different advertising agencies. Right now he is working on an elephant called "Tusk-Tusk" to advertise a breakfast cereal called Cocoa-Crispies.

Mr. Faulkner spent about twenty minutes showing us drawings that he had made. Many were from popular magazines. During his presentation, he chose two people—one boy and one girl—and he drew them right in front of our eyes. He says he likes his work very much. Mr. Faulkner drew some animals, and we tried to guess what they were—we knew right away! We had a great time listening to him talk and watching him draw cartoons for us.

Black and White Still Photography
by Hal Linde

In Miss Baird's science class we have been studying black and white still photography. We learned all about good composition and good technical quality. We also learned about the different parts of a 35 mm camera: focus, f stops, shutter speed, and film speed.

We divided into groups of 1–5 people and then the groups decided what phase of communication they wanted to cover. Some people chose pollution and one group chose communication with animals.

After we took our pictures, we developed and printed them in the school darkroom. So, you can see, our study of photography was not just in the snapping of pictures, but there was quite a lot involved.

Lights, Action, Camera . . .
by Maria Pum

Maybe you already know, but Team 8A has started a communications unit called Com-Com. Each subject is working on communications in a different way, and in Language Arts we are studying film-making.

We divided into groups of our choice after picking the type of film we'd like to make. For example, we could choose to make a color movie, a black and white movie, an animation, a filmstrip or a "movie without a camera."

That done, we then made a storyboard for the storyline of our movie. If we were having music, we had to put that on the storyboard with pictures of the scenes (what's happening), the type of shot and its angle, and the list of credits. If we were using a voice or speech, that too had to go on the storyboard. One problem is that we only have 3 minutes and 20 seconds of film to work with, unless we choose to buy extra film ourselves.

We learned how to work the camera and the tripod, and we learned about lighting and how to shoot. We saw some of last year's films and learned about some of the problems they had. We also saw movies on film-making and read articles about how to do it.

When we were finished rehearsing and filming, we had to edit our films and splice them together in order, then into one large reel of film to be shown to you tonight at the Tin Cannes Film Festival.

The competition will be great and tough, especially in the black and white movie category. So, sit back, relax and enjoy!

SOURCE: Glen Ellyn Junior High School, "The Reel Thing," Glen Ellyn, Ill., 1977. Used with permission.

Sample of School Improvement Plan • Staff Development Activities

IT'S IN THE BAG

SDTC

STAFF DEVELOPMENT TEACHER'S CENTER NEWSLETTER
STAMFORD PUBLIC SCHOOLS OCTOBER 1976 Vol. 2 No.2

WHAT'S NEW?

The Staff Development Center, which has serviced, for the past two years, our elementary schools, will this year be servicing our four middle schools. Through the redeployment of the ten Instructional Associates, grades K–8 will now be a part of the support system.

With this in mind, the scope and coverage of our newsletter will be increased. Therefore, we have devoted the center pages of this issue to the concept of "mapping"—giving you ideas for a mapping center as well as activities to enrich these centers.

So that the Staff Development Center can better coordinate its activities with those of the classroom, the Center will, for the next two months, be utilizing its workshop rooms for mapping activities within the four curriculum areas: Social Studies, Language Arts, Math and Science.

We hope that all teachers (K–8) will make use of the activities we have on exhibit. We are, of course, hoping that you will share your ideas with the rest of the Stamford Learning Community, either by sending them to the Center, or, better yet, why not drop them off when you are here looking at the exhibits.

LEARNING CENTERS

Learning Centers or Learning Stations, Interest Centers or Interest Stations are frequently heard terms which are usually used synonymously in today's education circles. Often teachers ask what a Learning Center is and find, to their surprise, that they have already been utilizing this approach, but have not referred to it as a Learning Center.

Simply speaking, a Learning Center is an area set aside in a classroom for a specific learning experience. That purpose may be to arouse interest in a certain subject area; it may be to teach a specific skill or concept; or it may be activities designed to reinforce skills or concepts already taught.

A well-designed Learning Center can provide some very positive experiences for the students. It allows them the opportunity to become more responsible for their own learning. It affords the students the opportunity to choose between alternative tasks and levels of materials, guaranteeing success. Centers allow students to work at a pace comfortable for them. Students are also responsible for (or at least involved in) the evaluation of their own activity.

Stamford Middle School Program Workshop Proposal

1. **Topic:**

2. **Participant(s):**

3. **Objective(s):**

4. **Action Plan:** (list activities and/or tasks which will be carried out)

5. **Time Required:** (In 1/2-day units)

6. **Personnel Resources Needed:** (list those people from whom you will need assistance to complete this project)

7. **Material Resources Needed:**

Implementation Plan: (To be developed during workshop for school-year implementation.)

SOURCE: Stamford Middle School (Stamford, Connecticut), 1969. Used with permission.

Middle School Teaming Workshop Evaluation

The objectives of the workshop this week were the following:

1. To identify elements of the middle school curriculum.
2. To explore the concept of "Team" and practice the Team-Building Process.
3. To facilitate development of leadership skills.
4. To look at ways of "How to get people to change."
5. To establish alternative patterns of Discipline and Motivation.
6. To develop interdisciplinary teaching skills and develop interdisciplinary units.
7. To participate in a variety of learning center activities:
   a. Setting up Learning Centers.
   b. Designing Creative Instructional Activities.
   c. Building Interdisciplinary Units.
   d. Examining Skill-Building Techniques.
   e. Facilitating Leadership Skills.
   f. Dealing with Reluctant Learners.
   g. Reviewing Grouping Techniques.
   h. Materials in Areas (Curriculum).

I. Have we accomplished these objectives?   Yes_____ No_____

Comments: _____

_____

_____

_____

_____

Middle School Teaming Workshop Evaluation—*continued*

II. Specifically, what did you like most about the workshop? What were its strengths?

_____

_____

_____

_____

_____

_____

_____

III. How might the workshop have been improved?

_____

_____

IV. What activities in the workshop do you feel might be beneficial to teachers *not* in the workshop this week.

_____

_____

V. Were the materials in the learning centers useful to you? Comments: _____

_____

Overall the materials were: Very useful _____

Useful   _____

Not useful   _____

Did not review materials _____

VI. What kind of follow-up activities would you suggest for fully implementing the team concept:

A. In your school?

_____

_____

B. At the District level?

_____

_____

VII. How would you rate this workshop on the following scale?

1	2	3	4
Poor	Fair	Good	Excellent

VIII. How would you rate the consultant team on the following scale?

1	2	3	4
Poor	Fair	Good	Excellent

SOURCE: Stamford Middle School (Stamford, Conn.), 1973. Used with permission.

Samples of Evaluation and Reporting • Instruments for Middle Schools

Team Effectiveness

We bring to new teams work rules that we think will make the team, and us, effective. Despite their importance, these rules are usually not written down, and are not talked about in the beginning.

To get some notion of the kinds of rules you have been accustomed to, and that others have been accustomed to, we have provided below some statements of rules for you to examine. After you have read the statement, please put a check mark in one of the blank statements beside the question or statement. If you agree with the rule, put your check under agree. If you disagree, put your check under disagree. If you are not sure, then mark the space under *not sure.*

Rules to follow when working in teams.

	Agree	Disagree	Not Sure
1. People with the most knowledge about a subject should do most of the talking.	____	____	____
2. Disagreement and conflict should be avoided whenever possible.	____	____	____
3. Decisions should not be made until everybody has been heard.	____	____	____
4. Keep your real thoughts and feelings to yourself.	____	____	____
5. The best way to handle conflict is to take a vote.	____	____	____
6. When you do not know anything about what is being said, the best thing to do is to keep quiet.	____	____	____

	Agree	**Disagree**	**Not Sure**
7. If someone looks like he is angry or upset, you should not ask what is making him angry.	___	___	___
8. When you do not like something that someone else has said, you should tell him in the most polite way you know.	___	___	___
9. You should encourage others to question you when they do not understand what you say.	___	___	___
10. Each member has a responsibility for dealing with members who want to talk all the time.	___	___	___
11. When you feel hurt, rejected, or put down by someone else, you should tell him your feelings.	___	___	___
12. Members should be interested in how other members are feeling, as well as in what they are thinking.	___	___	___
13. When several people are bored, or impatient, or asleep, it is a good idea to stop and find out why.	___	___	___
14. The chairman or leader should be responsible for getting members to pay attention to each other.	___	___	___
15. Trust others not to take advantage of you.	___	___	___
16. Do not question openly the power structure of a group or team.	___	___	___
17. People who have an interest in how problems are solved have as much right to talk about the problems as people who are experts in the problem area.	___	___	___
18. When team members have to do something about decisions made, it is best to have members in agreement about decision.	___	___	___
19. The best way to act in a team meeting is to stay cool.	___	___	___
20. Team effectiveness is improved when team members examine how they feel about working with each other, and what they think of their work procedures.	___	___	___

State Reporting Form—Florida Riviera Middle School

Grades: 6–8   Enrollment (October 11, 1975): 1125
Program Capacity: 1229*   Number of Teachers: 62
Number Other Instructional Staff: 10.3   Supporting Staff: 28.1
Acreage: 16   Original Construction Date: 1965
Percent Air Conditioned: 100%

*Not including 4 portables

COMPARISON INFORMATION

Category	This School	All Pinellas Middle Schools
Pupil Absentee Rate	5.8%	7.7%
Pupil Mobility Rate	24.3%	30.5%
Pupil Non-Promotion Rate	0.6%	1.8%
Pupil Drop-Out Rate	1.3%	2.6%

All data in the above four categories are from the 1974–75 school year; all data below are from the current year (1975–76).

Percent Non-White Pupils	16.0%	16.3%
Percent Non-White Faculty	5.8%	10.3%
Percent Male Faculty	42.0%	44.2%
Percent Faculty Holding:		
Bachelor's Degree	73.9%	66.4%
Master's Degree or Higher	26.1%	33.6%
Percent Faculty Teaching Experiences: Less than 1 Year	2.9%	2.1%
1–3 Years	17.4%	17.3%
4–9 Years	37.7%	30.2%
10 or More Years	42.0%	50.4%
Pupil / Teacher Ratio	18.1	19.8
Pupil / Other Instructional Staff Ratio	109.2	118.4
Pupil / Total Instructional Staff Ratio	15.6	17.0
Per Pupil Expenditures:		
Instruction	$ 789.35	$ 735.19
Instructional Support Services	87.82	76.63
General Support Services	209.43	199.99
TOTAL	$1,086.60	$1,011.81
Remodeling and Construction	$ 0.00	

Pinellas County School Attitude Survey 1975/76 for Riviera Middle School

Below are the results of this year's School Attitude Survey of students (S), parents (P), and teachers (T).

Percent Response	Strongly Agree			Agree			Uncertain			Disagree			Strongly Disagree		
	S	P	T	S	P	T	S	P	T	S	P	T	S	P	T
1. Enough time is available in this school for teachers to meet with parents.	8	17	35	40	67	45	44	8	5	6	5	15	2	3	0
2. Learning materials available to students in this school meet their instructional needs.	19	20	0	54	44	50	9	11	15	15	15	35	3	10	0
3. This school offers instruction which prepares students for daily living.	18	20	10	55	52	65	14	15	20	10	11	5	3	2	0
4. The guidance services offered in this school meet the needs of students.	30	15	0	42	60	20	19	10	20	8	13	45	1	2	15

Item															
5. The range of extra curricular activities offered at this school (clubs, sports, etc.) is wide enough to interest most students.	35	25	50	41	57	40	8	10	5	13	8	0	3	0	5
6. Students have a good feeling about attending this school.	20	26	70	43	64	30	24	10	0	9	0	0	4	0	0
7. Enough money is spent on this school's instructional programs.	17	16	5	27	36	30	38	25	15	14	18	45	4	5	5
8. The lunch program in this school serves good tasting food.	8	10	0	33	36	25	16	37	35	22	17	25	21	0	15
9. In this school, rules are enforced with fairness to all.	20	10	10	32	65	70	15	15	15	19	8	10	14	2	0
10. This school is kept in good repair.	29	31	15	47	57	55	12	10	10	9	0	20	3	2	0
11. This school communicates well with parents.	15	22	20	32	61	75	38	8	5	11	7	0	4	2	0

PRINCIPAL'S SUMMARY: The survey was completed by over 300 parents and students selected randomly and classroom teachers. Results show that approximately 95% of those participating do not strongly disagree with the school's overall position on the eleven items. This is a 6% improvement over the previous year. The lowest rated items are: by students, those dealing with lunches and school rules; by parents, those dealing with finances; by teachers, those dealing with availability of materials and services. However, the overall results are high and with gains in most areas. Student spirit is very high and students have a good feeling about attending this school. Teachers and parents feel there is a high degree of cooperation between home and school. The majority feel that the school is maintained well and communications and relations between community and school are excellent.

Riviera Middle School
Florida Statewide Eighth Grade Testing Program
February, 1976

Objective	% Reaching Mastery Florida	% Reaching Mastery Pinellas County	% Reaching Mastery This School
Essential Reading Skills			
1a. Labels—Caution	95.1	96.2	96.8
1b. Labels—Vocabulary	63.1	67.2	66.1
1c. Ingredients	88.3	91.8	90.7
1d. Medical Instructions	96.2	97.3	98.0
1e. Preparation Directions	89.9	92.4	94.1
2a. Driver's Handbook	89.9	92.6	93.9
2b. Transportation Schedules	54.1	60.8	61.5
3a. Job Want Ads	81.5	84.2	85.4
3b. Job Applications	90.5	92.7	93.9
3c. Tax Forms	66.5	73.5	76.3
4. Newspaper Reporting (Fact vs Opinion)	88.4	90.6	90.0
5. Store Directions	89.3	92.1	92.9
6. Outdoor Signs	83.8	87.5	90.0
7. Telephone Directories	89.8	92.2	92.7
8. Abbreviation Meanings	72.7	76.5	79.3
Essential Math Skills			
1. Rate of Interest	59.9	63.5	61.7
2. Discount Rate	40.9	47.1	43.5
3. Cost Comparison	86.7	90.2	89.1
4. Travel Time	75.0	79.5	76.5
5. Time Calculations	72.6	77.2	74.8
6. Spending Behavior	82.3	85.5	84.5
7. Sales Tax	56.1	63.4	56.9
8. Currency	93.7	95.4	95.1
9. Income Tax Calculations	45.4	49.7	49.6

School Board of Pinellas County Financial Statement
May 31, 1976 Riviera Middle School

	Year to Date			
	Beginning Balance	Receipts	Expendi- tures	Balance
INSTRUCTIONAL AIDS FUND Total	$ 1,265.30	$ 2,037.49	$ 2,441.65	$ 861.14
GENERAL FUND Total	2,200.48	2,128.79	2,802.22	1,527.05
CLASS, CLUB, TRUST FUND Total	8,020.03	30,971.46	27,851.40	11,140.09
COUNTY BUDGET TRUST FUND Total	0	4,982.00	3,851.55	1,130.45
MUSIC ACTIVITIES Total	1,805.52	350.10	1,081.90	1,073.72
ATHLETIC ACTIVITIES Total	49.15	153.45	120.95	81.65
TOTAL	$13,340.48	$40,623.29	$38,149.67	$15,814.10

Outstanding orders yet to arrive and be paid for	2,004.27
Projected Balance	$13,809.83

Parent Summary Form

Dear Parents,

This document was produced in compliance with Chapter 73–338, Law of Florida. We hope that the following report will assist our parents and school community to be informed of the progress at Riviera Middle School during the 1975/76 school year.

Achievement of This Year's Goals

The implementation of the Academic Centers Concept was our major goal for this school year. This has been successfully accomplished through the establishing of three centers which are actually three schools within a school. The fourth group, the teachers of Related Arts classes, supported all three teams.

The state-wide Attitude and Opinion poll supports the success of the new program by showing that Riviera students are proud of their school, and that Riviera out-ranked the county and state scores by a large percentage in almost all areas.

Absenteeism was very low and the number of suspensions was reduced. This can be attributed to the success within the teams of averting discipline problems and helping students with their social and emotional as well as academic growth.

Teacher Education Center: Staff Development

This year emphasis has been placed upon middle school certification. Many teachers attended the preschool workshop held here at Riviera and, during the year, completed other required courses. Others met the requirements through Staff Development courses. At this time it appears that all the staff have met, or are very close to meeting, the requirements for middle school certification.

Use of School Facilities

The building was used by the community for the following activities:

Jr. Raiders—Youth Association monthly board meeting, practice and ball games on our fields.

Northeast Little League—Practice on our fields.

Adult Education—Various night classes were offered.

P.T.A.—Four night meetings

Advisory Committee—Four meetings with the P.T.A. Executive Board

School System, County Wide—Meetings, workshops, in-service classes

Guidance

Riviera's Guidance Department has performed such guidance activities as counseling, orientation, registration, scheduling, dissemination and interpretation of information concerning student progress, parent/teacher consultation, and identification and referral of specific learning or adjustment problems. Testing for 1975–76 year included two state assessment programs; one in the sixth grade and one in the eighth grade. In the seventh grade the county testing program was administered. Occupational information activities and field trips have been an integral part of the year's program. Maintenance and updating of student records has also been a guidance responsibility. The Riviera Guidance Department has been staffed this year with two counselors, one occupational specialist and one records clerk.

Student Advisory Committee

In the various meetings chaired by Mrs. Antoinette Rambo, the Riviera Advisory Committee this year reviewed plans for the building program, viewed a slide presentation explaining the three academic centers program, and previewed the new middle school grade reporting form. In addition the members also discussed a variety of topics including: parent and student concerns with stolen and lost personal items, repair and restoration needs in the school building, effects of zone changes, changes to the Raider Football Field, proposal to form a comprehensive middle school in lower Pinellas County. The communication between the committee and the school staff has greatly aided all persons to understand the concepts of the school's program.

Curriculum Organization for 1976/77

Riviera Middle School will continue the 1976/77 school year with three cross-grade level centers. The three interdisciplinary teams within each center will provide learning experiences in Math, Language Arts, Reading, Social Studies and Science. There also is a Related Arts Team which covers courses in Humanities and Vocations. In addition, all students will participate in a Physical Education Program. The Exploratory Program, which we call RED period, includes Research, Enrichment, and Developmental classes, which are based on the abilities, needs, and interests of the students.

Accomplishments and Items of Interest

Open House in August.

Bicentennial Year Book published.

Band and Chorus presented Christmas and Spring Concert.

Candy Sales netted the school $5,456.47.

Student Council supported many school projects.

Orientation was provided for outgoing 8th graders and for incoming 5th and 6th graders.

Two school-wide field trips were conducted involving 320 students.

A total of 2,816 students went on 56 other field trips sponsored by the teams.

Sixteen activities other than field trips were conducted.

Honors were won in the Optimist Speech Contest, Spelling Bee, Math Competition.

Varsity Teams won Division Honors in Volleyball, Basketball and Track.

Bicentennial Celebration—April 9 was an all day Field Day honoring the spirit of the Bicentennial.

The Florida State-Wide Eighth Grade Testing Program was administered in February of this year. Results were expressed as percentages of students who have reached mastery level in certain essential reading skills and essential math skills. Riviera's percentages of eighth graders who have achieved mastery is greater than the county percentages and the state-wide percentages in a majority of the skills sub-tests. The opinions expressed by these students in the Opinion Poll section of this program indicate an extremely high regard for their school experiences, as do the results of the Student/Parent/Teacher Attitude Survey. Such enthusiasm and support of their school is due to a great extent to the attitudes and regard with which parents view the educational institution. With that thought in mind I would like to close this school year by expressing my heartfelt appreciation to you and your community for the time, effort, backing, and support without which no school can be successful.

Chalmers Coe
Principal

SOURCE: From Riviera Middle School (Pinellas County, Fla.), June 1976. Used with permission.

Azalea Middle School
Team D Newsletter

*A report of what your child is learning
in school the last six weeks*

ENGLISH

During the past six weeks our Language Arts program has involved a variety of activities. We have continued working in the Random House Skills Center. This is an individualized program of instruction in one of four divisions: Spelling, Vocabulary, Capitalization and Punctuation, or Grammatical Usage. As soon as a student completes the instruction he needs in one area he moves into another division. We have also continued working in the Picto-Cabulary Series and individualized vocabulary development program. Our main project has involved working in a delightful book titled *Imagination*. The students have signed a contract to complete work to earn an A, B, or C. They read selections from the text and then complete a written exercise in connection with a poem, short story, play, or thought-provoking article, drawing, or photograph. The students have enjoyed this book so much that thirteen copies have disappeared. I would appreciate it if you would check around your home to see if you find one.

Our team teaching projects in connection with Social Studies 8 have included two written book reports. We have just begun a careers unit with the aid of Mr. Schwark, our Occupational Specialist. We have had a speaker from Annapolis, the U.S. Post Office, The Police Department, The St. Petersburg Times, and a news reporter. We are taking a Kuder General Interest Survey to help determine in which occupations the students would be happiest.

SOCIAL STUDIES

In Social Studies 8 your child is completing the following learning projects:

LAB. WORK

A. Americans Text and Workbook
B. Newspaper Workshop
C. Black History Laboratory
D. Reading Enrichment Work Kit
E. Reading Contract

Your child should be able to show you a notebook with completion of a number of parts for each area, A through E.

During the next eleven weeks your child will have the opportunity to work with Mr. Mark Mallone, student teacher. Prior to Mr. Mallone's coming your child completed the following work:

A. Book Report.
B. Individual Project (research and public speaking techniques used).
C. Library Work—learning skills of research technique introduced by librarian.
D. Text Book Assignments—exploration and introduction to government.
E. Test.
F. Laboratory Work A through E.

Team D Newsletter—*continued*

MATHEMATICS

In Mathematics, seventeen students continued studying Algebra, solving equations and using equations to solve word problems. Kathy Anagnos, Ellen Greenbaum and Donna Hoyer were given a certificate of honor for their outstanding work in Algebra. Other students completed a unit of study to learn some simple concepts of probability by doing various experiments with coins, dice, cards, etc. They learned how the mathematics of chance is used in evaluating the results of ESP tests, since they were working on an imagination unit in English. One group of students has studied number theory, while another group has worked on meaning of rational numbers. Seven students have been given contracts for independent study in Prealgebra concepts. All students practiced basic computational skills using Cross-Number Puzzles and "Numbers in the News." Some of the students are beginning to accept more responsibility.

SCIENCE

We are delighted that our science teacher, Mrs. Pulkrabek, will return to the classroom on February 15, 1974. During her absence we have worked with a substitute on Introductory Chemistry I. We have completed units on "Chemistry of Matter;" "Chemistry and the Atom," and are beginning a unit on "Chemical Activity." We also have science-related current events at the end of each week.

You may use this newsletter to help you understand your child's present grades.

SOURCE: Azalea Middle School, "Team D Newsletter" (St. Petersburg, Fla., 1967). Used with permission.

Interim Progress Report—Riviera Middle School

To Parents or Guardian of _____   Date _____

From: _____   Subject: _____

I think it wise to keep you informed of _____'s need for improvement and extra effort.

ITEMS CHECKED BELOW ARE THOSE THAT NEED
IMPROVEMENT OR ATTENTION:

Home Preparation—
_____ Assignments not turned in.
_____ Assignments late.
_____ Assignments often incomplete.
_____ Needs individual help before or after school.
_____ Needs supervised study at home.

Class Work—
_____ Needs to bring necessary materials to class.

Interim Progress Report—(*continued*)

_____ Needs to use class time wisely.

_____ Makes careless mistakes.

_____ Needs to improve note taking.

_____ Needs to listen and follow directions.

_____ Low test grades (needs to review text/ take notes).

Class Behavior and Attitude—_____ Day dreams and appears disinterested.

_____ Talks and interrupts class.

_____ Rude and disrespectful.

_____ Lacks self-control.

_____ Has been given detentions for improper behavior.

Parent Action Request: Please sign and return to me_____

PARENT'S

SIGNATURE_____

If a conference is desired please call the Guidance Counselor to arrange a time.

Phone # - 527-8352 or 8656

SOURCE: From Riviera Middle School (Pinellas County, Fla.), 1976. Used with permission.

School Facility Checklist

Listed below are twenty-two premises regarding the middle school facility which are usually considered effective criteria for measuring the validity of the school facility.

Indicate by circling the particular number in the column to the right of each premise as to the degree of appropriateness to which that premise is considered valid in measuring the middle school facility. In order to be consistent with your opinion of the effective middle school facility, items may be modified and others added.

The descriptions of the numbers listed immediately below apply to the numbered columns to the right of the premises and should be remembered when marking the degree of appropriateness.

Degree of Appropriateness
1. Highly appropriate
2. Moderately appropriate
3. Slightly appropriate
4. Not appropriate

Degree of Appropriate-
ness

PREMISE

1. The school facility is arranged in such a manner as to allow implementation of the school's philosophy and objectives........................ 1   2   3   4

School Facility Checklist—*continued*

2. The school facility provides for individualized
    instruction as well as areas for large and
    small group instruction.. 1   2   3   4

3. The school facility offers an aesthetic en-
    vironment conducive to the social, emotional,
    and intellectual growth of the students............... 1   2   3   4

4. The thermal and ventilating systems of the
    facility meet the required health and comfort
    standards 1   2   3   4

5. The lighting of the facility meets approved
    standards 1   2   3   4

6. Acoustical treatment of instructional areas
    provides an environment conducive to learn-
    ing... 1   2   3   4

7. Instructional and service areas involving
    noise-producing activities are set apart from
    quieter classrooms.. 1   2   3   4

8. The design of the facility allows efficient traf-
    fic flow among students... 1   2   3   4

9. The design of the facility provides for
    emergency exits 1   2   3   4

10. Accessible and adequate storage areas are
    available for individual and general use............... 1   2   3   4

11. The design of the school facility has adequate
    provisions for future enrollment growth, if
    needed.. 1   2   3   4

12. The design of the school facility allows for
    present and future flexibility as the educa-
    tional program changes 1   2   3   4

13. The building(s) and outdoor facilities are so
    located on the site as to maximize educa-
    tional and aesthetic values 1   2   3   4

14. The school site is centrally located for the
    community that the facility serves 1   2   3   4

15. The school site is easily accessible to roads
    and/or streets... 1   2   3   4

16. The school site makes provisions for smooth
    and safe pedestrian traffic (where applicable) 1   2   3   4

17. The school site allows for accessible and safe
    bus loading and unloading (where applicable) 1   2   3   4

18. Adequate parking areas are located near or
    on the school site... 1   2   3   4

19. The school site reflects professional planning
    by providing outdoor educational facilities......... 1   2   3   4

School Facility Checklist—*(continued)*

20. Adequate and safe locations of public utilities
    have been provided at the school site.................... 1   2   3   4

21. Proper drainage creates a healthy environ-
    ment at the school site... 1   2   3   4

22. Professional planning of the school site is re-
    flected in the landscaping of the site.................... 1   2   3   4

Others:

Comments:

SOURCE: Developed by Dr. Fred Russell, University of Tennessee, 1973. Used with permission.

Middle School Review

NAME OF SCHOOL_____ DATE_____

Directions: With each of the following items, rate the school on the basis of the knowledge of and experience with the school that you possess. Place an "X" on the place on the continuum for each item to indicate how you believe the school is doing now.

Each continuum should be interpreted as follows;

NA: Not applicable to this school.

1: The school has made no progress in this area.

2: The school has made some progress in this area.

3: The school is about average in this area.

4: The school is doing well in this area.

5: The school is doing an outstanding job in this area.

A. *Focusing on the Emerging Adolescent*

1. The entire school program offers many opportunities for physical movement.

2. The school provides a variety of approaches to learning (e.g., problem-solving, laboratories, independent study).

3. Many social activities in and out of school, with special attention to their appropriateness for the age group, are encouraged and planned.

4. Learning tasks are individualized, to provide for maximum numbers of success experiences.

5. Cooperative planning between students and faculty, and student participation in the routine tasks of the school.

Middle School Review—*continued*

6. Community resources of interest to the students are utilized as fully as possible.

B. *Planning for Student's Individual Development*

7. Through a home-base, block of time, or other advisory arrangements, each learner is able to identify one teacher to whom he may turn for support and guidance.

8. Health and physical education are frequent and focus on the needs of learners.

9. Through exploratory courses, mini-courses, activities, and other arrangements, each learner has the opportunity to explore a wide range of possible interests.

10. Each student is involved in an independent study program.

11. Special group and individual instruction is provided for students who have explored, and who wish for extended study in the arts, foreign languages, prevocational areas, or other fields.

12. The school avoids situations and activities in which a few special students dominate everything, in favor of an attempt to provide success for greater numbers.

C. *Skills of Continued Learning*

13. The school provides special instruction, for students requiring it, in reading, math, study skills and writing.

14. Students are equipped with the skills which will enable them to become independent learners.

D. *The Areas of Organized Knowledge*

15. Through use of subject area planning teams, the school has identified the major themes, concepts and objectives of each school subject.

16. The aim of instruction is to foster an awareness of the system, order, and big ideas of the subject area.

17. Students are given directed practice in the use of materials and the "ways of knowing" appropriate to the subject (e.g., studying history as a historian would).

18. Occasional cross-subject theme units are carried on.

E. *Organizing for Instruction*

19. The school is organized into, and functions with, interdisciplinary teams.

20. The school sometimes places students into multiage groups to facilitate continuous progress.

21. Team planning time is scheduled during the day.

22. The school schedule permits time for recreation breaks or special activities.

Middle School Review—*(continued)*

23. Whether students are grouped by grades, years or teams, no individual is assigned to a groove in which he must inevitably remain from year to year.

24. Access to all learning resource areas (library, media center) is as immediate and open as the rights of learners permit.

25. Teachers use instructional methods more appropriate to this age group; not overly relying on traditional lecture-recitation models.

F. *School Facilities*

26. The school building is flexible; neither rigidly closed nor rigidly open.

27. Anticipating a team approach, students are housed in areas which enable them to identify with a smaller group.

28. Staff members have ample storage, work, meeting, and "retreat" space.

G. *Securing Community Cooperation*

29. Prior to the opening of the school, staff, parents and selected laymen undertook a year-long study of the concepts important to the development of a good middle school program.

30. A continual orientation system is maintained after the school opens.

31. A planned community relations program continues year after year.

H. *Planning for Continuous Progress*

32. Each curriculum area has prepared a statement of goals and a continuum of objectives.

33. Diagnosis of learner progress is keyed to the goals and objectives.

34. Instructional strategies emanate from and are consistent with the goals and objectives.

35. Reports to parents concerning learner progress are multi-dimensional and low inference evaluations.

36. Adequate record-keeping systems describe where a student is on a continuum of knowledge or skills.

37. Students are able to move along by a combined index of age, development, and academic progress.

I. *Staffing the Middle School*

38. Teachers have special training for middle school teaching, provided by the school system.

39. Teachers combine the strengths of elementary and secondary training by weaving together a warm concern for students and a love of academics.

40. Administrators and teachers understand and are committed to the middle school concept.

Middle School Review—*(continued)*

J. *Renewing the Program and Staff*

41. Innovations occur at a rate which does not exceed the capacity of the staff, student or the community to adjust.

42. A regular and organized method of total program evaluation is conducted and studied by all concerned.

43. Before middle schools were adopted on a systemwide basis, a pilot study utilizing one school was conducted.

44. Within the individual school new programs (e.g., activity periods, exploratory courses, etc.) are piloted with small groups or for a short time before being recommended for permanent schoolwide use.

45. Sufficient time and resources are provided so that curricular planning and teacher input are of value to the effort.

Middle School Review Profile Sheet

1	NA	1	2	3	4	5
2	NA	1	2	3	4	5
3	NA	1	2	3	4	5
4	NA	1	2	3	4	5
5	NA	1	2	3	4	5
6	NA	1	2	3	4	5
7	NA	1	2	3	4	5
8	NA	1	2	3	4	5
9	NA	1	2	3	4	5
10	NA	1	2	3	4	5
11	NA	1	2	3	4	5
12	NA	1	2	3	4	5
13	NA	1	2	3	4	5
14	NA	1	2	3	4	5
15	NA	1	2	3	4	5
16	NA	1	2	3	4	5
17	NA	1	2	3	4	5
18	NA	1	2	3	4	5
19	NA	1	2	3	4	5
20	NA	1	2	3	4	5
21	NA	1	2	3	4	5
22	NA	1	2	3	4	5
23	NA	1	2	3	4	5
24	NA	1	2	3	4	5
25	NA	1	2	3	4	5
26	NA	1	2	3	4	5
27	NA	1	2	3	4	5
28	NA	1	2	3	4	5

Middle School Review Profile Sheet—*(continued)*

29	NA	1	2	3	4	5
30	NA	1	2	3	4	5
31	NA	1	2	3	4	5
32	NA	1	2	3	4	5
33	NA	1	2	3	4	5
34	NA	1	2	3	4	5
35	NA	1	2	3	4	5
36	NA	1	2	3	4	5
37	NA	1	2	3	4	5
38	NA	1	2	3	4	5
39	NA	1	2	3	4	5
40	NA	1	2	3	4	5
41	NA	1	2	3	4	5
42	NA	1	2	3	4	5
43	NA	1	2	3	4	5
44	NA	1	2	3	4	5
45	NA	1	2	3	4	5

Student Questionnaire on Individualized Learning

To the students: We are interested in finding out to what extent the school has been able to individualize your learning to help you learn most effectively in your own way, at your own rate of speed. Your frank answers to the questions below will help us improve our program. Do not identify yourself or your teacher; in no way is this a rating of your classroom teacher.

1. Number of years you have been in school: _____
    5_____ 6_____ 7_____ 8_____ 9_____ 10_____.

2. In which of your classes is this questionnaire now being administered to you? (Check one)

    _____English   _____Science   _____Foreign Language
    _____Mathematics   _____Social Science

    ANSWER THE FOLLOWING QUESTIONS ONLY AS THEY RELATE TO THE
    SUBJECT YOU HAVE JUST CHECKED

3. In this subject I find that the pace or speed at which we must cover material is just right for me. YES_____ UNCERTAIN_____ NO_____

4. In this subject I find that the work I have is not too easy or too hard for me but is just right for me. YES_____ UNCERTAIN_____ NO_____

5. In this subject I find that the work we have interests me and will be useful in my future. YES_____ UNCERTAIN_____ NO_____

6. In this subject I feel that the teacher knows me as an individual and tries to suit the work to my ability and interest.
    YES_____ UNCERTAIN_____ NO_____

7. I think this subject could be individualized more effectively for me
    by _____

    _____

Student Opinion Survey—Azalea Middle School

Please check:

I am a   seventh grade   eighth grade
boy   girl

DIRECTIONS: We would appreciate receiving your opinions about the Azalea Middle School program to help us improve our school. It is not necessary to put your name on this survey.

Please answer by marking your answers from 1 to 4 on the answer sheet provided according to your degree of agreement or disagreement with the statement.

1—strongly agree; 2—partly agree; 3—partly disagree; 4—strongly disagree

I feel that:

1. At the present time, this school does not offer a large enough variety of courses.

2. Generally speaking, the academic courses offered in this school are of good quality.

3. Generally speaking, the related arts courses (courses other than academic and special interests) are of poor quality.

4. I did not get the special interest course that I wanted.

5. Special interest is rather enjoyable.

6. There are not enough areas offered in special interest.

7. Generally speaking, team teaching in this school works well.

8. Generally speaking, I don't get along too well with the teachers in this school.

9. Generally speaking, I get along pretty well with the other students in this school.

10. Overall, I like the program at this school.

Comments: _____

_____

(Continue comments on the back of this page if needed.)

Middle School Check Sheet

Below is a list of elements common to most middle schools. To help you informally evaluate your middle school check where you feel your school places on the continuum for each item. The definition of the terms used is determined by the person using the check sheet.

Directions: Place a check on the continuum which best expresses your feelings.

Middle School Check Sheet—*(continued)*

1. Is the schedule flexible enough to allow the manipulation of time, space, media, teachers, and students, for different purposes?

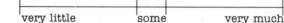
very little   some   very much

2. To what extent do you feel you are using time, space, teachers, and students flexibly?

very little   some   very much

3. To what degree is team teaching successfully used?

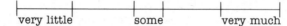
very little   some   very much

4. Is there adequate time or opportunity for common team-planning?

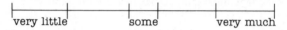
very little   some   very much

5. To what extent is team-planning time used successfully?

very little   some   very much

6. Are there efforts to implement an interdisciplinary approach where appropriate and natural?

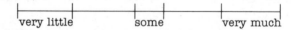
very little   some   very much

7. Student-centered curriculum:
   —Are there efforts to pretest students in skills areas to determine skills levels?

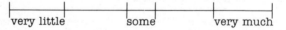
very little   some   very much

   —Are there efforts to concentrate on individual students' needs (profile folders, staffing, etc.)?

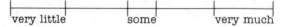
very little   some   very much

   —Does the curriculum emphasize student personal development (values clarification, communication skills, guidance, etc.)?

very little   some   very much

8. Are students given an opportunity to explore a wide range of offerings in academics, related arts, and special interest?

very little   some   very much

9. Do you feel your program adequately reflects the Azalea Middle School Philosophy?

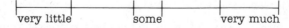
very little   some   very much

Middle School Teacher Competencies Self-Appraisal

NAME _____   School _____
Date _____   Grade _____

Directions: Below are a list of competencies deemed important for effective teaching in the middle school. Please examine each competency and appraise your own abilities in this area. Indicate whether the competency is an area of strength, adequacy, or weakness for you. Do so by using the following code to mark the boxes to the right of the competency: S = Strength, A = Adequacy, W = Weakness.

At the end of the list you are asked to select several competencies for further professional development. The competencies that you select may be strengths that you wish to capitalize on, or weaknesses you wish to erase.

Part One: Middle School Teacher Competencies   Appraisal

A. Competency Area: Interpersonal Relationships
   1. The teacher manages the classroom with a minimum of negative or aversive controls.
   2. The teacher creates a climate in the classroom which rests somewhere comfortably apart from an authoritarian tenseness or a laissez-faire chaos.
   3. The teacher uses himself (herself) as a tool in promoting the personal growth of students and colleagues.
   4. The teacher's relationships with colleagues, administrators and supervisors are harmonious and productive.
   5. The teacher is aware of the needs, forces, and perceptions which determine his (her) personal behavior.
   6. The teacher accepts behavior, and values individuals and groups which depart from his own.

B. Competency Area: Basic Instructional Skills
   1. The teacher exhibits variety as a basic facet of instruction both during the hour and from class to class.
   2. The teacher uses a multimedia approach.
   3. The teacher maintains a balance between teacher-directed learning and student-directed learning.
   4. The teacher individualizes instruction in the classroom.
   5. The teacher promotes student self-direction, initiative and responsibility.
   6. The teacher selects learning activities and executes them in a way that promotes student interest and involvement.
   7. The teacher's efforts in curriculum and instruction proceed from a problem-solving framework, involving the students in relevant inquiry.
   8. The teacher plans lessons thoroughly and in advance, using specific objectives and smooth transitions from one lesson to another.
   9. The teacher utilizes a variety of group sizes and devices in instruction.

Competencies Self-Appraisals—*continued*

10. The teacher possesses skill in asking questions which encourage student thinking beyond the level of "recall."
11. The teacher avoids common pitfalls of expository teaching, such as in faulty speech patterns, pacing the room, use of chalkboard, physical appearance of the classroom, etc.
12. The teacher knows about and applies modern learning theories in the classroom.

C. Competency Area: Curriculum
   1. The teacher knows what is relevant to the lives of students and finds ways to include it in the curriculum.
   2. The teacher chooses curriculum materials which are appropriate for the learning abilities and styles of the students.
   3. The teacher, individually or with a team of teachers, involves students in interdisciplinary studies.

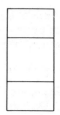

D. Competency Area: Relationships with the Community
   1. The teacher establishes positive relationships with the parents and families of students.
   2. The teacher works at understanding, accepting, and being accepted by members of the subcultures in the school and in the community.
   3. The teacher is interested in and participates in affairs of the community and school.

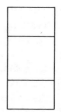

E. Competency Area: Understanding the Student
   1. The teacher understands the intellectual nature of middle school youth.
   2. The teacher understands the physical nature of middle school youth.
   3. The teacher understands the socio-emotional nature of middle school youth.

F. Competency Area: Commitment to Middle School Teaching
   1. The teacher is enthusiastic and vigorous in the daily activities of teaching middle school youth.
   2. The teacher understands the middle school concept and attempts to apply it in the classroom, and in the school as a whole.

Part Two: Areas for Development

Please list below the numbers of the competencies which you have selected for further development. They may be either strengths or weaknesses, and you may select more than five or fewer than five.

   1.
   2.
   3.
   4.
   5.

ASCD Paper—
"The Middle School: A Positive
Change in American Education"

INTRODUCTION

In 1977, the Association for Supervision and Curriculum Development (A.S.C.D.) Working Group on Research and Theory identified a set of "valued learning outcomes that reflected the 'holistic' nature of individuals." Ten goals with subgoals for each were identified by the Working Group. These goals could well become goals for American education.

Taking those ten goals and applying them to the middle school concept, the authors of this paper have attempted to demonstrate that the middle school is designed to help its students reach each of the goals.

The emergence of the middle school has offered an exciting challenge to those seeking a more relevant educational experience for youngsters between childhood and adolescence. Although much remains to be accomplished before middle schools everywhere achieve all of the goals discussed in this paper, the middle school has become something special, something significant, something stimulating in American education.

Goal One—Self-Conceptualizing (Self-Esteem)

Whom am I? That persistent question haunts youngsters during the period of transition from childhood to adolescence. The world of the emerging adolescent is an "I" and "me" world where a positive image of self is all-important. A positive image of self comes most often through peer acceptance, and conformance to the peer group often becomes more important than conformance to adult expectations. Presenting a positive image for their peer group results in conformity of dress, language, hairstyle and behavior on the part of emerging adolescents. The will of the group often determines a young person's response to others outside the group.

Combs, Kelley, Maslow, and Rogers, in the classic A.S.C.D. yearbook, *Perceiving,*

Behavior, and Becoming: A New Focus for Education, spoke of the importance of a positive view of self.[1]

Combs: "Extremely adequate persons seem to be characterized by an essentially positive view of self."

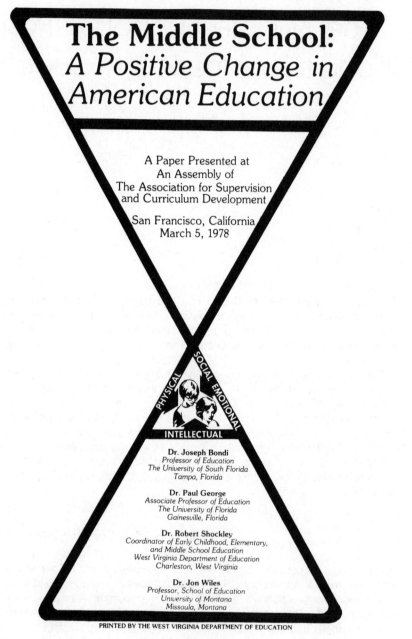

The Middle School:
A Positive Change in American Education

A Paper Presented at
An Assembly of
The Association for Supervision
and Curriculum Development

San Francisco, California
March 5, 1978

PHYSICAL SOCIAL EMOTIONAL
INTELLECTUAL

Dr. Joseph Bondi
Professor of Education
The University of South Florida
Tampa, Florida

Dr. Paul George
Associate Professor of Education
The University of Florida
Gainesville, Florida

Dr. Robert Shockley
Coordinator of Early Childhood, Elementary,
and Middle School Education
West Virginia Department of Education
Charleston, West Virginia

Dr. Jon Wiles
Professor, School of Education
University of Montana
Missoula, Montana

PRINTED BY THE WEST VIRGINIA DEPARTMENT OF EDUCATION

Used with permission.

---

[1] Arthur Combs et al., *Perceiving, Behaving, and Becoming: A New Focus for Education,* 1962 Yearbook (Washington, D. C.: Association for Supervision and Curriculum Development, 1962), p. 99.

Kelley: "The fully functioning self is motivated by the value of facilitating self and others."

Maslow: "Every person is, in part, his own project and makes himself."

Rogers: "Self and personality emerge from experience."

Coping with physical changes, striving to gain independence from family to become a person in his or her own right, and managing new levels of intellectual functioning—all are part of the lives of youngsters in the middle school. At no other time is an individual likely to encounter such a diverse number of changes simultaneously as he or she does during the middle school years.

The middle school is designed to provide opportunities for each individual to grow and develop according to his or her own unique abilities. The general atmosphere of middle schools is one of recognizing that each student is in the process of becoming a better functioning, more mature human being. It is interesting to note that when examining the philosophy or goals of a middle school, one invariably finds reference to the need of a middle school student to develop a positive self-concept.

The middle school concept, through its commitment to the personal development of each student, has been a positive influence on American education. Advisor-advisee groupings, shared decision making, strong guidance programs, and opportunities for interaction among students of differing age and physical development are a part of most middle school programs. The middle school has made a major effort to design activities in physical education, sports, and student activities that are appropriate to levels of maturity. Instruction, related to growth of the body, has been provided in many middle schools to help students understand normal changes in development.

In summary, the middle school concept is an approach that is consistent with basic democratic principles. Teaching-learning situations in the middle school are based on respect for others; and the environment of the middle school is designed to provide for positive individual personality development.

Goal Two—Understanding Others

The middle school curriculum seeks to promote human understanding through its programs and instructional technique. It is recognized that the preadolescent period is one during which the student is experiencing immense change; changes in body image, changes in social-emotional make-up, changes in intellectual functioning. As these changes occur, students realign most values and perceptions about others. The school program in the middle grades seek to make such a realignment a positive experience.

In particular, the middle school seeks to foster acceptance of human diversity, respect for others, and an understanding of the role of culture in values and behavior. It does so through a support of increased social awareness and through the promotion of self-realization.

As the preadolescent enters the middle school program there is still a significant dependence upon parents and family for role identification and a set of values. Ten and eleven-year-old children tend to think and act like their parents. Later, as the maturation process begins in earnest, the dependence on parents lessens and the preadolescent is faced with the momentous task of realigning beliefs, values, and thoughts about self and others.

To combat the decrease in social stability during this period, the student often aligns himself with a group of friends who provide support and stability while values are being realigned. The program of the middle school must, therefore, consider the impact of such temporary social relationships in assisting the student in understanding self and others.

In particular, middle schools address the development of social awareness by refinement of social skills, exploring social values, assisting in the development of interpersonal communication skills, aiding students to accept responsibility, and teaching human relations. These tasks are carried out in a program which uses peer influence and personal interaction to shape development.

Specific means of accomplishing social development are the use of such arrangements as a close student-teacher relationship (counselor model), the use of peer group counseling, an exploratory curriculum, time for value clarification and assessment, control of social experiences sponsored by the school, and some sharing of planning and evaluation of in-school activity.

Social awareness and development in the middle school is usually an outgrowth of self-realization. Until self-concept is crystalized, there is little hope that significant understanding of others can be accomplished. Middle school programs seek to promote self-realization by assisting students to gain confidence, by accentuating their personal strengths, by broadening their range of interests, and by providing an environment conducive to the exploration of personal values.

Curriculum arrangements to accomplish these tasks are multiple. Middle schools seek to restrict unfair competition among students by de-emphasizing competitive sports and social activities. Students are encouraged to discover strengths through mini-courses which are as social in nature as they are academic. Middle school buildings often provide for privacy and alone-time for students who need time for reflection and introspection.

Finally, middle schools attempt to promote an understanding of others by specific instructional techniques. Teachers model acceptance and understanding by recognizing the crucial role of affect in the classroom. It is recognized that peer group influence can aid social development. It is acknowledged that the cultural emphasis of language is legitimate. It is recognized that school motivation has a social quality. The diversity of intelligence, especially creativity, is accepted. In short, teachers in the middle school promote the understanding of others by being understanding themselves; by accepting their students for what they are.

Goal Three—Basic Skills

Skills development is one of the major foundations of the middle school program. It is a goal of the middle school that all students will acquire information, become reflective thinkers, be able to express themselves, and possess a basic ability in mathematical reasoning. The pursuit of these goals is vigorous in the middle school.

Instruction in the middle school places strong emphasis on the "patterns of learning" that have academic application both in present and future learning. Intellectual growth and school skills are stimulated through varied experience. The importance of out-of-school activity on classroom learning is acknowledged.

Through the formal academic processes, middle schools seek to develop sound foundations in information sources. Subject matter is introduced through a "process of learning" rather than as an artificial product of learning.

Specific skills of scholarship, such as reading and computation, are highly developed. In reading, for instance, both developmental and functional skills are taught:

Reading

Developmental—word analysis, comprehension, structural analysis, phonetic analysis

Functional—locating information, organizing information, interpreting information, evaluating information

In addition, other process skills essential to further learning and academic communication are also taught and practiced:

Speaking	*Spelling*
Informal	Familiarity
Dramatization	Utilization/application
Storytelling	
Reporting	*Listening*
	Appreciation and enjoyment
Writing	Critical and evaluative
Creative writing	Application
Notetaking	
Outlining	
Letter writing	

Beyond direct academic skills, middle schools encourage attitudes and habits that are supportive of learning skills. Through the use of learning contracts and independent study, students are supported in the development of "learning patterns" that are fundamental to academic success.

Teachers in the middle school assist in the development of basic skills by relating learning to the world of the student. As student needs, academic processes, and basic skills are combined into units of study, students master skill development as a part of the overall learning process.

Goal Four—Interests and Capability for Continuous Learning

A major theme of the middle school curriculum is the development of attitudes for continued learning in the individual student. Not only are such interests and capabilities necessary for later academic success, but also for a fully functioning adulthood. The middle school curriculum seeks to accomplish this end by ensuring that the student values the learning experience, by providing the learner with opportunities for autonomous learning, and by helping the learner appreciate the on-going quality of all learning experiences.

Middle schools, unlike other forms of intermediate education, make some basic assumptions about learning in school environments. First, learning is seen as a natural process; particularly at the preadolescent stage of development when much of all learning is of a survival nature. Second, learning revolves around self-adjustment and self-acceptance. This means that if learning is to be consequential, it must be relevant. Third, learning is perceived as a highly individualized act. Each student has his own style and rationale for learning. Taken in its totality, this belief about learning suggests that schools must provide opportunity for students to become skilled at learning. Learning experiences that are unnatural, irrelevant, or dependent on a single uniform style of learning discourage a pattern of life-long learning.

Middle schools build interests in continuous learning by several techniques:

1. Recognizing and responding to the uniqueness of each learner through a flexible, individualized program.

2. Presenting learning opportunities through a variety of learning mediums and allowing some degree of learner selection of learning medium.

3. Emphasizing the application of information whenever possible, thereby allowing the learner to draw conclusions about the utility of learning.

4. Beginning learning activities in areas familiar to the learner, and concluding learning activities in areas of possible future interest to learners.

5. Using an exploratory, inquiring, individualized approach to learning.

As the learner is allowed to find learning mediums that are comfortable to him, attitudes and habits of learning are established and find application both in school and outside of school. A goal for the middle school is, then, increasing learner autonomy and helping each student find an appropriate learning style.

Goal Five—Responsible Member of Society

The middle school has demonstrated its high esteem for the area of responsible membership in society. No concept of school organization has shown more concern, for example, for the significance of process, as opposed to product, when thinking about curriculum. Middle school educators have long acknowledged the importance of the "hidden curriculum" in early adolescent education. We recognize that schools shape their students' daily lives and personal futures by how they teach, and how they are organized, as well as by what they teach.

The middle school concept includes a strong commitment to model those processes that are necessary for life in a participatory democracy. Collaboration, power sharing, group problem-solving, good listening, effective interpersonal confrontation, sustained and stable face-to-face personal friendship and support—all of these are built into the middle school concept. Organizational components such as interdisciplinary teaming, advisor-advisee groups, multiage grouping, program improvement councils—all attempt to realize these important commitments. Students who experience life in a fully functioning middle school will experience those processes that produce active citizens capable of effective participation in a democratic society.

Goal Six—Mental and Physical Health

The core of the middle school concept, the main source of its designation as a positive change in American education, must be traced to its espousal of one central goal in the school program: the personal development of each student. The middle school concept boldly asserts its commitment to the mental and physical health of each child. In open defiance of traditionally dominant forces which would have it otherwise, the middle school concept holds up the banner of student personal development with a seriousness of purpose that surprises even the soundest defenders of academic lifelessness.

As Thomas Gordon, author of *Teacher Effectiveness Training,* says so well, "democratic" and "therapeutic" are synonymous. What is democratic will contribute to mental health and whatever contributes to mental health will have a democratic base. All of those programs which flow from the middle school concept's commitment to responsible social membership also contribute to personal mental health. What is socially healthy is also mentally healthy. Many middle school programs contribute.

Advisor-advisee programs that create a continuing support system for smaller groups of students help to create an atmosphere where individuals find warmth and understanding, as well as assistance in moral development and social-emotional education. Personal responsibility grows within a context of human caring, facilitated by the many varieties of advisor-advisee groups that are consistent with the middle school philosophy.

Interdisciplinary team organizations, in addition to their curricular and instructional justifications, promote a more manageable sense of community than can be attained with the traditional departmentalized format. A small group of teachers who share the same group of students, the same schedule, and the same area of the school, helps to disperse the amorphous anonymity which produces so much of today's student alienation.

Teachers need a support system and a sense of community in order to perform as effectively as their students. This is what the middle school concept provides.

In this regard, it has been said that multiage grouping is the best kept secret of the middle school concept. Organizing schools so that students of several grade levels are permitted to live and learn together is one of the most important elements of the middle school concept. It is this process that so strongly reinforces the success of other programs such as the advisor-advisee system and the interdisciplinary team organization.

Developing positive growth-producing relationships with young adolescent students takes time, often much longer than fifty minutes a day for thirty-six weeks. Multi-age grouping permits students and teachers to work together for two, three, and even four years. Time to "reach, touch, and teach." Without it, much of what is done if not a charade, is at least less effective than it should be.

Because the middle school concept emerged from a reconsideration of the nature of older children and early adolescents, it recognizes the significance of the goal of physical health far more fully than have other levels or organizational patterns of schooling. Middle school students are, more than anything else, physical beings. The rate of sexual, muscular, skeletal, metabolic, and organic development reaches dimensions unmatched during any other period, with the exception of the first year of life. Quite possibly the pubertal passage, with all of its attendant changes, is the most important but least understood (i.e., valued) transition human beings undergo. Until the middle school concept arrived, these physical needs were ignored. It is no accident that the only scholarly review of research on early adolescence has been titled *Growing Up Forgotten*,[2] and this book itself is largely unknown even among professionals in middle school education.

Goal Seven—Creativity

To be mentally and physically healthy is to be creative. To be a responsible member of a democratic society requires both creative thinking and creative activity. It is no wonder, therefore, that the middle school concept is concerned with the development of student creativity. It might even be said that the development of creativity is the central goal of middle school education.

From its infancy the middle school concept has advocated the cultivation of creativity. Even in a "back to the basics" milieu the terms "creativity" and "exploration" remain the keys to the mission of the middle school. The generation of creative minds and responsive bodies is the "raison d'etre" of the middle school.

As a result, attempts to determine the dimensions of a satisfactory middle school curriculum have always included a strong focus on the exploratory, the experimental, and the enriched. Decades of research make it clear that growth in both creativity and basic skills is very directly related to the depth of the exploratory phase of the curriculum.[3] As the curriculum of the middle school suffers from the devastation

---

[2] Joan Lipsitz, *Growing Up Forgotten* (Lexington, Mass.: D. C. Heath and Co., 1977).
[3] Wayne Jennings and Joe Nathan, "Startling/Disturbing Research on School Program Effectiveness," *Phi Delta Kappan,* March 1977, pp. 568–72.

forced upon it by the advocates of dullness and drill, educators become more aware of the need to "come to our senses in regard to the significance of the Arts in American education."[4]

Many schools have managed, in spite of all the pressure to the contrary, to establish and maintain exploratory and special interest programs that are often the highlight of the day for many of the schools' students and teachers. These programs are too frequently the only sources of creative renewal and personal enrichment in a curriculum which has been and will continue to be damaged by the forces of fear and frustration.

Social responsibility, mental and physical health, creativity—can the momentum that has been stolen from American education's movement toward these goals be reclaimed? The middle school concept answers affirmatively, with enthusiasm.

Goal Eight—Informed Participation in the Economic World of Production and Consumption

To adequately consider this goal as it may relate to the middle school, one must focus on the learner during this developmental period. The learner is in a transition period between childhood and adulthood. The learner is searching for ways to sample behaviors of the adult world. Exploration activities during this transition period have become a trademark of the middle school curriculum.

Activity periods that are integrated into the total curricular plan are a part of most successful middle school operations. These periods provide the learner opportunities to explore actively various hobbies, vocations, and interests.

This active involvement facilitates learning experiences in which the learner can broaden his horizons and further identify his weaknesses and strengths. Attitudes and interests evolve as they may relate to the student's possible vocational and educational experiences.

These experiences enable the transescent to sample the world of the adult. Career education, however, does not become an isolated or separate part of the middle school curriculum. It is integrated into the total curricular plan. The focus of the program then broadens beyond the quest of getting students into the right vocation or profession. The middle school curriculum is geared to assisting and guiding learners as they attempt to cope with questions of self-image and concept. The realization that these issues are extremely relevant to an individual's success or failure in school and life is reflected in the middle school curriculum.

The transition between childhood and adulthood begins as the child enters a period of rapid change and development called "transescence." The comprehensive exploratory emphasis of the middle school can enable learners to find their way while passing through this difficult stage of development. It can provide students opportunities to analyze themselves and their possible roles in the economic world of production and consumption.

Goal Nine—Use of Accumulated Knowledge to Understand the World

One of the exciting prospects of the middle school program is the potential to provide a broad general education in which the sciences, arts, and humanities can be taught

---

[4] David Rockefeller et al., *Coming to our Senses: The Significance of the Arts in American Education* (New York: McGraw-Hill Co., 1977).

to facilitate the learning of concept relationships between the various disciplines. This can occur through the blocking of instructional time into more effective and flexible units.

The traditional scheduling approaches in which instruction is packaged into neat little fifty-minute time slots where rigid departmentalization occurs, does not encourage students to apply the learned concepts of various subject disciplines to the following A.S.C.D. subgoals identified under goal nine.

    A. Interpret personal experiences
    B. Understand natural phenomena
    C. Evaluate technological progress
    D. Appreciate aesthetic events

These subgoals are not unique to any one subject area. It is through an interdisciplinary approach that these applications can be facilitated.

The middle school organizational pattern usually does not include grade nine. This allows for a greater flexibility in scheduling practices. For example, rigid state and college requirements usually require four years of "Carnegie Credits" for college admission and, in most instances, high school graduation. Additionally, vocational programs, which are to a great degree funded through federal funds are traditionally four-year programs. These, and other factors, have placed limitations upon school officials to provide flexible education for ninth grade learners. These limitations have affected the other grades as well. Once school officials have developed programs and allotted resources through facilities and time, schedules for lower grades are automatically determined and limited.

Flexible time blocks for scheduling and interdisciplinary team teaching can be easily implemented in the middle school. This presents a tremendous opportunity for middle school educators to relate the structure of various disciplines to the gestalt of human knowledge. It is through such an approach that school learning can be applied to life-related learning.

Goal Ten—Coping with Change

This particular goal is extremely relevant to the middle school curriculum. The middle school is predicated upon the fact that transescent students are progressing through a unique period of growth and development. Furthermore, this uniqueness has great implications for the educational programs that are offered to these learners.

The transescent learners are unique because during this period of development, there are more changes occurring physically, social/emotionally, and intellectually, than at any other time during their formal schooling. "Coping with change," then, becomes an intricate part of the middle school curriculum.

The curriculum focuses attention upon assisting learners to cope with changes occurring in their bodies. An important feature of this task is the issue of improving the learner's self-understanding and ultimately his self-image. Therefore, it is important that students develop a positive and realistic view of themselves, their roles, and their functions in a fluid and changing world.

The transescent period is an extremely formative one. The degree to which students are able to adapt to these changes and develop positive self-identities affect, to a tremendous extent, their later adaptability in a society which is changing at an accelerated pace.

The middle school program can assist learners in coping with the changes in their world. The flexibility and adaptability of the curriculum can facilitate the development of student attitudes and understandings so conducive to productive involvement in a rapidly changing society.

```
┌─────────────────────────────────────────────────────────┐
│                                        Appendix 12        │
│                                                           │
│   Definition of Pertinent Terms                           │
│                                                           │
└─────────────────────────────────────────────────────────┘
```

A MIDDLE SCHOOL GLOSSARY:
DEFINITION OF PERTINENT TERMS[1]

articulation: relationships with the elementary school, designed to make transition into the middle school easy; and relationships with the high school, to make transition of pupils into that school comfortable and effective. Of course, articulation is expected also in the middle school, between grade levels and learning levels, and in continuous progress programs.

block of time schedule: a "block of time" is placed in the schedule, in which one teacher or a team of teachers teaches a class in two or more subject areas, with the teacher or team determining the relative amount of time to be devoted to each subject, according to a daily estimate of needs.

cognitive learnings: a term commonly used for academic learning of a subject-matter nature.

core or fused curriculum: in this arrangement two or more subjects are "fused," or integrated. Examples could be English and social studies. Problem and theme orientations often serve as the integrating design.

deductive learning: the learning process that moves from larger generalizations and principles to illustrative examples and concepts.

departmentalization: students move from one classroom to another, with separate teachers for each subject.

discovery learning: a type of inquiry, often emphasized especially in individualized instruction, in which a student moves through his own activities toward new learnings, usually expressed in generalizations and principles, and typically involving inductive approaches.

feedback: evidences from student responses and reactions which provide indications concerning the degree of success being encountered in lesson objectives.

---

[1] William Cuff, *The Middle School: An Innovation With Possibilities,* vol. 18, no. 7 (Oregon Study Council, March 1975), pp. 30–32. Used with permission.

Teachers find feedback constantly in discussion, student questions, written exercises, and test returns.

house plan: a kind of organization in which the school is divided into units, with each house having an identity, and containing the various grades, and, in large part, its own faculty. The purpose is decentralization, closer student-faculty relationships, and easier and more flexible team-teaching arrangements. Frequently a vertical team-teaching plan is used.

independent study: work performed by students without the direct supervision of the teacher to develop self-study skills and enlarge and deepen interests.

inductive learning: the learning that results when individual concepts, in which examples, and illustrations, lead to larger generalizations and principles.

innovations: new instructional strategies, organizational designs, building rearrangements, equipment utilizations, or materials, from which improved learning results are anticipated.

interdisciplinary team: a combination of teachers from different subject areas who plan and conduct coordinated lessons in those areas for particular groups of pupils. Common planning-time, flexible scheduling, and cooperation and communication among team teachers is essential to interdisciplinary teaming.

learning media center: usually a large area containing books, audiovisual opportunities, learning resources of wide dimensions, independent study facilities, and research materials. It is designed to influence both learning and teaching styles.

middle schools: the term middle school designates a school in between elementary and high school, housed separately and, ideally, in a building designed for its purpose, and covering usually three of the middle school years, beginning with grades 5 or 6.

modular scheduling: the division of the day into modules, typically 15 or 20 minutes long, with the number of modules used for various activities and experiences flexibly arranged.

nongraded organization: grade levels are abandoned, and students move upward in continuous progress, associating in every subject field with those who are at approximately the same point of development.

performance objectives: the purposes pursued by the teacher expressed in terms of pupil behaviors, which in themselves act as evidences that the purposes have been achieved.

programmed learning: materials built on a rational step-by-step development basis, usually presented in the form of a workbook or for use in a teaching machine, designed for independent study and learning. Emphasis is on subject-matter development.

self-contained classrooms: students are housed in one classroom, with one teacher. Variations may occur in such subjects as music, art, shops, and physical education.

scope: the term refers to the parameters of learning. A subject-matter discipline sets its own scope, often by grade level. "Post-holing," the selection of certain spots within a discipline for depth study, has a scope of its own, as does the "structure of subject matter" approach of Bruner, which stresses underlying principles attached to a subject. The "needs" approach has its scope set by personal, social, and societal pressures.

sequence: this term refers to the organization of an area of study. Frequently the organization is chronological, often a movement from simple to complex. Some sequences are spiraled, using structure, themes, or concept development as guidelines. A few schools use persistent life situations to shape sequence.

subject-matter curriculum: in this organization the stress is emphatically on the mastery of subject matter. All other outcomes are considered subsidiary. The school may employ tracks, units within subjects, and ability grouping. There have been recent shifts from encyclopedic learning to structural recognition, from facts to understanding. But the center remains subject-matter mastery.

team teaching: a method of teaching which utilizes teacher strengths, and allows teachers to work flexibly with individuals, small groups, and large groups.

theme-oriented course: emphasis is placed on the principles that hold the subject together. The micropedagogy of textbook teaching is changed to the macropedagogy of underlying principles.

transescence: the period in human development which begins in late childhood prior to the onset of puberty and extends through the early stages of adolescence.

unified arts: usually refers to a grouping of subjects including art, music, industrial arts, drama, homemaking, etc., for which a time is scheduled with a team of teachers organizing the pupils into groups.

unified studies: a unifying theme is used to tie together many subjects. An example might be "conservation," which could attract contributions from many fields. Often team teaching is used for this type of organization.

unstructured time: unscheduled time used for independent study, individual projects, and open laboratory activities. The student assumes responsibility for his own learning.

wing plan: a number of classes of the same grade, housed in close proximity to each other, usually facilitating a horizontal interdisciplinary team-teaching arrangement. It can be part of a house plan.

Jon Wiles, a professor of education at the University of Montana, received his doctorate from the University of Florida. A former intermediate school teacher, Dr. Wiles has been active in middle school education since 1967. Dr. Wiles has served on numerous national commissions for middle school education and has worked as a consultant to middle schools in over twenty-five states. He is the author of *Planning Guidelines For Middle School Education* and, with Dr. Bondi, developed the film script for "Profile of a Middle School" (A.S.C.D. 1979). Dr. Wiles has served as the President of the Texas Middle School Association and Director of the Research Division of the National Middle School Association. He is the co-author of three other recent books, *Curriculum Development: A Guide to Practice, Supervision: A Guide to Practice,* and *Practical Politics for School Administrators.*

Joseph Bondi, a professor of education at the University of South Florida, has been a long-time leader in the middle school movement in the United States Dr. Bondi has both teaching and administrative experience in the middle grades and has served as a consultant in the development of middle school programs in over 350 school districts in 45 states and Canada. He served as President of the Florida Association for the Supervision and Curriculum Development and as a member of the Board of Directors and Executive Council of the Association for Supervision and Curriculum Development, A.S.C.D.

Dr. Bondi has authored or co-authored eight texts in education including *Developing Middle Schools: A Guidebook.* He chaired the State of Florida Middle School Committee that produced the first state guide on the middle school. He chaired the A.S.C.D. Working Group on the Emergent Adolescent Learner that produced *The Middle School We Need,* a national position paper of A.S.C.D. Dr. Bondi also co-authored the script and study guide of the first 16 mm. film produced by A.S.C.D., "Profile of a Middle School."

Name Index

Subject Index